Understanding
Database
Management
Systems

Trademarks

Database Products and Their Manufacturers. The following products are copyrighted by the companies that produce them. ADABAS—Software AG; (HP) ALLBASE/SQL, (HP) Open ODB, (HP) TurboIMAGE—Hewlett Packard; Alpha Four—Alpha Software; BTrieve—Novell; Clarion—Clarion Software; Clipper—Nantucket Corp.; Condor—Condor Computers; Data + Plus—Piano Computer Sales; Datacom, Datacom/PC, DBFAST, DB/VAX, IDMS, IDMS/PC, RAMIS—Computer Associates; DataEase—DataEase International.; Dataflex—Data Access; Datamanager PC—Timeworks; DataPerfect—WordPerfect; DayFlo Tracker—DayFlo Software; dBASE III+, dBASE IV, dBASE MAC, Interbase, Object Vision, Paradox, Rapidfile, Reflex—Borland International.; DBC1012—Terradata; DBMan V—Verasoft; DBMS, Rdb—Digital Equipment Corp.; dB VISTA III—Raima Corp.; DBXL—Wordtech Systems, Inc.; DB PLUS—Tominy, Inc.; DB2, IMS/DLI, OS2-EE-DM, SQL/DS, SQL/400, TPF—IBM Corp.; DB/SQL, INFOS/2—Data General; DM-IV, IDS-II, Interel—Bull HN; DMS II, DMS1100, RDMS 1100, SQLDB SIM—Unisys; Double Helix—Odesta Corp.; Empress Micro—Empress Software; FileMaker Pro—Claris; filePro Plus—The Small Computer Company; First SQL RDBMS—FFE Software; Focus, PC/Focus—Information Builders, Inc.; Force—Dvorak Software; Formbase—Columbia Software, Inc.; FormGen—FormGen Corp.; Fourth Dimension—ACIUS; FoxBASE, FoxPRO—Fox Software, Inc.; Gemstone—Servio; GURU—MDBS Inc.; IDOL-IV—Thoroughbred Software; IDENTITY—Horizons Unlimited; Information—Prime Computer; Informix—Informix; Ingres—Ingres; Integra SQL—Coromandel Industries; Knowledgeman, M/4—MDBS, Inc.; Magic PC—Aker Corp.; Model 204—Computer Corp. of America; MS File, SQL Server—Microsoft; Multibase—Cykic Software; My Advanced Database—MySoftware Co.; Nomad—Must Software; Nonstop SQL—Tandem Computer; Nutshell Plus II—Iris Software; O_2—O_2 Technology; ObjectStore—Object Design; Object View—Matesys Corp. N.A.; Objectivity DB—Objectivity, Inc.; Omnis 7—Blyth Software, Inc.; OnCMd—On-Linedata; ONTOS—ONTOS; Open Access III—Software Products International; Oracle—Oracle Corp.; PC-File—Buttonware, Inc.; Pace—Wang Laboratories; Postgres—UC Berkeley; Powerbase—Compuware; Prodas—Conceptual Software; Professional File, Superbase 4—Software Publishing; Progress—Progress Software; Q&A—Symantec Corp.; Q&E—Pioneer Software; Q-ProQ—NE International; Quadbase-SQL—Quadbase Systems, Inc.; R:Base—Microrim; Revelation—Revelation Technologies; SIR/DBMS—Sir, Inc.; SQL Windows—Gupta Technologies; Starburst—IBM Research; Supra—Oincom Systems; Sybase—Sybase, Inc.; System 1032—Compuserve Data Technologies; System 2000—SAS Institute; TAS Professional—Business Tools, Inc.; Team-UP—Unlimited Processing; Unify—Unify Corp.; Versant—Versant Object Technology; Watfile—Watcom Associates; WindowBase—Software Products International; Wintrieve—The Whitewater Group; Xerox Formbase—Xerox Corp.; XDB—XDB Systems, Inc.; XDP—Plexus; XQL—Novell.

Other brands and product names are trademarks and registered trademarks of their respective holders.

Understanding Database Management Systems

An Insider's Guide to Architectures, Products, and Design

Robert M. Mattison

Research by:
Michael J. Sipolt
Frank Mattison

Edited by:
James Bierbower

McGraw-Hill, Inc.
New York   St. Louis   San Francisco   Auckland   Bogotá
Caracas   Lisbon   London   Madrid   Mexico   Milan
Montreal   New Delhi   Paris   San Juan   São Paulo
Singapore   Sydney   Tokyo   Toronto

Library of Congress Cataloging-in-Publication Data

Mattison, Rob.
   Understanding database management systems: an insider's guide to
architectures, products, and design / Robert Mattison.
   Includes index.
   ISBN 0-07-040973-0
   1. Database management. I. Title.
QA76.9.D3M3879 1993
005.74—dc20   92-25971
                                       CIP

   2 3 4 5 6 7 8 9 0 DOC/DOC 9 8 7 6 5 4

ISBN   0-07-040973-0

The sponsoring editor for this book was Jeanne Glasser.

Printed and bound by R. R. Donnelley & Sons Company.

I would like to dedicate this work to three people, none of whom I can ever hope to repay for their timeless support and caring.

To Eleanor Kelly, whose consistent support over the years has made so many things, including this book, possible. To Brigitte Mattison, who managed to keep her patience and sense of humor through seemingly endless nights and weekends of meetings, late night phone calls, edit sessions, and temper tantrums. And to Carol Coon, who helped me learn how to live life in the here-and-now, and actually to enjoy the experience of writing this book.

Contents

Chapter 4. The Architecture Profile   69

Chapter 5. PC Architectures   89

Chapter 10. Data Storage Management

Chapter 11. The Administrative Profile

Preface

In my early days as a professional computer systems consultant specializing in the design, installation, implementation, and troubleshooting of large and small database projects, it had always been irritating to work with so many different products and still be unable to get a full grasp of the tools I was using. As time went on, this itch to understand databases became a passion resulting in the dedication of extensive amounts of time in post-graduate study, independent research, and pouring over hundreds of research papers. Ultimately however, I came up short. Somehow, a whole lot of things about databases were being missed. I soon discovered that this nagging problem was not mine alone. It seemed that many others had the same questions and concerns.

Clearly, there is something common to all of those software products we call databases, and yet, every time a pattern for understanding these becomes clear, a new product or approach comes up which invalidates the previous set of assumptions. It was in the spirit of resolving this dilemma that the Database Integration Research Team was born.

The Objective

At the beginning, our objectives were quite simple. We set out to research a "few" of the more popular database products and to develop a comprehensive, global set of terminologies and concepts that would help us understand how different products compared.

Of course, as the research continued and we progressed further and further into it, two things became clear:

- That there were clearly a lot more differences between database products then we had anticipated

- That in order to understand what really made databases alike or different was more than simply an architecture, platform or, vendor consideration

As a result of these findings, we decided to take a more scientific and comprehensive approach to the venture, and thus was born the database research project and this research team.

The Research

The research discipline that was developed in order to make our findings as comprehensive as possible was quite extensive.

First, a complete inventory of database products for all hardware environments was developed. This involved conversations with most hardware manufacturers and many software vendors as well. After the initial list was completed, a process of prioritizing those products by their efficiency, market share, usability, and uniqueness was undertaken. This weeding-out process continued up until a few weeks before the book was completed.

After an original triage of products, the researchers then proceeded to develop extensive research profiles on each of the products remaining. This research involved obtaining a complete set of supporting manuals from the product vendor, a copy of the database code (when possible), and contacting sites that used the product for production applications.

Armed with this input, the researchers were able to compile product profiles, which summarized the operation and organization characteristics of each product. (Appendix A provides a small subset of these profiles). For most products, a prototype application (Pete's Pet Shop) was developed and tested to guarantee that the researcher understood exactly how the product really worked. As the original population of more than 150 database products was trimmed, patterns of product construction and organization began to emerge, resulting in the finished product before you.

Based on the similarities and differences found between products, a significant amount of theory from published works and research papers within the ACM, IEEE, and standard industry periodicals (*Computerworld, Database Management Magazine, DBMS, Database Programming and Design*, etc.), and my experience working with multiple-database integration projects, the model of how to view a database product was developed.

The Accomplishments

Because of this thorough and unbiased approach, you should be able to develop an appreciation for the many database products that are available today from a new and, we hope, more objective perspective.

Among the more significant things that I hope this book will accomplish is to generate some credibility and consistency in the use of certain terminology in the database arena. Terms like database architecture, relational, object-oriented, and

GUI are used so often and with so little regard for meaning that they serve only to confuse an already greatly confused population. The relational architecture presents a particularly interesting problem because when applied too strictly, it serves to define no products at all; and when applied too loosely, it can be used to define all databases.

We have tried to take a neutral view regarding assigning an architecture classification to a database product. Unfortunately, this assignment is still subjective in many ways and is still subject to interpretation.

Another thing that I hope will happen is to grant some legitimacy to the many PC-based products that represent such a large share of the database population. These seem to get little treatment from the theoretical and academic communities.

Our presentation of the flat-file, XBase, and SBase architectures should help to fill the void left by this lack of attention. These products and their supporting architectures represent approaches to the storage and management of data that are as legitimate as any mainframe or relational database system.

The Three Schema Architecture

The discerning reader will notice an obvious relationship between 3 of the profiles of a database product (programming, architecture and data storage) and the classical 3 schema database architecture popular in database theory for some time now. This relationship is no accident. On the other hand the reader should not equate the two as synonomous. The profiles of a database product referred to in this book refer to a collection of characteristics that products share, not to a recommendation for how they SHOULD be built. The same could be said for our descriptions of the database design process. What we have tried to do is explain and illustrate how things are actually done today, not how they ought to be done. The ambiguity and inconsistencies that are exhibited here are nothing but reflections of how things are actually done today.

Future Works

I have come to view the completion of this book not as the end of a process, but as the beginning of one. I expect that its publication will spur some controversy in the data-processing community, and I look forward to hearing opinions from people about our approach, the findings, and ways that the discipline can be made sharper, finer, and more useful.

Regrets

Among my regrets are that we could not have published two or three times as much material as we finally produced. There is so much more that can be said, but not enough room for it all. I hope that in the near future we can produce additional works that will address, in more detail, the specifics about individual products, and the workings of the administrative profile. The incredibly complex world of distributed database systems presents more material to be covered, as does preparing a lot more detail and examples on the design process, especially the logical and physical design processes and the automating of those steps.

I am also very sorry that we could not include all of the products reviewed within our Appendix A. Because of space considerations we had to make some decisions based upon which products best represented the entire database market or which had some particularly distinctive characteristics.

Disclaimer

The nature of the computer software business today makes it impossible to report accurately all of the details about each of the products that we have reviewed. Although we have solicited the assistance of most of the vendors in reviewing our reports about their products in order to assure as much accuracy as possible, it could still happen that some details would be missed. In addition, the software industry is so volatile that some of the products may undergo serious reengineeriung by the time you read this book. Please keep this in mind while reading through any product specific information, and check with the products vendor for the most accurate and up to date information.

In addition, the author, publisher, and researchers can accept no responsibility for the reader's interpretation of the information provided here. This work is informational and general in nature, and should not be construed to be an instructional guide (we simply are unable to provide enough detail to do this kind of approach any justice).

The bibliography at the back of this book can provide you with additional, detailed sources of information about any of the subjects or products discussed within the context of this book.

Acknowledgments

There are so many acknowledgments to make I just hope I can remember them all. First, the Database Integration Research Team:

Frank Mattison, the PC products expert and desktop publisher guru. Frank's many hours of in-depth research, the installation and operation of dozens of PC database products, and persistent questioning of our professional assumptions helped give us all the PC end-user's perspective on how things work.

Michael J. Sipolt, the public relations, mini, Unix, and mainframe expert. Michael's dedication to this project and willingness to pitch in wherever required contributed significantly to the team's solidity. In addition to these soft skills, his dynamic, take-charge attitude paid big dividends in breaking through the platform barriers for many of the products.

James Bierbower, writing member of the team. Jim did an exceptional job of turning the technical rambling of a group of techies into a coherent, understandable, very readable literary work. In addition to this, he provided most of the charts and graphics seen throughout the book, and afforded the team an Apple voice through the melee.

I can not emphasize or credit these individuals enough for the hours of work, hundreds of phone calls, and dozens of working weekends they spent pitching in to make this book the quality product you see here. This is as much their work as mine, and it was only through everyone's patience, understanding, and dedication to the concept of creating a truly important piece of database research work that we were able to complete it in the fashion it deserved.

Vendor support

I would be greatly remiss were I not to credit the dozens of vendor employees, independent consultants, and industry experts who contributed materials and time to our undertaking. Although there are probably a few who will be missed, (and I apologize to them in advance) we owe a debt to each of those people who saw beyond the benefit to their own companies and products and helped us develop this truly global view of databases. We list these individuals by database product, vendor, or company name in a totally random order:

ADABAS (Software AG)- Mike Schiff, Hewlett-Packard; Lynne Hanson, Alpha Four; Bob Heibison, Clarion Software; John Herron, Data Ease; Denise Giakas, DataPerfect; Carrie Carter, Computer Associates; Bob Gordon and Dominique LaBourde, DB-Plus; Sandy Moonert, DBC1012; Mat Stankey, DEC; Brian Duggleby, Borland International; Nan Borreson, DBXL; Tyra Wright, Unisys; Ed Johnson, Unisys (DMS II and SIM); Doug Talbert, Unisys (DMS1100 and RD-BMS); Manual Lavin, Bull HN; Dan Traxler and John White, Double Helix; Julie Lyon, Focus; Judy Rattner, Formbase; Lydia Chaverin, FoxPro; Gloria Pfeif, Informix; Dan Black (the best SE in the USA), Ingres; Glynnis Sears, MDBS; Doreen Habben, Computer Corporation of America; Victoria Winston, MySoftware Co.; Kimberly Norris, Nomad; Pat Stites, NonStop SQL; Yvette Del Prado, Objectivity DB; Brian Clark and Craig Wood, Blyth Software; Jenny Blome, Ontologic, Inc.; Joshua Duhl, Oracle; Mat Duncan, Wang/Pace; Marty Saulenas, Buttonware; Dee Dee Walsh, Progress Software; Stephen Zamierowski, Symantec; Lisa Vermont, Microrim; Mickey Friedman, SIR; Dennis Grey, Supra; Dan Dyer, Unify; Mary Camarata, Versant Technology; Mary Loomis, Ph.D, WindowBase; Connie Roloff.

Other credits

I would also like to thank Jeanne Glasser and the support staff at McGraw-Hill for helping make this work possible, and special kudos to Wojtek Kozaczynski, Jeff Studer, Muriel Stone, Dennis Thanig, Dustin Mattison, the editorial staff of Data Base Management Magazine, Tom Sprague, John Killoren, Amy Birschbach, Janice Bushey, Patricia Miller, Robert Ice, Debbie Flatow, Don McMurray, Lori Cielinski and Thom Ferris; Dustin Mattison who remained supportive and undemanding throughout the many long months of work; Stephanie Yesulis, who provided us with many hours of badly needed typing support and of course to our wives, Margaret Bierbower and Mary Mattison, who tolerated the seemingly silly dedication to "the book" for so many months. These women, by virtue of their patience and understanding made it possible for us to get the job done with a minimum of stress and strain and a large deal of credit should go to them too.

Rob Mattison

Introduction

Mention the word *database* to a group of business people, and chances are good that each person, no matter what their vocation, will claim to know exactly what you are talking about. Unfortunately, for those people who must work with databases on a day-to-day basis, the term database can be used to describe several different things, depending upon with whom you are talking and what you are trying to accomplish. Although everyone can agree on some of the basic capabilities databases have, there is no true baseline understanding of exactly what a database is. What there is, instead of an overall database discipline, is an assortment of database product specialties. There are PC-based database products like dBASE III and Paradox. There are client-server databases like Oracle and Sybase. There are minicomputer databases like RDB and SQL400 and of course there are the mainframe database management systems like DB2 and CA-IDMS.

For the computer user, whether they be programmer, analyst, designer, architect, database analyst, or end user, it is becoming increasingly important to understand not just one database or another, but to understand databases themselves.

Let us consider some typical business data processing situations and see how the label of database can develop so many different connotations.

Situation 1

Sam is the manager of a small shoestore at a large shopping mall on the East Coast of the United States. Sam has been having a lot of trouble keeping track of the store's inventory. Whereas in the good old days a manager needed to keep track of only 40 or 50 styles of shoes at any one time, business conditions have demanded that the inventory be quadrupled in order to keep up with the competition. The old fashioned tally sheets upon which inventories were maintained are no longer adequate, and it has been decided that a database will solve the problem.

Sam visits one of the neighboring shops, a computer store, and asks for a database that will solve his problems. Unfortunately for Sam, it isn't that simple. To his chagrin, Sam discovers that there are several dozen databases from which he can choose. The prices range from $25 to more than $1000 and each seems to be able to do the job. Each also requires that Sam learn how to use it, which could take anywhere from several hours to several years. For Sam, the decision to buy a database is much more complicated than the decision to buy a cash register or a VCR. What Sam wants is to keep track of his shoe inventory. What Sam must do in order to accomplish this is:

1. Decide what kind of computer to buy.

2. Decide what database system to buy.

3. Learn how to write programs using that database.

4. Design the system he will eventually be using.

5. Write the system.

If Sam is an open-minded and energetic person, he will make all of these decisions and do it himself. More likely, he will hire a consultant to write the programs that he needs to make use of the database.

Situation 2

Mary is the chief information officer for a large manufacturing concern. Her responsibilities include the management of more than 350 computer systems running on IBM, Unisys, Digital Equipment Corporation (DEC), Wang and PC-based computer systems. In contrast to Sam, who had to choose one database, Mary must constantly decide between hundreds of products. When a new computer system is going to be built, Mary must decide which computer it will run on, which database product will be used to store the data, and how the application programs that run against it will be written. In one respect, Mary must make all of the same decisions that Sam does. On the other hand, the number of factors that Mary must consider when making those decisions is much greater. When the company's factory in Taiwan tells her that they need a newer and more powerful shop floor control system in order to reduce inventory costs, Mary must ultimately go through the same decision-making process that Sam does.

Situation 3

James is the computer systems manager for a large brokerage firm. For his organization, computers are a relatively new addition to the day-to-day business. The brokers in James's organization don't need a lot of data processing done for them. What they need is information, lots of it, and in a relatively short amount of time. In the world of trading stocks and bonds, brokers who know the current price of a given stock sooner than their competitors have an advantage that can easily be turned into millions of dollars of profit. For these system users, speed is the key ingredient.

By purchasing the right computer hardware (like scientific workstations from Sun Microsystems, Hewlett Packard, or IBM) and combining it with a powerful distributed database package (like Sybase, Oracle, Ingres, or Informix) James is able to provide up-to-the-second information about the changes in stock prices to hundreds of end users and give his firm the edge over competition that does not have this capability.

These situations have several things in common. First, the database alone will not solve the problems. The path to meeting the needs of the users encompasses selecting the right computer hardware, database product, and application development environment, then designing and building the system.

Second, evaluating the database without taking the other factors into account almost guarantees that the database application and the system will fail.

If the decisions are made poorly or do not fit within the environment into which they will be placed, the system could be an extremely expensive loss of money. In the worst case, a poor set of decisions could cost Mary her job, or cost Sam his business.

An Industry in Transition

The business computing industry is going through a metamorphosis. The rate at which technology changes is so great that no one using computers today can stay insulated from it. There are many good reasons for these changes. Computer hardware is becoming more powerful with each passing year. The desktop computer of today is thousands of times more powerful than the mainframe of the 1960s, and the mainframe computer of today is correspondingly more powerful still.

Along with the improvements in the raw power that computers provide have come rapid advances in the area of data storage and telecommunications. Satellite, microwave, and fiber optics channels make it possible for more people and computers to communicate at speeds higher then ever before and new data compression and storage media make it possible to keep millions of times more data then ever before imaginable.

These benefits are not without drawbacks, however. Because the technology is improving so rapidly, decision makers are faced with some very difficult challenges. For each situation, someone must decide which database to use and how it can best be applied to the problem. This decision cannot be based on the simple criterion of which product is best. It must factor in the risks involved in choosing a technology that might be too new and unstable to trust, too complicated and difficult to work with, or too old and close to obsolescence.

It is in the midst of this chaos that we find database management today. Business computer systems have one thing in common despite all of their technological differences. The unifying factor for all computer systems is the data that they process. The management of data, and therefore database management systems, is the glue that binds systems together.

Four Worlds Converging

If managing data is the mission of data processing, then who are the missionaries? There are really four segments of this industry, each vying for ultimate leadership in the direction of data processing. These four groups have thrived and survived for several years, existing in parallel universes. Each one has clung to its own direction, its own way of doing things, and each one has succeeded, for the most part, by ignoring the others.

With ever-increasing computer power and businesses' demand for more information, these groups are being forced to work together. The data processing world of the future will be made up of distributed databases that merge all of these approaches into one.

The first group comes from large corporate Management Information Systems (MIS) organizations. These individuals have been managing the corporations' data for years. Unfortunately, the cost of this service has increased drastically, forcing managers to search for alternate solutions to their mainframe data processing needs.

The second group comprises business users. They work with personal computers such as IBM PCs and Apple Macintoshes and a host of other systems. As the ultimate customers of the data processing services, they have begun to develop their own ideas about how data management should be done. With PC-based spreadsheets and databases, they have forged an entirely different data processing world than the one supplied by their mainframe counterparts.

The third group comes from the ranks of research and academia. These are the Unix and scientific workstation aficionados. Theirs is clearly a theoretical rather than a business approach to the problems faced by data processing and they have proved that their approach can yield amazing results when executed properly.

The fourth group includes the midrange systems supporters. Working with minicomputers like IBM System 3x, AS/400, as well as DEC Vax, Wang, and several other hardware environments, they represent yet another distinct set of solutions to data processing problems.

It is unlikely that any one of these four groups will emerge as the ultimate solution to all of the varying problems faced by the users of computer systems today. More likely, over time, all four of these worlds will continue to merge. It is on the database battlefield—specifically in the distributed database arena—that these groups have converged.

The industry is, to say the least, chaotic and confused when it comes to database systems. Unfortunately, the debates occur at so many levels simultaneously that very little communication actually takes place.

Purpose, Scope, and Organization

The Purpose of this Book is:

1. To provide you with an introduction to the diverse world of database products and the way that these products fit into a much larger data processing environment.

2. To review the different approaches that database manufacturers use to create the database products that make up those systems, and to develop a common vocabulary with which these products can be described.

3. To consider some of the techniques for the modeling, design, and tuning of those systems.

4. To supply an inventory of more than 75 of the most popular database products in use today in order to give you an appreciation for the similarities and differences between them.

This Book Should Help You Answer Questions Like:

- What does a database actually do?
- What is a database architecture and why is it important?
- What is the difference between an object-oriented, relational, and network database?
- Why are there so many different kinds of database products, what exactly are the differences between them?
- What are the advantages of using the one product over another?

It is our hope to provide a forum and a starting point for the common understanding of diverse database products and their application to specific business problems. This is rooted in the idea that database decisions and the effective building of database systems is a function of understanding how each database product really works.

How this Book was Developed: The Database Integration Research Team

It is our intention that you will find something distinctive in the way this book has been conceptualized and presented. This approach to the problem of understanding database systems is based upon the extensive experience of the author and the researchers who have prepared it.

Over the past several years, the author and a group of highly proficient data processing professionals, each experienced with a different assortment of platforms and database products, began meeting on an impromptu basis. The purpose of these meetings was a matter of simple survival. Being expert with one database or another was simply not enough to guarantee survival in the world of data processing. More and more, systems were being built that crossed the traditional boundaries of platforms and architectures.

In order to be a productive database expert in the future, it is necessary to understand not only how one database works, but how they all work, and how they can all be made to work together.

The culmination of these meetings was the establishment of the Database Integration Research Team, a non-profit, database research organization that set out to catalog, define, and explain as many products as possible—no matter what their platform or architecture— and to assemble this information into a coherent form. This book represents the fruits of these labors.

Database products included in the research

(an * indicates a product which has been included in Appendix A)

Product	Company
Access SQL	Software Products International
*ADABAS	Software AG
*(HP) ALLBASE/SQL	Hewlett-Packard
*Alpha Four	Alpha Software
*BTrieve	Novell
*Clarion	Clarion Software
Clipper	Nantucket Corp.
Condor	Condor Computers
Data + Plus	Piano Computer Sales
*Datacom	Computer Associates
Datacom/PC	Computer Associates
*DataEase	DataEase International
Dataflex	Data Access
DataManager PC	Timeworks
*DataPerfect	WordPerfect
DayFlo Tracker	DayFlo Software
*dBASE III+	Borland International
*dBASE IV	Borland International
dBASE MAC	Borland International
*DBC1012	Terradata
*DBFAST	Computer Associates
DBMan V	Versasoft
*DBMS	Digital Equipment Corp.
*dB_VISTA III	Raima Corp
*DB/VAX	Computer Associates
DBXL	Wordtech Systems, Inc.
*DATABASE-PLUS	Tominy, Inc.

*DB2	IBM
DG/SQL	Data General
DM-IV	Bull HN
*DMS II	Unisys
*DMS1100	Unisys
*Double Helix	Odesta Corp
Empress Micro	Empress Software
FileMaker Pro	Claris
filePro Plus	The Small Computer Company
First SQL RDBMS	FFE Software
*Focus	Information Builders, Inc.
PC/Focus	Information Builders, Inc.
Force	Dvorak Software
*Formbase	Columbia Software, Inc.
FormGen	FormGen Corp.
Fourth Dimension	ACIUS
FoxBASE	Fox Software, Inc.
*FoxPRO	Fox Software, Inc.
Gemstone	Servio
GURU	MDBS Inc.
IDOL-IV	Thoroughbred Software
ID_ENTITY	Horizons Unlimited
*IDMS	Computer Associates
IDMS/PC	Computer Associates
*IDS-II	Bull HN
*IMS/DLI	IBM
Information	Prime Computer
*Informix	Informix
INFOS/2	Data General
*Ingres	Ingres
Integra SQL	Coromandel Industries
*Interbase	Borland International
*Interel	Bull HN
*Knowledgeman	MDBS, Inc.
Magic PC	Aker Corp.
M/4	MDBS Inc.
*Model 204	Computer Corp. of America
MS File	Microsoft

Multibase	Cykic Software
*My Advanced Database	MySoftware Co.
*Nomad	Must Software
*Nonstop SQL	Tandem Computers
Nutshell Plus II	Iris Software
O_2	O_2 Technology
ObjectStore	Object Design
Object View	Matesys Corp. N.A.
Object Vision	Borland International
*Objectivity DB	Objectivity, Inc.
*Omnis 7	Blyth Software, Inc.
OnCMd	On-Linedata
*ONTOS	ONTOS
Open Access III	Software Products International
*(HP) Open ODB	Hewlett-Packard
*Oracle	Oracle Corp.
*OS2-EE-DM	IBM
*PC-File	Buttonware, Inc.
*Pace	Wang Laboratories
*Paradox	Borland
Postgres	UC Berkeley
Powerbase	Compuware
Prodas	Conceptual Software
Professional File	Software Publishing
*Progress	Progress Software
*Q&A	Symantec Corp.
Q&E	Pioneer Software
Q-ProQ	NE International
Quadbase-SQL	Quadbase Systems, Inc.
RAMIS	Computer Associates
*Rapidfile	Borland International
*R:Base	Microrim
*Rdb	Digital Equipment Corp.
Reflex	Borland International
Revelation	Revelation Technologies
*RDMS 1100	Unisys
*SIM	Unisys
*SIR/DBMS	Sir, Inc.

SQLDB	*Unisys*
*SQL/DS	*IBM*
*SQL/400	*IBM*
SQL Server	*Microsoft Corp.*
*SQL Windows (SQL Base)	*Gupta Technologies*
Starburst	*IBM Research*
*Superbase 4	*Software Publishing*
*Supra	*Cincom Systems*
*Sybase	*Sybase, Inc.*
System 1032	*Compuserve Data Technologies*
System 2000	*SAS Institute*
TAS Professional	*Business Tools, Inc.*
Team-UP	*Unlimited Processing*
* TPF	*IBM*
*(HP) TurboIMAGE	*Hewlett-Packard*
*Unify	*Unify Corp.*
*Versant	*Versant Object Technology*
Watfile	*Watcom Associates*
*WindowBase	*Software Products International*
Wintrieve	*The Whitewater Group*
Xerox Formbase	*Xerox Corporation*
*XDB	*XDB Systems, Inc.*
XDP	*Plexus*
XQL	*Novell*

Products were considered from the following hardware/operating system environments:

- IBM and compatible computers
- Amdahl
- Digital Equipment Corp.
- Unisys
- Bull
- Apple
- Cray
- Hewlett- Packard
- Tandem
- Several dozen Unix-based systems (AT&T, Next, etc.)

In order to help organize and systematically explore the many aspects of a database product's capabilities and idiosyncracies, we have implemented the concept of a database profile. The profiles identified help the reader and the system user to understand and compare database products on something closer to an equal footing. All databases have each of these profiles, though some rely more heavily upon one than another.

This book is organized around the exploration and understanding of these profiles. We begin in Chapter 2 by exploring the world of databases in a general sense and introduce you to some of the major issues and concerns of database users. It is in this chapter that we introduce the database profile and introduce the profiles to be considered: the programming, architecture, data storage and administrative profiles. We then define some of their characteristics.

In Chapter 3, the programming profile of databases is explored. There is a dizzying variety of ways that programmatic access to stored data can be managed. The programming profile of a database defines how that product treats the requirement that all databases have, to allow users to access and manipulate the data.

Chapters 4 through 9 explore database architectures. In Chapter 4 we define the term *architecture* and discuss how it affects the way a database can help develop useful and efficient systems. Chapter 5 defines the three primary PC-based architectures, the flat-file, XBase, and SBase approaches. These architectures describe the basic logical operating mode for most PC-based database systems (with the exception of some products that exploit non-PC architectures) and represent some of the newest and most revolutionary aspects of database processing. These products and their unique approach to architecture have managed to dominate the PC database market for some time, to the dismay of relational and other more *legitimate* architecture approaches. Chapter 6 reviews the traditional database architectures: the network, hierarchical, and inverted-list systems which represent the original database population of mainframe systems. These architectures have provided the foundation of database processing systems for decades, and continue to be used to support a large number of production application systems.

In Chapter 7 we begin the exploration of some of the newer architecture approaches with a review of the relational architecture, its theoretical foundations, and practical application. Chapter 8 provides the same kind of treatment for object-oriented databases and the distinctive twist they add to traditional data processing concepts. Finally, in Chapter 9, we review the hybrid and proprietary architectures and summarize the basic logic and operation assumptions of all of the architectures.

Throughout our coverage of database architectures and the other profiles, we develop examples of real-world application of these principles by using a prototype system for Pete's Pet Shop. Through this vehicle we demonstrate the building of a database system using products typical of each approach, including: PC-File (flat-file), dBASE III (XBase), DataEase (SBase), ADABAS (inverted list), IMS (hierarchical), CA-IDMS (network), DB2 and Informix (relational), Objectivity DB (object-oriented) and several products of the hybrid and proprietary classification.

In Chapter 10 we discuss the database storage management profile. This is the way that database products handle the physical storage and retrieval of data.

Surprisingly enough, and contrary to popular belief, the storage management and architecture profiles of database systems are, in fact, quite unrelated. Knowing the database's architecture tells a person very little about how data actually will be stored and retrieved. It therefore tells you very little about how well or poorly the system will perform. Products from almost every architecture category use almost every storage management technique. These techniques include blocking, buffering, compression, sequenced storage, indexing, hashing/scattering, pointing, and clustering.

Chapter 11 considers the database administrative profile and the ways that database products can help people administer systems by providing security, concurrency, and backup/recovery mechanisms. In Chapter 12, we conclude our profile analysis with a brief review of distributed database issues and their impact on database building and use.

After finishing our discussion of database products themselves, we return to our prototypical case and see how the database design process can be better understood and executed when viewed from the perspective of these profiles. Chapters 13 and 14 carry you through the three phases of database design: modeling or conceptual design, architectural design and physical design(referred to as implementation). We will then consider the impacts different profiles have on the effectiveness of the execution of each of these phases.

Finally, in Chapter 15, we return to the basic themes and issues brought up in Chapter 2, and examine how the information developed throughout this book can be utilized to effectively address those concerns.

It is our hope that you will find this reading interesting and informative.

2

Introduction to Databases

The database world is extremely complex, clouded with facts and opinions, fantasy and reality, and an abundance of *expert* opinion. Unfortunately, although there are definitely a lot of opinions about the do's and don'ts of databases, most of them are at best confusing and in the worst case downright contradictory. Database issues are involved, but the resolution of database issues does not need to be quite so complex.

Different Reasons to Study Databases

Choosing a Database

To start with, different people have different reasons for working with a database. Some want a database to provide them with the means to building an entirely new business system. These individuals are involved in the process of selecting a database. The database selection process occurs dozens of times a day, in about every business environment imaginable. From the one-person office to the *Fortune 500* corporation, everyone seems to be involved in the process of choosing a database product of one kind or another. For some, the database selection process is simply a matter of walking into the local software store, reading a few boxes, asking the salesperson a few questions, then closing the eyes and picking one. For others it is a lengthy, drawn-out process involving dozens of people, months of research and investigation, and hours of vendor interrogation; all just to come up with the right database product.

Using a Database

Others are not allowed the luxury of being involved in the process of selecting the database with which they will work. These individuals are called upon to develop new systems, making use of the database products selected by somebody else. Often, the people selecting the database are not the people who will be called upon to use it.

For example, a PC program developer may be told that the customer wants a new application system developed, and that it will be written using a preselected product like dBASE III or RBase, for example. Regardless of how good the developer thinks this selection is, chances are what the customer wants is what the customer gets.

Sometimes the situation is even more clear cut. A project manager for an IBM AS/400 system was left with the choice of using IBM's SQL/400 database for the AS400 or using no database at all; not much of a choice. In the mainframe development environment a preselected database technology is the rule, not the exception. Most shops have a database product of choice, like DB2, IMS, IDMS, or Supra. All systems will be built with the designated product.

People working with a preselected database product couldn't care less about what went into the database selection process. What they are interested in is finding out how best to make use of the products they have available to them. For them, understanding how the database works and how it will behave in different situations is critical to the successful completion of their mission.

Evaluating Databases

The last group, and equally common, are people called upon to diagnose existing database systems. These individuals, whether they be involved in performance tuning, system monitoring, or in many cases database system troubleshooting, must work within an environment where not only the database product is a given, but the application development code and database design decisions have already been made. Diagnosis can be either the most mundane or the most exciting of database evaluation situations.

Ongoing systems evaluation, standards reviews committees, and operations watchdog groups must understand as much about database systems as the selectors and builders did, but must also be able to piece together how all of the system's disparate components fit together into a cohesive, fully-functional database system.

System troubleshooting and project disaster recovery experts are often called in to quickly and efficiently determine what has gone wrong with a system that should have worked or used to work. When system owners spends hundreds, thousands, or sometimes even millions of dollars in the development of a system that their organizations depend upon, database problems are considered to be issues of critical importance.

Whether you are choosing, using, or evaluating database systems, the same basic understanding of database systems is prerequisite to the continuation of your task.

Not too surprisingly, the discipline and techniques that contribute to the successful selection of a database are the same ones that ease the burden of a system developer and expedite the task of the system evaluator. Understanding how databases work is the underlying assumption beneath each of these different objectives.

Ways of Dealing with Database Problems

Database Anxiety

One of the ways that people deal with the topsy-turvy, technologically overwhelming work of databases, is to very quickly develop an acute case of database anxiety. This anxiety can cause people to develop almost paranoid suspicions about the database decisions they make, or the decisions made by other people. There are so many variables that the database evaluator must deal with, and so little concrete fact upon which to base decisions, that it is surprising more people do not slip into this state. The condition can create a lot of problems, especially when there are many people involved, or when the system in question is especially large or complex.

One of the biggest contributors to this condition is the simple fact that database technology is relatively new. It changes so quickly and so often that it is literally almost impossible to keep up with it. In the 1960s there were perhaps a dozen Database products available to the system professional and personal computers were a pipe dream. By the 1980s, there were more than 100 database products available, boasting more than six basic architectures, hundreds of hardware platforms, dozens of operating systems, and more features, functions, bells, and whistles than a circus train.

As if this explosion of product availability wasn't enough, most database vendors release new versions of their products several times a year. And to make matters worse, the new technologies like relational and object-oriented databases require the use of new kinds of specialist professionals such as data modelers, process modelers, data analysts, and normalization experts. Most people can keep up with the new technologies, but these technologies bring with them new approaches to old problems and new ways of looking at computers, businesses, and the people within them.

Added to this already overwhelming ocean of information is the fact that most people working in data processing today received little or no education in these new technologies as they pursued their education. To make matters worse, few educational institutions are able to keep up with the technological advances.

So, our database evaluator shows up for work with very little history upon which to base the decision-making process, very little formal training in the disciplines required to execute it, and a continuously moving target of newer, better, and more complicated technologies to work with.

Some people respond to this anxiety by becoming the ultimate pessimists. These individuals question everything and everybody at every stage of the process.

Database Myopia

One of the greatest liabilities a person working with database products has to face, and one of the most common responses to anxiety about the explosion of database technology, is to develop a condition called *database myopia*. This condition occurs when a person learns how to use one database product well, but fails to take into account the ways that this particular database is similar to or different from other database products. Database myopia, or dependence upon knowledge of only one database product, makes it easy for a person to develop a large collection of false perceptions about what a database is and how it works.

For example, if you know the DB2 database product well, then you might assume that all databases are like DB2; a fatal assumption. Database myopia can take many forms:

> 1. The functions, features, and performance characteristics of the known database become considered the standard against which all other databases are judged. If the known database provides full backup and recovery, for example, then any database without this capability is considered inferior. If a product offers more functionality than the known database, then those features are considered trivial or unnecessary. The reason that this can happen is that a person views the database they know within the context of the system within which it operates.

If the known database provides no security features, for example, then the database system of which it is a part either has no security requirements or uses some other means to handle security. The fact that another database package might handle security in a better way is ignored, since this alternate way of doing things is foreign to the myopic individual.

In the personal computer market, database myopia leads individuals to see the product they learned first as the best product around. When you consider the hundreds of database products available for PCs today, it is hard to believe that anyone could find the best one, especially if they've only used one.

> 2. The architecture of the known database influences not only the database evaluator's view of database products, but influences the way users, programmers, analysts, designers, and managers view them as well. The infiltration of a database architecture into the very way that people view their systems, functions, and programs is called the *architecture paradigm*.

What is a Paradigm?

A paradigm (pronounced "pair-a-dime"), is a model or pattern used to help simplify understanding of complex things. Architecture paradigms describe how programs, programmers, and others involved in the building of systems tend to build their view of reality around the database architecture they use the most frequently. People who work with hierarchical databases all day long can hardly help but begin organizing their programs and data constructs into hierarchies. Individuals working with network databases consequently begin structuring their view of the business world around networks. Although quite useful for the building of the individual's known database system, when those same individuals are called upon to work with a new technology that requires a different set of paradigms, they often find it difficult to adjust their styles of execution.

This reliance on paradigms is by no means restricted to the developers of large database systems. Database experts in the use of XBase architectures like dBASE III or FoxPro, for example, have an equally difficult time adjusting to the new ways of doing things offered by products like RBase or Ingres.

3. Changing a database architecture can have a devastating effect upon users' perceptions of different products. If you think it is difficult for a programmer or analyst to learn and manage multiple paradigm sets when working with different database products, imagine what it must be like for users.

Despite the severe and often ignored problems created by myopia, new database products are constantly being introduced to the market while existing products are being upgraded, modified, and improved several times a year. This rapid rate of change only serves to make the task of understanding database products even more difficult.

Although database myopia offers people one way of reducing the anxiety that these systems can create for people, it is certainly not the only way.

The Search for a Database Guru

Some people decide that the only way they have a chance of getting a grasp on database issues is to hire an expert to explain it. They search for someone who has done it all and knows it all; someone who can be trusted without question to produce the right answers at the right time. There are several things wrong with this approach.

First, there is no way that any one person can possibly know everything there is to know about a database product. The subject is too complex and the expertise required to do everything well is too diverse. Databases are multifaceted, interconnected entities, not simple machines like toaster ovens. The effective use of a database involves not only technical expertise in several areas (operating systems, hardware internals, telecommunications, programming languages, etc.), but requires proficiency in political, organizational, theoretical, and practical applications as well.

Second, long-term dependence on an outsider to provide knowledge sets up a situation creating the need to learn how to do without them. This can leave the owners of the database with a system no one truly understands.

Third, people who depend upon experts often come to the point where they become disenchanted with that guru's opinions. If this happens, the owners of the database are left with no choice but to try to find yet another expert with better opinions.

Database Obsession and Technical Tunnelvision

Yet another way to try and relieve some of the anxiety database decisions place on people, is for those people to become obsessive about learning everything they can about the database product. These people become completely embroiled in the learning, understanding, and mastery of database concepts and technologies. They buy dozens of books, attend weeks of training classes, and spend an inordinate amount of time trying to assimilate all of the details they can about what a database is, how it works, and what it will do when some condition changes.

The net result of this kind of obsession can be that the person becomes extremely proficient in working with the database. The result might also be, however, that the person becomes so enmeshed in the details of how the database works and how things *should* be done, that they lose sight of what it is they set out to do in the first place. The details become so important that they fail to remember that they started out to build a system to meet some business objectives. Instead they try to build the perfect database and then find someone willing to use it.

Technical tunnelvision often results in the development of systems that are technically sleek but functionally cumbersome—or all too many times—totally useless.

The Search for the Perfect Database

For one subset of the database evaluator population, the solution to this anxiety becomes a process akin to the search for the Holy Grail. "If only I could find the perfect database then my life would be simplified," say proponents of this solution. They could then spend all of their time learning about that one product. Anyone else using anything else is obviously out of step.

So the search for the perfect database solution begins. Management consulting firms are paid large amounts of money to conduct studies on this subject. Think tanks command exorbitant fees to predict the future and point to the one true and best direction to go. Hours, days, and weeks are spent in research, investigation, and analysis. Unfortunately, when it is all said and done, two things have usually been accomplished. First, those who commissioned the study are more confused then ever about which database is best. Second, the technology changes, there's a new breakthrough, or a new functionality provided by a database vendor, and the process starts all over again.

Ultimately, the search for the ideal database product leads the investigator to the same place time after time. There is no such thing as a best database product. A database product is only one component of a much bigger database system. It is the behavior, performance, applicability, and functionality of the database system that people care about, not solely the database product itself. Failure to address the database system as a whole is failure to miss the whole point of your selection, implementation, or evaluation project.

What is a Database?

The question of what exactly a database is could in and of itself spark a lot of debate among data processing professionals. Depending upon what a person's experience is and what they are trying to accomplish, a database can be construed to be many things.

In the broadest sense, a database can be considered to be the sum total of all data that an organization keeps. This broad definition would include the data stored in traditionally defined databases, the data kept in different files and tapes kept throughout the organization, and would even include the data typed or hand written on forms, memos and other noncomputer sources. Although this definition can prove useful for certain kinds of discussion, it is certainly too broad a definition for our purposes.

A narrower definition, and the one to which we will adhere follows:

A database is a collection of data organized logically and managed by a unifying set of principles, procedures, and functionalities that help guarantee the consistent application and interpretation of that data across the organization.

Given this definition of a database, we continue by defining a database product:

A database product is a computer software product (a program or collection of programs) that manages the storage and retrieval of a set of data, organizes it logically, and provides the user with certain functionalities to guarantee that the data will be logically organized and consistently applied.

There are several different ways that database products can be categorized. We can classify them by the platforms on which they run, by the functions they perform, or by their architecture.

What is the Difference between a Database Product and a DBMS?

Another way that a database product might be marketed is to refer to it as a database management system (DBMS). There is no clear definition for what the difference between one or the other may be, but in general, when a product is called a database management system, it usually has built into its capability more than just simple data storage and retrieval functions. These products usually include robust backup and recovery capabilities, logging, locking and concurrency control, and security mechanisms that the lighter database product does not have. Although a few of the database products we consider might not be classified as database management systems, for the most part, database products do provide these functions in one form or another.

All databases, no matter what their architecture, platform, or individual features, can provide the same basic functionalities. We must stress that these products *can* provide, not *will* provide because only the designer or builder can guarantee that these benefits are actually exploited by the system.

The Profiles of a Database System

Databases are usually designed to:

- Make it easier to provide information to the users of the system
- Organize the data a system uses
- Control the storage and retrieval of data
- Improve the system's overall performance and maintainability

Let's consider how a database can be used to provide these benefits.

The Programming Profile

By organizing things so that they can be found more readily, and by establishing a standard procedure for input to and output from the system, the database is able to make it easier for applications to be developed. Existing programming tools, whether they be 2nd-, 3rd-, or 4th-generation products, query managers, or utility products, can be modified to work with the database easily enough. But more importantly, the job of locating where the information to be processed is stored and what the rules are for changing it is made significantly less bothersome. The bigger and more complicated the system gets, the more benefit a database provides.

We refer to the collection of characteristics that help end users and programmers with the processing of information as the *programming profile* of a database system. The programming profile consists of the programming language interfaces, built-in user access facilities, and the database's own programming functionalities.

Computer programs are an integral part of every database system. When we refer to programs here, we in fact refer to several kinds of programs.

Programming Languages

First, those collections of code (be they assembler, COBOL, PL1, Pascal, BASIC, or others) which provide the user with a way to work with the database. Programming languages represent the biggest expense of most computer systems in operation today.

Interface Management Systems

Also included in *our* definition of programs are those that are prewritten by software manufacturers and that work with a given database product. This kind of program, or collection of programs, is usually referred to as a *package* in the mainframe world, or a prewritten application in the PC arena. Software manufacturers write programs that handle accounting, human resource management, inventory control, and a host of other specific business functions. Although the database evaluator may not have full control or a full understanding of programs of this nature, they are still an important part of the evaluator's mix.

User-Friendly Interfaces: Programming Languages in Disguise

We include under this description those programs referred to as *user friendly* or *report- generation* programs, which claim to eliminate the need for a custom-written program. These programs that eliminate the programmer are really nothing more than half-completed application programs that the user is then taught how to use. More often than not, user-friendly interfaces simply force the user to become the programmer. This user-friendly input, whether it is the SQL language, a query by example, or query by form screen, is simply a type of program that the user writes and, as such, is included as a program, not a part of the database product itself.

Data Delivery Vehicles: Not a Part of the Database

This area can become particularly confusing since many database manufacturers market these user-friendly *front ends* as the most attractive component of their database product offering. For our investigation, it remains critical to separate the user-interface programs from the database products themselves if we are to have any chance of comparing databases from so many different environments.

Also included in our category of program components are those languages, products, and approaches for delivering data from the database in some kind of mixed collection of procedural language commands, screens, and/or key words. Products like CA-ADS, SQL-Forms, or CASE (computer-aided software engineering) products that generate programs and database components are considered here to be a very important part of the database system they belong to or work with, but are also considered to be something separate from the database.

Database Programmability

These program products and approaches are not to be confused with another set of customizable or programmable business logic built into databases themselves. Stored procedures, referential integrity capabilities, triggers, and a plethora of object-oriented and intelligent database capabilities *are considered* to be part of the database itself. The distinction between internal and external programming capabilities is made based upon where the logic is executed (within the database or outside of it) and how the timing for the execution of that logic is controlled (whether by a data-determined event, a transaction, or event-driven event).

The Architecture Profile

What is the difference between an environment with a database and one that does not? Imagine that all of the names in a phone book were kept on 3″ x 5″ index cards, with one card for each person's name. Imagine further that you divided up these cards between 100 people, each one deciding where and how to save 1/100th of the cards. It would certainly be possible to find somebody's phone number with this arrangement, but it would be difficult. First, you would have to determine who has the cards containing the name you are looking for. Then you would have to ask that person how they arranged their cards. One person might keep them well organized alphabetically in little file cabinets. Another person might sort them by address and keep them in a shoe box. Eventually you could find what you wanted, but it would be confusing, disorganized, and inefficient.

Imagine that we collect all of these cards and put one person in charge of them. We tell that person to sort the cards alphabetically and keep them in a chest of drawers that we have put aside for that purpose. In this situation, finding a name or address will be much easier.

Our first example describes an environment without a database, while the second describes how it would be organized with a *well-run database*. Unfortunately, a database is not magical. Just because you put all of your information into it does not mean that it will automatically become organized. You must not only put data into the database, but you must also tell it how you want it to be managed.

The method that a database uses to organize data is defined by its architecture. We refer to this as the *architecture layer* of a database.

Architectures

The architecture of a database describes the basic operational and logical organization that a particular database will assume in the execution of the tasks required of it. Some of the principal architectures include flat-file, XBase, hierarchical, network, relational and object-oriented.

It is the database architecture that dictates how the database will be perceived by users and programmers. It is around the architecture that logical and physical database design decisions are made. We devote several chapters of this book to the investigation of several of the aspects of architectures as they relate to overall database systems.

What is a Database Architecture?

In its fundamental form, the word architecture refers to the style or method of building something. We use the term database architecture with two distinct meanings.

First, in its singular form, a database product's architecture refers to the specific way it has been put together and the method of use and style to which users of that product must adhere.

Second, and more commonly, we use the term architecture to refer to the loosely-defined grouping of database products into families or related sets of database products that share some common characteristics.

Comparing the different database architectures is not a simple task. We can compare the architecture of second-century Romans and to Frank Lloyd Wright's Prairie Style architecture of the twentieth century, and note that there are some common characteristics. But there is a lot more about each that is unique.

The term database architecture refers to the method and style of building a system that a particular database product will support. Although there are several hundred database products on the market today, there are fewer than a dozen architectures that they use. We discuss eight of these architectures in detail: flat-file, XBase, SBase, inverted list, hierarchical, network, relational, and object-oriented. Although it is possible to break down the classifications of architectures to a much finer level of detail, it is our intention to review only these major classifications. Architecture tells us something about the way a database product accomplishes its primary objective, which is to manage data. It also indicates something about the environment in which it runs, the platforms it utilizes, and the other functions it will provide.

The Storage Management Profile

Databases are able to manage the data stored within them because they establish the control points through which users are allowed to place things into them or take things out again. When you decide to store things in a database, you tell everyone using it that they must always go through the same procedures.

Building on our index card example, the decision to store the cards in one place and keep them arranged alphabetically was the way that the we organized things. However, if we allowed anyone to go through the drawers and look for cards, remove them, and replace them at their whim, our system would begin to deteriorate. Someone might file cards in the wrong place or not replace cards at all. To prevent this, we could assign a librarian who could handle locating cards and filing them. This librarian could also then make sure that the person taking the cards signed them out properly, and returned them on time.

Databases establish this control over storage and retrieval through the use of several mechanisms. Indexing, hashing, clustering, and compression are only a few of the techniques that the databases use to guarantee that access is as quick and efficient as possible. These devices are implemented through the use of the database's own language for building data structures. These languages, referred to as the data definition language, schema generators, or simply the *gen-specs,* make it possible for the database administrator to control and vary the physical organization of the database independent of its logical organization. We refer to this collection of features and capabilities as the *storage management profile* of a database system.

Figure 2-1 shows a diagram of a database system in regard to the three layers of control it enforces. As you can see, we view the user of the system as requesting that information be processed through the *processing layer.* This layer is usually either a customized, prewritten application program or a user query tool—a product that makes it easy for users to write their own programs. The processing layer then determines what data is required, and formulates a request for it as defined by the database's architecture. The product itself is then able to efficiently retrieve this information from a storage medium (usually disk) through its *storage management layer.*

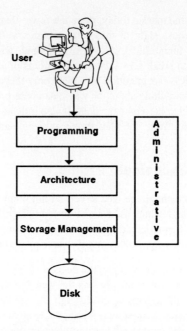

Figure 2-1: Database access through the profile layers

Database Functionality

Along with making it easier to find the data and keeping it in an orderly condition, the database actually provides the additional benefit of speeding up the process of finding and replacing information. It does this in three ways:

1. It finds things faster than you could without its help.

Imagine that our librarian kept a cross-reference sheet of where different cards were located. One sheet for names, one for addresses, and one for phone numbers. You could then ask her to find all of the names of people living in New York, and she could tell you immediately, because she figured it out ahead of time. The database provides this capability through the use of indexes. An index is an internally-controlled reference list that the database uses to find things quickly.

2. It arranges the storage of things so that related things are easy to combine.

Assume that we decide to expand our librarian's function to keep two sets of cards. Not only do we want all names from the phonebook tracked on cards, but we also want a set of cards holding information about every car registered in the state. These cards, one for each car, will also have the owner's name and address on it.

If people frequently asked the librarian to find certain people's names, phone numbers, and the cars they own, a good librarian might rearrange the file drawers so that the car owners' cards were located close to their phone number cards. There are several ways that this might be accomplished. We could mix the phone cards with the car cards in alphabetical order and keep them all in one very large file cabinet, or we could place the drawer with cards of car owners whose names begin with the letter A next to the drawer holding the names of phone owners beginning with the same letter, or we might simply color-code the drawers. The way we choose to do this will depend on several factors, but in the case of a database, it is determined by a combination of the database's architecture, and the design approach used.

3. It makes it easier to get the information in the order you want it.

If our librarians are really conscientious, they might allow us to ask that they not only locate the cards we have requested, but actually sort them in a certain order before giving them to us. Not all databases will do this, but most will do it in at least a limited fashion.

Most large-scale applications in use today could not exist without the presence of some kind of database management system. The processing would simply be too complex and too resource-intensive to be practical.

Just as the benefits we get from our card catalog depend upon the librarian and how conscientious the librarian is with our requests, so to does the selection of a database product determine how much benefit will be provided.

Administrative Profile

Administrative Functions

Although the layers of control exercised by a database define a large amount of the justification for using them in the development of systems today, there are additional functions that many databases provide that make them even more valuable. We recognize four groups of these capabilities:

- Backup and recovery
- Security enforcement
- Improved data concurrency
- Memory management

Backup and Recovery

Having all of the data kept under the control of the same database product allows the system developer to take advantage of some additional capabilities that would otherwise not be possible. One of these is the ability to keep track of what happens on the system and to recover should anything go wrong.

Continuing with our librarian example, we might decide that the cards in the system are too valuable, and that we cannot afford to lose any. What would happen if there was a fire and one of the file drawers was destroyed? The easiest way to protect ourselves is to have the librarian make copies of the cards and keep the duplicate set in some other building. That way, if a fire did occur, we could always use the old versions.

In the database world, this capability is referred to as backup. Most databases provide some kind of backup capability. For some, it is nothing more than a warning that you should copy your files every once in a while. For others, it is an extremely sophisticated, automatic function.

Of course, after the librarian has copied all of the cards, our information will remain safe until someone changes a card. When this happens we have a new problem. Now the backup copy of the card does not match the current copy. One way to guarantee that they stay synchronized is to have the librarian copy every card every night. Sometimes this is done, but what if only one card was changed? In this case, the librarian could simply make a copy of the new card and store it with the backup copy.

When the system keeps track of each change occurring on the system, it is called a logging capability. Logging is often a more efficient way to protect the identity of the data than a backup copy is. Using logs and backups to restore the system to the way it used to be is called recovery.

Computer system failures are a lot more common than many people think. If Pete's Pet Store loses an animal database because a floppy disk was defective or damaged, a backup copy will be good enough. If your bank does not keep logging facilities on the system that tracks your checking account, however, you still want them to be sure that no matter what happens, your account information is safe.

The other side of the issue is that backup, logging, and recovery take up a lot of system resources. The decision to use them or not depends upon the requirements for the system.

Security Enforcement

One additional benefit that the database can provide system builders is a better and more efficient way of handling data security than would be possible in a non-database world. Since the database is providing the control point through which all requests for data must pass, it is possible to create the database software so that you can decide in advance who is eligible to see, erase, or modify particular data. Although not all databases have a security capability, and even though not all systems that have it available make use of it, it can be critical to the success or failure of a database project.

Improved Data Concurrency

Data concurrency refers to the ability of the database product to allow several users to operate on the same piece of data at the same time. Although few PC databases provide this capability, the vast majority of workstation, minicomputer, and mainframe databases must include it in their product mix.

Concurrency can be an extremely complex capability to provide, especially since concurrent activities must all be logged, backed-up, and recovered just as they would normally. Concurrency is accomplished through the use of *locking* and *deadlock detection* mechanisms.

Memory Management

In order to provide all of these different capabilities, and to allow for the efficient accessing of data through its storage management capabilities, the database usually provides for some kind of computer memory management. The creation of buffers, caches, queues, and other types of memory allocation devices make it possible to tune the system to an optimum level of performance.

We can now add the *administrative profile* to our diagram of database organization. As you can see, the administrative capabilities overlap all areas of the database, helping make all of them run more smoothly and allowing for centralized control over the entire environment.

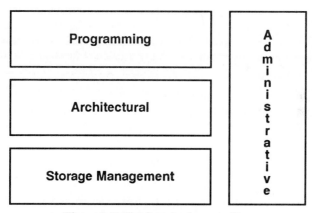

Figure 2-2: The four database profiles

The Synergy of Database Systems

By combining the processing, architecture, storage management and administrative capabilities of a database, the system developer is able to capitalize on a synergy that could not be experienced by making use of simply one feature or another. The database makes it a lot easier to build, design, and maintain a system than could be accomplished without it. It is here, in this synergy, that the database really pays off.

It is our proposal that by examining the capabilities of each database product as regards these three layers of functionality (processing, architecture, and storage management) and the administrative profiles of each, that we can develop the means to compare products in a meaningful and constructive way, regardless of their platform, idiosyncrasies, or marketing hype. The fact is that databases are databases, and they share a lot more similarities than differences. By reducing your view of them to these basic terms, it is possible to separate the facts from the impressions about how effective each one can be.

Database Functions and Requirements

Each of the functions a database provides can be related to a set of requirements that the system is expected to meet. If the system has no requirement for security, then whether a database product can provide that functionality or not is immaterial.

If the system is small enough, or simple enough, then there is a very good chance that no database will be required at all. If the requirements for the system cannot be addressed by a database product, then there is no reason to use one. Even if the database does provide a function that the system requires, that does not necessarily mean that the developer will take advantage of it. Why not? If database products can provide all of these enhanced capabilities to a system, then why doesn't everyone use them?

It's simple. The benefits that databases provide to the system have detriments associated with them. Databases are not magical panaceas that meet requirements at no cost. The decision to use a database in order to meet a requirement brings with it a trade-off that the system designer must take into account before deciding whether to use it or not. When developing a database system, the designer always has the option to place responsibility for a particular function—the meeting of a requirement—on the database or not. This delegation of functional responsibility may not be viable or attractive for any number of reasons, but they are always possible.

Determining what the trade-offs are when faced with the decision to choose between a platform, database product, programmed, or people resolution of a system requirement is the art and science of the system designer.

Building Database Systems

When you consider how complicated databases can be, it should come as no surprise that building these systems can be extremely complex as well. There are almost as many design methodologies as there are database systems. However, over time three categories of techniques have been developed to help the builder of a system in the process of deciding what particular arrangement will be best. These are *modeling*, *design*, and *tuning*.

Conceptual Design - Modeling

Modeling is the discipline utilized to help turn very complex and hard-to-understand business procedures into easy-to-understand abstractions that the system designer can then use to develop an optimum organization of database elements. Modeling is therefore concerned with users, their business processes, and the logical relationships between them.

Several approaches to modeling have been developed. These include *entity-relationship modeling*, which involves reducing the complex nature of business processes into entities (real world *things* that the system works with) and the relationships between them; *semantic data modeling*, which tries to capture the full complexity of these relationships by using a semantic or word-based approach; and object oriented modeling.

These modeling techniques, though quite different in their assumptions and execution, have several things in common. First, they emphasize the logical and abstract nature of the real-world system being modeled. They are not to be influenced by the way things are done, but instead, upon how things are really are. This characteristic is referred to as *process independence*. Second, they are used to develop a model that is equally useful no matter what database product or architecture is to be used. This is called *database independence*. Process independence and database independence are the characteristics that differentiate modeling from design techniques.

Logical Design and Architecture Mapping

The term *logical design* is used to define many different kinds of design processes. In fact, any design process that is logical in nature can legitimately refered to in this way. In an attempt to clarify the readers understanding we will try to de-emphasize the use of the word logical when referring to the design process, and will instead consider the processes of archictectural mapping. This is the process of determining how data will actually be grouped, named, and stored within the system, according the the assumptions dictated by an architecture. When performing architecture mapping , the user, programmer, or database administrator actually builds the data constructs (physical data organization structures) that make up the database system. Different database products and architectures make use of different kinds of constructs, but each involves the creation of storage components (tables, databases, or files), which are collections of data elements (fields, attributes, or columns).

In order to design effectively, a person must be familiar with the conceptual models developed for the system, the architecture of the database being utilized, and the nature of the applications that will be using the system.

Physical Design

While modeling and logical design are usually performed once in the life cycle of a database, tuning and physical design is a process that is conducted continually throughout its life. Tuning, sometimes referred to as design optimization or physical design, involves the modification of the database's storage management capabilities and the administrative profile parameters to help optimize system performance by varying the way the database operates physically. In order to conduct tuning, a person must know how the database stores and accesses data, manages memory, manages transactions, and handles logging and locking mechanisms.

Exposure to System-Building Disciplines

The use of these disciplines (modeling, logical design, and physical design) depend largely upon the size, type, and complexity of the system being built. For smaller and less complicated systems, it is usually unnecessary to undergo the rigors of formal modeling and design. In these cases, the design of the database will be intuitively obvious. As the number of users or complexity increases, however, so does the need for this type of discipline. For very large systems, whole teams of modelers, designers, and tuning experts will be employed to help derive the best database possible.

Advanced Topics and Future Directions

Although it is beyond the scope of this book to cover them in much detail, the following subjects are also of particular importance to the student of databases.

Distributed Database Systems

Distributed databases involve systems that span multiple hardware platforms, but which provide the user with transparent access to all of the data within. In the ideal distributed environment, users would be totally unaware of the actual physical location of the data that is being accessed. Instead, the system itself actually manages that information dynamically. The presence and increasing popularity of these systems present the database system builder with unique challenges and opportunities.

Gateways

Several database manufacturers have begun to dedicate a significant amount of their development efforts to the area of gateway capabilities. In its capacity as a gateway, the database serves as the focal point, allowing access to the products of other database vendors. Several products already excel at this, while others are just beginning to develop it. Although this feature is certainly related to distributed database operations, the implications and application of the technology can be quite different, but as distributed database approaches grow, so shall the gateway capabilities of many products.

Repositories

While distributed database and gateway capabilities seem to be the areas of keenest interest for database software vendors, the development of repositories, or super-database management systems represent the biggest trend for hardware manufacturers. Both DEC and IBM, two of the biggest hardware manufacturers in the world, have presented their versions of a repository product. A repository is designed to function as yet another layer of software in the database world, serving as both a superdatabase, which controls the access to all databases under its span of control, and as the place where business definitions for the treatment of data can be stored and enforced. This occurs regardless of the hardware or database that happens to hold a particular piece of data. Although it is unlikely that any but the largest of organizations will be making use of these repositories in the near future, they definitely represent a trend with which all should be aware.

Database Machines

Finally, no discussion of databases would be complete without mention of the database machine. This platform provides a unique blend of hardware, operating system, and database management system all within one dedicated unit. Although most database machines are built on the relational architecture, their unique ability to make full use of its hardware capabilities make them another significant force in the ever-expanding realm of database systems.

Conclusion

We have considered the different ways that people might approach the appraisal of database products, choosing the products, using them, or evaluating their performance, and many of the ways that people can become overwhelmed by the process. Anxiety, myopia, and technical tunnelvision all serve to make the process of working with databases more difficult.

It is proposed here that one of the most effective ways to reduce the amount of time and energy spent sorting through the many different features and functions of so many products, is to examine them all and develop a consistent and comprehensive body of knowledge that takes them all into account. That is the purpose of this book.

Earlier, we proposed that a database could be viewed as providing for three layers of influence over the management of data and three corresponding profiles that define how those layers work: the processing layer (programming and user access), architecture layer (logical organization and rules), and storage management layer (the physical storage and retrieval of data). We also considered the role and synergy provided by the database's administrative profile (the collection of memory management, backup, recovery, security, and concurrency management), and suggested that all products could be defined as a collection of these attributes and features.

We also considered the process of building database systems as regards modeling, the development of process- and database-independent views of the business environment; design, the development of a physical layout for the database; and tuning, the customization of storage management and administrative parameters. These processes provide the ability to optimize the performance of the system.

In the chapters to come, we will examine each of these layers and approaches in detail.

3

The Programming Profile

No aspect of database systems tends to be as confusing as that of databases and the ways to process data with them. This is not surprising when one considers how important the relationship between programming and databases is, and how many ways there are to do it. The ease or difficulty with which people can make use of the information stored within a database provides most people with their lasting impression of how good or bad the product really is. The availability of an easy-to-use programming interface is often the main selling point for one database over another. Because of this fact, database vendors spend a great deal of time, money, and marketing resources on the development of an impression that their product is the easiest to program with.

For the student of databases, however, this emphasis on the programmatic side of the database's capabilities can create many misconceptions about what is really going on with the system. This confusion is often exacerbated by the fact that vendors sometimes are clever in the way they package application development capabilities into a single, seamless database product.

Internal vs. External Database Programming

The first delineation to make in order to help the uninitiated understand the differences between the methods used to perform data processing with a database, is to clearly define the difference between the processing that occurs external to the makeup of the database itself, and that which is internal to it.

The external processing of database data occurs whenever an end user, program, or interface management system makes independent requests for the addition, deletion, modification, or retrieval of data within the database. In these cases, which define the vast majority of database processing done today, the process that makes these requests is outside of the control of the database itself.

In the case of internal processing, which is conducted through the use of triggers, stored procedures, and object-oriented database systems, the code or system intelligence is built into the very structure of the database itself.

We begin our discussions with the issue of external processing, and then proceed with the definition of the internal processing options.

External Processing and the Database

In order to understand external processing, we have divided the subject into three areas.

First, we discuss basic database access. Basic access is the fundamental ability to read and write from the database. All databases provide up to three forms of basic access; the ability to perform calls from within a program (the PDML); the ability to access the database with a special language (the UDML); or the ability to access the databases through special screens (the database access facility).

Second, we consider programming languages. These come in three forms (2GL, 3GL, and 4GL); three preparation/execution techniques (compiled, pseudo-compiled and interpretive); and are designed for use by programmers or users.

Third, we consider interface management systems, which are those products which make it easier to process data through the use of screens, menus and icons.

Before discussing the many ways that databases and external programs can be combined to provide the information management services required, let us start by examining the underlying facility that makes any kind of database access possible.

Basic Database Access

Despite the great variety of platforms, architectures, and profiles that the many database products work with, all database activity can be simplified to this basic element. In order to get things into or out of a database, there must be some fundamental language or mechanism that makes it possible for users and programs to work with the database. There are three ways that products provide for this baseline functionality: database calls (program data manipulation languages or PDMLs), user data manipulation languages (or UDMLs), and database access facilities (DAFs).

Database Calls

The first, and still the most popular way to allow external resources to manipulate the database, is through the database *call*. Database calls, as opposed to the other two basic access techniques, can be used only from within a program. These access methods are referred to as calls because the programs execute a call to the database, and ask it to perform some kind of operation.

The syntax for database calls is pretty consistent no matter which database you are using. Because of the nature of many programming languages, the syntax usually will be the keyword CALL (or some other term), and a list of instructional parameters.

```
CALL EMPLOYEE, ADD, EMP_REC
```

Figure 3-1: A generic database call

In some cases, with a language like C, the keyword CALL is eliminated and the name of the database function being performed is used in place of the word CALL. For example, if you wanted to add a record to a database file named EMPLOYEE, and the information was stored in a record layout named EMP_REC, then the instruction to the database would be something like the previous example while for other databases it will look like this:

```
ADDREC EMPLOYEE, EMP_REC
```

Figure 3-2: Alternate database call syntax

Of course, not all databases are organized this simply. In many cases, the parameters included with the database calls are really the names of program variables that hold the name of the database structure being accessed, the name of the operation to be performed, and all of the other processing information embedded within them.

This technique for accessing database data is often referred to as the *parameterized call syntax* or the use of a *program data manipulation language*.

Below are some examples of database calls from several different environments to delete a record for Parts:

C++ delete from a Versant database. (Part* is a pointer to the Part record.)

```
delete (Part*) partLnk;
```

Figure 3-3: A Versant database delete instruction

PASCAL delete from a Turboimage database:

```
DBDELETE (,PART,1,HOLD_VAR)
```

Figure 3-4: A Turboimage database call

An assembler language delete from an ADABAS database. (CB, FB, and RB represent the names of variables that hold the database call parameters). In this case, the variable CB would hold the delete command as well as the name of the record being deleted.

```
CALL ADABAS,(CB,FB,RB)
```

Figure 3-5: An Assembler language/Adabas command

A COBOL language delete from an IMS database. (As with the ADABAS example, the name of the record to be deleted, and the delete command are stored in variable structures.)

```
CALL 'CBLTDLI' USING (variable names)
```

Figure 3-6: A COBOL language/IMS database call

Although the exact syntax for these calls depends on the architecture of the database and the vendor's idiosyncrasies, the parameterized call has been the most popular means of database interface for some time. In fact, one of the quickest ways to determine exactly what a database can or cannot do, is to simply review a list of its call parameter options. Of particular interest are those commands having to do with the location of records.

Unfortunately, the user of a database will find that the parameterized call technique for working with the database has many shortcomings. Among them are:

- Calls must be placed within application programs

- Calls are usually too complicated for users to work with without some kind of help

- Calls are very rigid in their structure, and therefore can be very limiting and complicated

User Data Manipulation Languages

Given the inherent shortcomings of the called method of database access, it is not too surprising that an alternate method was developed. This method has been provided by the invention of user data manipulation languages, or UDMLs. UDMLs make the process of getting things into and out of the database easier and friendlier. This is accomplished by replacing the rigid, parameterized syntax of a database call with a relatively free form, data manipulation language, which allows both programmers and system users to perform their operations with a more English-like language.

The most prevalent of the data manipulation languages is the structured query language, or SQL, which provides the user access to relational databases. Whether it's SQL, EZQL or GDML, user data manipulation languages make the database easier for everyone to use by decoding the manipulation process. Unlike calls, data manipulation languages are used frequently by end users, ergo the name USER data manipulation language.

Below we have listed some examples of how some of the more popular UDMLs locate a Part record with a Part identification number of 123456. (Please note that user data manipulation languages come in two forms, the first form is where the language is its own , free standing database access mechanism. The other, are a collection of commands which are in fact a subset of a more robust User programing language (i.e., the FOCUS language) :

The SQL Language

```
SELECT PART

FROM PART_DB

WHERE PART_NUMBER = 123456
```

Figure 3-7: The SQL language (relational databases)

The FOCUS Language

```
TABLE FILE PART_DB
PRINT PART
IF PART_NUM IS 123456
```

Figure 3-8: A FOCUS language database call

The NOMAD Language

```
select part_number eq 123456
list part
```

Figure 3-9: The NOMAD user language with database call

The Interbase GDML Language

```
print part with part_number 123456
```

Figure 3-10: The Interbase GDML access language

Database Access Facilities

For several database products, the challenge of making things as easy as possible for the user is taken to the extreme. For these databases, there is no data access language of any kind provided. Instead, the vendor provides a collection of menus and screens, which guide the user through the process of getting information into and out of the system. With products of this type, there is no other way to manipulate system data. Because of this limitation, databases of this type have a very limited applicability to the development of any but the most rudimentary of systems. The tieing together of database access and database programming into one seamless package makes it difficult to classify these databases in the traditional view of data processing. We classify these databases as having built data access into a user-interface management system. Databases of the flat-file and SBase architectures fall into this category.

Developing a Taxonomy of Programming Profiles

Although being aware of these differences between database products and their programming profiles can be informative, there is a much bigger reason for our spending time on it at this juncture. The programming profile of a database management system is one of the four criteria upon which your appraisal of any database system must be judged. In order to appraise these products equilaterally, we must establish a taxonomy of the ways that these profiles are expressed.

The first component of our programming profile taxonomy is basic database access. We have defined three ways that this can be accomplished: with a database call, which is usually embedded within a program; a data manipulation language, which either is used within a program or directly against the database; and a database access mechanism.

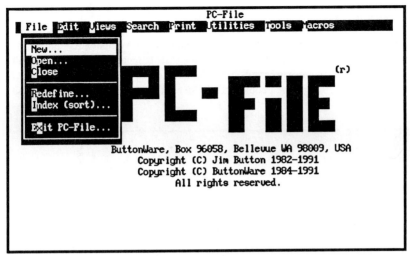

Figure 3-11: PC-File and its database access facility

As far as function is concerned, we can see that the taxonomy of database access and programmability can be viewed as a succession of three layers between the stored data and the end user.

I. External: Access only (no processing)

    A. Database access methods

        1. Calls (Program Data Manipulation Languages)

        2. User Data Manipulation Languages

        3. Direct Access Facility

Now let us proceed to build on this foundation with the next level of operational complexity: the addition of programming languages.

Programming Languages

When we refer to programming languages we refer to that collection of data processing mechanisms that allow the user or programmer to get the computer to do some kind of real work. Whereas the database calls and manipulation languages previously discussed allow for the simple retrieval and manipulation of data within a database, programming languages allow the user to actually add, subtract, move, and otherwise process that basic data. Languages require the programmer to create comprehensive collections of computer instructions, which tell the system what to do and when to do it.

Compiled, Pseudo-Compiled and Interpretive Languages

When discussing languages, the terms compiled, pseudo-compiled, and interpretive are referred to frequently. Let's take a moment and explain these terms in more detail.

Compiled Languages

The initial programming environment developed for computers required that programmers write their programs using an English-language syntax, like COBOL or C, and then turn those programs into something computer-readable. The process of turning something from people-friendly to computer-friendly is called compiling.

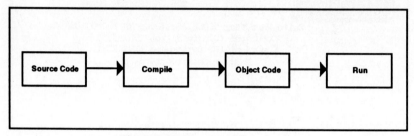

Figure 3-12: The compiling process

In order to perform the compile process, the programmer must first write the program using the selected language. This is called *source code*. After it is completed, the programmer runs a special program, called a compiler, which reads the English-language instructions and turns them into machine-readable instructions. The output of the compiler is referred to generically as *object code*. It is actually this object code that is run by the computer when a program is executed, not the original source code.

Interpretive Languages

As programming languages advanced, and computer power increased, it was no longer a prerequisite that languages be compiled. This new generation of languages, called interpretive languages, are executed directly from the English-language commands by the machine. Of course, the computer does not actually learn how to read English. Instead, a special minicompiler is built into the system. The computer is able to compile commands one line at a time. There are numerous interpretive languages and products in use today, including BASIC under PC DOS and the Focus database report generation language.

Whereas compiled programs must be completed and compiled before they can be run, interpretive languages can be run interactively by the user. In other words, the users can write the program as they go along, entering one command at a time. This makes it possible for users to experiment with programs and their desired results, making interpretive languages the choice for user-based programming languages.

Pseudo-Compilers

In a pseudo-compiler environment, when the program is ready to be used it is partially compiled into a form that is somewhere between interpretive and object code. An additional product (either a database environment or fourth-generation language program) is then required to run the program. These products are usually either a database environment or a fourth-generation language shell. The shell takes care of the rest of the compile process while the program is actually running.

The pseudo-compiler option obviously has some of the advantages and some of the disadvantages of the compiled and interpretive environments.

Procedural vs. Nonprocedural Languages

A procedural language or approach demands that the programmer or user define the specific step-by-step logic that the computer use in order to perform specific tasks. Here is an example of a BASIC program, written with a procedural language.

```
100 INPUT ,"WHAT IS YOUR NAME?", $NM

200 INPUT ,"WHAT IS YOUR AGE?", AG

300 PRINT "HELLO," $NM, "ARE YOU" AG "YEARS OLD?"
```

Figure 3-13: A Basic program

This program asks the user to enter their name and age and then prints a message on the screen. If a user named Joe, who is 12 years old, was to run this program he would see HELLO, JOE ARE YOU 12 YEARS OLD? on the screen.

The logic of the program is explained by the order in which the program's instructions are executed.

A nonprocedural language does not care about the logical order in which things are done. Data manipulation languages are a good example of a nonprocedural languages. For the purposes of our database and its programming profile, let us say that when referring to the expression *programming languages*, we will be discussing procedural languages. The other types of languages fall under the categories of data manipulation and user-interface management system languages, which although similar to programming languages, have a different purpose and function.

Definitions for the Programming Environments

Second-Generation Languages

The second-generation languages (2GL), better known as *assembler languages*, were the original set of what are now known as application programming languages. Assembler languages are an integral part of the operating system and hardware on which they run. As such, they can be written and run on only one type of hardware, whatever type they are made for. This means that an assembler-language program has no portability. Assembler code for one machine is useless on another machine.

In addition to the fact that assembler programs are not portable comes the additional constraint that they are incredibly complex and cryptic languages. Assembler language programs are written in a form that is very close to the way that the computer hardware itself works. Therefore, assembler programming is usually done only when very efficient, or very sophisticated operations must be accomplished.

Assembler languages are compiled and work with many, but not all, database products. They are platform-specific, command-driven, and procedural.

Third-Generation Languages

Third-generation languages (3GL) are those languages that have come to be traditionally known as application programming languages. COBOL, C, PL1, Pascal, RPG, BASIC, FORTRAN, and many more languages make up the 3GL ranks. Although each of these languages has some unique characteristics, they have several things in common.

- They are procedural languages.

- They are relatively independent of the platform. In other words, they generally can be written on one platform and then run on another. Although this is not 100% true, it is a stated objective for most of them.

- They are compiled.

- They have robust command sets. They can perform numerous functions.

- They run autonomously. They are separate from the database with which they work.

Third-generation languages are command-driven, procedural, compiled (usually), are platform-independent (usually), and database-independent.

Fourth-Generation Languages

It is in the category of fourth-generation programming languages (4GL) that we find a large group of new application programming tools. Fourth-generation languages differ from the 3GLs in several ways:

- They are usually interpretive or pseudo-compiled, though some are compilable.

- They have a far smaller command set than their 3GL counterparts. However, the commands they do have are more powerful.

- They are often tightly coupled with databases. It is not uncommon to find a 4GL with a special set of instructions specific to a database product.

- They are often packaged as part of a particular database product. In these cases, they are of limited usefulness without the database with which they are associated. The dBASE III and Informix 4GLs are good examples of this kind of product.

Examples of the three types of programming languages are shown below:

Assembler (2GL):

```
START:   MOV   Byte ptr PLG,0
MOV   PL,Byte Ptr
CMP   Pl, 20H
ARC   EQU   25
BUL   EQU   14
INT   BDDB
JMP   EXIT
```

Figure 3-14: An assembler language program

COBOL (3GL):

```
100-MAIN-ROUTINE.
MOVE NEWNAME TO OLDNAME.
OPEN FILE IN-FILE.
READ IN-FILE USING HOLD-RECORD-FOR-INPUT-PARM.
MOVE 12 TO HOLD_VARIABLE(COUNT).
MOVE INPUT_VALUE TO OUTPUT_VARIABLE.
IF OUTPUT_VARIABLE IS EQUAL TO 10 THEN
PERFORM LOW-VALUE-ROUTINE
ELSE
PERFORM HIGH-VALUE-ROUTINE.
```

Figure 3-15: A cobol program

dBASE III a fourth generation language (4GL):

```
CLEAR
SAY "ENTER THE ACCOUNT # DESIRED"
ACCEPT TO ACCOUNTFIELD
STORE ACCOUNTFIELD TO ACCOUNTFILE
```

Figure 3-16: The dBASE III programming language (4GL)

These short samplings of programs written with each type of programming language help illustrate some of the differences between them. As you move from 2GLs to 3GLs to 4GLs the language becomes less cryptic and easier to understand. At the same time, this progression from one type of language to the next also means that the programs written are less flexible and more expensive in regard to the computer resources necessary to execute them.

Using the Database with a Programming Language

Whether the programming language is 2GL, 3GL, or 4GL, it depends upon the same set of data manipulation languages or database calls in order to work with a particular database. These calls or requests are simply coded within the program, as any other operation would be.

When calls or requests are placed within a program, however, that program requires several modifications in order to allow it to work with the database effectively. No matter what database you are accessing and no matter what type of programming language you are using, those programs must be modified to include:

- Some kind of database input/output (I/O) area—a place within the program where the data placed into or taken out of the database is stored.

- A database communications areas, called the DBCOMAREA, SQLCA, or some other semidescriptive abbreviation. This communication area allows the program running to check on the status of each database operation it requests.

- The presence of a linkage section to include the file or a precompiler that binds the independently running program to the database with which it is communicating.

The decision to use a programming language to provide access for the processing of database data is dependent on several factors. For the vast majority of situations, these decisions are made automatically based on the environment within which you are working. Most organizations have standards that give direction to the decision maker. In other situations, only one of the options is available, making the decision quite simple. In situations where some programmer discretion is required. The following guidelines can be helpful.

Assuming that all three types of programming language access to a database are available, the decision to use one over the others can be based on a simple trade-off, that of efficiency compared to ease of use.

These three approaches to programming can be reduced to a simple continuum of efficiency/ease-of-use trade-offs. Assembler, or the 2GLs are the hardest to use, but the most efficient. Third-generation languages are much easier to program, but use more computer resources. Finally, 4GLs provide the simplest kind of programming, but also use the most of the system's memory and speed resources.

The Different Ways Programming Languages can be Used

Programming languages can be used in several ways in conjunction with the database. They can be used as the principle means of providing user access to the system through the writing of prepared application programs. They can be given to end users as a means to access database information directly. Or, they can be used to build certain processing capabilities into the database itself. (This application of programming languages will be considered under the Internal Database Access section of this chapter.)

Table 3-1: Programming language comparison

Type	Complexity	Flexibility	Difficulty	Examples
2GLs	Most	Most	Most difficult	Assembler languages for each hardware platform
3GLs	In between	In between	In between	COBOL C Pascal BASIC FORTRAN PL1
4GLs	Least	Least	Least	Informix 4GL Paradox Pal

Programming Languages Used in the Development of Applications

The most commonly defined means of providing users access to database data is through applications programs. Truly, when you say the word *programming* the first picture that comes to mind is legions of application programmers writing hundreds of millions of lines of code in order to develop the many different business computer systems in use today. The 2GLs and 3GLs are used exclusively for these purposes, and approximately half of the 4GLs exist for this same reason.

Programming Languages Utilized by End Users

Another aspect of 4GLs is the way that they can be modified for use by business users themselves. Of special interest to the student of database systems is that of the end user 4th generation languages in popular demand today. The vast majority of these are tied to database products. Databases like Focus, Nomad, RAMIS, SAS, DBase, Knowledgeman, Paradox, and dozens of others are marketed with a big emphasis on the end-user 4GLs that work with them.

Expanding the Taxonomy of Database Programming Profiles

Given the inclusion of programming languages to our taxonomy of the database's programming profile, we can incorporate more detail on our basic diagram.

I. External: Access Only (no processing)
   A. Database Access Methods
      1. Calls (program data manipulation languages)
      2. User Data Manipulation Languages
      3. Direct Access Facility (user-interface management system)
II. External: Processing and Access Combined
   A. Programming Languages
      1. User Languages
      2. Programming Languagses

Another way of looking at database programming accessibility is by categorizing these methods by whom the intended user is. From this perspective, we can see that end users can directly manipulate data by using:

- User Data Manipulation languages (UDML)

- User Programming Languages (4GLs)

Programmers can use these, but also have the additional availability of:

- Database Calls (PDML)

- Application Programming Languages (2GLs, 3GLs, and 4GLs)

Interface Management Systems

In recent years, the use of conventional programming languages has begun to lose ground to a new kind of data processing option, called the *interface management system*. Whereas a programming language allows users and programmers to process data by defining a series of computer instructions, the interface management system streamlines and simplifies the process by presenting them with a series of screens, menus, or other kinds of fill-in-the-blank interfaces. There are two kinds of interface management systems:

1. The programming-interface management system—This includes CASE, fourth-generation products and other kinds of advanced programming tools

2. The user-interface management system—This provides the end user with the means to develop applications on-the-fly without needing to understand a language of any kind.

Characteristics of Interface Management Systems

As opposed to programming languages, interface management systems:

- Are usually not procedure-based. They often do not require that the user do things in any preset order.

- Are usually form- or menu-driven as opposed to being language-driven. In other words, while a programmer must know the language and be able to build instructions based on that language, an interface management system usually builds applications by offering the user menu options or forms. The interface management system itself then builds a machine-understandable program, which it executes transparent to the user or programmer.

- Are more resource-intensive than the programming languages.

- Exchange flexibility for this ease of use.

Many interface management systems are built to capitalize on the new generation of graphical-user-interface (GUI, pronounced "GOOey") environments, including the Apple product line, X-Windows, Microsoft Windows, and OS/2 Presentation Manager. Because of this, these products often offer whole new frontiers of programmability never before available to the humble programmer or end user.

There are, in fact, three types of user interfaces that interface management systems can use: the graphical or GUIs (already discussed); text-based or TUIs (text-based user interfaces), such as IBM's CICS ; and GLUIs (graphic-like user interfaces). GLUIs look and act like GUIs, but actually are sophisticated TUIs.

The terms interface management system and user interface are in fact two completely different concepts. The user interfaces (TUI, GUI and GLUI) tell you HOW the database data is going to be presented to the user, while the interface management system is in actuality a system written to make use of that interface.

Programming-Interface Management Systems

Programming-interface management systems (PIMS) allow the programmer to build systems through the use of menus and fill-in-the-blank screens. Several products of this type have been in use for many years, but the approach has seen a resurgence in popularity as computer costs are reduced and as GUIs gain popularity. These two factors contribute to making programming-interface management systems attractive, powerful, and easy to use, while at the same time sparing large shared systems the additional expense that they usually incur.

There are several types of products that fall into this category, including code generators, CASE tools, forms-based interfaces, and hybrid interfaces.

Code Generators

The oldest and most common form of a programming-interface management system is the application code generator. These products allow the programmer to specify the logic, data elements, and screen aspects of an application, and define how they should work together *without ever writing code*. Instead, the programmer is prompted for identifying information, which the system itself then turns into executable program code. The code generated is usually a 3GL or 4GL, but there is no reason that assembler language applications could not be developed as well.

Since code generator packages create 3GL and 4GL programs, they must also generate the database calls or data manipulation languages required for database access, just as any normal 3GL or 4GL would.

Examples of this type of programming-interface management system include Computer Associates' ADS (Application Development System) and IBM's CSP (Cross System Product).

CASE Tools

CASE tools, or Computer-Aided Software Engineering tools, allow the developer to build applications by first capturing all of the logical and business requirements of a system. Then the tool drives these high-level definitions down to the level of programs. One way to look at CASE tools is to consider them as very sophisticated application and database system generators, with the emphasis on keeping track of the logical relationships between programs and databases. This makes it easy for analysts and programmers to make the changes at a high level and automatically have the changes applied to the lower, coded level.

Although the majority of CASE products available in the market today are sold separately from the databases they work with, some vendors have begun to include CASE capabilities in their product offerings. One example of this is the Mantis product from Cincom, the makers of the Supra database. Through Mantis, Cincom offers system developers an integrated CASE/database environment.

The blending of CASE products into database products is a logical progression when you consider how critical an integration of this kind is to the successful implementation of CASE technologies.

From the database programmability perspective, a CASE product generates code like any normal code generator. As far as programmability is concerned, the product must include database calls or user data manipulation language statements in the same way that a code generator must.

Forms-Based Programming Interfaces

With a forms-based programming interface, applications are built to run directly from the specifications entered into the system by the programmer. While code generators and CASE tools generate 3GL or 4GL programs that are in turn compiled and run, forms-based products execute directly from the screens of which they are made.

Of all of the types of programming methods considered, the forms-based programming interfaces are the easiest to use, the most restrictive, and the least efficient in regard to computer resources.

Systems that are built to make exclusive use of forms-based interfaces are often referred to as nonprogrammable databases. Their ranks include a fair number of PC-based databases including the Formbase product from Ventura Software and DataPerfect from the makers of WordPerfect.

Hybrid Systems

Of course, in the computer business nothing is simple. Along with these specific types of programming interface systems, there is also a sizable collection of products that use a combination of forms, 4GLs, CASE, and code generation approaches in order to offer an even richer set of options from which to choose.

Included in a list of these hybrid systems are the Q&A database, which combines forms and 4GL interpretive execution, and the Paradox PAL environment which includes forms, a programming language, and the ability to compile both.

User-Interface Management Systems

The programming-interface management systems (PIMS) make it easier for the programmer to develop applications, which can then be run for end users. An even more direct way to make the database accessible is through a product that allows the user to access and process the data directly through the same kinds of friendly screens and menus. User-interface management systems can be classified as query

managers, report writers, simple programming products, and cross-function interfaces.

Query Managers/Report Writers

The simplest type of user-interface management system is the query manager. A
query manager provides the user with the ability to enter user data-manipulation
commands onto a blank screen, or to build data requests interactively using a form.
In either case, these requests for data are applied directly to the database, and the
user is immediately presented with the results.

Most query managers include some form of rudimentary data formatting, so that
the information returned can be made presentable. Resulting data can be modified
through the addition of report headers, footers, column headings, and other basic
cosmetics. To be classified as a query manager, however, the product must not
allow the inclusion of processing logic or the building of extremely sophisticated
output reports.

Query managers often have the word *query* in their names, like the IBM QMF
(Query Management Facility) and the dBASE IV QBE (Query By Example)
offerings.

Simple Programming Environment

Although many of the tasks an end user would like to accomplish can be handled
by the query manager or a user programming language, many database products
have enhanced the capabilities of their menu-driven systems to allow users to build
simple programming logic into their systems. There is, of course, a fine line
separating those systems that offer application programming capabilities and those
we would consider to be simple user-interface programming products. The difference between the two has to do with the level of complexity they can handle. For
the simple programming environments, only the basic mathematical and conditional instructions can be utilized, while in the full programming interface management system, these capabilities are quite robust.

In this category we include products like the Alpha4 or Q&A flat-file database
systems. Although they have programmability, it is at such a rudimentary level that
an end user could perform all of the programming needed without assistance.

Executive Information Systems

The executive information system represents the deluxe version of a user-interface
management system. Within these systems, the user finds query management,
report writing, and simple programming capabilities. Also included are the ability
to perform in-depth statistical analysis and to create graphical displays of the data
being operated on. As is true with the CASE products, the majority of executive
information system products are produced by non-database vendors who make their
products connectable to almost any database in existence. However, several database manufacturers have begun to package their products with these features as
well.

Cross-Function Interfaces

Another fast-growing area of user-interface systems is that of cross-function system interfaces. The two principal types of products are the spreadsheet and word processing packages. Under this arrangement, spreadsheet products like Lotus 1-2-3, Quattro Pro, or Wingz, or word processing packages like WordPerfect, WordStar, or Microsoft Word are able to function as user-friendly front-ends to database systems. This allows the end user to build requests for database data from within the spreadsheet or document and then import the information from the database directly.

New cross-function interfaces are being built daily between the more popular spreadsheet, word processing packages, and many of the database products on the market today.

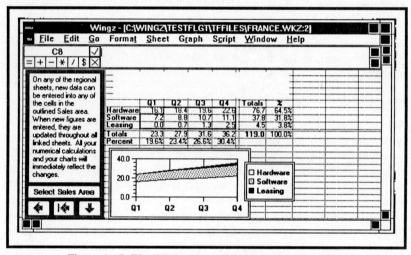

Figure 3-17: The WINGZ spreadsheet/database interface

One of the more integrated of the cross-function interfaces is the Wingz spreadsheet from the makers of the Informix database. In this case, the spreadsheet and database function as one seamless user environment. Another highly-integrated combination can be found between WordPerfect and the Dataperfect database, both from WordPerfect Corporation.

User Interfaces and Windows DDE

The users of interface management systems that run under a windowing environment, (like Microsoft Windows, X-Windows, and OS/2 Presentation Manager) now have an entirely new level of interconnectivity between their applications and the world of databases, no matter what the platform. This interoperability is defined by a facility referred to as dynamic data exchange.

Dynamic data exchange (DDE) allows the user of a spreadsheet, word processor, or other user-interface system to share memory with a database. This means that two unrelated products, including database products, are able to establish *hot links* between them. When these links are established, a person working on a spreadsheet can have data destined for storage in a database added, changed, or deleted from that database by simply changing the spreadsheet value. No intervention is required on their part.

Although DDE is still in its infancy, its continued propagation across platforms and products opens up an entirely new world of possibilities regarding user access to database-stored information.

When to Use Interface Management Systems

Because of the power, flexibility, and user-friendly characteristics of interface management systems, they are best used whenever:

- The user or programmer is interested in drastically reducing the time necessary to develop applications.

- The types of operations to be performed are more easily handled by a system of this kind.

- Performance and efficiency are secondary to appearances and user friendliness.

The continuum of programming approaches and their applicability can be summarized by three characteristics: ease of use, efficiency, and manageability. Each product offers a unique combination of these attributes, and it is the challenge of the product selector to determine which product strikes the right balance of the three.

Filling Out the Taxonomy

Our database product's programming profile can now be expanded even further. We are ready to add yet another layer of complexity to our already complex diagram.

II. External: Processing and Access Combined
    A. Programming Languages
       1. User Languages
       2. Programming Languages
    B. Interface Management Systems
       1. Programming-Interface Management Systems
          a. Code Generators
          b. CASE-Tools
          c. Forms-Based Programming Interfaces
          d. Hybrid Approaches
       2. User-Interface Management Systems

    a. Query Managers/Report Writers

    b. Simple Programming Products

    c. Executive Information Systems

    d. Cross-Function Interface Management

Users can gain access to the database directly through:

- Direct access facilities

- Data manipulation languages

- User-programming languages

- User-interface management systems

User can gain access to the database indirectly through:

- Applications prepared for them which use either application programming languages or programming interface management systems

By adding interface management systems, we complete our development of a model of external access and processing with the database. The only component of a database product's programming profile yet to consider is that of direct database programmability. With database programmability, system administrators are able to take the logic out of the hands of programmers and users and place it all under the control of the centrally-defined database itself.

Bundled, Packaged, and Third-Party Products

Before wrapping up our discussion of the external programming interfaces, it is critical that we consider one other aspect of those interfaces. This concerns the way that these products are marketed and made available to the user of the database.

In its simplest form, a database product can be viewed as totally independent of the application programming languages and the interface management tools that work with it. Only database programmability functions can legitimately be considered to be part of the database. All types of programming interfaces, languages, and interface management systems can be offered for sale in at least three ways: bundled, packaged, and as third-party products.

Bundled Programming Interfaces

Product bundling occurs when the product vendor decides to include a programming interface (language or interface management system) as an integral component of the database product being sold. This approach, found most frequently among the PC-based systems, presents the purchaser with a database, an access method, and a programming language as one seamless product offering.

There are several advantages to this approach for both the vendor and the user. The vendor is able to guarantee that whoever uses the system will have a well-defined, user-friendly environment in which to work. It also gives the vendor more control over the quality of the product.

For the system user, bundling provides simplicity—there is only one product to learn. It also provides dependability, because there is only one product that can go wrong, and accountability, since there is a single place to turn if things do not work right. The disadvantages of bundling often outweigh these advantages, however. For one thing, products that are bundled together too tightly, where the database can be accessed only by the programming product, leave the system user with very little room for system expansion when new requirements crop up.

All too often, database products are purchased based upon the attractive bundling provided by the vendor. In a large number of these situations, the purchaser finds out much later that the product does not allow for the expansion of the system into other areas. Of course, when this happens, the purchaser is left with no choice but to purchase yet another package based upon still another set of criteria, and the cycle starts over again.

This cycle is responsible more than most other factors for duplication of data and programming effort within most organizations. It is for this reason that we are spending so much time discussing programming profiles and separating them from the other characteristics of databases.

There are several examples of bundling, including:

- PC flat-file databases, which are packaged with a user friendly front end

- The XBase family of products, which tend to be considered as programming languages first and as databases second.

- Mainframe and minicomputer database packages like Focus, RAMIS, Nomad, and SAS, which concentrate more on the processing of data than they do on the management of it.

There is nothing wrong with this kind of product bundling. Indeed, the creative marketing ideas simply provide more variety for the purchaser. However, this bundling tends to make it difficult for the student of databases to compare one group of products to another.

Packaged Programming Capabilities

Whereas bundling includes programming capabilities as a part of the database, a much more common way for a vendor to offer databases and their complementary products is by packaging and selling them separately. This is by far the most common technique for several reasons. The packaging approach allows the customer to purchase only what is needed and allows the vendor to sell two products, a programming product and a database, instead of only one.

These package approaches include most of the mainframe and minicomputer 4GLs and interface management systems, and many of the workstation and PC platforms. Products like IBM's Cross System Product, Cincom's Mantis, Computer Associates' Application Development System, and Informix's Wingz are good examples of products sold to work with one database, but which are able to work with others.

Third-Party Products

Another huge market for programming software is in the area of what are called third-party products. Third-party products are developed by companies not in the database business at all, but which are in the business of developing programming interfaces that work with several databases equally well. Although a detailed exploration of these products is beyond the scope of this book, suffice it to say that third-party products expand the usability and effectiveness of any database product they work with.

Included in the ranks of third-party software are the spreadsheets and word processing packages referred to earlier, as well as a great many of the CASE, executive information systems, and interface management systems. Also included are the vast majority of the 2GLs and 3GLs.

In order to understand databases in a way that makes sense across all platforms and architectures, it is useful for us to unbundle or disassociate these products from the databases they work with whenever possible. The unbundling we perform here is something that many database vendors have already done with their products. Previously bundled products, like the XBase, systems are constantly being unbundled by vendors in order to increase their market share. This is why a database product like Focus is able to process data from dozens of other database products as well as its own.

Another way to look at the bundling and unbundling of programming capabilities with a database product is to consider it in terms of the built-in (bundled) and potential programmability provided.

For example, you might prefer using a database that offers a very friendly user-interface management system. After purchasing the product and developing the initial applications, you might decide you would like to expand your application in order to do some things the this interface management system cannot provide. It is at this juncture that the potential programmability of the product is important. Can you access the database using the C language? Can you access stored data through a Lotus 1-2-3 spreadsheet? Does this database prevent you from using other interface management systems you might like to use?

We can now add this aspect, the packaging and availability of programming interfaces, to complete our taxonomy of external programming capabilities.

I. External: Access Only (no processing)
   A. Database Access Methods
      1. Calls (program data-manipulation languages)
      2. User Data- Manipulation Languages
      3. Direct- Access Facility
II. External: Processing and Access Combined
   A. Programming Languages
      1. User- Access Languages

2. Application Programming Languages
B. Interface Management Systems
  1. Programming-Interface Management Systems
     a. Code Generators
     b. CASE Tools
     c. Forms- Based Programming Interfaces
     d. Hybrid Approaches
  2. User-Interface Management Systems
     a. Query Managers/Report Writers
     b. Simple Programming Products
     c. Executive Information Systems
     d. Cross-Function Interface Management
C. Types of External Programming Capabilities by Availability
  1. Bundled
  2. Packaged
  3. Third-party

Internal Processing and the Database

Database Programmability: Data Processing Internal to the Database

Given our overview of the *external* processing options for working with a database, we can turn now to the *internal* ones in greater detail. You will recall that we defined the internal database processing options as those procedures giving the database full control over the execution of procedure logic. *

Where is the Logic Stored?

One way of classifying programmability is to consider where the logic or intelligence of the system is stored. Internal programmability is provided when the database itself stores, manages and runs programs. By examining systems in this light, we can see a logical progression in the development of database capabilities and derive a basic understanding of how databases and their processing capabilities vary. To help illustrate this, let us follow the development of application programming and databases in a brief historical review, keeping in mind the location of the system's logic and intelligence as new technologies are presented.

The Business World before Computers

In the precomputer business world, businesses had to function without the benefit of the data processing function. Most small businesses today still operate without it. In these situations, the rules necessary to run the business must be kept in one of two places: either on pieces of paper, or within the minds of the employees. The owner of the business is subject to the efficiency and accuracy of the employees in order to be sure that those rules are enforced.

The Computer-Managed Business

When businesses began using computers, it was discovered that one of the advantages was that the enforcement of rules and policies could be enhanced by the computer system.

For example, assume that a company has a policy that no orders are to be taken from customers who are overdue in their payments. Despite a policy like this, without a well-developed computer system, there are many ways that a customer might get around it. The customer might be good friends with a salesperson, or the person taking the order might forget to check the delinquent accounts list. If the company uses a computerized order entry system that checks on the status of a customer's account, then management is guaranteed that the rule will be enforced no matter what.

The Addition of Databases to the Business Environment

When databases were added to the business data processing environment, organizations found an even better way to keep track of information and store some of the business logic. Some of the burden for keeping track of how things are organized and enforced is captured by the structure of databases themselves.

Advanced Database Functionality

As databases have become more sophisticated, so too have they taken on more of the responsibility for cataloging and controlling not only the data itself, but the processes that use the data as well. The object-oriented database architecture and repository management products move the database to a level of almost full responsibility for this.

Therefore, the history of database technology can be viewed as a progression of ever-increasing dependence on a centralized data management facility that makes processing larger amounts of data easier.

Another way to view this is by looking at programs and their functionalities. From this perspective, we can say that programs have four functions:

1. To access data (Access)

2. To enforce business rules that protect data from corruption (Enforcement)

3. To prepare and process that data for users (Preparation)

4. To prepare a screen or printed display of the results (Presentation)

The second pair of functions, presentation and preparation, define things that programs do to make it easier for users to work with information. The first two, enforcement and access, are concerned with the integrity and efficiency with which that is handled. When considering the evolution of database products and their relationship to programs, we can see that the first generation of databases concentrated on the data access functions, leaving the other three areas to external programs. The newer database products, however, are beginning to concern themselves with the enforcement of business and integrity rules in addition to the more traditional database functions.

It is unlikely that the developers of database products will stop there. Already, some database products are concerned with some of the presentation and preparation aspects of the data that they work with. It is safe to assume that this encroachment on the world of application development will continue.

Reasons to Use Database Programmability Options

There are, of course, many reasons people would want to take advantage of a database's programmability. In its broadest definition, database programmability offers the developer yet another tool for the development of applications. Programmable databases allow the system to manage the centralized storage and execution of often-used programs, and to make those programs easy to identify and maintain.

In a more theoretically-defined form, the facility makes it possible for developers to place the data protection processes under the control of the database, while allowing programs to concentrate on the preparation and display of data to the end user.

Types of Business Rules

Since most database programmability is concerned with the enforcement of business rules, we begin with a description of what they are.

The definition of what business rules are and how they can be enforced is in the early stages of definition as a computer science topic. However, between the many vendors and theorists, the following types of rules have been identified:

1. **Data Identity Rules** — A requirement that data entities be stored and tagged as being unique. Identity rules guarantee that no duplicate values for the same elements are allowed on the system. In physical terms, this type of rule is usually enforced through the use of indexes. For example, if you had a database that held information about cars, and wanted to make sure that no one added the same car twice, we might put a unique index on the Serial Number field. That way, any attempt to insert two records with the same serial number would result in an error. Almost every database in existence provides this minimal level of business rule support.

2. **Domain Enforcement** — The identification of all the valid values that a given field can have, and the enforcement of those constraints. For example, you might want the Color field of a car database to have only the values blue, red, or green. These values are said to describe the domain of the car color field. With domain enforcement capabilities, the database will make sure that only those values can be entered.

3. **Referential Integrity**— This capability allows the developer to set up permanent relationships between different fields of the database and make sure that the *integrity* of their relationship is preserved. For example, if you wish

to require that in order to add a car to our database, there must be a record for its owner already on the system, referential integrity will guarantee it.

4. Complex Interdependencies — There are dozens of other ways that databases can be used to help assist the developer of a system in protecting the integrity of system data. Most of these more advanced options are handled by the object-oriented databases.

Only a very limited subset of database management systems use most of the internal processing options. The greatest population of products using internal processing can be found among the newer relational databases, which use it intermittently. On the other hand, the most dedicated users of this approach are the object-oriented databases, which are designed to use it almost exclusively. Although the detailed dynamics of the way object-oriented databases use this option really falls under the topic of database architectures, we mention it here for completeness. The split personality of object-oriented databases—that is, their dual role as data storage mechanisms and processing managers—is what makes their architecture unique.

Mechanisms for the Execution of Internal Database Processing

Different database products use different mechanisms in the provision of internal processing capabilities. There are four primary mechanisms used by most.

These include Stored Procedures (Command and Event-Triggered), rules built into the database structure, rules interface management systems and object oriented approaches.

Stored Procedures

The most frequently used mechanism for the handling of database programmability is for the vendor to build special tables or storage areas within the product itself. These areas hold programs. Once stored, these programs can be executed by a variety of mechanisms, including the use of special data manipulation commands or the creation of triggers. We refer to these as stored procedures.

The main difference between stored procedures and the more traditional programming techniques is therefore twofold. First, for external programming products, the programs are stored and executed outside of the database, whereas these are managed totally within the database product. The second is that while external programs are told to execute by way of a user- or system-generated command, the database's internal programs are controlled through special database execution commands or through a command generated by the database itself.

The biggest differences between stored procedures on different databases have to do with the languages that make them up, and the ways that they are executed. Some databases allow only the SQL language as its storable language, while others make use of a fully-functional 4GL. Obviously, the more powerful the stored procedure language, the wider the variety of business logic that can be captured.

Command-Triggered Procedures

Command-based stored procedures are executed whenever the specified key words or data manipulation language syntax is executed by an end user or from within a program.

Because command-based stored procedures can be executed at any time, they are most often used by system developers to function as remote application programs, rather than in the more rigorously-defined business rules enforcement role. With the command-based procedure, few of the previously-stated advantages of using database programmability are enjoyed, but the facility does allow system designers to redistribute the execution load from an application to a database. It also allows them to develop and store often-used queries and programs for centralized access by users and programs. The following example of an Informix stored procedure is really a program which checks for cancelled customers and deletes them from the table. This procedure, stored on the database, can be run whenever the *delete_customer* command is issued.

```
create procedure delete_customer(purchaser_name);
     define sql_err int;
     define p_purchaser_name char(20);
     define change_date int;
foreach select purchaser_name
     into p_customer_name
     from customer
     where status = 'cancelled'
end foreach;
delete from customer
     where purchaser_name = p_purchaser_name;
```

Figure 3-18: An example of an Informix stored procedure

Event-Triggered Procedures

Procedures triggered by some kind of internal database event, on the other hand, provide much more functionality to the developer. In these cases, programs are executed whenever a data value specified by the trigger command is modified by an outside source. For example, a database with a field that holds people's last names can be set up so that when someone changes the spelling, a message is sent to a security terminal.

The following example shows an event-triggered procedure in the Interbase database. In this case, the trigger will be executed whenever a customer's status gets changed to cancelled automatically. This will then *post* the customer_alert event which will notify all concerned parties of the fact that this customer is no longer a valid customer in good standing.

Whereas the command-based procedures are best viewed as little more than an enhancement to the developer's programming options, the trigger-based procedure

```
define trigger check_status for customer
   modify:
       if customer_status = 'cancelled'
          then post customer_alert
end trigger
```

Figure 3-19: An example of an Interbase trigger

opens a whole new world of programming possibilities. Triggers are used to provide many kinds of business rule enforcement capabilities, including constraints and referential integrity. They also serve as alarms and notifiers, detecting conditions like low stock levels, security access violations, and many events that used to be missed by more passive systems.

Rules Built into the Database's Structure

Another other way that business rules and logic can find their way into the database is through the use of special database structure components. Using the structure of a database to help define its use is nothing new. All databases from the simplest flat-file to the most complex object-oriented are able to influence and dictate how data is to be used.

In order to expand this rules enforcement capability, database vendors have added new kinds of structures that help impose new kinds of constraints on the users of the system. Indexes, data field constraints, referential integrity structures, and cross-reference tables are only a few of the many ways that this is accomplished. See Figure 3-20 for an example.

```
CREATE TABLE CUSTOMER
   (
   NAME   CHAR (15) ,
   CITY   CHAR (10) CHECK CITY IN
                    (CHICAGO, NEW YORK, LOS ANGELES)
      . . . .
      . . . .
   )


(An Informix "Check" statement, which guarantees
that only customers from Chicago, New York or Los An-
geles will be added to the CUSTOMER table.)
```

Figure 3-20: Structurally defined business rules

Structure-based enforcement of business rules has had a turbulent history. While placing business-defined constraints and referential integrity into the database's structure makes it highly enforceable with a minimum of maintenance, they also degrade system performance and make it difficult to change any of those rules.

Rules Interface Management System

For a select few database manufacturers, the problem of how to allow the database more control over processes is handled by the creation of an additional layer of software. This layer manages the creation, modification, and execution of all of the rules as a separate process on top of the database's normal functions. These products, which include the Unify and Pace databases, and the IBM Repository Manager, provide the system manager with a customized interface management system dedicated to the collection and enforcement of many kinds of business rules.

Rules management software has both positive and negative impacts on the overall management of the database environment. On the one hand, an approach of this kind makes the administrator's job much easier. Instead of having to track down the location of business rules in programs or within stored procedures, the software allows all rules to be managed from one place.

On the other hand, the additional system overhead implicit in the approach forces the user to ponder the consequences for long-term system efficiency. Ultimately, the decision about whether the rules interface management system approach to rules management will be only be determined by continued development and exploration of the possibilities.

The Object-Oriented Approach

The natural progression of database programmability reaches its maturity in the construction of object-oriented databases. In these databases, there is no question about where the system's logic resides. It will, by definition, be a component of the database itself.

In order to provide this functionality, the object-oriented database must have an additional software control layer, similar to the one used by the layered programmability approaches. In this case, however, the amount of additional overhead is reduced because application programs themselves have a greatly reduced role.

The object-oriented approach to programming with databases is still in its infancy. However, it is making significant headway in several specialized application areas including medical, design, scientific, and engineering applications. The dominance of object-oriented databases in these fields can probably be attributed to several factors, emphasize the strengths of the object-oriented approach.

- In these areas, the cost of hardware, software, and system development is minor compared to the importance of the processing that needs to be done. In these systems, accuracy and precision are imperative.

- These applications tend to have well-understood and relatively rigidly-defined parameters. This clarity of purpose and stable requirements make object-oriented programming much easier to accomplish than it would be in a typical business application. Usually, accuracy is less important and the cost of the system is much more important is business system.

- It requires a great deal of sophistication and a large amount of training and experience to build object-oriented systems well.

Choosing and Using Internal Database Programming Functions

For the person unfamiliar with the many ways that databases can be internally programmed, the subject of which one to use and why can be befuddling. In order to do this decision-making process any justice, we must begin by identifying the reasons that anyone would want to use these approaches in the first place. With the exception of triggers, which offer a new kind of functionality, the database's internal programmability options are nothing more than alternative ways of doing the same things that have been done with programming languages and interface management systems for years. There are two sets of valid reasons for making use of these functionalities, one strategic and one tactical.

Tactical Uses of Database Programmability

Organizations or individuals can make use of this programmability whenever there is a short-term desire to simplify the system for users. This can be done by storing often-used procedures in the database and making them available to all, or by building identity, domain, and referential integrity rules into the structure. This way, users can freely manipulate data directly without fear of impacting other users or processes.

If the system being built is expected to have a lot of direct access by users, then using database programmability makes good short-term sense.

On the other hand, if the system is expected to be accessed primarily by prewritten application programs or packages, then using these capabilities simply adds overhead to the system.

Strategic Uses of Database Programmability

If the system being developed is intended to satisfy longer-term objectives, then the importance of using these facilities takes on a new importance. Very large, or very long-lived systems—even if they are developed with the utmost of care—tend to collect multiple versions of business rules within multiple generations of application programs. In cases like these, the longer the system exists, the more bogged down in maintenance it becomes. This occurs because more and more programs must be changed whenever business conditions change. It is in an attempt to address these concerns that database programmability came into existence in the first place, and will probably continue to be an attractive alternative for the development of large, complicated systems.

The Internal Programming Taxonomy

The taxonomy for the last area of consideration in our development of a comprehensive description of the database's programming profile is made up of those components relating to internal database programming and logic capabilities.

III. Internal Characteristics
  A. Reasons to Use Internal Database Programmability
    1. Centralization of Program Execution and Management
    2. Ease of Use
    3. Enforcement of Business Rules
      a. Identity Enforcement
      b. Constraint Enforcement
      c. Referential Integrity
      d. Complex Interdependencies
  B. Mechanisms for the Execution
    1. Stored Procedures
      a. Command-Driven
      b. Event-Driven (triggers)
    2. Structural Enhancements
    3. Rules Interface Management Systems
    4. Object-Oriented Databases

Programming Choices From a Business Perspective

Now that we have explored many of the ways that databases handle programmatic and logical processing, we can consider what all of these things mean to the businessperson, making decisions about the systems being built.

Consider Sam, the manager of the shoe store mentioned briefly in Chapter 1. Sam had never worked with a computer before, and decides to purchase a PC to help him manage his business. After Sam purchases his computer, he must decide on the method that will be used to process his information for him.

His first option is to write a series of customized application programs using a language like BASIC or C. If he does this, he will need to figure out, in detail, in advance, exactly what functions and operations he wants to perform, and then write the programs that satisfy the requirements.

On the other hand, Sam might decide to use a prewritten end-user tool like the Paradox QBE (query by example) facility, or a Lotus 1-2-3 spreadsheet with database access capabilities. In this case, Sam does not need to write any programs at all. All he would need do is learn how the tool works and then get it to work with the database. In this case, Sam is using an Interface Management System (Lotus or QBE) in order to provide direct user access to the system.

Obviously, these two approaches create an entirely different environment for Sam to work in. In the first case, he will reduce his initial system expenses by avoiding the purchase of a user tool. However, he will end up investing a lot of time and energy in the development of customized applications. In the second case, he will reduce the expense and bother of the customized application, but will need to learn all of the idiosyncrasies and operating assumptions of the tool that he purchases. Each option offers advantages and disadvantages that he must weigh when making the decision.

Let's consider Situation 2 mentioned in Chapter 1: Mary, the chief information officer of a large corporation. From Mary's perspective, the issues of database programming are much more complex than they are for Sam. Mary faces an organization that could not exist without millions of lines of COBOL and assembler code, which run the organization's mission-critical applications on a daily basis. To Mary, these programs represent a mixed blessing. On the one hand, there is so much business intelligence and organizational structure built into these applications that the business literally could not survive without them. On the other hand, there are so many of them and they are so complex that it is almost impossible to maintain them all, let alone keep up with the frantic pace of enhancements that are being demanded.

This dilemma provides Mary with a justification for considering a second option: using interface management systems for direct user access. By allowing system users to take advantage of these tools, Mary is able to reduce the backlog of application program enhancements that are demanded, while allowing the users to get the information they need in a timely manner.

Unfortunately, this too provides a paradox. Although allowing end users to get their own information and to write their own programs reduces the strain on the application development staff, it also creates an additional and unpredictable strain on the computer system's hardware and telecommunications facilities.

While the rest of the computer system's environment runs according to schedule, an end user, armed with the ability to run programs at will, can very quickly bog down the system with too much activity. Along with this negative impact, comes the fact that end users who write their own programs are not subject to the rigid discipline and rules that application programs follow. This means that there is no way to guarantee that the information being handled by those end users is accurate and meaningful. Worse than that, there is no way to assure that these amateur programmers will not inadvertently slip up and erase, change, or insert invalid data. User tools, for the most part, allow for only a minimum of business logic within their definition, and therefore, allowing access to important information, utilizing tools of this kind, can be a highly risky undertaking.

For Mary, neither the application programming nor the user-interface management system solution seems to provide a good answer to her problems. Mary must turn to our third alternative, database programmability, for this.

By placing the business rules, procedures, and constraints that are critical to the operation of the business into the definition of the database itself, Mary accomplishes several things.

First, she can now instruct the application programmers to remove complicated business rules and procedures from within the programs where they currently reside. This will make those programs smaller, easier to write, and much easier to maintain. It also guarantees that only one version of those rules is in force at any one time.

Second, she can now allow end users to access the data using their tools much more freely. This is because the database itself, not the application programs or the users themselves, will be responsible for seeing to it that these business rules are followed.

For the builder of computer systems, the availability of different programmatic interfaces can become the most important selection criteria. In these cases, the packaging of those products (bundling, packaging, and the availability of third-party products) and their internal programmability can spell the difference between a successful implementation and a dismal failure.

Summary

In our coverage of the individual database products, we refer consistently to each product's external and internal (when applicable) programming profiles. In noting these profiles and the bundling or unbundling that the vendor provides with the product, you should be able to develop an appreciation for how each of them compare on this important issue.

A Complete Taxonomy of Database Programming Profiles

I. External: Database Access
   A. Database Access (no processing)
      1. Calls (program data-manipulation languages)
      2. User Data Manipulation Languages
      3. Direct Access Facility
II. External: Processing and Access Combined
   A. Programming Languages
      1. User Languages
      2. Programming Languages
   B. Interface Management Systems
      1. Programming-Interface Management Systems
         a. Code Generators
         b. CASE Tools
         c. Forms-Based Programming Interfaces
         d. Hybrid Approaches
      2. User-Interface Management Systems
         a. Query Managers/Report Writers
         b. Simple Programming Products

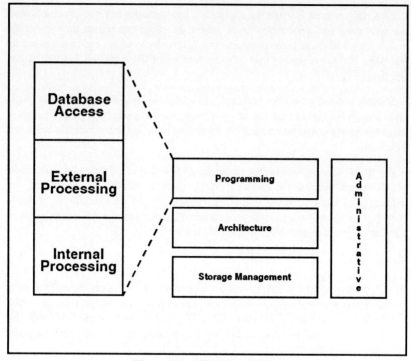

Figure 3-21: The four profiles

    c. Executive Information Systems

    d. Cross-Function Interface Management

  C. Types of External Programming Capabilities by Availability

    1. Bundled

    2. Packaged

    3. Third-party

III. Internal Characteristic

  A. Reasons to Use Internal Database Programmability

    1. Centralization of Program Execution and Management

    2. Ease of Use

    3. Enforcement of Business Rules

      a. Identity Enforcement

      b. Constraint Enforcement

      c. Referential Integrity

      d. Complex Interdependencies

  B. Mechanisms for the Execution

    1. Stored Procedures

      a. Command-Driven

      b. Event-Driven (triggers)

2. Structural Enhancements

3. Rules Interface Management Systems

4. Object-Oriented Databases

Throughout our coverage of databases, we refer to this taxonomy in order to help define how each product works with programs. We define each product's capabilities in three respects: external access directly to the data, external access through interfaces, and Internal database programmability. In order to facilitate this, we use the following tables:

First, when considering the ways that a particular product allows for direct access to the stored data, we will use this table:

Table 3-2: Direct access method criteria

Database Access Method	
Program Data Manipulation Language (PDML)	
User Data Manipulation Language (UDML)	
Direct Access Facility	

When considering the different ways that programmatic access to the database can be accomplished, this table is used:

Table 3-3: Language and interface criteria

Languages and Interface Management Systems	
User Languages	
Programming Languages	
User Interface Management Systems	
Programming Interface Management Systems	

And finally, for those databases that provide the functionality, we will use this database programmability table:

Table 3-4: Database programmability criteria

Database Programmability	
Command-Based Stored Procedures	
Event-Driven Stored Procedures (triggers)	
Structurally-Defined Business Rule Enforcement	
Rules Interface Management System	

Each database manufacturer offers its customers a different combination of built-in (bundled) and potential programming capabilities. When comparing databases it is important to keep both the built-in and potential capabilities into account.

The sum total of the built-in and potential programming capabilities that a database product facilitates is referred to as its complete programming profile. This profile defines one of the four profiles that allow the database selector, developer, or evaluator to objectively ascertain the value and fit that a product will have for the application being considered.

4

The Architecture Profile

Having completed our examination of the programming profiles that a database may present, we can turn now to its second profile, the architecture. As we have previously stated, an architecture defines the way that a database is logically organized, and defines the interface between methods of programming and the actual physical storage and retrieval of data.

Products and Architectures

As a direct result of the extensive research done in the preparation of this book, eight architectures have been identified as having the most significance to the student of database technologies. The architectures that we have chosen to highlight here were selected for one of three reasons:

1. The group of products share the same architectural approach and represent a significant portion of the database market of today.

2. The architecture has a history of providing a sound and time-tested organization that makes it worth further study

3. It represents the leading edge or current direction into which database products are headed.

The Value of Understanding a Database Architecture

Although not all databases fit neatly into one of the families we have described, by examining the database products in this way, we have been able to develop a set of operational characteristics, terminology, and logical data organization assumptions that can provide us with several insights.

First, although all products do not fit into these categories, all products exhibit some unique combination of these operational characteristics: terminology and logical data assumptions. This allows us to compare one database to another on equal footing. In other words, our dissection of these architectures into their component parts provides us with a set of building blocks with which to build meaningful descriptions of all database products.

Second, armed with these building blocks, the selector, builder, or evaluator of database systems can better understand how each database works by comparing it to databases that look and act in similar ways.

Finally, by better understanding the paradigms that each database works with, the process of learning how to use a database other than the familiar one becomes much simpler.

Categorizing Databases

Any attempt to classify the vast majority of database products into one of the categories we have considered will, for the most part, be a fruitless endeavor. The point is not to determine which database falls into which category; but to understand how the individual database works; and how the database practitioner can best take advantage of it.

Unfortunately, not all database products fit neatly into one of these categories. The approaches each architecture advocates are quite flexible. Many databases conform to no formal architecture whatsoever, just as some buildings cannot be said to belong to any architecture category.

It is also common for database manufacturers to modify their products in an attempt to make their products more marketable or more efficient. These hybrid products, which combine two or more architectural approaches, are becoming the norm. In recent years, there has been a major trend on the part of manufacturers of nonrelational database to make their products relational. At the same time, relational database manufacturers are beginning to turn their products into object-oriented systems.

Architectural Approaches and System Requirements

Each database product meets the requirements placed upon it in a different way. Much of the functionality that it will provide will be determined by the underlying architecture. The key to matching architectures to requirements lies in the practitioner's ability to match those requirements to the performance characteristics of the database product. Remember that in the first chapter of this book, we said that there was no such thing as a best database product or approach. Now we are able to back-up that statement up with some specific explanations.

Control vs. Flexibility

The builder of any database system must decide in one way or another what the economic value of system flexibility will be. This must be weighed against the benefits gained by allowing the system to exert more control, and provide more structure over the entire system's environment. These two characteristics of a system, flexibility and control, are diametrically opposed to each other. The more control the system exerts, the less flexibility it will have and vice versa. The decision to build a system that enforces more or less overall control should of course be made based upon the requirements placed on the system. The control/flexibility trade-off can be experienced in several ways.

System Performance and the Trade-Off

Providing flexibility can be very costly to the system as far as the performance is concerned. The equation is very simple: the more flexible a system is, the more overhead (memory, speed, disk space, etc.), is required to accomplish the same things it could do quickly in an inflexible environment.

One way to consider architectures then, is in regard to how flexible and/or efficient they can be.

For example, a hierarchical database is more restrictive than an object-oriented one. To perform a search for the same data, the hierarchical database produces results using fewer system resources than the object-oriented database does. The tradeoff cost of this efficiency is, of course, that a different search, not in alignment with the hierarchical database's structure, will be much more costly.

Therefore, a decision on optimum database/system performance should be made based on the designer's best approximation of the importance of performance compared to the importance of system flexibility. If a system has a high performance requirement, and the requirements are stable, then a more rigid database product is a better choice.

For example, an airline reservation system that is consistent in its structure and requirements from one year to the next, but which also requires thousands of transactions per minute, is better served by using a more rigid architecture like hierarchical or network.

On the other hand, a system that allows airline executives to analyze ticket sales, places a premium on the system's flexibility. The population of users (airline executives) is relatively small, so the transaction rate they require is thousands of times lower than for the reservation system. Conversely, these executives will want to analyze information many different ways.

System Manageability and the Trade-Off

Another consideration when determining which database architecture best meets the needs of the organization is to take into account how manageable the environment created by the database is. The more flexible a system is—the easier it is for users and programmers to create customized mini-environments—the more difficult the job of management and administration.

This can show itself in several ways. In the case of an XBase architecture, where programmers can build indexes, copy files, and associate files on demand, the system can quickly become populated with many more indexes and copies of data than are required. The database architecture does not support centralized management and control.

In the case of a relational database, it is possible for users to build SQL queries that tax the system immensely. Additional administrative responsibilities are required if the system is to remain manageable.

Consequently, the database practitioner must consider not only the direct data-access requirements the system must meet, but should also consider these broader factors when analyzing systems.

Fitting the Database to the Processing Requirements

Sometimes the fit between processing requirements and database architectures can be well matched. For example, a system that keeps track of an operation already hierarchically organized is best suited to a hierarchical database. A system that tracks military reporting structures, or which captures information about hierarchies (national, regional, state, county, and city for example) are good architectural fits.

Systems requiring *ad hoc* query capabilities and other kinds of decision support usually fit well with relational or XBase databases.

Choosing the Best Architecture

When it comes to understanding and deciding on the best architecture for a given database system, the story is the same as it has been throughout this book. The database product and its architecture are only one of the four profiles that make up a database system. A database's ability to perform its job is dependent on the ability of the system designer to blend the people, program, product, and platform components into a homogenous operating environment. In other words, there are no easy answers to the questions that plague builders of database systems to be found in the theoretical profiles that products offer. There are only capabilities, tradeoffs, and ultimately, compromises.

Architectures and Environments

While considering the databases sharing the same architecture, we describe the environments, applications, and functionality that these groupings tend to provide. The fact that *most* of the products sharing an architectural approach:

- Happen to run on the same platform
- Provide the same kind of user interface
- Have the same strong or weak points

does not mean that these things are a function of the architecture itself. How an architecture happens to be packaged by a group of vendors does not indicate what the architecture is capable of if packaged differently.

We provide this environment information only because it can help you better understand some of a technology's background and practical application.

Jargon and Terminology

The other area that we consider is that of the terminology typically associated with each of these kinds of databases.

- XBase databases use records, fields, primary and secondary pointers

- Inverted list databases use the associator area, inverted list indexes, User-views, and Dataviews.

- Hierarchical databases are made up of segments, parents, children, and peers.

- Network databases include record types, pointers, and *walking the sets*.

- Relational databases use joins, tables, columns, and rows.

- Object-oriented systems use objects, classes, and hierarchies.

These keywords and phrases also communicate much about the database's organization and operation paradigms.

Data Organization Assumptions

Last but not least, are the assumptions about data organization that each adheres to, the most clearly-defined being hierarchical and network.

- XBase supplies the ability to thread multiple files into one long relationship string.

- Inverted Lists require mapping relationships through inverted list indexes.

- Relational databases require the SQL join.

- Object-oriented databases require associations.

Database Systems and Multiple Paradigms

To fully appreciate the environment within which a system developer must work, these database product paradigms provide only a small percentage of the necessary information. The platforms upon which a system runs and the programming, data storage, and administrative profiles each provide their own paradigms. What's more, different combinations of these paradigms result in unique, full-system paradigms.

For example, a database system on a mainframe platform, using the COBOL language and an IMS (hierarchical) database, create an operation environment quite different from a system built on a minicomputer platform using a Focus database (also hierarchical). The fact that the database in both cases is hierarchical provides only one piece of the information necessary to understand how the system will work its performance characteristics. By combining the architecture profile with the others, we develop a more precise description of what the system is and how it will work. All paradigms are equally important in making this determination.

Ways of Distinguishing Database Architectures

In order to distinguish between one architecture and the next, we need to develop a vocabulary that describes the components of a database based on some common ground. We accomplish this by considering:

- Terminology that identifies the principal objects utilized by the database system, specifically data objects and database constructors.

- Navigation paradigms and cross-file capabilities, which define the way the architecture expects data retrieval to be managed.

- Some of the basic operational characteristic that make databases of this type stand out from the others.

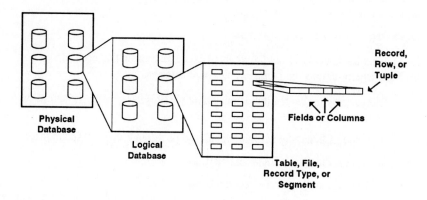

Figure 4-1: Data constructs

Data Constructs

Data constructs are the primary building block of any database system. Although different architectures may use different naming conventions to communicate subtle distinctions in the meanings of these terms, it is important for our investigation that we establish a baseline description that can be used for comparisons.

The lowest-level building block of a database is the individual data element, which is stored and processed for the user. These data elements are referred to as fields in most systems, but are also called attributes, columns, or data element instances in some architectural frameworks. We will stick to the term *field* as much as possible. A collection of fields is most often called a record, but can also be called a tuple, row, occurrence, or object instance.

A collection of similar records (records having the same field identifiers) can be stored in a file, a database, a record type, segment type, table, or object. We refer to these generically as files, tables, or record types depending on the context. (Incidentally, we use the term *table* in the logical sense, not in the relational database's literal sense.)

A collection of related tables or record types is usually classified as a database, or a logical database, We define a collection of logical databases as the database system or physical database. A physical database is the collection of all data managed by the same database management system.

Throughout our discussions of each architecture, we will refer back to these terms in order to help identify the differences.

Building Data Constructs using Database Constructors

Database constructors are those things the database uses to build a functional system. Database constructors define data constructs to the system. It is within the syntax of a data constructor that fields, records, files, and databases are given their names. Here too, we find different architectures using different terminology for the same logical concepts. We use constructors to build data constructs. Constructors are used to define the real database to the real system.

A database is defined to the system using one of three methods, either with a data-definition language (DDL), through system generation (SYSGEN), or by using a collection of screens (a user-interface management system).

The result of these operations is the definition of logical arrangements of fields, records, and tables into physical database components.

These logical/physical definitions of the database are referred to as *data descriptors, system gens, table layouts, schemas,* or *persistent object descriptors*. It is the data constructor that maps logical data constructs into the actual physical storage of data. Because of this, data constructors are an aspect both of the database's architecture profile and its storage management profile. We will discuss these constructs in much more detail in Chapter 9.

Navigation Paradigms and Cross-File Capabilities

Although the understanding of the varying database terminology is certainly helpful, of much greater importance is developing an appreciation for the differences in the ways they manipulate the data. Each architecture defines certain ways that the database product is expected to behave when a request for information is made. These differences in behavior can be summarized as having to do with:

- **The search profile**—How will the database handle a request to search for a specific record within the entire population of records?

- **Data cross-referencing capabilities**—When the programmer or user wants to relate data from two different collections of records, how will the database help or hinder that process?

- **Dynamic mapping vs. static mapping**— Mapping defines the way that a database aids in the processing of cross-construct information. Static mapping establishes permanent relationships between collections of records. Dynamic mapping capability allows the programmer or user to declare spontaneously that some relationship between two collections of records be made.

- **Record vs. set processing**—This indicates how data is provided to the user or program: one record at a time, or in complete sets.

The assembly of these capabilities into a consistent operation model defines a given architecture's paradigms. By doing so it defines how the data can best be arranged when stored within a given architecture, and the kinds of processing that are most efficiently handled by that architecture.

Pete's Pet Shop

Perhaps the easiest way to begin describing the different architectures and how they provide navigation services is to begin with a simple case study. This will show how increasing demands on a system can create a need for increasingly robust databases.

To help explain the concepts of database functionality and architecture, we begin by considering a business that does not have the benefit of a database.

Our imaginary company, called Pete's Pet Shop, shows how we can build some systems for Pete without a database. The first system that Pete needs must help him keep track of what pets are in his store at any given time. In order to do this, we will write two simple programs, one that allows him to enter the name, animal type, color, and price of each pet, and one that prints a report listing these items.

A Simple Applications Example

Obviously, Pete does not want to type in the list of animals every time he wants to print the report, so our first program will write everything to a file, which the second program will then read.

The first file will have a section reserved for each animal and physically will look like Table 4-1.

Unfortunately, when we print Pete's list, he sees all of the animals listed in the same order as he originally typed them. If Pete decides that he wants to see only animals of a certain color, we will have to run another program—a search program—that looks through all of the records to find the right color animals, writes

Table 4-1: Pete's animal file

Name	Animal Type	Color	Price
Sammy	Shark	Gray	25.00
Billy	Goat	White	120.00
Roger	Rabbit	Black	5.00
Phillip	Fish	Green	0.50
Dan	Dog	Brown	99.00

this output to a second file, file 2 , and then run the report program to produce the listing.

Obviously, in the case of Pete's five pets, this is not a problem. However, if Pete had several thousand pets, then this extra job of finding certain animals and creating an additional file for each new report could take a significant amount of time. In order to print the second report quickly, Pete might decide to save the second version of the data. That way, he can get the report either way he wants it in a short amount of time.

Search Capability

It would be helpful for Pete's system to find all of the pets of a certain type without requiring him to run a special search program and writing results to another file. The process of scanning through all of the records every time a report must run can obviously be quite costly. The ability of a database to locate certain records based on specific field values is called a *search capability*. There are two kinds of search capabilities: limited and full.

In a limited search arrangement, a special auxiliary file, called an index, is created for a field (or fields). When Pete wants to find the record associated with that field, the system is able to search through the index first, and then follow a *pointer* to where the actual record is stored. With an architecture that provides only limited capabilities, Pete can perform searches only on those fields identified in the index. In an unlimited, or free-form, search arrangement, the database does exactly what Pete's programs did. Pete tells it which value for which field to locate, and it reads through all of the records and finds the ones that Pete wants. All fields can be used as search criteria.

Architectures and Search Profiles

Although there is some variance among particular architectures in the enforcement of these criteria, for the most part the flat-file, XBase, SBASE, relational, and object-oriented architectures support full search capabilities. Any program or user can request a search based on the value in any field. The other architectures, inverted list, hierarchical, and network provide searches only on indexed or keyed fields.

Table 4-2: Search capabilities by architecture

Full Search Capability Architectures	Limited Search Capability Architectures
Flat-file (most)	Inverted List
XBase	Network
Relational	Hierarchical
SBase	
Object-Oriented	

Some minor, programmatically enhanced capabilities used by these architectures can provide full search capabilities, but these are the exception, not the rule.

With search capabilities, full or limited, programs like the Pete's search program need not be written. Instead of writing a search program and making the entire system more complicated, the report writing program can simply be modified to take advantage of the database's search functions. If Pete was to stop now and build no additional systems, or remain satisfied with the kind of processing he is doing today, then the search capabilities provided would be enough.

At some point, Pete finds that his system has grown. The list of animals has grown considerably and he is keeping more information then ever. Because of his increased operating efficiency, Pete is keeping more animals than ever in the store and he has decided to add a customer file to his system. The animal file with fields called, Name, Type, Color, Price has been joined by a customer file. This file holds information about each of the people who have bought an animal from Pete, as well as the name and type of animal they bought.

Pete soon becomes disenchanted with his simple search capability. He still ends up doing a lot of information manipulation with a pencil, paper, and calculator. There are just too many things that he would like to do with the data, but his choice of a databases prevents him from doing so.

He would also like to make some new reports that perform some simple analysis on the data he has captured. How many cats were sold in November? What is the best month for selling Gila monsters? The answers to questions like these cannot be determined without some expanded capabilities.

Pete needs the ability to operate on both the animal and customer file at the same time. This can be accomplished in one of two ways.

The first method is to simply write a program that finds the desired record in the first file, and then goes to the other file and finds the records that match. When the program is done working on the second file, it goes back to the first and picks up where it left off. Although this method can be used, it obviously results in very complex programs, and much time being spent by the system reading the same files over and over again.

The second method is to use a database, which allows the system to relate two files to each other. This facility, which we refer to generically as *data cross-referencing*, can be accomplished using several commands, depending on the architecture of the database. The term data cross-referencing describes the way a database relates one type of data construct (record, tuple, row, or segment) to another. In Pete's case, it would be relating an animal record to a customer record.

Data Cross-Referencing

The Easy Way Out: Data Duplication

Before considering the ways a database can manage the data cross-referencing process, let's determine the alternatives to using a database. The system requirement is to give Pete a way to generate information about the relationship between two sets of data. The easiest way to accomplish this is by keeping information about customers and the animals they buy in the same file.

The Superfile Solution

Suppose Pete would like to know the name, address, and phone number of each person purchasing an animal at his store. One way to capture this information is to add some additional fields to the animal file currently in use.

Table 4-3: Pete's superfile solution

Animal Name	Animal Type	Animal Price	Color	Purchaser Name	Address	Phone Number
Sammy	Shark	25.00	Gray	Joe	111 w 25th	803-4390
Billy	Goat	120.00	White	Larry	2 W Beacon	609-6969
Buster	Rabbit	5.00	Black			
Phillip	Fish	.50	Green	Joe	33 w 33rd	615-4390
Dan	Dog	99.00	Brown			
Sammy	Salamander	.25	Green	Joe	111 W 25th	803-4390

Obviously, this file allows Pete to capture and retrieve all of the information he desires. If Pete never expects any more out of this system, then this solution will be sufficient. If Pete's system becomes much larger, however, then this same solution will begin to create problems.

What will happen if Pete decides to add supplier information, veterinarian reports, and accounting information to the system? Eventually, this simple little file will grow so large and complex that Pete will need a bigger machine just to read it. Unfortunately, as files become larger, the system becomes correspondingly slower. Not only will the performance of the system degrade, but in addition, the complexity of programs and the chances for errors within the system become greater, too.

Look at the address listings for Joe. Why is Joe listed as living on 25th street twice and 33rd street once. Did Joe move? Is it a data entry error? Either way there is a problem. By duplicating the information about Joe several times in the same file, Pete has a condition called *data redundancy*, which is guaranteed to increase the chances for errors within the system.

There are many reasons that the superfile approach to building systems should be avoided. Some large systems could never be physically built this way, there is simply not enough disk space available in the world to hold all of the data.

Creating Two Files and Linking Them

Another way for Pete to solve this problem is to add a new file for customer information to this system.

Table 4-4: A separate animal file (no references)

Animal Name	Animal Type	Animal Color	Animal Price
Sammy	Shark	Gray	25.00
Billy	Goat	White	120.00
Buster	Rabbit	Black	5.00
Phillip	Fish	Green	.50
Dan	Dog	Brown	99.00
Sammy	Salamander	Green	.25

Table 4-5: Customer file (referenced via animal name)

Purchaser Name	Address	Phone Number	Animal Name
Joe	111 w 25th	803-4390	Sammy
Larry	2 W Beacon	609-6969	Billy
Joe	33 w 33rd	615-4390	Philip
Joe	111 W 25th	803-4390	Sammy

By creating a separate file, we make each one smaller and easier to handle and make it possible to expand the system to include as many additional files as we want.

Although the information that Pete wanted has now been collected, he still cannot get the cross-file information that he is interested in. How can you tell which animals Joe bought from this file arrangement? You cannot. A connection between the two files is required. The most common way of establishing a relationship between two files is to place an identifier from one as a field in the other. This is called establishing a logical relationship or adding a reference field.

One way would be to place the name of the animal purchased in the customer's record (see table 4-5). Another way is to place the customer's name in the animal file (see table 4-6).

Table 4-6: Animal file (referenced via purchaser name)

Animal Name	Purchaser Name	Animal Type	Animal Color	Animal Price
Sammy	Joe	Shark	Gray	25.00
Billy	Larry	Goat	White	120.00
Buster		Rabbit	Black	5.00
Phillip	Joe	Fish	Green	.50
Dan		Dog	Brown	99.00
Sammy	Joe	Salamander	Green	.25

Although these two alternatives might, on the surface, seem to be equally viable, they are definitely *not* equivalent.

Under the first option, placing the animal name on the customer list, we are able to capture only the name of one of the animals that Joe bought. In order to save the names of all the animals a person has purchased we must either add a field to the file for each additional animal (animal 1, animal 2, etc.) or we must duplicate the row several times, once for each animal that is added. Neither solution is a good one. In the first case, we will never be able to predict how many animals a person might buy, so we must keep adding fields every time a purchase is made. In the second case, we will have begun to duplicate customer information again, something we wanted to avoid.

The second alternative file layout, the one where purchaser names go onto the animal file provides a much better solution. Since an animal can only be purchased by one person, you do not have to worry about multiple occurrences for that value.

Although in this case, we were able to reason the best way to establish the logical link between these two files, there should be some kind of guideline that can be used to guarantee that we arrange multiple files the right way. Fortunately, there is.

Database Design

Although in the example presented here we are trying to determine the best way to relate two nondatabase files to each other, when working with databases we are confronted with the same problem. How do you determine how to make these files as compatible and useful as possible, without wasting programming activity or disk space. The technique of analyzing the relationships between constructs is called database design. The topic is so important that we have dedicated a large portion of the chapter about Modeling, Design, and Tuning, to this issue. For our purposes now, let us stick with simple business situations where the design decisions should be intuitively obvious.

Using Programs to Cross-Reference Data

Assuming that we have determined the best arrangement of the data, we can now return to our original question. If a database is not used, how will Pete generate reports that refer to two discrete files?

There are two ways this can be accomplished without a database. Both of these programming solutions require a large amount of programming to be done, and both will take up a significant amount of the system resources.

Sort Merge

One programming technique is called the *sort/merge*. With this method, the programmer begins by sorting the two files, both ordered by the field they have in common. In the case of Pete's files, we would sort the animal and customer files in Purchaser Name order.

After the files are in the same order, another program would be written. This program reads through the two files simultaneously, writing out a new combined record each time there is a match.

Nested Loop

The other programming technique is called the nested loop. With the nested loop approach, the program reads through the first file (the animal file) until the first desired record is found. It then scans through the second file (customer file) looking for any matches. When the first record is finished, it reads the second desired record in the animal file, and then finds any matches for it in the customer file. The program continues looping through the files until both files have been read completely.

Hybrid Searches

It is also possible to combine the sort/merge and nested loop methods of matching in several ways to make the process even faster. For these hybrid methods to succeed, the programmer must know a lot more about the nature of the data being merged.

How do Databases Accomplish Cross-Referencing?

Assuming that we would like to avoid the use of extremely complicated and resource-intensive programs as much as possible, let's see how the different database architectures get the same job done with a lot less effort.

Each database architecture takes a different approach to the mapping of relationships between data constructs. Underlying any of these approaches are two basic techniques: relating files logically or physically.

Physically Relating Data: Static Mapping

One way to create a database system that allows for the efficient cross-referencing of data is for that database to establish a physical relationship between the two objects being related. This can be done using pointers (physical addresses that point from one record to another) or through proximity (storing related records in the same physical area).

The *proximity method* of physically relating different record types is logically the same thing as the superfile solution we discussed earlier.

The *pointer technique* allows the data to be stored in physically diverse locations while maintaining a high degree of accessibility.

Table 4-7: Pete's database using pointers

The Animal File					The Customer File		
Animal Name	Animal Type	Color	Animal Price		Customer Name	Address	Phone Number
Sammy	Shark	Gray	25.00	---->	Joe	111 W 25th	803-4390
Billy	Goat	White	120.00	---->	Larry	2 W Beacon	609-6969
Buster	Rabbit	Black	5.00				
Phillip	Fish	Green	.50				
Dan	Dog	Brown	99.00				
Sammy	Salamander	Green	.25				

Relating the Customer and Animal Data Constructs with Pointers

The advantage of physical, or static mapping, is that access using these techniques is very fast and resource-efficient. Because the system does not need to do much processing in order to ascertain which two records need to be related, it can operate at peak efficiency.

The disadvantage of static mapping is that it is a relatively permanent arrangement. Once relationships are physically mapped, it is very difficult to unmap them without rewriting application programs. With a physically-mapped relationship, the programmer or end user is dependent upon that mapping in order to perform any processing. If the mappings change, existing applications will no longer work. They must be rewritten in order to make use of the new mapping.

Logically Relating Data: Dynamic Mapping

Another way for the system to relate records is to use the same technique as the programmer at Pete's Pet Shop. In a dynamically-mapped environment, the programmer need only tell the database which records to relate, and the system determines how to relate them. This can only work if there are fields in each of the files or tables that can be logically related to each other.

The first advantage offered by the dynamic-mapping facility is that the mappings can be changed by the programmer or user at any time. The database administrator need not make a commitment to any one organization scheme. Another obvious advantage is that the job of the programmer or user is greatly simplified. There is no need to be concerned with issues of indexes, keys, or other kinds of requirements that hamper the person using a statically-mapped system. In the dynamically-mapped database, the database takes care of finding and associating data, and the programmer concentrates on processing the results.

The misleading thing about dynamically-mapped systems is that although the programmer doesn't have to program them, it doesn't mean that the work is no longer being done. To the contrary, the locating of records that match, the sort/merge, or nested loop operations have simply been shifted from the programmer to the database. This means that a dynamically-mapped system has much more system overhead built-in than a statically-mapped system.

Which Technique is More Efficient?

There is significant controversy about which of these methods is the more efficient. Is the statically-mapped system, with low system overhead and high performance more efficient, or is the dynamically-mapped system, with low application program overhead and greater processing burden to the database? The answer to this question is not simple.

On a call-per-call basis, the statically-mapped system outperforms the dynamic approach every time. It is a matter of simple physics. The dynamic system must build additional intelligence software into its structure to respond to all of the requests that it might be asked to answer. The static system is concerned with only a small subset of commands.

	Static	Dynamic
System Resources	Low	High
Proficiency	Low	High
Stability	High	Low

Figure 4-2: Characteristics of Static vs. Dynamic

Conversely, as systems become larger and more complex, it becomes increasingly difficult to guarantee that the programmers and users accessing the system will do so efficiently. As the number of inefficient users increases, the performance advantage of the static system is minimized.

From yet another perspective, if the system is to be used directly by end users, then the efficiency of static mapping is almost meaningless if the users are unable to understand it or use it effectively.

Therefore, the decision to use a static architecture or a dynamic one depends on:

- The amount of system resources available

- The proficiency of the programmers and end users

- The stability of the system (how often mappings must be changed)

Mapping and Architectures

With these mapping schemes in mind, let's examine how varying architectures address them. Flat-file architecture usually provides no mapping at all. The network, hierarchical, and inverted list architectures use static mapping. The XBase, SBase, relational, and object-oriented usually take advantage of dynamic mapping.

Table 4-8: Architectures and Mapping

Static Mapping	Dynamic Mapping
Hierarchical	XBase
Network	Relational
Inverted List	Object Oriented
Object Oriented	SBASE
Flat File (Does not apply)	Flat File (Does not apply)

Navigational vs. Non-Navigational Mapping

When discussing the subject of mapping, two other terms are recognized: navigational and non-navigational. Statically-mapped systems are also known as navigational systems, and non-navigational applies to the dynamically mapped. Unfortunately, the connotations of these terms can be misleading. The word navigation refers to the way that a programmer or user must follow the physical path, defined by the architecture, to locate the data. In a statically-mapped system, the person accessing data must know what pointers have been established and how they relate to each other to find anything. In the non-navigational system, the user simply asks for data, and the system conducts the navigation instead. A more meaningful pair of terms to define these differences might be to call the navigational systems *user-navigated*, while calling the non-navigational ones *system navigated*.

We will continue to use the terms static and dynamic mapping, because they provide a clearer understanding of the differences.

Record vs. Set Processing

Although search capabilities, data cross-referencing, and dynamic and static mapp

ing define a great deal about how a system works with data, there is another aspect of equal importance. There are two ways that the data a user (or program) requests can be provided. The records can be returned to the requestor one at a time, or the

Table 4-9: Record vs. set processing by architecture

One-Record-at-a-Time Processing	Set-Based Processing
Flat file (most)	Flat file (some)
XBase	Relational
Inverted List	Object Oriented(some)
Network	SBASE
Hierarchical*	
Object Oriented (some)	

* There are some exceptions to these declarations, for example: the FormBase product by Ventura Software does have set processing capabilities.

whole set of data being searched for can be displayed at once.

The traditional way that applications programs have dealt with reading and writing data has been on a one-record-at-a-time basis. This is because almost the entire body of theory about computers and how they work has been based on the principals of Van Neuman processing logic. Van Neuman, a famous mathematician and computer theorist, defined the single-threaded, one-task-at-a-time logic on which most 2GLs, 3GLs, and 4GLs are based.

With the creation of user-interface management systems, and graphically-based applications, it was discovered that database processing did not have to be restricted to this simple concept. Many of the newer databases (hybrid and relational) are based on the concept of set processing. Set-based processing works on entire blocks of information simultaneously. So instead of requesting and working on data one record at a time, the programmer or user can simply ask for everything at once.

Most of the flat-file databases return all of the information requested by the user at one time. How the database goes about assembling this set is immaterial; what is important is that one request is made to the database and all of the data comes back.

When using an XBase, inverted list, hierarchical, or network database, data is returned one record at a time, not in a set. The programmer or user must explicitly ask that each record be read. In this particular case, the records returned are determined by the position of a program pointer, which moves through the different files being accessed.

Relational databases, some of the object-oriented databases, and several hybrid databases work with data in sets as opposed to one-record-at-a-time access.

A Taxonomy for Database Architectures

In order to help define the differences between databases based upon their architectures, we will again develop a simple taxonomy. So far, we have determined that an architecture defines terminology for data constructs and data constructors, and provides search, data cross-reference, mapping (static or dynamic), and processing (record vs. set) capabilities. When considering individual database products and their architectural profiles, we will utilize Table 4-10.

Table 4-10: Architecture profile criteria

Architecture Characteristics	
Data Constructs	Fields, records, files, etc.
Data Constructors	Data Definition Language, System Generated or Interface Management System
Search Capability	Full or Partial
Data Cross-Referencing (Mapping)	Dynamic or Static
Processing Mode	Record at a time or set at a time

Architecture Taxonomy

I. Terminology

  A. Terminology for Data Constructs

  B. Data Constructors

    1. Data Definition Language (DDL)

    2. System Generated

    3. Interface Management System Defined

II. Capabilities and Paradigms

  A. Search

    1. Full

    2. Partial

  B. Data Cross-Referencing/Mapping

    1. Dynamic

    2. Static

  C. Processing Mode

    1. Record at a Time

    2. Set at aTime

Of course, still missing from our discussion of architectures is the most important part, the navigational paradigm. These thought patterns and assumptions tell the user exactly how to get the desired information out of the system. We will delve into that discussion, along with more generalized descriptions of each architecture in the following chapters. We will consider each architecture in detail and develop a sample application using a typical database product.

5

PC Architectures

In this chapter we consider the PC-based architectures: the flat-file, XBase, and SBase systems. Of all the architectures that we consider, these architectures are the least formally defined and the least understood.

Personal computer database architectures are as distinctive and user-friendly as the computer platforms on which they run. As opposed to the other architectures, which have their own roots in historical or theoretical foundations, the PC architectures have always placed their priorities on making data processing easier and more intuitively obvious for the end user.

Coupled with this user-friendly imperative has been a tendency for these products to be less concerned about high volumes (since it is only recently that PCs could hold megabytes of data) and multiuser processing (since it has only become an issue since the recent popularity of local area networks). These issues have traditionally been the concern of only the bigger systems.

In recent years, however, many of these products have become retrofitted to address these kinds of concerns as well.

In today's business world, PC-based architectures represent a huge market and a significant percentage of all databases in use. Because of this, and the ever-increasing demand to integrate PC products with more traditional platforms and software, the PC architectures have become important to everyone involved in building computer systems.

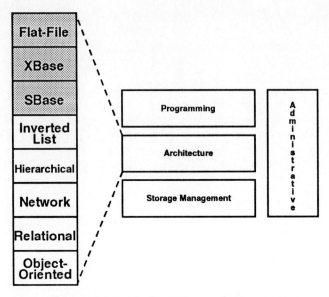

Figure 5-1: The Flat file, XBase and SBase systems

Flat-File Databases

Under the heading of flat-file databases, we include PC-File, Q&A, Reflex, Rapidfile, My Advanced Database and FileMaker Pro. These products, like the vast majority of flat-file databases, run only on personal computer platforms like the IBM PC, IBM-compatibles and Apple Macintoshes. These databases are most often used for simple, stand-alone applications, such as list managers, electronic rolodexes, card files, and other simple data entry and reporting applications.

Flat-file databases represent the low end of the database products market. They are inexpensive—many cost less than $100—and are very user-friendly. Because of this, they are often the first database product purchased by an individual new to the computer world. (Recently, the term flat file database has fallen into disfavor by many of the product manufacturers, the terms programmable v.s. non-programmable being used to separate the flat-file (non-programmable) databases, from the rest).

The Programming Profile of Flat-File Databases

Flat-file databases provide the narrowest programming profile of any of the database products. All come with a user-interface management system. This defines the data access method, the sole method of programming, and provides no database programmability. They also provide no programming languages, or the ability to obtain access with third-party languages or interface management systems.

Unfortunately, this simplicity of design carries with it the inability to do much more than the simple operations provided by a menu or screen. Despite this fact, many users develop extremely sophisticated applications using the very simple toolkit provided.

The Architectural Profile of Flat-File Databases

These products define data constructs with the terms field, record, and file. They enable building data constructors through the same screens that are used to perform data storage and retrieval. They usually provide only partial search ability and provide little or no data cross-referencing services Therefore mapping does not have to be considered. More often than not, processing occurs by the set, but some record-at-a-time systems do exist. Most flat file databases provide a full search capability.

Based upon its limited capabilities, one might wonder why a flat-file database would be used at all, or even considered in this book. Well, the fact of the matter is, that more flat-file databases are in use today than most of the other architectures combined. This is because they are so inexpensive and easy to use, and many people use them on a daily basis.

Navigation with a Flat-File Database

The name *flat-file* database can be a bit misleading to the average user. The term flat-file itself is data processing jargon for a simple data file having no indexes or other access-enabling structures. Flat-file databases manage simple data structures, but do use indexes to speed processing. In addition to this capability, the flat-file system typically provides the user with simple, screen-based programming capabilities and no access is available through 2GLs, 3GLs, or 4GLs. With the flat-file database, the programming capabilities provided by the product itself represent the full extent of the programming that can be done.

The one thing that really distinguishes the flat-file system from all other database management approaches is that systems of this type can provide access only to one construct (file) at a time. Whereas the principal reason that many people use databases is to ease the processing of multiple files at the same time, the flat-file database provides none of this power.

So, to summarize, the flat-file database is one in which:

- There are no program or user access languages
- Data constructs are built using the system's own forms
- No (or very limited) cross-file capabilities exist

These databases do provide:

- User-friendly screens for the manipulation of data
- A built-in User Interface Management System
- Simple query and report writing capabilities

The PC-File Database

The PC-File database, from Buttonware, Inc., is typical of the flat-file architecture family. Its simplified structure and user-friendly services make it a popular choice for many first-time computer users.

For a detailed look at the characteristics of PC-File, refer to Appendix A for the PC-File listing.

Building Constructs with PC-File

In order to do anything within the PC-File environment, the user begins with the system entry screen. From this screen you can use the slide bar menu across the top of the screen to select the database functions you wish to perform. Included in PC-File's main menus are the File (for the creation, modification, indexing, and opening of files), Edit (for the insert, update, and delete of data), Views (for access to customized views of the files), Search (for *ad hoc* query execution) , Print (for generating printed output and the creation of reports), Utilities and Tools (for maintenance functions), and Macros (for the execution of keyboard macros; the only kind of programming capability available to the user). To build files with PC-File, the user selects the File menu option, and then chooses the New sub-menu option. (See Figure 5-2.) Notice how easy it is to move around the system. Main menu options are selected by simply moving the cursor keys (the small arrows) from left to right. When the option desired is highlighted the user can hit Enter and the drop down sub-menu options will appear.

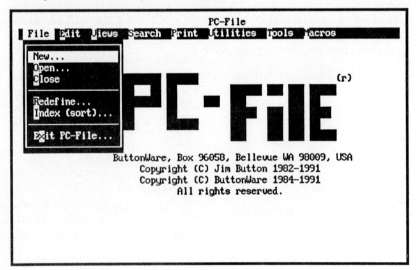

Figure 5-2: The PC-File logon screen-create a new file

After selecting the New... option, the user must decide whether to take advantage of the FAST DEFINE or normal file definition options. Figure 5-3 shows the FAST DEFINE screen. This screen allows you to quickly and efficiently input the names and characteristics of the file's fields and generate the file description quickly.

This allows the new user the opportunity to learn the basics of how the system works without needing to learn a lot of commands. Otherwise the FAST DEFINE option is invoked.

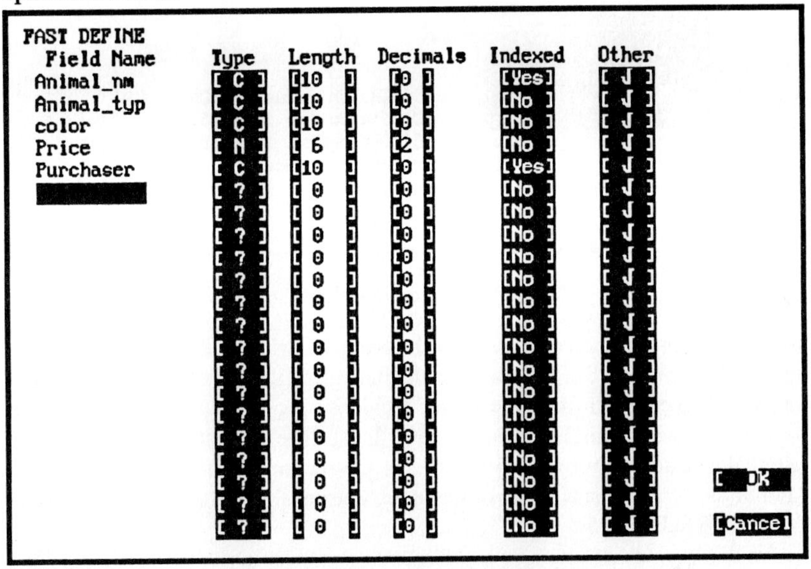

Figure 5-3: PC-File's field definition screen

With this option the user simply types in the names for each of the fields that are going to be added. After that the user simply "fills in the blanks".

Included on this field definition screen are columns for designating the type of data that the field will hold (C for Character or N for numeric), the Length of the field, how many decimal places it will have and whether the field should be indexed or not.

Loading Data into PC-File

The PC-File system user will in most cases load the data one record at a time, using the Edit - Add option. This is accomplished by first choosing the Edit option from the slide bar at the top, and then selecting the Add sub-option (see Figure 5-4).

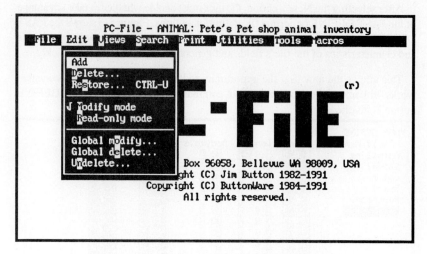

Figure 5-4: Adding a record to the PC-File system

After selecting this choice the user will be presented with a preformatted data entry screen. Data records can be input into the indicated field areas and saved into the system. Notice how the database system provides a pre-formatted data entry screen with the file name and field names already listed. The generation of this screen is handled automatically by the database. No programming effort is required. This kind of user-friendliness is one of the major reasons that flat file databases are so popular. (See Figure 5-5.)

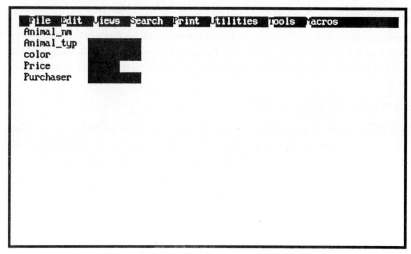

Figure 5-5: The PC-file data entry screen

```
                    PC-File - ANIMAL: Pete's Pet shop animal inventory
 File  Edit  Views  Search  Print  Utilities  Tools  Macros
Animal_nm    Billy
Animal_typ   Goat
color        White
Price          125
Purchaser    Bob
```

Figure 5-6: A new record for the animal file

Other Database Functions with PC-File

After creating and loading files, users can take advantage of the insert, update, and delete capabilities to maintain the file. These functions operate using the same principles as those exhibited by the Edit-ADD operation, providing the user with pre-formatted screens with which to work. They can also use the Search options to query for particular records, or create customized output report forms that can be written to the screen or to a printer using the Print option.

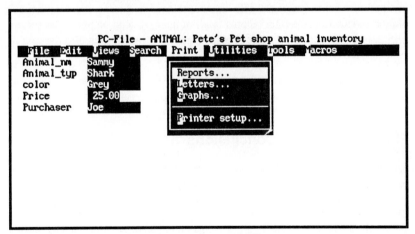

Figure 5-7: Starting a PC-File report

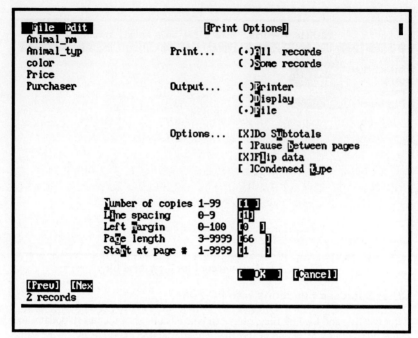

Figure 5-8: The PC-File output report specifications

In Figure 5-8 you can see all of the different output reporting options that can be invoked in order to create PC-File output. Included in the specifications are the ability to output only certain records or all of them, to send output to the screen, printer or a file, and to calculate subtotals, pause between pages, flip the data or condense the type.

Limited processing capabilities include the ability to do simple mathematical operations, to sort the data before reporting, do page layouts, report break layouts, mailing labels, or free-form reports and to access a report-writing language.

Flat File Database Conclusions

Although the flat file databases offer a considerably *friendlier* environment than any of the mainframe systems that preceded them, the systems are unfortunately limited in their ability to provide all of the functionality that computer users require. The next two architectures to be considered, the XBase and SBase approaches provide near mainframe functionality but maintain a lot of this user-friendly profile.

XBase Databases

The XBase database, like the flat-file, represents an extremely large market. There are probably more XBase and flat-file databases in use today than all other databases combined. The number of licensed users for popular products in these classes are counted in the hundreds of thousands, as opposed to the tens of thousands for the next most popular group. Included in the ranks of XBase databases are dBASE II, III, III+, IV, Alpha IV, FoxBase, DBExcel, Multibase, DBMan and DBFast. These products are the most prevalent on the IBM PC, PC-compatible and Apple Macintosh platforms, However, several XBase products have begun to *up-size*, whereby the vendor issues code that runs on larger platforms. It is now possible to get XBase databases that run under Unix, on IBM mainframes, in client-server arrangements and on many other popular platforms.

Because of its very powerful programming language and otherwise robust programming profile, the XBase database is utilized for the development of complex applications. XBase systems typically provide full support for reporting, transaction processing, and all other business functions. Many small businesses are run solely with databases of this type.

Because of the historical preference for PC platforms, most applications are single-user, but not stand-alone. Multiuser applications are possible and several exist.

Programming is usually provided by a fully-functional, procedural 4GL bundled with the product. More often than not, the selection of an XBase database has as much to do with the 4GL capabilities provided as does with the ability of the database engine to make that programming easier. This can probably be attributed to several factors. One of the biggest could be that until the advent of database packages and their 4GL capabilities, the programming environment on the PCs was quite unfriendly to the typical user.

Not only do these databases come with a 4GL, but 2GLs and 3GLs can also be customized to work with the database. This customization is not simple, but many applications written in C or assembler can be used with XBase databases.

There are many application packages that can use an XBase database, and the vast majority of the fourth-generation products and utility products (spreadsheets and word processors) have developed XBase interfaces. XBase databases do not typically have any programmable capabilities of their own.

Architecture Characteristics

The XBase approach to data management allows the programmer/user to work with several files simultaneously. This cross-file capability is what makes the XBase database, or any database, an extremely powerful and useful addition to a system.

XBase databases store data in separate, physical database files. Each file is a collection of records that are made up of individual fields. Navigation is accomplished by establishing a *logical relationship* between files and by the movement of a *current record pointer*.

File Navigation With an XBase Database

Under XBase organization, the system is made up of a collection of autonomous files, each holding a collection of records whose fields are related. In the case of Pete's Pet Shop, the animal and customer flat-files could simply be moved into the XBase environment. Since each file is autonomous, the programmer or user can always work with any file as if it was the only one on the system.

Searching for a Record (Single File)

In order to locate a particular record in an XBase file, the programmer must:

1. Create the file

2. Load the file

3. Open the file

4. Create a primary index for the file(unless one already exists). This index tells the system which field(s) will be used for primary search and navigation operations.

5. Define a variable to hold the value for which a search will be made. (Optional)

6. Move the search value into the variable. (Optional)

7. Use a search command, which instructs the system to retrieve the row that matches the value.

8. When the record is retrieved, the system's current pointer is now situated at that place in the file.

After performing a search, the programmer can then perform whatever processing is required, then reinitialize the variable and conduct another search.

Walking the XBase File (Single File)

Sometimes, the programmer will not wish to simply search for particular values, instead preferring to walk through the file—that is, move from one record to the next in sequential order. The database provides several *move pointer* commands that move it forward or backward one record at a time.

Establishing the Search and Sequence Parameters

Indexes are the primary means by which the XBase database can determine the search or sequencing order. These indexes, which can be created and dropped at will, are actually physical reference files that store a sorted copy of the index fields as well as internal pointers to the areas where their source records are stored. It is the dynamic use of indexes that give the XBase database its efficiency and flexibility.

Multiple File Processing

In order use several XBase files simultaneously, the system utilizes *base* and *related* files. A base file is the first file opened by an XBase program and serves as the file that maintains the current pointer positioning. No matter how many files have been related, one base file drives the processing.

After opening the base file, the XBase programmer can then relate several additional files to it. When a file is related, the XBase system is told that a field on the base file has a matching field on the related file. Given this information, the database moves a secondary pointer within the related file every time the pointer in the base file is moved. After opening a base file and relating another file to it, the programmer can then proceed with processing.

Search Using Multiple Files

Searching multiple files is similar to single file handling. As in the single file search, the programmer opens a file and creates a primary index. In this case however, before proceeding, a command that relates this file to another is executed. Then a search variable is created and initialized, followed by the execution of a search command. This time, when the current pointer is moved to the desired base file record, a secondary pointer is also moved to a record in the secondary file that has a value matching a field in the base file. As the programmer moves the current record pointer in the base file, all secondary pointers are moved correspondingly.

Walking Through Multiple Files

When several files have been related, the system maintains all secondary pointers in positions parallel to wherever the base file pointer is located. This way, no matter where the program happens to navigate, all files stay in synch.

dBASE III

In order to help illustrate the workings of an XBase database, we will begin to develop a simple case study, using the dBASE III database and programming language, which are typical for XBase databases. We begin by reporting on the programming and architectural profiles of the dBASE III database, using the direct access method, languages and interface management systems and architectural characteristics tables. Refer to the Appendix for a description of the Dbase III product

Given this basic knowledge of how an XBase database is put together, let's develop an application using the dBASE III programming language and database. We will write a program that finds the "JOE" customer record and all animals he purchased, from the Pet Shop example we developed earlier.

The first step in this process must always be to create and load the database files that hold the data. With dBASE III this is usually accomplished through the interactive CREATE database file command. After issuing the CREATE command, the user is prompted for the information necessary to build the data constructs. The result of this process is two database file definitions, one for the animal file and one for customers.

Creating Data Constructs With dBASE III

The animal database file:

```
Structure for database : ANI.DBF
Number of data records : 5
Field       Fieldname      Type          Width Dec
- - - - - - - -   - - - - - - - - - - -   - - - - - - - - - - -   - - - - -   - - - - -
1           Animalname     Character      10
2           Animaltype     Character      10
3           Color          Character      5
4           Price          Numeric        6        2
5           Purchaser      Character      10
```

Figure 5-9: A dBASEIII description of "animal file"

The customer database file:

```
Structure for database : CUS.DBF
Number of data records : 2
Field       Fieldname      Type          Width Dec
- - - - - - - -   - - - - - - - - - - -   - - - - - - - - - - -   - - - - -   - - - - -
1           PurchaserN     Character      10
2           Address        Character      20
3           Phone          Character      8
```

Figure 5-10: A dBASEIII description of "customer file"

Along with his interactive capability, dBASE III data structure definitions can be created by simply copying existing ones and modifying them.

Loading Data into a dBASE III File

After creating the files, they can be loaded using the interactive INSERT command, or by using the COPY or APPEND commands, which allow for the copying of data from or to external sources.

Writing a Program Using the dBASE III 4GL

Assuming that our dBASE III files have been created and loaded, we can now proceed to do some programming with them. dBASE III provides two modes of operation with which the programmer or user can work: interactive and programmed.

In the interactive mode, a limited number of commands can be used. These allow the programmer to open, navigate through, and process dBASE III data all from a command prompt line. In the programmed mode, a much fuller set of commands allow the fully operational 4GL to do almost anything a 3GL can do.

Interactive dBASE III and Some Simple Operations

Assume that Pete would like to review all of the animals in inventory and change some of their names. Under interactive dBASE III, all he would need do is type the following commands:

```
USE ANI
EDIT
```

Figure 5-11: A very simple dBASEIII program

The USE ANI command makes the animal file the base file. The EDIT command moves Pete into an interactive edit mode where all records in the file are presented. From the edit mode screen, Pete can make changes to the system at will and save those changes easily. Interactive dBASE III commands include SET, APPEND, ASSIST, BROWSE, CHANGE (field), CREATE, EDIT, HELP, INSERT, MODIFY, READ, and REPORT.

Programming With dBASE III

In order to help illustrate how navigation is performed, let's build a small program that:

1. Establishes the customer file as the base file

2. Creates an index on the purchaser field, establishing the name of the purchaser as the primary search field

3. Creates a second work area, and opens the animal file

4. Establishes a relationship between the two files

5. Finds the record for the purchaser named Joe in the customer file

5. Prints the names of the animals that Joe purchased (from the related animal file)

The scaled down program would look like the code shown in Figure 5-12.

```
* Open the customer file as the base file (A)
USE CUS
* Create an index on the purchaser field
INDEX ON PURCHASERN TO PURCHASER
* Moves to next work area
SELECT B
* Opens the animal file
USE ANI
* Establish the relationship between the two files
SET RELATION PURCHASER INTO CUS
* Switch back to the base file
SELECT A
* Find the JOE record
SEEK "JOE"
* Print the name of Joe's animal
@1,1 SAY B -> Animalname
```

Figure 5-12: A larger dBASE III program

As you can see, the logical relationship between animal and customer is established dynamically within the program by using the SET RELATION command. The FIND command moves the primary pointer to the correct record and the secondary pointer moves with it.

dBASE III Programming Commands

Although a complete list of the dBASE III programming language commands would be quite extensive, this small sampling should help you develop an appreciation for the scope of the language.

Database file opening and closing is handled by the USE command, which makes a file available for use by a program, and by the CLOSE or CLEAR commands, which make them unavailable. The APPEND and INSERT commands add records to a file, DELETE in combination with PACK drops one record, and ZAP erases all records.

Data search and navigation are handled by the LOCATE (sequential search), SEEK (indexed search) and FIND commands. In addition the SET FILTER command identifies a subset of records within which the program is told to work.

The relations between files are set by the SET RELATION commands. A relation set between two files guarantees the synchronicity of their pointers no matter where the base pointer is moved.

XBase Architecture Conclusions

As you can see, the XBase architecture provides a dynamic and powerful mechanism for the processing of multiple-file database situations. The architectural approach and mechanisms that support XBase systems are as powerful and flexible as many of the more traditional database management systems. As the XBase database manufacturers continue to upgrade and up-size their products, we will see more of the approach.

SBase Databases

The term SBase, or screen-based databases, has been coined to identify a large group of PC-based products that provide significant ease-of-use capabilities like those of the flat-file databases but with the power and flexibility of the XBase systems. The ranks of SBase databases include the DataEase, Paradox, Omnis 7, Formbase, and Double-Helix products.

These products represent some of the newest entries to the database marketplace and therefore tend to capitalize on the power and friendliness afforded by the GUI and GLUI front ends.

The SBase database is similar to the flat-file system in that data construction and the accessing of data is handled through screens. The difference lies in the programming and cross-file capabilities that the database can muster.

Programming Characteristics

The programming profile of an SBase database is far more robust than that of the flat-file systems, and almost equal to that of the XBase systems. SBase systems force all data access through user-defined screens, but provide users and programmers with a much richer set of programming options. Most SBase systems come with some kind of 4GL or macro language. *Macro language* is a term borrowed from the spreadsheet and word processing product environment. A spreadsheet or word processing macro is a program made up of a collection of codified system keystrokes. In other words, a macro remembers the keys you press and their sequence to perform some work, and repeats the sequence for you automatically.

While some flat-file databases also have limited 4GL or macro access, the SBase systems' versions of these languages are more inclusive; they have more commands and more capabilities.

Architecture Characteristics

The SBase architecture system provides only a direct access facility for reading and writing data. Data constructs are never operated on directly, but are created and envisioned through the creation of screens or forms. This insulates the user from the constructs. One screen defines one construct. Along with the basic construct creation capability, however, the SBase system allows users to map relationships between constructs through modification of screens themselves. In this manner, the

SBase system provides the ability to map hierarchical, network, and simple relational logic constructs into the logical organization of the screen system.

Since this is done through screen definition, and not through the creation of special data constructs or other typical architecture devices, the SBase system accomplishes its navigational capabilities from its programming profile, not its architecture profile.

SBase systems work with set- or record-at-a-time processing, and usually provide for a screen-definable and therefore dynamic-mapping capability.

The DataEase Database

To help illustrate how a typical SBase system works, let's use the DataEase database to develop a Pete's Pet Shop application similar to the ones we did with the flat-file and XBase systems. For specific information about DataEase, see Appendix A.

The DataEase Main Menu consists of the Form Definition and Relationships, Record Entry, QBE, DQL (DataEase Query Language), Menu Definition, Database Maintenance, and System Administration options.

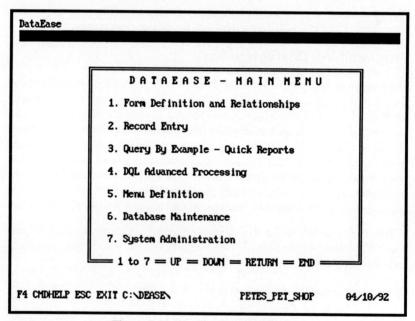

Figure 5-13: The DataEase main menu

Form Definition and Relationships provide the user with all of the options necessary to create and modify data constructs and their interrelationships within the DataEase Database.

The Record Entry option takes users into a series of predefined screens which allow for the rapid input, update or delete of database records.

Query by Example-Quick Reports is an option for the development of reports and ad hoc queries. The QBE or Query by Example format provides users with pre-formatted but blank screen layouts, allowing the user to specify the search values required.

DQL Advanced Processing and Menu Definition are programmability features that enhance the users ability to build sophisticated menu driven application programs.

Database Maintenance and System Administration provide the means to maintain control over the entire system, users and the backup/recovery environment.

Creating Data Constructs with DataEase

Under the control of DataEase, data constructs are built using the Form Definition and Relationships options.

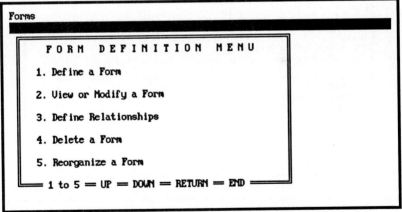

Figure 5-14: The DataEase Form Definition Menu

From this form you can define all of the fields that a file can hold along with the characteristics. Under DataEase as with all screen based systems, the definition of a screen automatically defines the underlying construct at the same time.

```
┌──────────────────────────────────────────────────────────────────────┐
│     Form: PURCHASERS            R 1 C  1                                │
│                                                                        │
│  ████████████████████████████████████████████████████████████████     │
│                                                                        │
│     PURCHASER NAME                                                      │
│     ADDRESS                                                             │
│     PHONE NUMBER                                                        │
│                                                                        │
│                                                                        │
│                                                                        │
│                                                                        │
│                                                                        │
│                                                                        │
│                                                                        │
│                                                                        │
│     F4CMDHELP ESCEXIT F2SAVE F3CUT F5COPY F6PASTE F7DELLN F8INSLN F9SUBFRM F10FIELD │
└──────────────────────────────────────────────────────────────────────┘
```

Figure 5-15: Form definition for the Purchaser file

```
┌──────────────────────────────────────────────────────────────────────┐
│  Form: ANIMAL                                                          │
│                                                                        │
│  NAME ███████████████████                                              │
│  ANIMAL TYPE                                                           │
│  CO┌────────────────────────FIELD DEFINITION──────────────────────┐   │
│  PR│  Field Name                      PRICE                         │   │
│    │                                                                │   │
│    │                                                                │   │
│    │  Field Type                      Number                        │   │
│    │  Number Type :                   Fixed point                   │   │
│    │  Max. digits left of decimal :   6                             │   │
│    │  Digits to the right :           2                             │   │
│    │                                                                │   │
│    │  Required? yes      Indexed? no       Unique?  no              │   │
│    │  Derivation Formula                                            │   │
│    │  Prevent Data-entry? no                                        │   │
│    │                                                                │   │
│    │  Lower Limit                                                   │   │
│    │  Upper Limit                                                   │   │
│    │  View Security                   Write Security                │   │
│    │  Field Help                                                    │   │
│    │  Field Color                     Hide from Table View? no      │   │
│  ALTF1HELP ESCEXIT F2SAVE F6CLEAR FIELD F7DELETE          9:07 pm     │
└──────────────────────────────────────────────────────────────────────┘
```

Figure 5-16: Field definitions for the Price field

Defining Relationships with DataEase

After defining the individual screens to be used as the base descriptions for the
system, relationships between these screens can be defined using the Define
Relationships menu option.

With the relationships screen, the user can name each of the files to be joined
together, the common fields to be used to link them, and the referential integrity
that this relationship must maintain.

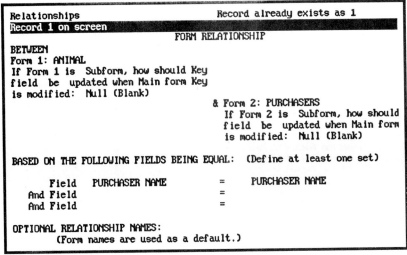

Figure 5-17: Defining the relationship animal/purchaser

Clearly, of all of the methods to defining the relationships between constructs that databases have exhibited, the DataEase technique is the simplest, most intuitively obvious and easiest to maintain.

The relationship created with this screen is available to users of the system as simply another screen name.

Other Functions Using DataEase

While the user of the DataEase system can certainly load data one record at a time using the Record Entry option, a much easier way to load the system, assuming that a load file is available, will be through the Utilities Menu. This menu allows data to be imported or transferred from outside of DataEase into its own internal format.

Along with the load utility, comes the ability to make backup copies of the database, retrieve those copies and make them current and a sophisticated security system which allows different users and passwords to have access to different parts of the system.

Key to the functioning of the entire DataEase environment is the products control tables which track data, backups, screens, relationships and indexes. These control tables make it possible for the system to be administered from one centrally defined point.

Although an entire book could be written about the many different things that
DataEase can do, we will at least make note of the QBE Quick Reports option (see
Figure 5-18).

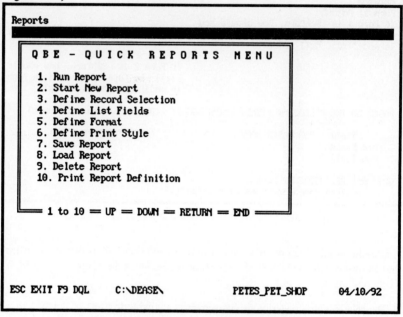

Figure 5-18: The QBE quick reports menu

Figure 5-19: A complex report with DataEase

The DataEase Reporting screen makes it possible to create almost any kind of report in a short amount of time.

Many times, users can take advantage of the inherent DataEase edit capabilities to get report type information out of existing utilities. (See Figure 5-20.)

SBase Conclusion

The SBase architecture can therefore be categorized by the following characteristics:

1. Data access is accomplished with a direct access facility

2. Data constructs are screen generated and screen based

3. Mapping relationships between constructs is managed with screens

4. Powerful, fully functional GUI, GLUI, and 4GL programming capabilities

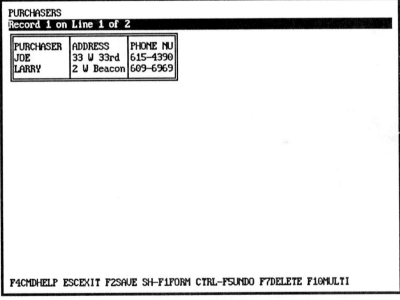

Figure 5-20: A Table View of the Purchasers table

PC-Based Architecture Conclusions

The SBase architecture represents the last of the PC-based architectures that we discuss. This is not to say that only these three architecture approaches can be found on personal computers. It is possible to find inverted list, hierarchical, network, relational, and object-oriented databases on these platforms as well. We single out these three because they are the most likely architectures to be found on a PC and the least likely to be found on any other platform.

These products have been responsible for sparking a veritable revolution in the data processing and database fields. They have significantly altered people's experience of and expectations for database systems of all types, and will continue to exert a stronger and stronger influence on the industry.

6

Traditional Architectures

While the three database architectures considered in the previous chapter are relatively new, extremely easy to use, and usually found on PCs, the three architectures we consider next, the inverted list, hierarchical, and network have entirely different backgrounds and capabilities.

These *traditional* architectures represent the original approaches to database management. The traditional database architectures, and most of the products that use them today, can trace their origins to systems developed in the 1960s and 1970s. At that time, computers and the data processing industry were very different than they are today. In those days, the only computers were *big* computers the mainframes and mini's. They were also very expensive. At that time, with comparatively small CPUs (8k-64k) and slow processing speeds (measured in microseconds as opposed to the nanosecond and Hertz measurements used today). Programming was also a lot more complicated and involved using only 2GLs and 3GLs.

Because of these constraints, many things about the way that databases were designed were different as well.

First of all, the emphasis for the database product was almost completely centered around the minimization of access time and the maximization of processing speeds. The architecture had to support *fast* processing.

Second, because the platforms were big and expensive, the emphasis was on being able to process incredibly large volumes of data at high speeds.

Third, user friendliness, programmer ease of use and fancy trimmings were dismissed as being trivial and inefficient extravagances.

As of result of their history, the database products in use today that are based upon these architectures exhibit a lot of the characteristics carried over from their earlier days. Although most manufacturers have undergone the process of retrofitting these products into newer, sleeker, friendlier versions, the underlying assumptions of the architectures remain the same. The emphasis is on speed, efficiency, control, dependability, and the ability to work with large volumes at high speeds.

Consistent with these traits is the fact that these databases exhibit:

- Rigid, highly structured mappings between constructs
- Complex, fine-tuned construction methods
- The ability to manage high volume, high-transaction-rate systems well
- Rich and mature administrative profiles and utility sets based on decades of experience working in these environments

For our investigation we use the ADABAS database to illustrate the workings of an inverted list database, the IMS database for a hierarchical example and the CA-IDMS system for the network database perspective.

Inverted List Databases

Whereas the flat-file and XBase architectures are most commonly found on the personal computer, the inverted list architecture databases are usually associated with large mainframe computers. These databases, which were partially responsible for the growth of the mainframe database environment, have been on the decline. This is primarily because the inverted list database manufacturers have been converting their products into the relational type of database. This process of conversion is a relatively simple process for inverted list manufacturers since the physical implementation of these types of databases are very similar. The only difference between them is that the relational model offers a richer set of functionalities then an inverted list database alone does.

Currently offered inverted list database products include the ADABAS and Model204 databases. Also included is Computer Associates' Datacom database, which formerly was inverted list, and is now recognized as a hybrid inverted list/relational system.

The thing that makes the inverted list approach unique is the way in which it internally organizes its files or tables. The inverted list architecture is similar to XBase in that each file is built and can be treated as an autonomous data construct. Another unique quality is that as opposed to allowing for dynamically-defined indexes and the creation of dynamic relationships between files, the system uses a special index—called an inverted list—which provides access to the system. The list also relates multiple files to each other.

Programming inverted list databases is defined as much by the environments they run in as by the database itself. Being a mainframe-based product, the only programmatic accesses to the database are provided by the traditional 2GLs, 3GLs, and 4GLs. Very few interface management systems, other then those provided by the vendors themselves, are available.

The Inverted List Index

The one truly distinguishing characteristic of the inverted list databases are the indexes they use. Under a typical indexing scheme—that used most often by the flat-file, XBase, hierarchical, network, relational, and object-oriented databases—an index is a special file. It holds a copy of the values of an indexed field from each record in the file, as well as a pointer, which tells the system where each record holding that value can be found. In other words, if a file has 2,000 records, its index will have 2,000 entries, one for each record.

Of course, if the value being indexed is different for each of these records, then the use of 2,000 index entries makes perfect sense. On the other hand, if the field being indexed is, for example, a color field, and if for those 2,000 entries, only three colors can be found, then the use of 2,000 index entries is not an optimum arrangement.

An inverted list index for this color field would contain only three entries, red, blue and green. Associated with each of those entries would be not one, but as many pointer values as necessary to point to each record that has that color value associated with it. In other words, it is an inverted list, a list with only one row for each distinct index value.

Inverted List Architecture Characteristics

The inverted list architecture makes use of these inverted list indexes to provide an optimum database environment. These indexes are used in two ways: as free-standing indexes used to help the system provide search capabilities, and as cross-file references, which are used to relate two files together in a fashion similar to that of the XBase database.

Single File Navigation with Inverted List Systems

Searching for a specific record with an inverted list system is just like searching for it in the XBase system. A FIND or SEARCH command is issued, which includes in its call parameters, the name of the index field being searched, and a value to match for that field. The system then checks the inverted list index, finds the appropriate data record, and returns it to the requesting program.

Walking through the inverted list system can be accomplished using the index (the default) or can be performed using sequence numbers. Sequence numbers are added to each record inserted to the database in the same order as they are loaded.

In all cases, a programmer must open a file, specify the type of search to be conducted (index or sequential) and the issue a call command to execute it.

Multiple File Navigation with Inverted List Systems

Just as the programmer can use only the indexes that have been predefined to perform a single file search, so too must any cross-file capabilities be established prior to running a program that must take advantage of it, most of the time.

There are three ways that inverted list databases provide the programmer with cross-file capabilities.

With the first technique—called coupling—two files with a common field description (like the customer and animal files in our previous example), are permanently associated through the creation of a special coupling index. This index relates every record in the first file with the records that have matching values in the second file. After the index is created, programmers can take advantage of it by using the coupled command as part of the syntax of their database call. This approach is similar to that used by the XBase databases. The differences between the two are that while the XBase database allows the programmer to create these indexes at any time, the inverted list programmer can use only coupling indexes that have been previously defined. While the XBase database uses simple index structures, the inverted list database uses the existing inverted list indexing scheme. The inverted list database returns data to the requestor through its own internal memory and data management scheme. This means that access can be much faster and more efficient than in the XBase case.

Another method of associating files is through the creation of userviews or dataviews. These views, which like coupled indexes must be predefined, provide the programmer with an easy-to-reference userview name, which can be used instead of a filename within a database call. When a call is executed referring to a userview name, the database internally recognizes it as an alias name for the joining of two files into one, and performs that joining operation automatically. As far as the programmer is concerned, the userview represents a superfile, made up of all matching entries from both files. As far as the system is concerned, a coupling index must exist, and the two files are dynamically associated internally.

The third and most flexible method for coupling files is by using *logical coupling* commands, which dynamically link two files. These commands identify the two files to be coupled and the relationship they should be coupled by.

While it is true that the coupling of files in an inverted list database is less flexible then dynamically associating them in the XBase fashion, it is important to remember that inverted list databases are built to handle data volumes and transaction rates much higher than an XBase database. Also, the logical coupling commands provide the same kind of flexibility anyway.

Inverted list databases can be tuned more precisely to meet the predefined navigation requirements.

Pete's Pet Shop and ADABAS

To illustrate the workings of a typical inverted list database, let's convert the animal and customer files from Pete's Pet Shop to the ADABAS database, a typical inverted list system.

Remember, just as with the dBASE III database definition, ADABAS can only couple files with a common field. Therefore the identity of the data loaded into the system and the field layouts of the ADABAS database will be similar to that of the dBASE III example.

The ADABAS Database

Refer to the Appendix for a description of the ADABAS product.

The ADABAS database, manufactured by Software AG, is distributed to run on the MVS, VM, and DOS operating systems on the IBM mainframe, as well as the Fujitsu OS4/F4 and Siemens BS2000 systems. During its relatively short history, ADABAS—with its popular Natural programming language environment has captured a respectable portion of the mainframe database market. ADABAS's inverted list architecture makes it well-suited for the support of several business data processing needs, and it has developed a reputation for solid customer support and canny product offerings.

ADABAS Physical Components

The ADABAS database is made up of the following major physical components

- Three types of data storage areas (associator, storage, and work)
- A data dictionary that holds information about the database itself
- The database nucleus, or engine (the database code)

The ADABAS database provides a much more complicated collection of operating characteristics than the previously discussed architectures. This is because it is designed to handle large volumes of data and higher transaction rates, and this level of complexity is required to take advantage of inverted list technology. Let's review the services provided by each of these components.

The ADABAS nucleus is the actual executable database software that manages the entire environment. A request for database services will be sent to the nucleus from any of a number of sources (programs running on this system or from any other system that is attached). The nucleus upon receiving this request (which will be in the form of an ADABAS call, will check the Data Dictionary tables for information about the different access methods that are available. Upon examining the alternatives, the nucleus will proceed with command execution via the following steps:

- The associator area (where all inverted list indexes are stored) will be checked and a collection of the physical storage addresses of the desired data will be extracted.

- Upon obtaining these addresses, the nucleus will revert to the main data storage area to retrieve the desired data items.

- If the complexity of the request is too great, the nucleus will make use of the work data sets as its own personal read/write area for the further processing of the information request.

- What will then be returned to the user (or requesting program) will be exactly the information requested.

Building the Animal and Customer Files

In order to build the files necessary to support Pete's system, we will use the ADABAS system called PREDICT, which is the vendor-provided interface management system for handling database activities.

```
15:51:52              ***** P R E D I C T *****          92-01-22
                       - File Maintenance Menu -              PRMF


   Code        Function          File-ID C-file-ID Type File-nr in DB
   ---- --------------------------------- ----------- -------------- ------- --------- --------
   A  Add a file                    R              O    O   O
   C  Copy file                     R       R      O    O   O
   D  Display file                  R
   E  Edit elements of a file       R
   G  Push backward                 R       R
   M  Modify file                   R
   N  Rename/Renumber file          R
   P  Purge file                    R
   S  Select file from a list       *              O    O   O
   U  Edit owners of a field        R

   ?/. Help / Return to maintenance menu

   Please enter code: A              Parameters: O = Optional
   File-ID: ANIMALS                           R = Required
   Copy-file-ID:
   File of type: A (?) File-nr:  5
```

Figure 6-1: Predict - Creating the animal file

The database files themselves are created by filling out a series of screens, which prompt the database administrator for information critical to the building of a file structure. After defining the file, fields are defined in a similar manner.

Upon completion of the file creation process (see Figure 6-1 to see the first of several screens involved in that process), the database administrator will be ready to begin the process of loading and activating the database.

If at any time, however, the definition of the database must be altered, the "E" option of the main Predict screen will allow the administrator to modify these definitions. Figure 6-2 shows the modification of the animal file using Predict.

```
>                    > + Fi: ANIMALS           L: 1   S: 5
   All  Ty L       Name              F  Length D U DB  S
   ----- --- --- ----------------------------------- -- ---------- ---- --- ----- ----
          1 ANIMALNAME               A   10.0        AA  N
          1 ANIMALTYPE               A   10.0        AB  N
          1 COLOR                    A    5.0        AC  N
          1 PRICE                    N    6.0        AD  N
          1 PURCHASER                A   10.0  D     AE  N
```

Figure 6-2: Using Predict to modify the animal file

Figure 6-3 shows a similar modification for the customer file.

```
>                    > + Fi: CUSTOMERS          L: 1   S: 3
   All  Ty L       Name              F  Length D U DB  S
   ----- --- --- ----------------------------------- -- ---------- ---- --- ----- ----
          1 PURCHASERNAME            A   10.0  D     AA  N
          1 ADDRESS                  A   20.0        AB  N
          1 PHONE                    A   08.0        AC  N
```

Figure 6-3: Using Predict to modify the customer file

Relating Data Constructs with ADABAS

After creating and or modifying the animal and customer files, there are several ways that they can be related. One option is via the ADABAS ADAINV utility.

With this utility, the files that are to be coupled and the matching fields of each, are converted by the nucleus into coupling index entries. In this case we will couple the animal and customer files through the purchasername field.

Syntax for the ADAINV utility, which couples the animal and customer files:

```
ADAINV    COUPLE    FILES =1,2
          DESCRIPTOR = 'PURCHASER, PURCHASERNAME'
          .......
```

Figure 6-4: Beginning the ADAINV utility

The animal file (file 1) and customer file (file 2) are coupled through the purchaser and purchasername fields.

An alternate way to join two files together is through the ADABAS *logical coupling* option. Whereas the example given above defines a STATIC join of the two files, the logical coupling option allows the programmer to create a DYNAMIC join at the time of query execution. (Of course STATIC joins are more resource efficient then DYNAMIC joins). The syntax for a logical coupling command is:

Loading the ADABAS system

```
FIND (file name) WITH first_column = second_column
```

Figure 6-5: Syntax for logical coupling

An ADABAS file is loaded by using the ADALOD utility, which allows the database administrator to load preformatted flat files into their designated ADABAS files.

Programming with ADABAS

After defining and loading the ADABAS database, a program can be written to access these files using the Natural programming language. Natural is a fully-functional 4GL favored by the majority of ADABAS users.

In order to find all of the information about a customer named Joe, a Natural program need only prepopulate a search variable field, and then execute the FIND command using the following syntax.

```
FIND CUSTOMERS WITH PURCHASERNAME = 'JOE'
```

Figure 6-6: A sample FIND command

Other ADABAS database manipulation commands include Record Update, Backout Transaction, Close Session, Write Checkpoint, Write Data to Log, Delete Record/Refresh File, Hold Record, Read Record, Read Physical Sequential, Read Logical Sequential, Read Descriptor Values, Read Field Definitions, Add Record, Sort ISN List and others.

To help show how a more robust version of an ADABAS program might look we have provided a small program which lists all customers and the animals they purchased. This program is written with the Natural language, the ADABAS 4GL.

```
0010 READ CUSTOMERS BY PURCHASERNAME
0020    FIND ANIMALS WITH PURCHASER = PURCHASERNAME(0010)
0030        DISPLAY PURCHASERNAME ADDRESS PHONE
0040                ANIMALNAME ANIMALTYPE COLOR PRICE
0050    CLOSE LOOP (0020)
0060    CLOSE LOOP (0010)
0070 WRITE 10T 'NUMBER OF CUSTOMERS='*COUNTER(0010)
0080 END
```

Figure 6-7: A natural program (ADABAS 4GL)

Please notice that this program makes use of a logical connection to elicit the desired information.

Inverted List Architecture Conclusions

The inverted list databases, represent a big step up in both the performance that the product can provide, and the sophistication necessary to work with it. As we proceed with the other architectures you will see this trend continuing.

The Hierarchical Architecture

Hierarchical databases are dedicated to the capture and control of one specialized type of data relationship called a *hierarchy*. Data organized this way assumes that there is an order of precedence between data. One data structure is *superior* to another.

- All data is in one-to-many relationships.

- All relationships are one-way. They move downward from the highest level structure, called the *root* or *parent*, to the lowest level called *children*.

- Hierarchical relationships are usually modeled using a *tree* structure diagram.

Hierarchical databases were the first kind of database to achieve commercial popularity. Because of their long and productive history, there are many production systems running with these databases today. There is substantial evidence to indicate that, in the mainframe environment, there are more hierarchical databases in use than any other architecture. Among the products researched for this book were the IMS and DMS II products for mainframes, and the Formbase and DataPerfect products for PCs (these PC products, though SBased in their principle organization, rely heavily upon a hierarchical structure for the data that they manage).

Hierarchical databases have achieved this popularity for several reasons. First, they are incredibly fast and efficient. Second, they are among the most easily maintained of the database architectures. They can be tuned to run at a peak performance and then left alone. Third, hierarchical navigation is both powerful and flexible. Fourth, the logical relationships mapped in a hierarchical database are the most easily understood. Hierarchical relationships are intuitively obvious to most people.

Organizing a Hierarchy

To build a hierarchical database, the database administrator begins by determining what the one-to-many relationships are, and then arranging them hierarchically. There are several rules that must be adhered to. First, the highest segment type in the hierarchy, the parent, must have no peers. In other words, the parent (topmost) record must be higher then all other records. In the case of the animal and customer files, it is easy. The customer (the one) is the parent, and the animal (the many) are the children.

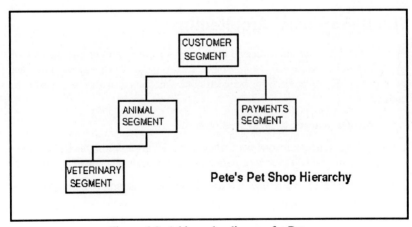

Figure 6-8: A hierarchy diagram for Pete

In the hierarchical world, data fields are grouped together to form a *segment* and a group of logically connected segments is referred to as a database. One system is usually made up of several databases, each holding a different cluster of segments.

If we add animal veterinary records to the customer/animal database, we still see the *customer segment* as the parent, the *animal segment* as a child to that parent, and a *veterinary segment* as a child under that.

Segments can also have peers. For example, we might want to attach a segment that keeps track of a customer's payments, with one occurrence for each check. This segment would be attached beneath the customer segment parent, but as a peer to the animal segment.

Using this relatively complex database with customer, animal, payment, and veterinary segments, we can now navigate through the database.

Each database product has its unique set of navigation commands, but they all accomplish the same thing. They move the program or user up, down, left, and right through the structure.

It is important to note that the hierarchical database does not allow the builder to create autonomous files the way the flat-file, XBase, and inverted list architectures allow. In the hierarchical world, and the soon-to-be-considered network world as well, whole groups of logical file definitions are clustered together into large databases.

The IMS Database

We will use the IBM IMS (Information Management System) database, to illustrate how a hierarchical database can be used to build a system for Pete's Pet Shop. We begin with the characteristics table for IMS. (Refer to the Appendix for a description of the IMS product.)

The IMS database uses the Get Unique (GU), Get Next (GN), Get Next Within Parent (GNP), and several other commands to allow navigation. By combining the request for a record (one of these commands) with a database return code that tells the program what happened when the command was processed, the program can determine where it is currently positioned in the hierarchy. Let's see how these can be used to get information about Joe and the animals he bought.

We will use the hierarchy previously developed, with segments named CUSTOMER, the ultimate parent; ANIMAL, a child under CUSTOMER; PAYMENTS, also a child under CUSTOMER and a peer to ANIMAL; and VETERINARY, a child to ANIMAL.

In the following examples we will paraphrase the IMS calls in order to illustrate the logic represented in each command. In the next section, we will consider the actual syntax for these calls.

To find information about anything in the database, we begin by locating the ultimate parent record in which we are interested. In this case that is the *Joe* record. In order to find this record and make it the current segment, we issue the following command:

```
Get Unique CUSTOMER where Purchaser Name = "JOE"
```

Figure 6-9: An IMS GET UNIQUE (GU) command

This makes Joe's record current. After reading any information about Joe into the program that is needed, we now want to identify any animals he purchased. We do this by issuing the command:

```
Get Next within Parent for ANIMAL
```

Figure 6-10: A GET NEXT WITHIN PARENT (GNP) command

The first ANIMAL record under Joe's segment, in this case, the Sammy the Shark record, becomes current. To find the next animal purchased by Joe, we say:

```
Get Next ANIMAL
```

Figure 6-11: The IMS GET NEXT (GU) command

Phillip the Fish is now the current record. To find any payment information for Joe, we would issue:

```
Get Next within Parent for PAYMENT
```

Figure 6-12: IMS - An alternate GNP command

Joe's payments now become the current set of records.To identify the records for Larry, we simply move the current pointer to the top of the Larry hierarchy with the command:

```
Get Unique CUSTOMER where Purchaser Name = "Larry"
```

Figure 6-13: A qualified GET UNIQUE command

As you can see, navigation through a hierarchical database is quite different from an XBase or inverted list structure. In this case, the options available to the programmer are quite limited.

In a hierarchical database, the programmer or user knows what the logical relationship between the current segment and any other segments are by where they show up within the hierarchy. In the case of hierarchical databases, a significant amount of the logic used to drive programs is dedicated to the task of getting around the maze created by the hierarchy.

IMS Structural Components and Navigation Control

The paraphrased commands we used to show navigation within an IMS database are not the real syntax. IMS databases, like inverted list and many network databases, require that the programmer codify the database call and pass it to the database from a control area.

In order to make the construction of an IMS database as efficient as possible while allowing programmer access to be as simple as possible, the database is made up of three components: a data storage area, a database definition, and a collection of program control blocks.

The data storage area is the place where an IMS database administrator actually places the files that hold user data, the indexes, and pointers that relate them to each other. These data storage structures could include pointers, hashing routines, and indexes in a unique combination tuned to the needs of the particular system.

This unique arrangement of files and indexes is identified by a special file called a database descriptor (DBD). The database descriptor identifies the name of the database, the name of each segment, the keys that identify each segment, and the relationship each segment has to others. In addition to this logical information, the DBD also dictates the name, size, and structure of each of the physical files within which the data will be stored.

The DBD for the CUST database involves the definition of every single aspect of the database environment. In a hierarchical or network database everything about the databases physical and logical organization must be *hard coded* into the system.

It is this hard coding of the database description that makes the hieracrchical and network databases so inflexible for modern day database requirments. While the relational databases can be altered (fields can be added or deleted, indexes added or removed) while the data is still available for user access, this hardcoded database definition technique means that all user access must stop, the entire database must be unloaded, the database regenerated and the data reloaded into the system.

```
DBD    NAME=CUSTDBD, ACCESS=...
DATASET DD1=DS1,DEVICE=DISK,RECORD=3000
SEGM   NAME=CUSTOMER,BYTES=38,FREQ=100,PARENT=0...
FIELD NAME=PURNAME,BYTES=10,START=1,TYPE=C
SEGM   NAME=ANIMAL,BYTES=41,FREQ=50,PARENT=CUSTOMER
FIELD NAME=ANINAME,BYTES=10,START=1,TYPE=C
SEGM   NAME=VET,BYTES=122,FREQ=5,PARENT=ANIMAL
FIELD NAME=VETNAME,BYTES=20,.....
SEGM   NAME=PAYMENT,BYTES=100,FREQ=5,PARENT=CUSTOMER
FIELD NAME=PAYDATE,BYTES=20,.....


DBDGEN
FINISH
```

Figure 6-14: An IMS DBDGEN -- making an IMS database

Notes on the DBDGEN for CUST

The Parent=0 entry identifies the CUSTOMER segment as the ultimate parent.

The FREQ=value, requires the DBA to determine, in advance how many occurrences of this segment will occur underneath its immediate parent. For example, the ANIMAL entry will show up 50 times for each customer and the Vet entry will be, on the average 5 times per animal.

Only the key fields, the FIELD entry lines, for each segment are managed by the database. All other fields are left up to the program to control.

After completing this description, the database administrator runs a special job, called a DBDGEN or database descriptor generation job, which creates the files, indexes, and other physical constructs.

After generating the database, the administrator creates a number of program communication blocks (PCBs), which define the different logical relationships that programs will be able to utilize. Programs are allowed to access the database only through these PCBs. Each program has within it one or more program specification blocks (PSBs), which work as the interface to the PCBs.

Loading the IMS Database

After generating the database, data is loaded from a flat file, and is executed through the use of a LOAD utility.

Other Set Up criteria

It should be quite apparent that the work involved in setting up a hierarchical database is much more complicated than that required for XBase or inverted list structures. In those cases, the programmer or administrator could modify the structure of the database and the relationships between data constructs without having to worry a great deal about its impact on the structures that are already built. In the case of the IMS database and most hierarchical databases, it is not possible to change a logical relationship between two data constructs without affecting all others in the database. To change an IMS structure requires that the entire database be regenerated.

IMS Calls in a COBOL Program

In order to use the IMS database, a program must have special working storage constructs, which provides communication functions. There are two such constructs: the segment search argument (SSA) construct, and a PSB.

The PSB becomes the doorway through which commands pass back and forth between program and database. It will be referred to as part of any database call. The SSA construct is where a command is built (just like the control area in the inverted list program).

An SSA, ready to be used to find the Joe record would look like this:

```
SEGNAME   CHAR(8)  VALUE "CUSTOMER".
FILLER    CHAR(1)  VALUE "(".
KEYNAME   CHAR(8)  VALUE "PURNAME".
OPERATOR  CHAR(1)  VALUE "=".
SSAVAL    CHAR(10) VALUE = "JOE".
FILLER    CHAR(1)  VALUE ")".
SSAEND    CHAR(1)  VALUE " ".
```

Figure 6-15: An IMS SSA for Pete's database

To execute the command to find the Joe parent record, the command would be:

```
CALL 'CBLTDLI' USING GU, PCBNAME,....,CUSTOMER-SSA.
```

Figure 6-16: An IMS/Cobol "Call"

This tells the database to perform the Get Unique operation using the command found in the CUSTOMER-SSA and through the doorway created by the PCB-NAME.

It is not our intention to describe in a great amount of detail how to code an IMS program. The point of these examples is to give you a chance to appreciate the wide range of variance that exists in the way database products approach the problem of data storage and access control. In the three architecture examples cited so far, we have seen vast differences in the complexity required not only to build databases using each, but to use the database through a program. Luckily, the IMS database, along with some of the inverted list and network types, represent the most complicated arrangements. That is not to say that all hierarchical and network databases actually *are* this complicated, just that the more complicated implementations show up in these areas.

The Network Databases

Network databases go back almost as far as hierarchical databases do. In fact, for a long time, they were the only two kinds of database that you could purchase, and they operated only on mainframes. Just like the hierarchical databases, network systems are extremely fast, are responsible for the support of a great number of large, fast production systems today, and continue to be selected for the support of many new systems being developed.

While the XBase and inverted list databases allow the designer to establish several kinds of relationships between data constructs, and the hierarchical architecture supports only one, narrowly defined type, network databases tend to split the difference between the two.

Included in the ranks of network databases are the Image database from Hewlett Packard, the Superbase 4 product running on the PC and Computer Associates' CA-IDMS, which is a hybrid network/relational system.

Data Constructs in a Network Database

A network database is organized into *data items* (fields), *record types* (collections of similar records), and *sets* (logical relationships). While the hierarchical database demanded that each one-to-many relationship be only a one-way relationship (a child cannot be parent to any of its parent segments), the network database allows a *recursive* relationship along with any normal hierarchical one. A recursive relationship is one where a child segment can be parent to its own parent.

Network logical arrangements are usually diagrammed using simple bubble charts or entity-relationship diagrams. The chart below shows the relationship between the CUSTOMER, ANIMAL, VETERINARY, and PAYMENT record types.

In this arrangement we do not have to declare an ultimate parent, or highest-order record type. Each record type can be considered a peer to all others. This flexibility can be quite useful.

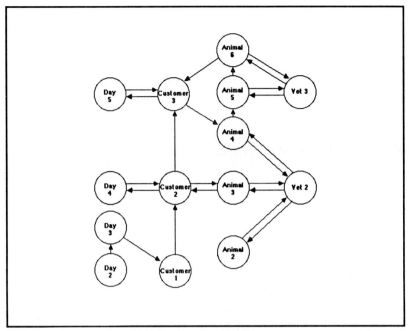

Figure 6-17: A network diagram

In the hierarchical example, we had to declare the customer segment as the parent. By doing this, by definition we made it impossible to store on the database animals not yet purchased. There was no customer (parent) segment to attach it to. Under a network arrangement, this constraint does not exist. An animal can be added to the system whether it is related to a particular customer or not.

Programming Profiles

The programming profile of a network database is highly dependent on the platform it runs on. Those running on PCs come equipped with fully-functional interface management systems with little or no third-party connectivity. The mini and mainframe systems provide robust third-party support 2GLs and 3GLs, and are often packaged with optional 4GLs or interface management systems.

The network architecture allows the designer to capture many more kinds of relationships than could be captured under the hierarchical scheme, especially recursive relationships. In the case of recursive relationships, no other architecture is able to manage them as effectively or efficiently as the network system.

Recursive Relationships

A recursive relationship is one where the child can be the parent of its parent record. For example, in the relationship between departments and employees, the manager of a department is a member of that department (a child segment under the hierarchical scheme), but is also the manager and therefore has a parent relationship to that department. With a network arrangement this double identity is easily captured. Typical recursive relationship applications include Bill of Materials or "Parts Explosions".

Navigating a Single Record Type

To locate a single record in a network database, the user or programmer must know what the predefined key for that record type is, and then prepopulate a search parameter before executing the call. To walk (browse) the record type, an OBTAIN NEXT or GET NEXT command moves the program forward through the file.

Establishing Search Sequences

Programmers can specify a customized search sequence, which allows the program to walk the file in any order defined in the command.

Cross Record-Type Capabilities

In order to relate two record types, the database administrator must create a special link between them within the data constructs. Once this linked relationship, called a *set*, is in place, programs can build complex relationships between different records by capitalizing on them. If a linkage exists between two records, programmers can *walk the set* by simply issuing an OBTAIN WITHIN SET command.

Whereas hierarchical databases enforce only one-to-many relationships in one direction from parent to children, a network organization allows the designer to do away with these restrictions. In a network database, different data constructs can be related to each other in any way desired.

How does this differ from the XBase approach? In only one significant way. The network, like the hierarchical architecture, demands that all potential relationships between data constructs be understood and structured ahead of time. How does this differ from the inverted list approach? The inverted list database uses inverted list indexes, and provides links between files based on matching index values of the two files being associated. The network database, like the hierarchical, uses direct pointers and data proximity to associate different record types.

How does the Network Database Work?

A network database establishes the relationship between record types by allocating a pointer from every record to every other record it is related to. In the case of Pete's Pet Shop, the one-to-one relationship between animals and customers (one animal can be purchased by only one customer), the relationship is captured by placing a pointer on the animal record, which provides the location of the purchaser record.

The one-to-many relationship that customers have with animals is accomplished by:

1. Placing a pointer from the customer record to the first animal purchased.

2. Placing a pointer on this animal record to the next animal purchased by the same person.

3. The last animal purchased obtains a pointer that refers back to the purchaser.

By navigating through this chain of records, the program can read all animal records for a given customer. When the program returns to the customer record, it is known that all animal records have been read. Following a chain of records like this is called walking the set.

CA-IDMS (Pre12.0) Database

To illustrate the network method of building a database, let's use Computer Associates' CA-IDMS database. The current release of this database (release 12.0) has a hybrid network/relational architecture, but the database's fully-functional network capabilities remain intact. In the current CA-IDMS environment, the database administrator can choose to use the database as a network database, relational database, or a combination of the two. We will consider CA-IDMS from only the network perspective here. Refer to the Appendix for a description of the CA-IDMS product.

The CA-IDMS database (prior to release 12.0), was a full network database. The database is made up of *pages* (blocks of records) and *areas* (a collection of pages). All of the data managed by a database is defined within a *schema*. This schema is made up of several *subschemas*, which define the areas, sets, records, and data items that will be made available to an application program. The device media control language maps areas to physical files.

To set up an CA-IDMS database, the administrator must:

1. Define the overall system schema and compile it.

2. Define the device media control language and compile it.

3. Define all subschemas and compile them.

The output of these compile processes is a series of entries in the CA-IDMS data dictionary, which monitors and controls database access activity.

As with the IMS database, the CA-IDMS database must be completely mapped out and generated before it can be used. The CA-IDMS schema defines all of the sets (relationships between two record types) that the database will capture. It is within the schema that the administrator sets up all of the pointers between different records.

```
SCHEMA DESCRIPTION
SCHEMA NAME IS CUSTOMER.
FILE DESCRIPTION.
FILE NAME IS IDMS-FILE1  ASSIGN TO DEVICEX.
                         DEVICE TYPE IS DISK.
FILE NAME IS IDMS-FILE2  ASSIGN TO DEVICEY.
                         DEVICE TYPE IS DISK.
AREA DESCRIPTION.
AREA NAME IS CUSTOMER-ANIMAL
RANGE IS nnnnnnn TO mmmmmmm
WITHIN FILE IDMS-FILE1.
AREA NAME IS ANIMAL-VET
RANGE IS nnnnnnn TO mmmmmmm
WITHIN FILE IDMS-FILE2.
RECORD NAME IS CUSTOMER.
RECORD ID IS 620.
LOCATION MODE IS ....
WITHIN CUSTOMER-ANIMAL.


       03 PURCH-NAME      PIC X(10).
       03 PURCH-ADDRESS   PIC X(20).
       03 PURCH-PHONE     PIC X(8).


RECORD NAME IS ANIMAL.
RECORD ID IS 730.
LOCATION MODE IS ...
WITHIN CUSTOMER-ANIMAL.


       03 ANIMAL-NAME     PIC X(10).
       03 ANIMAL-TYPE     PIC X(10).
       03 ANIMAL-COLOR    PIC X(5).
       03 ANIMAL-PRICE    PIC 9(5)99.
   .
   .
   .

   .
SET DESCRIPTION.
SET NAME IS CUSTOMER-ANIMAL.
   .

   .
OWNER IS CUSTOMER ...
MEMBER IS ANIMAL   ...
```

Figure 6-18: A CA-IDMS(pre 12.0) for Pete's Pet Shop

A typical CA-IDMS schema definition has sections of code defining the physical files within which data will be stored, the areas into which pages will be placed the layouts for each record type, and the different sets the schema will support.

Physical definitions are defined in a different file called the DMCL. (See Figure 6-18 for a full CA-IDMS schema layout.)

Navigating an CA-IDMS Database

The CA-IDMS database uses the FIND or OBTAIN command, with several variations.

```
FIND name  -  (conducts a search for the record specified.)
```

Figure 6-19: The IDMS FIND command

As with the IMS database, a program must navigate through the database, aware of the identity of each record based on its position relative to the record it is approached from.

Given the schema listed above, a program can now be written to access the database. Within the program is a copy of the schema definition. This allows the program to prepopulate the key fields that will be used to instruct the database about which records to retrieve.

To find the Joe customer record we would code:

```
MOVE "JOE" to PURCH-NAME.
FIND#CALC#CUSTOMER.  /PURCH-NAME IS THE CALC-KEY/
```

Figure 6-20: Finding the "Joe" record

After locating Joe's record, we can walk through the animals he purchased by coding:

```
FIND NEXT RECORD WITHIN CUSTOMER-ANIMAL.
```

Figure 6-21: Finding the next record

This finds the first animal record within the customer/animal set for Joe.

After reading through all of the animal records, Joe's customer record will ultimately be reached. When the customer record is again obtained, we know that all animal records have been read.

As with the IMS database, the CA-IDMS database uses no internal work areas in the processing of database requests (when fulfilling network requests). This means that an CA-IDMS database is extremely fast and efficient for the processing of very large volumes of data.

Program Communication with the Database

In order to allow communication between a program and the database, a special communication area called the CA-IDMS communication block is utilized. It is used to pass commands to the database and to receive status information.

The CA-IDMS Communications Block

```
01  SUBSCHEMA-CTRL.
03  PROGRAM-NAME     PIC X(8).
03  ERROR-STATUS     PIC X(4).
03  DBKEY            PIC S9(8) USAGE COMP.
03  RECORD-NAME      PIC X(16).
03  AREA-NAME        PIC X(16).
03  ERROR-SET        PIC X(16).
......
......
03  DATABASE-STATUS PIC X(7).
......
```

Figure 6-22: The IDMS communications block

By prepopulating, and referring to this communications block, the CA-IDMS programmer can operate effectively with the database.

Database Calls Using CA-IDMS

While the IMS database required the programmer to codify a call using the CALL command word and a storage variable holding the actual database instructions, the CA-IDMS programmer is allowed to use the database command words directly within the program. Database commands include FIND, GET, and OBTAIN to locate and retrieve a particular record. Several variations on these commands perform different kinds of movement through the database (next, prior, first, last, etc.).

A COBOL program that navigates the animal/customer set by finding the record for "JOE" and then finds the first animal record attached (*/ indicates comments).

```
PROCEDURE DIVISION.
/* This line ties the database to the program */
COPY IDMS SUBSCHEMA-BINDS.
/* This line primes the search key */
MOVE "JOE" TO PURCH-NAME.
/* This line actually performs the search */
OBTAIN#CALC#CUSTOMER.
/* After finding the record, this line finds the first animal */
OBTAIN FIRST ANIMAL WITHIN CUSTOMER-ANIMAL.
```

Figure 6-23: A portion of a CA-IDMS/Cobol program

The program can now proceed to process these records.

Network Database Conclusions

A competition for the *fastest database in town* would be a hard-pressed contest between the hierarchical and network architectures (from among the traditional architectures, specialty databases like IBM's TPF can be much faster, but only for specific kinds of situations). Both of them, with their rigidly-defined relationships between files, and their extremely fast accessing techniques, can store and access complex data relationships faster than any of the other architectures. Of course, this speed is purchased with the price of reduced system flexibility and increased programming sophistication.

The great number of large and effective network databases in production today in the Hewlett-Packard and IBM mainframe arenas, guarantees that network databases will continue to be important participants in data processing for some time to come.

Conclusion

In this chapter and the previous chapter, we have reviewed the flat-file, XBase, SBase, inverted list, hierarchical, and network database architectures. The products that use these architectures represent the vast majority of database management systems in use today. In general hey are flat-file and XBase on the PC, and inverted list, hierarchical, and network on the mini and mainframe platforms.

Each of these architectures represents a different strategic approach to the storage, management, and retrieval of data. Each has inherent strengths and weaknesses. All can be utilized effectively in order to support many of the systems in use today.

In the next two chapters we will consider the newest of the architectures, relational and object-oriented. Each of these architectures represents an attempt to take advantage of the strengths that each of the previously discussed architectures has, while minimizing the weaknesses as much as possible. In each of these newer approaches, you should be able to see similarities to these *older* technologies.

Relational Databases

The term *relational* has been used to describe more kinds of products than any other term in the history of databases. Although the discussions, debates, trials and tribulations of those individuals can be quite interesting and emotionally charged, it is not our desire here to muddy the water by defining yet another standard about what a relational database is or is not. What we will provide is a basic description of the architecture and approaches manufacturers take in the creation of products that attempt to adhere to this standard. We will in no way become involved in the process of declaring one database relational and another not. Nor will we give much credibility to the terms *truly* relational or *nearly* relational. As we will show, judgements about what is more or less relational are subjective, and of very little value to anyone but the vendors. Included in our discussion of the relational database architecture will be those products that conform to a minimal set of criteria; specifically that the product:

Uses the SQL language as its only data manipulation language (DML). (Except in those cases where this language is *hidden* from the user because of front-end products.)

Uses the SQL data definition and data control languages (DDL and DCL) to manage the creation, manipulation, and securing of database components.

Products Using the Relational Architecture

There are literally dozens of database products that claim to be relational, and yet, none is actually able to comply with all of the standards set forth to define a *truly relational* system. A partial list of relational database products could include DB2, SQL/DS, SQL/400, and OS/2 EE-DM all from IBM; Nonstop SQL from Tandem;

Allbase by Hewlett-Packard; Interbase, Informix, Oracle, Sybase, Ingres, and a long list of others.

Besides these products, there is an even more exhaustive list of products that are unconcerned with the architecture, but which use the SQL language as a secondary data access language. Included among these products are FoxPro, DBase IV, Omnis 7, Focus, and many more.

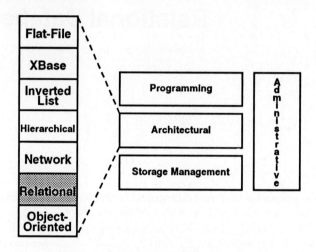

Figure 7-1: Relational database architectures

In addition, there are products that claim to have a double identity, the hybrid databases like IDMS and Datacom from Computer Associates. The impartial observer will rightly note that there seems to be many database products associated with the term relational in one way or another. This observation is valid.

There are several reasons for the stampede of vendors to the relational field, some valid and some not so valid; some theoretical, and some practical.

Tangible Benefits of the Relational Approach

By far the most substantial contribution the relational approach has made to the database industry has been the creation of SQL (structured query language). This language has established itself in a relatively short time as the *de facto* standard database language. By doing this, it gave all database vendors a common standard to adhere to. It is in a vendor's self interest to adhere to a standard access language because it guarantees that the programming profile is consistent with that of the other vendors. This means that you can buy any user interface management system or programming language and get it to work with several databases. This makes the potential market for both database and programming product vendors much larger.

Compliance with standard SQL language also means that users can change from one database product to another. When you know the SQL language, you know how to use several dozen databases equally well. Not only does standardization on SQL make programming and user interfacing easier, it makes the new generation of distributed database environments more feasible. Since most databases now speak the same language, they can talk to each other.

Soft Benefits

The other equally significant but less obvious benefits of the relational approach have to do with the long-term manageability of large database systems. In order to understand how relational databases can help people manage large systems, we must go back and examine the origins of relational theory, and the premises upon which it is based.

The Database World Before Relational Technology

In the days before the development of relational databases, data processing was a very different world. The business world was full of mini and mainframe computers, and the scientific workstation and PC were little more than drawing board sketches.

The computers that ran large business organizations had enjoyed a period of explosive growth as they built more and bigger systems. Part of the reason that these systems were able to grow as quickly as they did was because of the pre-relational database architectures. Without these products, it would have been impossible to manage the incredible volumes of data involved.

Unfortunately, while these systems were being expanded, no one considered the long-term implications of how they were being built. Inverted list, network, and hierarchical databases could be built and implemented quickly, and then enjoy several years of service. What was not anticipated was that these systems would continue to grow even after the business reasons for building them changed.

For example, the longer a navigational database exists, the more programs will be written against it. The more programs written, the more difficult it is to change the database in response to business demands. This is because a change to the database requires a change to all of the programs that already use it. If you want to change a database to help one program run better, and it could require that you rewrite 500 other programs. What are the chances that the database change will be made? Not very good.

So what happens when a new database structure is required to meet a new business need? Do you modify the existing structure? No, that is too expensive. Do you eliminate the existing system and write a new one? Not likely; the system still has value, it's just not a good fit for the new requirements. So, what do you do? *Make another database!*

That's right. The longer an organization's systems have been in existence, the more databases they will have and each of those databases will hold copies of information in the others. To say that this is a monumental waste is an under-statement. Unfortunately, until several things happened almost simultaneously, there was nothing to do but keep letting the systems grow.

The Relational Revolution and Related Events

As if someone had planned it that way, several revolutions occurred in the computer industry simultaneously. First of all, computer memory and disk space became less expensive while the maximum memory and speed of mainframe and minicomput-ers increased dramatically. Second came the invention and popular acceptance of PCs and scientific workstations in many business and engineering circles. Third, and of particular interest to us, was the creation of the relational approach to data processing.

Dr. Codd's Paper

It is against the backdrop of these events, and the condition of large data processing organizations at the time, that Dr. Codd wrote a landmark paper. Most people consider the birth of relational databases to have been heralded by Dr. E.F. Codd in his paper *A Relational Model of Data for Large Shared Data Banks*. This article was originally published in 1970 by the Association for Computing Machineries, a special interest group for databases.

In this paper, Codd laid out his reasons for proposing an entirely different approach to database management. He clearly cited the problems found in existing database approaches, how these problems could be eliminated, and even proposed a new access language to get that data. Codd described a condition called *data dependence*. This occurs when the users of a database need to know the internal representation of stored data in order to access it. In other words, the databases are navigational. He continued by proposing that a database that could be utilized without prior knowledge of the internal representation would be more flexible in the long term. He also described *data redundancy*, the storage of the same data in many different places.

The Cost of Data Redundancy

Before proceeding with any further examination, let's stop and contemplate for a moment. Are data independence and data redundancy all that important?

Redundancy is what happens when an organization stores the same information in more than one place. For example, in a world where only flat files exist, it is not uncommon to find an employee's phone number stored in hundreds of places throughout the system. The number is repeated because several programs need to read that information, so it is copied to wherever necessary.

This is fine until that phone number needs to be changed. When that happens, someone must find every place that phone number has been copied to and change it to the new number. This, of course, is a very costly operation and it is unlikely that you will actually change it to be correct in every place. You will only change it where it is important. Unfortunately, this means there is a good chance that sometime in the future the wrong phone number is going to be sent out for this person. Obviously, the fewer places you store the number, the easier and cheaper it is to maintain it correctly. So by using a relational approach to data management, you can eliminate a lot of the extra costs involved with this duplication.

On the other hand, by storing this number only once, I guarantee that numerous people and programs will need to access the same table to get that information, and *that* can be expensive too. Therefore, although redundancy is bad and has some high costs, so does eliminating it.

The Cost of Data Dependence

Another thing addressed by relational databases is, in theory, data independence. Data independence is achieved when the programs and users asking for data do not need to know how it is stored. Data access languages, before SQL, assumed that the person asking for information knew about the indexes, the relationship of the data to other types of data, and the order in which the data was loaded. Asking for data from a database when you have to know about its location before asking is called *navigation*.

The real cost of navigational access to data is not thecost incurred when actually getting the information you want. Navigational access is actually quite inexpensive when compared to SQL access. Instead, the cost to an organization when using a navigational data storage method is the cost it incurs each time a database needs to be changed. When a navigational database needs to have its segments moved, indexes changed, or keys altered (something that happens quite often) all of the relevant application programs must be modified so that they can still access the data they need. Data independence allows you to change database structures without changing application programs.

Protecting and Minimizing Programming Efforts

One of the justifications for relational databases has to do with the application programs that use it. They are developed in order to reduce the cost of application development and maintenance. It is easy to see how this can have value to an organization. Application development costs are skyrocketing. The more programs you write, the more maintenance headaches you have. The elimination of redundancy and dependence are just what the overwrought MIS organization ordered.

What is Relational?

The word *relational*, when applied to database systems, has several definitions;

> *It is a math/computer science theory developed by Dr. Codd. This approach submits a data representation and storage scheme that attempts to use advanced relational algebra and its corresponding mathematical and logical properties as an optimum means of storing and accessing data in a database system.*

Based upon these originally proposed ideas it has come to serve many purposes.

- It has been cesponsible approach for the development of several approaches to data definition and data administration theory. When coupled with other theories (entity-relationship and the ANSI 3 schema approach, for example) it can yield powerful insight into the nature of stored non-numeric data representation, and provides many guidelines for the actual performance of these tasks.

- It is useful in the design of databases themselves, whether they are relational or not.

- It is a type of database management system that attempts to incorporate those originally proposed relational theories into a physical and, we hope, efficient data storage and access method.

Relational Theory

In practice today, relational theory as proposed by Dr. Codd is applied to form what we can loosely identify as a practical relational approach to data management.

In general, this approach states that if data is stored according to Codd's original rules of structure and integrity, then the resulting database management system will be the most efficient organization of data possible. For simple purposes, an efficient system is defined as one that uses the smallest amount of computer resources (disk, CPU, and programming) to achieve the most work.

Codd's relational model addresses many areas and facets of data management and it is not our objective to oversimplify or minimize the significance and depth of the work. Neither is it our objective to get into too much detail about it. Of particular interest to the casual observer of relational theory are the three areas of data management that are addressed.

These are:

- Data Structure (how data should be stored)
- Data Integrity (how data should be keyed)
- Data Manipulation (how data is accessed)

Data Structure Rules

Data structure rules define a terminology and a set of rules for the building of data constructs. Data is viewed in terms of individual data elements. These elements are *atomic*, that is, they cannot be broken into smaller meaningful pieces. Each data element is said to have a *domain*, which is a pool of values considered valid for that element.

Any data elements sharing the same domain can use mathematical comparison operators (such as greater than, less than, equal, not equal, etc.), to generate information.

A *relation* is a collection of *attributes* (data element types) that are related in some way. For example, the attributes Name, Address, and Phone could form a relation called Customer Information.

A *tuple* is a single occurrence of a relation. In the Pete's Pet Shop example, Shark, Sammy, Gray, $25 would be a tuple from our animal relation.

Data Integrity

Having defined the rules for the building of data constructs, Codd's paper continued to define guidelines determining which fields should belong to which table.

In order to achieve relational efficiency in the storage and relating of data elements, the designer begins by identifying *base* tables. Base tables are stored representations of real world relations. For example, a company might have base tables for employees, customers, and products.

These tables should all be keyed by the following integrity rules:

1. Every *relation* has a series of *candidate keys*. A candidate key is any attribute or combination of attributes that identify the tuples.

2. Every *relation* has one and only one *candidate key* that serves as its *primary key*. A primary key is that candidate key that uniquely identifies the tuple and distinguishes it from all other tuples.

3. Any *attribute* of a *relation* can be a *foreign key*. A foreign key is an attribute of a relation that is the primary of some other table.

4. Every *relation* can have many *alternate keys* that are candidate keys not qualifying as primary keys but still identifying tuples in some way.

Data Manipulation

With the construction and relationship between data constructs established, Codd's paper continued by defining a series of operations that can be used with the database to extract the information required. Having created tables representing relations, data can be accessed using the eight relational operators. The traditional operators, based on algebraic set theory, include the union, intersection, difference, cartesian product, select, project, join, and divide. These operations are then defined using a data access language called SQL.

This collection of rules and guidelines became the foundation upon which all of the ensuing relational technology has been built.

The SQL Language

The SQL language is divided into three parts, the data definition language (DDL), data control language (DCL), and the data manipulation language (DML).

Data definition language commands are concerned with the creation of tables and other data constructs. The CREATE TABLE command that we will be discussing is a good example of DDL.

Data control language is concerned with security and data access control. Under the SQL language, security is granted and revoked with the GRANT and REVOKE commands.

The data manipulation language, the most critical of the three, is concerned with storing, modifying, and retrieving data from the database.

SQL and Navigational Characteristics

Relational navigation is completely defined by the SQL language itself. As opposed to the previously considered data access languages, which were often not user friendly, and usually tied to programming languages, SQL can be exploited by end users themselves.

Like the XBase and inverted list systems, relational tables are autonomous. Cross-table capabilities are established by the issuer of the SQL command.

SQL Syntax

Data retrieval using SQL is accomplished through the execution of simple commands, all of which share the same core syntax. All SQL queries begin with the phrase SELECT something FROM somewhere.

Scanning an SQL Table

To see a list of all animals in the animal table, the following command provides the required results:

```
SELECT ANIMAL_NAME FROM ANIMAL;


ANIMAL_NAME
- - - - - - - - - - -
Sammy
Billy
Roger
Phillip
Dan
```

Figure 7-2: Simple SQL query example

Notice that all of the previously discussed architectures returned one record for one execution of the data access language. In the case of SQL however, all rows that meet the criteria of the query are returned immediately. So for the relational database there is no use or need for walking the file. Every query results in the return of all the data that applies.

Searching for a Particular Row

Assuming that you wish to locate only one of the animals in the animal table, the SQL language provides an additional clause, called the WHERE clause. This allows search conditions to be added.

To find out what color Sammy the Shark is you would type in the query:

```
SELECT COLOR
FROM ANIMAL
WHERE ANIMAL_NAME="SAMMY" AND ANIMAL_TYPE="SHARK";
```

Figure 7-3: Specific SQL query

The results will be:

```
COLOR
- - - - - - - - - - -
GRAY
```

Figure 7-4: Result of Sammy Query

It's that simple. The user of the SQL language need not be concerned with indexes, keys, or any other kind of navigational construct. To the SQL user, every field can be a key.

Cross-File Capabilities Using SQL

In order to relate two of more files, the query need only name all of the tables from which records are required in the FROM clause. For example, to see names of all of the animals and their owners' phone numbers, which requires information from both the ANIMAL and CUSTOMER tables, the following query would be used:

```
SELECT ANIMAL_NAME,ANIMAL_TYPE,PURCHASER_NAME,
PHONE_NUMBER FROM ANIMAL, CUSTOMER
WHERE PURCHASER = CUST_NAME;
```

This provides the list below:

ANIMAL_NAME	ANIMAL_TYPE	PURCHASER_NAME	PHONE_NUMBER
SAMMY	SHARK	JOE	803-4390
BILLY	GOAT	LARRY	609-6969
PHILLIP	FISH	JOE	803-4390
SAMMY	SALAMANDER	JOE	803-4390

Figure 7-5: Relational Join in SQL

Notice that we had to tell the database to relate these tables by their matching columns. If we had not done this, the answer from the system would be incorrect. Notice also that Joe's name and phone number are repeated several times. This is because Joe purchased several animals.

When two or more tables are related with the SQL language, it is referred to as a JOIN.

The Implications of Using Relational Technologies

Based on the work of Dr. Codd, relational databases attempt to postpone the mapping of relationships between data structures until the moment that someone wants this to be done. This approach gives the relational database several advantages over the others.

First, the database administrator is not required to pre-establish all of the potential logical relationships that programs and users may need to exploit. The system designer can concentrate on optimizing those relationships between structures that are key to the successful implementation of a system. This allows the database itself to provide services dynamically to meet *ad hoc* requirements.

Second, the system can provide a consistent face to the users. The syntax for an SQL command does not change when the database administrator changes the underlying structure of the system (adds/removes indexes). It provides a database that is much more user friendly.

Third, relational databases are non-navigational. In other words, the user or program need not step through the process of translating a logical relationship between data structures into a series of navigational machinations. If users want the database to relate customer records to animal records, they simply ask to see this relationship.

Fourth, this characteristic of relational databases—to hide the internal workings of the database from the requestor—is called data access independence. The request for data is independent of the physical organization of the data. This independence makes relational databases the ideal platform for the building of distributed database systems. We will discuss distributed databases at length in a separate chapter.

Relational databases have become the choice for thousands of computer system end-users. Although the SQL language is not incredibly user friendly, its operation is intuitively obvious for many people, and is certainly less demanding than most procedural access languages. These databases are also a popular selection for systems dedicated to the creation of reports and decision support. The flexibility of the SQL language and the power that a sophisticated user can bring to bear on a complicated, free form analysis, make it the best option available in many situations.

Because of these factors, relational databases dominate the personal computer and workstation markets. They also play an increasingly large role in the building of minicomputer and mainframe systems.

Conformance to Relational Standards

As is always the case when many people are involved, the industry is having some trouble developing a 100 percent standard that all vendors will accept. Full compliance with a standard by all vendors is highly unlikely, but even today, there is a very high degree of concurrence on the majority of SQL syntax issues. There is even an ANSI SQL standards committee that continues to publish updated versions, and this standard-setting work will probably continue.

When it comes to SQL and relational standards it should be noted that:

- No manufacturer complies with relational standards 100 percent.

- Many manufacturer comply significantly.

- Many products conform at least a little bit.

What is really important about relational theory and practice is not how well a product conforms, but what the purchaser of the database intends to do with it. If the system is to be a small, stand-alone application, then compliance with standards is meaningless. If the system is to participate in a distributed database architecture, then it is critical that the product comply on the distribution and interconnectivity issues at least. If the system is to be a large production application, then the long-term relational benefits are of particular interest.

The best advice for someone struggling with these issues is to recommend utilizing those aspects of a relational system that are useful to your application, and not worry about those that are not.

Relational Reality

As we have already stated, there is a downside to the great power, versatility, and flexibility of relational systems. When relational systems are built properly, utilized intelligently, and managed conscientiously, they can be the most effective database systems. When these criteria are not met, however, the result can be quite the opposite.

User Friendly can be User Dangerous

Just because the SQL language is user friendly does not mean that users are database friendly. Whereas in an inverted list, hierarchical or network database it is impossible for a user to make requests inefficiently (because the only way they can ask for information is through the navigational paths established), in a relational database the user can build a query that is very inefficient. This is the biggest liability that free-form database types like XBase and relational have. Empowering users to access data any way they want means that they can access it incorrectly.

Overexerting the System

Another way that users and programmers can abuse a relational database is to try to make it do too much. Although a relational database *can* manage multiple depth hierarchies and extremely complex relationships, trying to make the system do this on a regular basis can result in poor response times and complicated SQL command structures. At some point, the flexibility and power of relational databases is offset by the clumsiness and complication of the system.

The Programming Profile of Relational Systems

Because of the standardized database access that SQL provides, the programming profile of most relational products is more robust than for the non-relational products. The fact that, by definition, all relational databases use the same data access language means that third-party vendors can build interface management systems and languages that can easily be plugged into any number of them. This greatly expands their markets.

The coupling of local-area network (LAN) technology with relational databases has made it possible for dozens of PC-based interface management systems to tap into the power of remote relational systems in a way never previously imagined. In fact, many of today's spreadsheet, word processing, and executive information systems are built with this kind of interconnectivity in mind.

Besides this influx of third-party software, almost every relational database manufacturer bundles or packages its own 4GL and interface management system solutions.

The Structural Components of a Relational Database

Most relational databases share a common arrangement of internal components. The database system is made up of tables, which are stored within one or several physical files. Each of these tables is created by a CREATE TABLE SQL command, which not only builds the underlying file structure, but also stores all of the information about that table in a set of special system-controlled tables called *system catalogs*.

When an SQL command is executed against this database, a special program called an *optimizer program*, checks the catalog entries and determines the best way to carry out that request. When the method for retrieving the data is determined, it is turned into a special program called a *plan*. The plan is executed, the tables are searched and manipulated to return the requested information, and the system ends the request.

In order to dynamically respond to a database request, relational databases have a common working area, or scratch pad called *temp tables*, *work areas* or some other similar term. In order to execute its functions, the database uses this area.

Relational databases have indexes as all other databases do, but programmers and users never need to know about them, or refer to them explicitly. The optimizer program decides at the time of the request what the best way of responding should be.

The relational database allows all types of relationships to be accessed at any time without predetermination. This is different from the XBase database, which requires the user or program to build indexes and use them explicitly in order to map all of the relationships, and different from the inverted list, hierarchical and

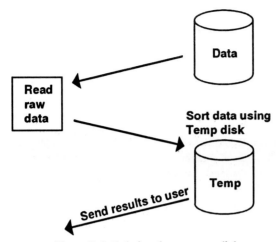

Figure 7-6: Relational temporary disk usage

network databases, which only allow certain predefined relationships to be manipulated.

This flexibility has been one of the largest factors in the increased popularity of relational databases over the past several years.

This begs a question: *If relational databases are so powerful and flexible, why have they only recently become available?*

There are many ways to answer a question like this. There are two very good reasons that are immediately apparent.

First, relational databases are exceedingly resource intensive. They require lots of memory, lots of speed, and lots of disk space to operate effectively. The platform configuration that can support a relational database did not exist a few years ago.

Second, because they are so resource intensive, relational databases are not for everyone. Many applications need every shred of computer memory, speed, and disk space they can get. If a system is strained for these resources, either because the existing hardware is all that can be afforded or because the size of the application is bigger than any computer configuration can currently handle, then the other database architectures begin to be look more attractive.

Third, flexible is not always synonymous with good. Many organizations decide that the organizational constraints that a less flexible system offers make it easier to build, administer, and secure. Flexibility brings with it a requirement for responsibility and proficiency on the part of those people who use it. If those characteristics are lacking, then a relational database can create a disaster instead of a system.

Fourth, relational databases *can* do a lot, but they *cannot* do everything. And they certainly do *not* do everything better than XBase, SBase, inverted list, hierarchical and network databases can. Many applications need the structural stability that a hierarchical or network database can offer, or the cross-referencing speed of an inverted list, or even the flexibility and user friendliness of an XBase database. Relational databases are powerful and flexible, but they are not miracle-makers. Every benefit that a relational database offers carries with it a cost.

The DB2 Database

IBM's DB2 database is considered by many to be the product that moved relational databases from the ranks of experimental systems to those of the serious production databases. The DB2 product has quickly become a standard fixture at many mainframe sites. Although DB2's history has been rocky a times, it continues to grow in popularity.

See Appendix A for specifics on the DB2 product.

The DB2 database has become both the hub for the IBM distributed database strategy and the largest selling mainframe relational database product. Because of its popularity, DB2 has become, in many cases, the standard against which other relational databases are judged.

DB2 can be found in many of the large mainframe-based organizations today. It is used to support transaction processing, process control, and decision-support systems of many kinds. A large amount of its acceptance can be seen in the area of user-friendly reporting systems.

Programming Products

The DB2 database boasts the ability to handle exceedingly large volumes of data (for a relational database) with a minimum of impact on performance. DB2 can be purchased as a stand-alone database product or with any of several accessories. Assembler language and most 3GLs, including COBOL, PL1, and C can be used to access DB2 databases. On-line programming services are usually provided by the TSO/SPF, CICS, or IMS/DC text-based user interfaces. Related IBM products include CSP (Cross-System Product) a 4GL code generator, Application System, a business analyst's workbench and QMF (Query Management Facility). QMF is by far the most popular of the IBM-provided user-friendly interfaces to the DB2 database.

Physical Components

Physically a DB2 database is made up of:

- STOGROUPS—which define disk storage space to the database
- TABLESPACES—which are the physical files within which data is stored
- TABLES—the logical components upon which the SQL language works
- INDEXES—which are created to help speed command execution

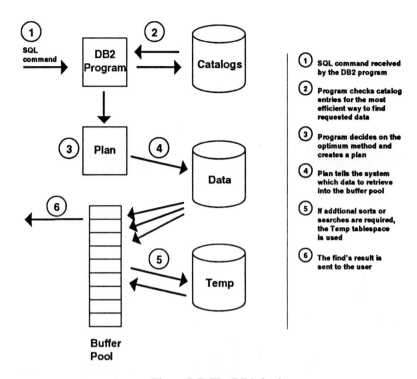

Figure 7-7: The DB2 database

Logical Components

Logically a DB2 database is made up of:

- User data - which is stored in the tables previously described

- System catalog tables - which identify all of the physical and logical components of the database

- Buffer pools - memory areas used to expedite physical I/O

- The database itself - which manages and coordinates all activity within the database

Building Data Structures

Data structures and indexes are built using the SQL data definition language. We will build another version of the customer/animal system, this time using the DB2 database to help show how relational databases work. Let's start by building the tables using the SQL language.

These commands can be executed interactively (as in the XBASE case), or can be submitted through a special batch job, as in the other architectures). Data is loaded into the tables from a sequential dataset with the Load utility in the majority

```
CREATE TABLE ANIMAL
(ANIMAL_NAME    CHAR(10),
 ANIMAL_TYPE    CHAR(10),
 ANIMAL_COLOR   CHAR(5),
 ANIMAL_PRICE   DEC(5,2),
 PURCHASER      CHAR(10))

CREATE TABLE CUSTOMER
(CUSTOMER_NAME CHAR(10),
 ADDRESS       CHAR(20),
 PHONE         CHAR(8))
```

Figure 7-8: DB2, Data Definition commands

of cases. After loading the tables, we can start asking the system for information that we want.

Programming with DB2

If we wanted to see a list of all animals in the ANIMAL table, we would simply enter the command:

```
SELECT ANIMAL_NAME FROM ANIMAL;
```

Figure 7-9: Simple DB2 query

The command could be typed on a query management screen by the end user, or embedded in a program. Either way, the results would be a list of animal names.

To get the list of animals that Joe has bought, we enter:

```
SELECT ANIMAL_NAME FROM ANIMAL,CUSTOMER
WHERE PURCHASER = CUST_NAME
AND CUSTOMER_NAME = "JOE";
```

Figure 7-10: Joe's animal query

Notice that in the first line we tell the database which columns of data we want to see. In the second line, we tell it which tables to use to find the information we want. In the third line, we identify, dynamically, how these two tables are to be related (where the PURCHASER and CUST_NAME match). Finally, in the fourth line, we tell it to provide only this matching information for Joe.

Obviously, the SQL language is substantially different from any of the other access languages we have discussed. It is the SQL language with its implied non-navigational set processing and non-procedural applicability that make relational databases so radically different from other databases. They are therefore correspondingly difficult to learn how to manage. The relational paradigm is also radically different from the paradigms for the other database architectures discussed.

Reporting

Although a report could be done using a COBOL program or any other number of third-party products, it is likely that the QMF product from IBM or QMX from Oracle would be used. In order to produce this report with a query manager, we would do the following:

1. Log on to the system and then choose the *query option* by pressing a specified PF key.

2. Fill out the QUERY screen with the SQL command that produces the information requested and execute the report RUN command by pressing the PF2 key.

```
SQL QUERY                                              LINE 1

SELECT ANIMAL_NAME, ANIMAL_TYPE, CUSTOMER_NAME
FROM   CUSTOMER, ANIMAL
WHERE  CUSTOMER_NAME = ANIMAL_NAME




*** END ***

1=HELP        2=RUN       3=END      4=PRINT    5=CHART      6=DRAW
7=BACKWARD    8=FORWARD   9=FORM    10=INSERT  11=DELETE    12=REPORT
OK, QUERY is displayed.
COMMAND ==>                                     SCROLL ==> PAGE
```

Figure 7-11: SQL query example no. 1

Just imagine how much simpler this method of creating reports is for the typical large computer driven organization.

No more need to call up programmers, request that customized reports be generated. No more filling out of report generation request forms.

Most importantly, there is no need for the user to wait. The data that a user requires can be requested as soon as they think of the needs they have.

3. View, modify, or simply print the resultant report (pressing the PF4 key prints the results).

```
REPORT                                        LINE 1    POS 1    79


ANIMAL       ANIMAL            CUSTOMER
NAME         TYPE              NAME
-------      ---------------   ---------------
Sammy        Shark             Joe
Billy        Goat              Larry
Phillip      Fish              Joe


*** END ***



1=HELP      2=           3=END        4=PRINT     5=CHART     6=QUERY
7=BACKWARD  8=FORWARD    9=FORM      10=LEFT      11=RIGHT    12=

OK, this is the REPORT from your RUN command.

 COMMAND ===>                                    SCROLL ===> PAGE
```

Figure 7-12: SQL report example no. 1

The advantages of using a relational database like DB2 become quite apparent when considering how a product like QMF or QMX simplifies the process of developing reports.

The Informix Database

The Informix databases, manufactured by the Informix Corp., represent another set of the early entrants in the relational database world. While DB2 is designed to run on IBM mainframes, Informix databases are built to run in the Unix (minicomputer and workstation) world.

Product Profile

See Appendix A for Informix Product details.

Since its creation, the manufacturers of Informix have been dedicated to the concept that Unix systems would be the wave of the future. In many ways these predictions have proved to be true. The Informix database therefore offers a mature, time-tested product in a relatively young field of competitors.

In regard to administration, logging/recovery, and internals management ,the Informix database is a mainframe-caliber database that runs in the Unix environment. The Informix administrator has as precise a level of control as any adminis-trator could wish. Included in the list of database capabilities is its ability to store and retrieve BLOBS (Binary Large Objects), which are used to allow for the manipulation of graphical items in a database environment.

Outstanding Characteristics

The Informix product offers cost effective client-server solutions for distributed database opportunities. It has a history of supporting high-transaction-rate, high-volume distributed systems. Included in the list of things that make Informix stand out from its competitors is a reputation for responsive and productive field support and the ease of use provided by the Wingz (PC-based product) and 4GL products.

Programming Products

The Informix database can be purchased with up to three different programming- and user-friendly environments, along with the capabilities provided by 3GLs. These products include:

ISQL—The interactive SQL product, which allows users, programmers, and administrators to execute SQL commands against the Informix database and create simple reports. In addition to this basic functionality it also provides a forms system, reporting, menuing and interactive schema editor.

4GL—A fully-functional fourth-generation product, which lets programmers build simple or complex high-level language programs that can do almost anything a 3GL can do, but with a fraction of the coding. 4GL can be purchased with the optional Rapid Development System, (RDS), which allows developers to use interactive debugging and other functions. It also has its own TUI (text-based user interface) screen generator that works intimately with the 4GL language. One of the most powerful selling points for the Informix 4GL is the fact that the code generated runs without modification on any of the platforms supported by the Informix database.

Wingz

Wingz is a GUI- (graphical user interface) based product, which works within MS-Windows, Presentation Manager, Macintosh, and X-Windows environments with the same code portability that the 4GL product provides. This product, a powerful combination of spreadsheet, a macro language called Hyperscript, and a GUI presentation builder toolkit, allows programmers to build highly sophisticated and user-friendly applications in a short amount of time.

Physical Components

An Informix database is made up of:

- CHUNKS—A large contiguous section of disk space.
- DBSPACES—A logical description of a collection of CHUNKS used to store normal data.
- BLOBSPACES—A logical description of a collection of CHUNKS used to store BLOB data.
- TBLSPACE—The logical collection of EXTENTS assigned to a table.
- EXTENTS—A continuous segment of disk space allocated to a TBL-SPACE.

- TABLES—The logical components upon which the SQL language works, these are stored within tablespaces.

- INDEXES—These are created to help speed command execution and reside within the same tablespaces as the tables they point to.

Logical Components

Logically an Informix database is made up of:

- User data—which is stored in the tables previously described.

- System catalog tables—which identify all of the physical and logical components of the database.

- Shared memory—memory areas used to expedite physical input/output and to assist in system management (see the section about system administration for a complete list of buffer areas).

- The database engine—which manages and coordinates all activity within the database.

- Network management products—INFORMIX*STAR and INFOR-MIX*NET, which provide for both distributed database and client/server physical configurations.

Building Data Structures

Data structures and indexes are built using the SQL data definition language. (See the example under DB2; the syntax is the same.)

A Data Input Program

To help show how the Informix database can be used to develop applications, let's define a screen for Pete's Pet Shop. This screen will allow Pete to view and insert new animal records into the animal table. We will develop it using the Informix Rapid Development System. The RDS system is entered by typing the command R4GL at the system command prompt and pressing Enter. After login the programmer is presented with the screen shown in Figure 7-13.

As is apparent from this screen, the Informix environment represents a user (or in this case) programmer friendly environment for the creation of application programs. Though certainly not as simple as the query manager style of database access, this technique does offer a lot more power and flexibility.

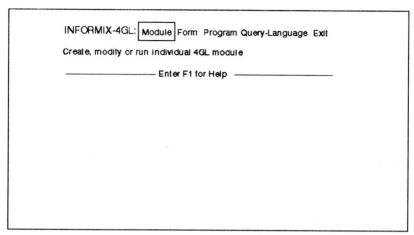

Figure 7-13:INFORMIX 4GL programmers interface

The slide bar menu across the top of the screen is typical for Informix applications. From this screen the programmer can choose to work on Modules, Forms, Programs, run SQL commands with one of the components of the ISQL product, or Exit the system by moving the highlight box to the preferred option. On the screen shown here, the Module option was chosen. By moving the selection box (using the arrow keys) to the Form option and pressing Enter, the programmer can put in a screen description.

```
database animal
screen
{
          ANIMAL INVENTORY
    Animal Name      :   [f000      ]
    Animal Type      :   [f001      ]
    Animal Color     :   [f002        ]
    Purchaser Name   :   [f003        ]
}
tables
animal
attributes
f000 = animal.animal_name
f001 = animal.animal_type
f002 = animal.animal_color
f003 = animal.purchaser_name;
```

Figure 7-14: INFORMIX 4GL programmers interface 2

After defining, saving, and compiling the form under the name bait_form, the programmer can select the Program option and enter a program similar to the one in Figure 7-15.

This application program could then be saved, compiled, and run.

Conclusions about Informix

It should be apparent that although DB2 and Informix are indeed both relational databases, their overall profiles are quite different. Informix, with its position in

```
DATABASE ANIMAL
GLOBALS
DEFINE p_animal RECORD LIKE animal*
END GLOBALS

MAIN
   OPEN FORM animal_form FROM "animal"
   DISPLAY FORM animal_form
   MESSAGE "Enter animal name,type,color and purchaser "
   CALL enter_name()
   MESSAGE "End program."
   SLEEP 3
   CLEAR SCREEN
END MAIN

FUNCTION enter_name()
   INPUT BY NAME p_animal.animal_name THRU p_animal.purchaser_name
   INSERT INTO animal VALUES (p_animal.*)
   MESSAGE "Row added."
   SLEEP 3
END FUNCTION
```

Figure 7-15: Informix 4GL program

the Unix and PC markets, assumes a totally different kind of operating environment
than DB2 with its mainframe leanings.

Database Programmability and Relational Databases

You may recall from the third chapter that we defined a set of programmability
features that are utilized almost exclusively by the relational databases. These
internal programmability functions were defined by the following taxonomy:

III. Internal Characteristics

   A. Reasons to Use Internal Database Programmability

      1. Centralization of Program Execution and Management

      2. Ease of Use

      3. Enforcement of Business Rules

         a. Identity Enforcement

         b. Constraint Enforcement

         c. Referential Integrity

         d. Complex Interdependencies

   B. Mechanisms for the Execution

      1. Stored Procedures

         a. Command-Driven

         b. Event-Driven (triggers)

      2. Structural Enhancements

      3. Rules Interface Management Systems

      4. Object-Oriented Databases

Let's apply this list to our understanding of relational databases and the relational architecture to develop the full picture of a relational database's unique approach to data management.

DB2 and Programmability

DB2 and Referential Integrity

The current release of the DB2 product itself provides a referential integrity facility as part of its standard offering. You will recall that the term referential integrity is the facility of keeping matching columns on autonomous tables in synch by logically linking them. DB2 handles the logical linking of tables through a modification to its standard data definition language (the CREATE TABLE statement). When the administrator wants to tie two tables together in this kind of relationship, a clause is added at the bottom of the statement to inform the database of the special arrangement they share. The clause tells the system which columns of the table are tied to some other table.

For example, if you wanted to relate the animal and customer tables making sure that the PURCHASER column on the animal table is always in synch with the CUSTOMER_NAME column on the customer table, the syntax would be as shown in Figure 7-16.

Based on this input, the DB2 system not only builds the tables requested, but builds the facility guaranteeing that:

- No animal row can be added without a valid purchaser value. The name of the purchaser of that animal must exist in the CUSTOMER table.

- If anyone was to attempt to change a purchaser name, it would have to be changed to one that can be found on the CUSTOMER table.

Besides this basic default capability, additional clauses can instruct the database:

- Not to allow the deletion of a CUSTOMER row if any animals match it

- To set the PURCHASER field to a null value if its matching CUSTOMER row is deleted

- To delete the rows of the animal table associated with a CUSTOMER that is deleted

Obviously, the DB2 version of referential integrity is only one of several ways that the integrity of the relationships between tables can be guaranteed. Although this particular method is limited, it does represent a big step forward in mainframe database programmability.

DB2 and Stored Procedures and Triggers

The DB2 database has had, almost from its original release, the built-in ability to store code within the database. These facilities, called Editprocs and Validprocs, are really prewritten and compiled assembler programming modules, which DB2 executes when data is added or modified within the tables. Unfortunately, due to

```
CREATE TABLE ANIMAL
(ANIMAL_NAME   CHAR(10),
 ANIMAL_TYPE   CHAR(10),
 ANIMAL_COLOR CHAR(5),
 ANIMAL_PRICE DEC(5,2),
 PURCHASER         CHAR(10))
FOREIGN KEY(CUSTOMER_NAME)
REFERENCES CUSTOMER;

and

CREATE TABLE CUSTOMER
(CUSTOMER_NAME CHAR(10),
ADDRESS      CHAR(20),
PHONE        CHAR(8))
PRIMARY KEY (CUSTOMER_NAME);CREATE TABLE ANIMAL
(ANIMAL_NAME   CHAR(10),
 ANIMAL_TYPE   CHAR(10),
 ANIMAL_COLOR CHAR(5),
 ANIMAL_PRICE DEC(5,2),
 PURCHASER         CHAR(10))
FOREIGN KEY(CUSTOMER_NAME)
REFERENCES CUSTOMER;

and

CREATE TABLE CUSTOMER
(CUSTOMER_NAME CHAR(10),
ADDRESS      CHAR(20),
PHONE        CHAR(8))
PRIMARY KEY (CUSTOMER_NAME);
```

Figure 7-16: DB2 Referential programmability

several severe limitations on the flexibility and applicability of this facility, it is not utilized very often.

The IBM Repository

Of special interest to data administrators and users of the CASE approach to systems design has been the recent release of the IBM repository. This product is built to provide the DB2 user with a separate and all-encompassing rules interface management system, which keeps track of the many relationships between tables and enforces those rules independently of the database itself. Although the Repository Manager does more than just enforce rules, and even though it is still a relatively new product, its appearance opens new horizons for those organizations that wish to capitalize on the centralized management approach to databases.

Informix and Database Programmability

The Informix database provides several kinds of database programmability, including constraint enforcement, referential integrity and stored procedures of a very different kind then the ones under DB2.

Constraint Enforcement

In the Informix database, constraint enforcement is made possible through the modification of the standard SQL data definition language. In this case, if a specific set of values constitute the population of all valid values for a given column can be identified, the definition of that column is appended with the CHECK phrase. This phrase provides the database with a list of values that must be checked whenever a value is added or changed.

```
CREATE TABLE ANIMAL
(ANIMAL_NAME   CHAR(10),
ANIMAL_TYPE   CHAR(10) CHECK (ANIMAL_TYPE IN
("fish","dog","cat", "goat","shark", "salamander"
"snake"))
ANIMAL_COLOR CHAR(5),
ANIMAL_PRICE DEC(5,2),
PURCHASER      CHAR(10))
```

Figure 7-17: Informix database constraints

Assume that Pete's Pet Shop decides that only certain kinds of animals should be allowed within the system. Pete wants to see only fish, dogs, cats, goats, sharks, salamanders, and snakes in his system. In this case, we would simply adjust the CREATE TABLE statement to include this information. (See Figure 7-18.)

The check phrase tells the database not to allow any other values but those listed into the table. Any attempt to insert a different value will result in an error condition.

Referential Integrity and Informix

Under Informix, the referential enforcement scheme is similar that of DB2. Informix CREATE TABLE statements are modified in order to provide the linkage.

```
CREATE TABLE ANIMAL
(ANIMAL_NAME   CHAR(10),
 ANIMAL_TYPE   CHAR(10),
 ANIMAL_COLOR CHAR(5),
 ANIMAL_PRICE DEC(5,2),
 PURCHASER      CHAR(10))
FOREIGN KEY(CUSTOMER_NAME)
REFERENCES CUSTOMER CONSTRAINT FK_CUSTOMER_NAME;
```

Figure 7-18: Informix referential integrity commands

While DB2 referential integrity provides three options for deletion criteria in this type of relationship, the Informix database has only one. When these tables are linked:

- No animal can be added if a valid customer record does not exist

- No customer can be deleted if a matching animal record exists

Stored Procedures with Informix

The Informix stored procedure facility is much friendlier easier to use and applicable than the DB2 Editprocs and Validprocs. These procedures consist of SQL statements and/or code written using the special stored procedure language (SPL). To add a procedure to the system, the administrator uses the CREATE PROCEDURE command.

```
CREATE PROCEDURE name
(statement(s))
END PROCEDURE;
```

Figure 7-19: Informix procedure syntax

Each procedure must be given a unique name and there is no practical limit on the number of statements that can be included. After running this command, the statements section is stored within the database. It can then be executed at any time using the EXECUTE name command.

An example should help illustrate the usefulness of these stored procedures. Assume that the system's users are constantly needing to write queries that display a list of all customers and the animals they have purchased. Although it is a relatively simple query, it can become quite bothersome to be typing it in over and over again. One way to help make the system friendlier might be to save that query as a stored procedure called REPORT1. That way, whenever someone wanted to see the report, all they would need to do is type in "EXECUTE REPORT1" instead of the full query.

To store this procedure, the administrator would input the command in figure 7-20.

```
CREATE PROCEDURE REPORT1
(SELECT CUSTOMER_NAME, ANIMAL_NAME, ANIMAL_TYPE
FROM ANIMAL,CUSTOMER
WHERE PURCHASER = CUSTOMER_NAME);
END PROCEDURE;
```

Figure 7-20: Informix, Stored procedure commands

After successfully executing this command, the REPORT1 procedure is available.

Database Programmability with Other Databases

The DB2 and Informix approaches and offerings in database programmability are far from extensive or truly representative of all the ways that this facility can be implemented. Many database products, including Sybase, Interbase, Nonstop SQL, and most of the other relational products have distinctive and quite clever approaches to the same problems.

Relational Databases Conclusion

There are several things about the relational architecture and the databases that use it that are of particular importance to the student of database technologies and architectures. First and foremost, it is critical that the person trying to understand how a relational database works understand the SQL language and the unique style of navigation it provides. Second, it is also important to keep in mind the way that relational databases attempt to simplify the process of managing large systems in the long run with data independence. Third, remember that there is no such thing as a *truly* relational database, only products that conform more or less closely to the ideals established in Dr. Codd's paper. Because of this, the performance of a relational database, like all others, should be considered based on all of the product profiles (programming, architecture, data storage, and administrative), not just the architecture itself.

Although the relational approach to database architectures represented a radical and significant change in the ways that organizations made use of databases, these changes are still not too easily understood against the demands of day-to-day data processing realities. In the next chapter, which is about object-oriented architectures, we will see a group of products that take even bigger steps in the direction of database programmability, database management of an entire environment, and the use of even more abstract and cumbersome paradigms.

Extended Relational Systems

There is a special kind of relational database organization, called the extended relational approach that should be mentioned at this point. The extended relational architecture, though based upon many of the same concepts as the normal relational systems, includes in its make up, a whole set of functionality based upon the object-oriented database approach. Different manufacturers provide different combinations of these two, oftentime contradictory architectures. The products of this type are very new, most are in the laboratory stage, but should become more popular over the next several years. The extended relational system is both relational and object-oriented and therefore a hybrid architecture.

Products of the extended relational family include Postgres from UC Berkeley, , and Starburst from IBM Research.

Chapter

8

Object-Oriented Databases

The latest generation of databases has sprung up around the object-oriented approach to data processing. Referring to object-oriented databases and the object-oriented approach as being an architecture is at best a liberal interpretation of the term architecture. Object orientation, and the use of objects in programs and databases, is simply too new a concept for there to be any set architectural principles upon which to draw. The best that we can do at this stage, is to develop an understanding of what the basic principles are, and how different vendors are applying them to database technology.

Object-oriented approaches were first developed as the result of research into more effective programming techniques. As a spin-off from this approach, a set of criteria for the development of object-oriented databases have begun to develop.

Object-oriented databases are still in the early stages of development. There are several PC and workstation versions that are commercially distributed, but in general, the products are simply too new to determine how marketable the approach will be.

Among the ranks of object-oriented databases are Versant, Ontos, Objectivity DB, and Open ODB. These products can be found on PCs, Unix-based workstations, minicomputers, and mainframes. The most popular of the products currently run on Unix platforms.

Object-oriented databases are currently being used to develop a number of useful applications. At this point, due to the newness of the environment and lack of programming expertise, mass production development has been restricted to lower volume and lower transaction rate applications. You will not find many airline reservations systems using object-oriented databases, but there are a few object-oriented specialty consulting firms with impressive applications in place.

Because of the sophistication and subtlety of the approach, object-oriented systems work best in environments that are extremely complex, but that have well-defined operation parameters. Therefore, the medical and engineering fields have provided the most frequently targeted environments for the application of these techniques.

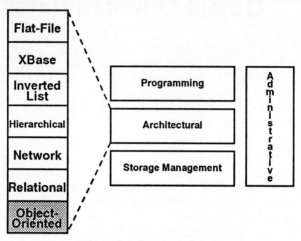

Figure 8-1: Database chart

The Programming Profile of Object-Oriented Databases

The paradigms necessary to work with object-oriented technology require a specific set of operators within the languages and interface management systems that work with them. For this reason, the field of available programming products is quite narrow. Some of the more popular third-party programming languages include C++ and Object-Oriented COBOL. Third-party interface management systems include Smalltalk, a programming interface management system, and several other object-oriented products.

Of course many object-oriented database vendors market programming products with their databases.

Definition of Terms

Object-oriented databases, like so many other areas of leading-edge technology, are fraught with confusion and misunderstanding. This is due to the broad-based nature of the approach and the immaturity of supporting theories and products. In a very real sense, the object-oriented approach is still being defined, just as relational technology is still being defined.

As opposed to relational theory, which has been based on one major work—Dr. Codd's paper—object-oriented technology has no such foundation upon which to build. Only time and concentrated efforts by vendors, theoreticians and standards groups will be able to develop the same kind of consistency within object-orientation that exists today for relational systems.

What does Object-Oriented Mean?

To begin with, the term *object-oriented* can be used to refer to several things. There is both a broad-based application of the term and several specific ones. Each of these brings with it its own set of paradigms and rules for adherence. In the broadest sense, the term object-oriented refers to the concept of reducing the identities and complexities of all of the things within a system to the single status of objects. In the object-oriented world, all people, places, things, events, and transactions are considered to be objects. This approach is diametrically opposed to the more traditional approaches, which concentrated on *separating* data from processes. The complex nature of the relationships between these objects is considered to be nothing more than characteristics of those things. By viewing the world in this way, the object-oriented theorist believes that the design and implementation of systems can be greatly simplified.

The Object-Oriented Approach: Specific Applications

The broad-based principles of object-oriented concepts can, of course, be applied in several different ways to the building of computer systems. The approach has been used to help the define several environmental characteristics of a system, including:

- The way that computers are actually put together
- The way that operating systems work
- The way that screens are presented to end users
- To define the way that applications are actually built

This is accomplished through object-oriented modeling and design, object-oriented programming, and object-oriented databases.

All of these different applications, are based upon the same basic set of principles, upon which object-oriented theory is based.

Object-Oriented Principles

When considering the object-oriented systems and approaches, we enter a new level of sophistication and complication when compared to the other data management approaches. Object-orientation is based upon the concepts of:

- ABSTRACTION—the principle that a system design should be based on the abstract attributes and characteristics of an operation rather than the short-term tactical implementation of a set of tasks. Abstraction attempts to get behind the meaning of processes.
- ENCAPSULATION—this principle requires that as much of the system as possible be built as a collection of *black boxes*. Each operation should be independent of all others. All activities should be autonomous.

- SHARING—this principle requires that no function or data be stored, moved, or manipulated more than absolutely necessary.

In a very real sense, these three characteristics are nothing more than a restatement and revalidation of good systems and database design principles as they have been developed over the years.

Polgmorphism

Another important concept is that of polymorphism—the characteristic that operations (code) and objects (data) should be bundled as one thing called an object. In other words, in the object-oriented world, the programmer never works directly with a database table, but instead works with the object that is a combination of the programs and tables that make it up.

For example, in the object-oriented world, activities having to do with employees would be directed to the employee object for handling instead of within a program itself. While traditional programming languages and interface management systems work directly with a database, object-oriented applications defer this work to objects, which manage the data and the transactional operations related to it.

To add an employee record to a table in the nonobject-oriented world, a program must collect all of the information about the employee, validate that all spellings, classifications, and interdependencies between this record and the others on the system have been met, and then finally proceed with the insertion of the record. Under object-oriented programming, an employee object is created. This performs all of these validation routines and inserts the record into the database for the program.

Obviously, under the principle of polymorphism, the job of end-user application programs is reduced dramatically. It is polymorphism that makes object-oriented data management so different from previous approaches.

Inheritence

- INHERITANCE—the principle that involves the identification of objects as having a hierarchy of membership in different superclasses, classes, and subclasses. All of these help define what the object really is. After tieing individual things to the classes of which they are members, the system uses inheritance to minimize the data storage and retrieval required to gather information about it.

Inheritance defines a different way of dividing up and *tiering* the complexity of applications and data storage.

An Example of Inheritance Principles

We will use our simple animal table to help underscore the significance of inheritance. A casual glance at the animal table of Pete's Pet Shop shows that we are not able to save a lot of information about the animals that Pete sells. Even though we have information about the names, types, and colors of animals, it would be helpful to be able to store information about the care and feeding of these animals as well. Of course, if we tried to work with our animal table, and simply add columns to save animal care information we would create a problem. The care and feeding of fish is very different from that for goats. More importantly, the information is not simply different, but is a different *kind* of information.

For fish, we need to know whether it is a fresh water or salt water fish and whether it is from a tropical or a temperate zone. For goats, on the other hand, temperature and water salinity are meaningless, but preferred diet (tin cans or old shoes for example) might be important. Even though all of the things listed in the animal table are animals, they are also different kinds of animals.

```
ANIMAL  ANIMAL       ANIMAL  ANIMAL   WATER   TEMP        PREFERRED
NAME    TYPE         COLOR   PRICE    TYPE    ZONE        FOOD
------  ----------   ------  ------   -----   -----       ---------
Sammy   Shark        Gray     25.00   Salt    Tropical
Billy   Goat         White   120.00                       Boots
Roger   Rabbit       Black     5.00
Phil    Fish         Green      .50   Fresh   Temperate
Dan     Dog          Brown    99.00
Sammy   Salamander   Green      .25
```

Figure 8-2: The animal database with inheritance data

For our system to store all of the information about all of the animals, we need to add several dozen columns to the table. In order to add information about fish and goats only, we would have to add at least three.

Notice that not only has the table grown significantly, but there are also a lot of blanks. Dan the Dog is neither a fresh water nor a salt water dog. The terminology does not apply. So the typical data management approach will not allow us to capture this kind of information easily.

In an inheritance hierarchy (not to be confused with a database hierarchy), the different categories to which an animal belongs are identified as *classes*. For example, Sammy the Shark belongs to the classes of animal, fish, saltwater, and tropical, while Billy the Goat belongs to the animal, mammal, and herbivore classes.

By categorizing the different animals in Pete's table by the different classes to which they belong, the object-oriented system can then keep track of the characteristics of each class, independent of the animal itself.

In this case, classes for fish, goats, dogs, and cats could be defined, and information about them stored separate from the individual animal records.

Having categorized the animal and defined the classes to which they belong, the you can then access that information through the inheritance facility. Inheritance brings in all information about all of the classes that an animal belongs to each time it is referenced.

```
ANIMAL    ANIMAL        ANIMAL   ANIMAL
NAME      TYPE          COLOR    PRICE
-------   ----------    ------   -------
Sammy     Shark         Gray      25.00
Billy     Goat          White    120.00
Roger     Rabbit        Black      5.00
Phillip   Fish          Green       .50
Dan       Dog           Brown     99.00
Sammy     Salamander    Green       .25

The class of fish information:

WATER     TEMP
TYPE      ZONE
-------   ------
Salt
Fresh
          Tropical
          Temperate

The class of goat information:

PREFERRED
FOOD
-----------
TIRES
BOOTS
TIN CANS
```

Figure 8-3: The Animal Object with fish and goat class

Applying the Object-Oriented Approach to Different Problems

The Construction of Computer Hardware

By applying object-oriented principles to the building of computer hardware, manufacturers have been able to streamline, modularize, and improve the overall efficiency and expandability of their platforms. In a very real sense, the open systems movement in data processing is an attempt to apply object-oriented principles to the building of hardware and the interconnecting of that hardware to build an information infrastructure.

Under open systems, computer infrastructures are built so they are composed of self-contained component parts (encapsulation), which can be used by all other members of the system (sharing), and that function as autonomous black boxes (polymorphism) in the execution of their tasks.

The Development of Operating Systems

The Unix operating system is a good example of object-orientation in action. Even though Unix was around before the object-oriented approach was developed, the principles upon which both are based are basically the same. Under Unix, printers, disks, tapes, terminals, programs, files, and byte streams are all considered to be objects. A Unix shell script uses the same basic syntax to manipulate all of them.

Although Unix falls short of perfect adherence to object-oriented principles, it does conform to a great degree.

The benefits gained by Unix programmers by keeping the system modular, interchangeable, and concise certainly helped inspire the developers of some of the newer operating systems and window-based systems to use the same principles in their design.

The Building of Graphical User Interfaces

One place where object-orientation can be seen in action with great success is in the areas of graphical user interfaces and windowing products. The success of these products has been spearheaded by the acceptance of the Apple Macintosh, X-Windows, Microsoft Windows, and OS/2 operating systems by large numbers of end users. These products have been built using the object-oriented approach.

These environments define a world for the user that is made up of objects (files, programs, databases, etc.), and events (point with arrow, click mouse button, etc.). Based upon these two simple premises, an incredibly easy-to-learn and powerful interface management system can be built.

Products developed under this discipline retain certain characteristics, as defined by several seminal research papers published over the past several years. They combine object-orientation, computer-human interaction and the exploitation of high quality graphics terminals to create a truly user-friendly environment. These characteristics are typified by the following acronym:

WIMP— Windows, Icons, Menus, and Pointers

Under the WIMP scenario, applications are based upon a point-and-shoot or user-friendly basis, which uses these four characteristics. Psychologically, WIMP interfaces allow users to:

- Visualize operations
- Recognize operations dynamically, as opposed to recalling commands
- Transfer knowledge about the interface from one environment to another (only if applied consistently)
- Achieve high compatibility between stimulus and response

The WIMP characteristics can be found in:

- The Apple MacIntosh
- X-Windows
- MS-Windows
- OS/2-Presentation Manager

To capitalize upon the WIMP characteristics, simply use windows, icons, menus, and pointers in the building of an application.

Another acronym presents a different set of characteristics.

NERD—Navigation, Evaluation, Refinement, and Demonstration

The NERD characteristics define more than the simple physical totems with which an application and user work, but instead define the intention and arrangement of those WIMP elements into a meaningful organization.

NERD characteristics and rules give the object-oriented developer a set of guidelines for the combining of objects and processes into a meaningful whole. It is the availability of new operation totems (WIMP) characteristics, that when combined with the NERD characteristics, give the object-oriented display products their potency.

Although the application of object-oriented approaches to the building of computers, operating systems and graphical user interfaces helps explain how these abstract concepts can be applied to real problems, it does not help us understand how they are applied to the building of application systems, the areas of object-oriented design, programming and databases. The issues revolving around modelling and design will be addressed in a later chapter, but we will spend a considerable amount of time here with the other two.

An Overview of Object-Oriented Design, Programming, and Databases

It is important for the person struggling with object-oriented application development to keep in mind from the start that object-orientation is more an *approach* to doing things than a *method*. Just as the previously discussed database architectures built on the functionality of their predecessors, so to does object-orientation add more options to choose from.

Perhaps the easiest way to envision how the object-oriented approach builds on earlier technologies is to review the continuum of programming functionalities as they apply to databases.

We will take a moment from our current line of investigation and go back to examining some of the earlier days of the data processing world.

Through this investigation we should see how the capabilities of the last few generations of database products is nothing more than a logical extension of the direction that data processing in general has been moving for some time.

The Predatabase Data Processing World

**The scope of control by programming languages
in the prerelational database world**

Programs and Programmers

Presentation of the Data	Preparation and Processing of the Data	Enforcement of Business and Integrity rules	Management of Access to the Data

Figure 8-4: Programming before database management

In the world before databases were invented, programmers wrote programs that handled user presentation, calculation, data integrity protection, and the physical reading and writing of records to files.

In this environment, programs have full responsibility for the insertion, deletion and management of data stored on disk. The programmer must be aware of everything about that environment in order to write an application.

The Early Database Environment

When databases were introduced to this environment, this functionality began to be split between programs and databases, and operationally between database administrators and programmers.

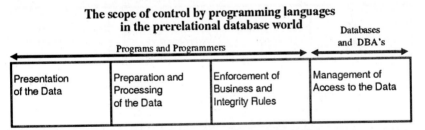

**The scope of control by programming languages
in the prerelational database world**   Databases
                                                   and DBA's

Programs and Programmers

Presentation of the Data	Preparation and Processing of the Data	Enforcement of Business and Integrity Rules	Management of Access to the Data

Figure 8-5: Prerelational database programming

In this world, the burden of data storage management is removed from the program and placed on the database software. The intricacies of data management are reduced to a number of calls to the database software, which manages it for the program.

The Relational Database Environment

In today's relational database environment, the enforcement of business and integrity rule functions are also being picked up through referential integrity, constraints, and other rules-based enhancements. In effect, the database is in the process of taking over control of that whole portion of the system.

**The scope of control by programming languages
in the relational database world**

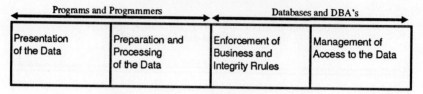

| Presentation of the Data | Preparation and Processing of the Data | Enforcement of Business and Integrity Rrules | Management of Access to the Data |

Figure 8-6: Relational database programming

By using stored procedures, referential integrity, and the other means of rules enforcement, programmers are relieved of the burden for an additional set of logic. When databases were first introduced, a lot of code was replaced by a database call. In this case, the transformation is even simpler. The programmer simply does not worry about the predefined business rules anymore, the database manages it automatically. Violations of business rules simply result in error messages.

The Object-Oriented Environment

In the object-oriented environment, the preparation and processing of data, is also taken over and managed by new, powerful object-oriented databases.

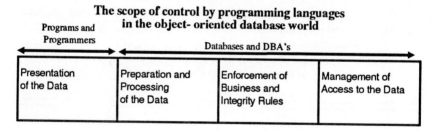

Figure 8-7: Object-oriented database programming

Under object-oriented programming, the additional logic removed from application programs is again replaced by a simple call to the database. This time however, that call, like a call to a programming subroutine, simply passes-off the information required by another program—in this case the object program—to do the processing.

Stated in very simple terms, object-orientation attempts to shift the responsibility for preparation, processing, enforcement, and data management onto separate specialized called routines, which then handle everything for the application.

Of course the exact dynamics of how this shifting of responsibility takes place is still far from clear. At this time, object-oriented languages and databases only scratch the surface of the ultimate organization consequences of this kind of shift.

The Future Environment

If the implementation of these technologies and the development of object-oriented databases is consistent with their current direction, the ultimate organization will probably involve the creation of new categories of job functions including object

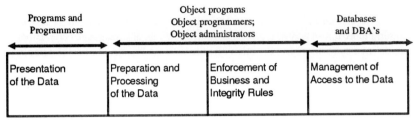

Figure 8-8: Future object-oriented programming

programmers (who concentrate on the building of objects), application programmers (whose specialty will be the development of GUI interfaces and reports), and object administrators (who will work with database administrators in the development of systems).

Object-Oriented Programming

Even though object-oriented terminology requires that we speak of objects as some combination of processing and data management logic, in reality, objects are simply specialized programs, separated from the flow of a normal program in order to help modularize the processing as much as possible. This approach to managing large data processing environments is not new. What is new is the syntax, language constraints, and supporting paradigms, which make it easier for organizations to do things this way.

As we consider the different object-oriented databases, we will see a considerable difference in the ways that they attempt to help manage things this way.

C++: An Object-Oriented Programming Language

In order to help develop an appreciation for the ways that object-orientation can work, let's take a moment to consider the C++ language. Unfortunately, under object-orientation, programming and databases are so tightly bound that we cannot hope to explain the one without a rudimentary understanding of the other. We choose C++ for several reasons. First, it is by far the most popularly accepted version of an object-oriented programming language today. Second, it is a hybrid language, combining the features of both the traditional 3GL C language and some object-oriented extensions. This makes C++ easier for programmers from a non-object-oriented environment to understand than the more non-traditional pure object-oriented languages.

Features of the C Language

A C program consists of 2 major sections: the *includes* and the *main* sections. In the *includes* section are declarations that locate for the program different libraries to which it should attach. The libraries included give the program access to all kinds of commands and functions not part of the base C language. The *main* section is the bulk of the C program. Within it, the programmer defines all of the variables and procedure code that runs the program.

The Main section is divided into logical subsections called blocks. A block is nothing more than a way to logically organize sections of C language code. Blocks are defined by surrounding a section of code with the bracket ({ and }) symbols.

```
#include <stdio.h>
#include <util.h>
main()
{
printf ("Hello");
}
```

Figure 8-9: A typical skeleton C program

This simple program prints the word Hello to the terminal. Notice the Include and Main sections. Notice also that Main is itself a block as indicated by the brackets.

Within the body of a C program, or as part of an included library, can be small mini-programs called functions. Functions are written to provide an easily reusable collection of code, which can be called by C programs and other functions. Functions can be defined with their own sets of variables, and can be built to receive parameterized input and to send parameterized output. To execute a function, the program need only refer to its name and pass it any variables it might require.

```
#include <stdio.h>
#include <util.h>
void printgreet()

main()
{
    printgreet;

void printgreet()
}
printf ("Hello");
}
}
```

Figure 8-10: C program with "Printgreet" function

This simple program that accomplishes the same thing as the last one by creating a function called printgreet. Although in this example the addition of the printgreet function is a waste of effort, the reason to write these functions is so that the same section of code can be executed over and over again, with a simple reference to its name.

For example, if you wanted to print Hello on the screen 3 times, all we would have to do is type printgreet; printgreet; printgreet; within the text of Main.

Making a Program Object-Oriented

Given this simple framework of a C program, we can now consider how the language is modified, in the form of C++, to provide object-oriented capabilities. In order to get a C program to manage objects, the C++ language provides for the creation of a special kind of called program called a *class*. The class is a mini-program that takes responsibility for the management of objects.

Classes are defined in basically the same way that programs are, with the exception that a new statement, the CLASS statement, is added to the Include section of the program. This differentiates CLASS programs from regular programs. It also defines two kinds of functions and variables within the class: those that the class program can use itself (private), and those that any calling program can use (public).

```
Definition of a class called animal

#include <stream.hpp>

class animal {
   public:
         char type[10];
         char name[30];
         void printname(name);
};

main()
{
/* - code which performs animal processes - */
}
```

Figure 8-11: Definition of a class called animal

Notice that in the public section we define two variables and one function. These variables and functions are made available to any calling program because they are public.

In order to make the animal class usable by a program, the name of the class is added to the Include section of a program, (animal.h) and declared as a class with a variable structure. This declaration makes it possible to invoke the class program through the use of a special syntax.

Notice that in this program, we include the animal.h class name and the phrase *animal callanimal*. This statement tells the program to treat the prefix callanimal, as an instruction to invoke the animal object.

A program that uses the animal class

```
#include stream.hpp
#include animal.h

animal callanimal

main()
{
    callanimal.printname

}
```

Figure 8-12: Usage of the animal class

Under the Main section of the program we see *callanimal.printname*, which tells the program to call the animal object and invoke the printname method.

Although there is a lot more syntax to be considered in the development of C++ programs, this introduction should give you an appreciation for the basic approach. In summary, under C++, classes (objects) are defined as autonomous programs of a special type. These programs can be called from within a C++ program by invoking their names. Programs can use both the variables and the functions within a class through the use of those invocation commands. A function that has been declared to be a part of a class is known as a class method.

Object-Oriented Database Terminology

Unfortunately, there is yet another set of concepts that must be considered in order to discuss the ways that object-oriented databases work. We must define more of the terms that make object-oriented databases unique.

Constructors and Destructors

In order to work with database records, programs must have a storage area prepared that matches the layout of the individual structures (record definitions) to be used. In order to initialize this area, programs use special commands called *constructors*. A constructor is a function with no input or output. When it is invoked, it simply initializes the appropriate storage area. *Destructors*, obviously, have the opposite effect.

Instances and Persistence

Because the object-oriented environment is so much more dynamic than a traditional one, the permanence of the data stored in a program's memory is considered to be transient. In other words, the values for a row of data are assumed to be temporary. The existence of values within a data structure is therefore called an instance (or occurrence) of the object.

If, on the other hand, the structure is assumed to be permanent (i.e., stored on disk when you are through working on it), then it is said to be a persistent object.

The Object Engagement Language (OEL) and Object Definition Language (ODL)

Since the object-oriented approach requires that an additional layer of software be added to the system, we create an entirely new set of commands that work with it. We refer to these new terms as the object engagement language and the object definition language.

The object engagement language consists of those terms that invoke, manipulate, or in any other way refer to the objects or object management portion of the system. Commands like CREATEOBJ and DELETEOBJ are used in the Versant database environment to create and destroy objects. Remember that in the object-oriented world, application programmers no longer work with database calls. Objects work with databases, and programs work with objects. This does not mean that the object-oriented database is without a data manipulation language. They certainly have that too. The person programming the objects must be familiar with them, while the application programmer need not worry about it.

Just as there is a separate language for the building of database constructs, so too is there a language dedicated to the construction of objects. The example cited earlier, of creating an animal class, shows how the C++ language expects objects to be defined. As we will see, the object definition language often accomplishes both the definition of the processing part of an object and the data construction part at the same time.

Given this preparatory information, we can begin to consider how some of the many object-oriented databases actually function.

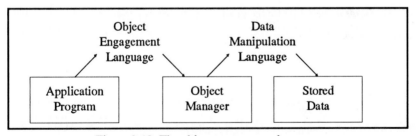

Figure 8-13: The object engagement language

The Objectivity/DB Database

The Objectivity/DB database, is marketed by Objectivity, Inc. The product is designed to provide a fully-functional, object-oriented environment for workstation platforms, and runs on the RS6000, Sun3, SPARCstation, HP9000 (300, 400, 700, 800), DEC RISC, VAX/Ultrix, Silicon Graphics, Vax/VMS and Sony NEWS. As with the previously considered database products, it may be helpful if the readers begins by reviewing the profile found in the Appendix.

The Objectivity/DB database can be viewed in terms of modules that provide specific database services. At the highest level is the application interface. The interface calls specific runtime services that manage the retrieval and storage of objects. These modules are:

- Object manager—which responds to requests for objects

- Type manager—which is responsible for the storage and retrieval of class definitions

- Lock manager—which guarantees the concurrency of the system

- Storage manager—which takes care of physical I/O operations

Data administration tools are also provided for browsing data and data types, checking on locks requested by users, moving data, and backup/restore operations.

Applications use either a C or C++ application programming interface (API) to manipulate objects. The API works directly with the object manager and type manager. In addition to working with the type manager, the object manager interfaces with the lock manager and the storage manager. If the system is running as part of a distributed database configuration, then of course, the Network manager is also invoked.

Objectivity/DB Logical Storage Model

Objectivity/DB uses a four-level hierarchy. Basic objects, containers, databases and federated databases.

The basic object provides the mechanism for storing user defined objects (data and methods). Basic objects correspond to tables or files in the previously discussed database architectures. In the case of Pete's Pet Shop, we will create two basic objects, the animal and customer objects.

Containers are a collection of one or more basic objects. Placing more than one basic object in the same container guarantees that the data being managed will be stored in proximity. Placing two or more basic objects in the same container object improves performance when both are likely to be accessed simultaneously.

Databases are a collection of containers, and can be tied to the definition of a physical file. All of the basic objects within the same database can be found in the same file.

The federated database maintains control over all databases within the same system. It is at the level of the federated database that all database class descriptions are stored and managed in the form of one or more schemas.

So an Objectivity/DB system is made up of basic objects, which are grouped into containers, which are grouped into databases, which are grouped into *the* federated database.

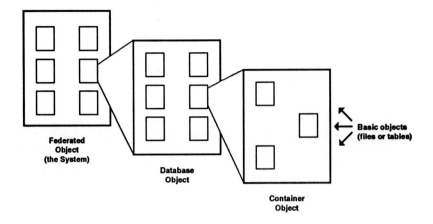

Figure 8-14: Objectivity objects

Types of Files Under Objectivity/DB

Objectivity/DB works with five types of file structures. These are the bootstrap, federated, database, journal, and lock files.

The bootstrap file holds the information to start and stop the database environment. It functions as the primer, holding the information necessary for the system to open the database.

The federated file contains the system-wide database, which holds information about all of the schemas within the objects that the database manages.

A database file holds all data associated with a database object. It is the database files that hold user data.

The lock and journal files hold locking information and logging information, respectively.

Gaining Access to Objects from a Program

Programs gain access to objects and navigate using a "handle" interface. Handles provide a level of indirection that allow the programmer to refer to an object logically, by some identifier, rather than having to know where an object is physically stored, or the machine architecture it is stored under. A handle is a smart pointer.

Developing an Application with the Database

In order to develop an application using this product, the following steps should be followed:

1. Determine the nature and identity of all basic objects that the application must access. This involves the development of both the procedure and data construct characteristics.

2. Write descriptions of the classes using an object definition language. This is referred to by the manufacturer as DDL. This DDL is used to create the schema.

3. Process the schema file to create the necessary programming subroutines and library members.

4. Write the application program and compile it.

Pete's Pet Shop

Now let's develop an extremely simple application using Pete's Pet shop to show some of the basics of how an object-oriented database can be used. We will create an object called oanimal, which will handle, among other things, the locating and retrieval of animal information based on the animal's name.

Creating the Schema File

Objectivity/DB uses the C++ class description syntax as the basis for a schema, but it also takes advantage of some of its own extensions for added functionality. To convert the existing animal file into an animal object, we could enter the code in Figure 8-15.

This schema file is then prepared and stored within the appropriate libraries and database objects. Given that this object has been created, we can now attempt to implement it using the C++ language.

To invoke this method, the programmer will code:

```
animal.printani(animal_name)
```

Figure 8-15: Command to invoke animal object

This command will:

- Invoke the animal object
- Execute the print and method within that object
- Use the animal_name value passed as an input parameter

Getting Data from the Object into the Program

The previous example shows us only how to pass a parameter to an object's method for invocation. Since objects are responsible for handling communication with the physically stored data, the first thing a programmer needs to know when considering how to get data back into the program after it has been found, is to determine how data is made available to a program. Luckily, the technique for doing this is

```
#include oo.h
//This line names the oanimal class, declares it a
//public object with public par5ameter and declares it a
//persistent, basic object with the ooObj parameter

class oanimal: public ooObj {

public:
  char animal_name[10];
  char animal_type[10];
  char animal_color[6];
  int animal_price;
.........


//Methods (functions) to be associated with this object
//include a method (printani) which prints out the
//animals name and type based upon the animal_name
//passed to it

void printani(animal_name)
{
// The lookupObj command, will return the animal
// information based upon the animal_name parameter
//passed to it. If a matching animal name is found
//the name and type will be printed
if(animalH.lookupObj(scopeH,animal_name))
  {
    ...
    printf(animalH->animal_name,animalH->animal_type)
  }
}
```

Figure 8-16: Object schema definition

the same as the technique for invoking a method within an object. To make data that has been obtained by a method available to the originating program, the programmer can use either the period (.) or arrow (->) syntax of C++, specifying the object's handle and the name of the field being requested. For example, to make the animal_name field available to our C++ program we could code:

```
animalH -> animal_name
```

Figure 8-17: C++ Command to invoke field

Of course, in order to use this access technique, a method that accesses stored data must have first been invoked.

Navigational Characteristics of Objectivity/DB

There are several ways to navigate through, or more importantly, gain immediate access to related data constructs under the Objectivity/DB database. These include simple access, scope names, the use of relationships, iterators, composite objects, and inheritance.

In order to find things in the system, we must first determine how they are identified. Other database management systems use file names, segment names, or table names to drive navigation between different collections of data. With Objectivity/DB, federated databases, databases and containers are provided with system names. Objectivity/DB also provides a predicate query capability using the SQL "Where" clause, conditional scan using C++, keyed lookup, and named lookup for navigating to basic objects.

Unique system identifiers are given to every object instance stored within the federated database. Therefore, one way to tell the system you want some data out of the object is to use this unique identifier.

Simple access to basic objects is handled with access commands (open, update, close, delete, and lookupObj). These commands are used to directly access the object if its identifier or name is known. Using these commands is more direct than using the simple sequential access or search commands of the other database architectures.

As an alternative, the database allows programmers to define any number of keys for each basic object. Each key can consist of any number of fields.

The other kind of names, scope names, are unique to object-oriented databases. An object is allowed to have several scope names, and each of those names can be considered to be an alias, or nickname, used by some other object. For example, a woman named Mary has a husband and child. The husband calls her Darling and the child calls her Mom. We could assign a husband->wife name of Darling, a child->mother name of Mom and a business->employee name of Mary, all to be associated with Mary's object.

Key access and scope name access are both accomplished through special commands. Scope names can be used only when the object resides in a *hashed* container container. We discuss more about hashed system access in the chapter on data storage and management. At this point, it is sufficient to know that hashed access is very fast, though somewhat limiting.

Keyed access is also supported through B-tree indexes.

These scan and search capabilities are useful but more limited than those found in more mature database management systems. However, keyed access is very efficient. Another, more effective way to speed access is through the use of composite objects and associations.

Associations

Objectivity/DB allows database designers to create logical relationships between objects on the system to speed process of finding and retrieving them. The linking of two objects is referred to as an association. These associations function in basically the same way as pointers in a network database, allowing the programmer to skip between object instances (records) based on navigation using these pointers. In fact, from the perspective of a student of databases, we could say that the object oriented databases have two overlapping architectures: the object-related architecture and an underlying network architecture.

Given the understanding that the Objectivity/DB database supports network-like navigation, it can be viewed as a superset architecture from the data management perspective.

Associations are specified within the schema file, and indicate which object classes can be linked to one another.

For example, to enable bi-directional associations between our animal class and a customer class we could code:

```
ooHandle(Animal)  animal  <--> customer;
```

figure 8-18: C++ association code for Objectivity/DB

This is part of the public declarations of the customer schema file. This will define an association between the two.

You can navigate associations just as you would a network database by invoking commands that traverse (walk) the relationships.

Another way to gain access to related objects is through the creation of composite objects. A composite object is a collection of associated objects whose relationships have been flagged as *propagated*. A propagated relationship is one for which delete, lock, and unlock operations apply to all objects in the composite. The effect of doing this is similar to that of defining referential integrity constraints between a group of related tables in a relational environment.

The creation and exploitation of inheritance and composite objects provides the user of the Objectivity/DB database with an high degree of flexibility and powerful database access.

Object-Oriented Databases Conclusions

You might conclude that the object-oriented approach to database management is very different from any of the architectures previously discussed. Although this is certainly true, this impression is exacerbated by several factors.

First, the preponderance of C and the C++ language in the object-oriented world tends to discourage any but the bravest of organizations from experimenting with the approach. For a typical user, PC programmer, or mainframe systems analyst, the pointers, Varrays and obscure syntax can seem quite cryptic. This will be lessened as more object-oriented products with friendlier syntax and structures become available.

Second, object-oriented technology is new. Many standards, conventions, and shortcuts to understanding are as of yet undefined. As time goes on, and a body of knowledge and experience is gathered, it will become easier to handle.

Third, the new terminology of instances, objects, handles, etc., is so far removed from most mainstream technologies that it will remain difficult to cross-pollinate between the object-oriented and nonobject-oriented worlds for some time.

These factors notwithstanding, we have seen by following the evolution of databases from simple file handlers to complex business rules enforcers, that the object-oriented databases are a step in the right direction.

Comparing Object-Oriented to the Other Architectures

One way to quickly appraise the differences between architectures is to consider the complexity of the paradigms necessary to work with them, and their corresponding ease of use.

Clearly, of all the architectures considered, flat-file, XBase, inverted list, hierarchical, network, relational, and object-oriented, the object-oriented is the most complex. Not only does it involve an extremely complex paradigm, it requires the most significant shift in the assumptions that programmers and users make about the way a system should be built and should act.

While the pre-relational databases provided alternate ways of accomplishing the storage and retrieval of data efficiently, the relational and object-oriented databases challenge the basic assumptions most people make about the relationship between programs and databases. Perhaps at some point we should stop calling them object-oriented databases and start calling them objectbases or relationbases.

In the next chapter we will consider the hybrid and proprietary architectures and draw some conclusions about architectures overall.

Hybrid/Proprietary Architectures

Before developing a set of conclusions about the many different architectures we have considered, it is important, for the sake of thoroughness, that we at least touch on the issues of non-standard architectures. Although the majority of databases can be classified as belonging to one of the eight architectures discussed, there are products that defy these classifications. These include hybrid databases (databases that utilize two or more architectures) and proprietary architectures (architectures that are the exclusive property of one product).

Hybrid Architectures

As we have mentioned, there are some database vendors who have attempted to combine the strengths of two or more architectures into one product. There are two ways that this is commonly done. One way is to establish two equivalent database call gateways into the product, one for each architecture. This approach, called parallel hybridization, allows the database purchaser to use two access languages instead of just one. The other approach, called superimposed hybridization, replaces the native access language of the database with a superset language, which provides more functionality than the basic access language provides.

Parallel Hybridization

The most common form of database hybridization is to parallel two or more architectures under the same product. The current trend for many manufacturers over the past couple of years has been to develop architectures that use an existing architecture and add a parallel relational architecture to it. Although each vendor may have their own reasons for taking this approach, two obvious explanations come to mind immediately.

One reason could be that the vendor wishes to offer customers the ability to buy one product and then choose to use one architecture or another on an application-by-application basis. For the purchaser, this is a powerful and economically attractive solution to an otherwise perplexing problem. Few organizations or individuals know in advance what kinds of applications they will be building in the future. The parallel hybrid architecture allows them to postpone a decision until more facts are available.

Another reason for this approach might be that many vendors found their market share slipping as relational databases became increasingly popular. For some time now, relational databases have been the hot item in database circles. In response to this slippage (or potential slippage), vendors may have moved to reclaim their markets by claiming that they were relational too!

For many organizations, the biggest reason to make use of a dual-architecture database, is to allow for the preservation of their investment in existing applications, while providing for the ability to capitalize on newer approaches.

The reasons for parallel hybridization are not as important as the effect it has. The effect is that purchasers of these databases get more flexibility and options to choose from than they do with a single architecture product.

On the downside, they also purchase a product that requires learning how to work with two paradigms instead of one. This means more training, more abstraction, and for some, more confusion about which way is best.

The CA-DATACOM Database

A good example of a mainframe hybrid database is Computer Associates Datacom/DB database. This product capitalizes on both the inverted list and relational architectures in its operation profile.

Note: To indicate that a database utilizes a hybrid parallel architecture, we use the notation architecture1||architecture2. In the case of Datacom, it is an inverted list||relational database.

The CA-DATACOM product started out as a very popular inverted list database. It is built to run in the IBM mainframe environment including the MVS, VM, and VSE operating systems. Several years ago, the product was enhanced to provide its users with both inverted list and relational access to stored data. Database administrators can choose to build data structures using either set of commands (SQL or inverted list), and programmers and end users can access the system using either set of data manipulation commands.

The Programming Profile of CA-DATACOM

For end users, Computer Associates offers the separately packaged, CA-DATAQUERY product. It has been an integral part of CA-DATACOM for some time. It works in two modes: Guided (for the novice) and expert. CA-DATAQUERY reports are built in two phases, the data extract request phase and the data formatting phase.

For data extraction, a user can implement the data query language, SQL, or both in the preparation of the data extract phase. In guided mode, the user is carried through a series of menus that request specific criteria important to the building of a query. In expert mode, the user is presented with an editor screen into which a query can be keyed and executed. CA-DATAQUERY has versions for the PC and Vax that allow the remote environment to access mainframe-stored data transparently.

The application programming environment includes Ideal, which is marketed as a complete life cycle development tool. It allows access to sequential, VSAM, DB2, and CA-DATACOM data. Ideal is often used in conjunction with 2GLs and 3GLs in the development of systems.

Creating Data Constructs with CA-DATACOM

Because the CA-DATACOM database is truly a parallel hybrid architecture, the database administrator can choose to use either architecture's methods for the creation of data storage structure. To create our animal table in the inverted list mode, the administrator would take advantage of the CA-DATADICTIONARY product, which provides a series of screens. These can be filled out to create the structure. When defining the structure with the inverted list facilities, the administrator must fill in all pertinent information about the building of inverted lists (indexes), describe how files will relate, and tie the specific database components to disk storage.

On the other hand, the administrator might choose to simply create a table using the syntax we used earlier for the relational databases. In this case, the system translates the SQL command into a definition recognized by the database itself.

Accessing Data with CA-DATACOM

Of course, the ability to create data constructs with two different command structures is not the reason to choose a hybrid architecture database. The reason to choose it is so that both the navigational efficiencies and the relational ease-of-use features can be exploited. The inverted list syntax for accessing the database, uses the standard database call facility, and can take advantage of LOCATE, READ, ADD, DELETE, and UPDATE commands. Cross-file access is provided by the creation of static *dataviews*.

The other option for accessing the table is to use the same SQL commands we considered under the relational databases.

The Impact of Using Parallel Hybrid Architectures

Parallel hybrids can be a blessing or a curse when it comes to system performance. If the product is built well with a balance of both architectures built into the system, then the developers and users will be able to take advantage of either facility without adverse effects. As we discussed in earlier chapters, there is a definite trade-off in performance between record-at-a-time and set-processing systems. With a parallel hybrid architecture, a developer should be able to take advantage of either with a corresponding performance improvement.

The administration of hybrid architectures can, unfortunately, be more complicated than for a single architecture database. The database administration staff
needs to learn two sets of system operation commands, and must learn to work with
two navigation paradigms. This can be particularly tricky when a cross-architecture
call (SQL call to inverted list file, or database call to relational tables) is involved.

Parallel hybrid architectures are, and will continue to be, extremely popular
solutions to database problems. Other products using this approach include Com-
puter Associates' IDMS (network||relational), Software AG's Adabas (inverted
list||relational), and Omnis 5 (a network||hierarchical||relational architecture).

Superimposed Architectures

Another way that two architectures can be merged is for the vendor to superimpose
one architecture method on top of another. The most common way that this happens
also involves vendor attempts to make non-relational databases appear to be
relational. Superimposing one architecture over another usually involves replacing
the original navigation commands with a proprietary superset of the original
language. This is done in order to simulate more functionality than the original
architecture could offer or to enhance its performance. A good example of a
superimposed or enhanced architecture is the FormBase Database by Columbia
Software Corp.

The FormBase Database

The FormBase Database offers the ease of use of a Screen based database, with the
strict data management rules of a hierarchical database. With FormBase, a user/pro-
grammer can quickly define the data, and it's appearance, along with the ability to
create all of the necessary data files, and their mapping, all on a single screen.

Creating a File with FormBase

With FormBase, the databases and the forms are one in the same, when a user/pro-
grammer creates a new database, FormBase creates an blank form for the user to
define. Users place the cursor on the form, type the name of the item, and specify
what type of data is to be stored in that location.

After the main form is defined, the user simply needs to specify where fields,
subtables, and subforms are shown. The data definition process is interactive, and
the user can enter and update the data during the definition process, providing the
ability to make exactly the type of form required.

Proprietary Architectures

In addition to hybrids, one last group of architectures that we need to consider are
the proprietary architectures. These approaches to database management are based
upon principles of navigation and management that are unique to an individual
database product.

When you consider the amount of flexibility that vendors have in creating their
own architectures (they can basically make the database any way they want), it is

actually quite surprising that more proprietary architectures do not exist. Most proprietary architectures are found on PCs, but an occasional workstation, mini or mainframe product may also be identified. Let's look at an example of this type of architecture to show just how different they can be.

The SIM Database

The SIM (Semantic Information Manager) database takes an entirely different approach to data management than the other products considered. SIM, which is distributed by Unisys, runs as a part of the InfoExec environment. InfoExec includes a data dictionary, the SIM database, user and programmer interface management systems, and other information management features. The InfoExec environment attempts to provide a fully-integrated platform from which all data processing operations can be driven.

The makers of the SIM database have attempted to combine many of the concepts of object-oriented databases with a special data modeling technique called semantic data modeling. (For details on the Semantic Data Model see the chapter on modeling and design). By combining these two approaches, they have created a distinctive, powerful, and flexible architecture unique to the industry.

The SIM architecture is probably best described as an object based data management system. This is in contrast to the object-oriented databases already discussed, which manage both data and processes. SIM manages objects through the definition of classes, superclasses and subclasses, and through the definition of rules for their use.

The Development of a SIM Database

The basic building block of a SIM database is a class. One class is used to represent one logical collection of data. Using the Pete's Pet Shop example, we would create two classes, one for animals and another for customers. These classes are defined using the ODL (Object Definition Language) and are built into a file called a schema, which is used as input to a database generation procedure. The schema, in turn, creates the database. The syntax to create our classes would be:

```
CLASS Animal
   (Animal-name:  string[10];
    Animal-type:  string[10];
    Animal-color: string[5];
    Animal-price: number[5,2];);

CLASS Customer
   (Customer_name: string[10];
    Address  :     string[20];
    Phone :        string[8]; );
```

Figure 9-1: SIM data definition syntax

Of course, the definition of our database does not stop here. What makes the SIM database so unique is the way that we are able to build business rules into the schema definition and relate different classes to each other. The data values we have defined here are referred to as Data Value Attributes (DVA). This is to distinguish them from another kind of attribute definition called an Entity Value Attribute (EVA), which are used to relate two classes. In this case, the two classes defined are referred to as *base classes* because they stand alone and are subservient to no other class.

Building Business Rules into the Schema

There are several ways to build the enforcement of business rules into the SIM schema. The first way is through the use of ranges.

A range clause, which can be appended to any attribute description, tells the database what range of values will be accepted as valid for that field. To add a range to the Animal-price attribute so that all values fall between $1 and $1000, the Animal class schema would be modified to look like this:

```
CLASS Animal
  (Animal-name: string[10];
  Animal-type: string[10];
  Animal-color: string[5];
  Animal-price: number[5,2]  (1..1000););
```

Figure 9-2: SIM object definition syntax

In order to establish the values that the elements of a string variable can have, the database designer uses the TYPE clause. TYPE clauses are named as part of the schema, and can then be referred to within the CLASS description. For example, to guarantee that all Animal names are made up of letters A through T, we would create a TYPE of Name-chars, and then refer to it as shown below.

```
TYPE Name-chars = CHAR("A".."T");
CLASS Animal
  (Animal-name  : string[10] of Name-chars;
  Animal-type  : string[10];
  Animal-color : string[5];
  Animal-price : number[5,2]  (1..1000););
```

Figure 9-3: SIM TYPE syntax

Another way to place logic into the database's definition is through the addition of VERIFY clauses to the schema. Each class is allowed to have associated with it any number of verify statements, which check and enforce logical assertions about the data being modified or added. Verify clauses work in very much the same way that triggers do.

For example, another way to enforce the same constraint defined by our range example (price between $1 and $1000) could be through the use of a VERIFY clause.

```
Verify Animal-price-check ON Animal:
      Animal-price LEQ 1000 AND
      Animal-price GEQ 1
      ELSE "This price is invalid";
```

Figure 9-4: SIM data Verify procedure

This clause would be placed in the schema file after the definition of the Animal class itself. Notice that the verify command is given a unique name (Animal-price-check), checks whether the price is less than or equal to (LEQ) 1000, or greater than or equal to (GEQ) the value 1 and issues an error message if the price is out of range.

Defining the Relationships between Classes

Besides this built-in integrity checking, the SIM database provides two ways for the establishment of relationships between classes. One way is to define classes to be subclasses to other ones. Another way is to establish bi-directional pointers (relationships) between classes.

In general, the creation of subclasses allows the database designer to develop hierarchical relationships between classes. To make a class that can be identified as a subclass of another, a special subclass declaration statement is used. This statement defines the subclass, which is also a class in its own right, and uses most of the same syntax as base class definitions except for the use of the keyword SUBCLASS.

For example, let's redefine our SIM animal/customer database so that the animal class is a base and the Dog class is a subclass.

```
CLASS Animal
   (Animal-name : string[10];
    Animal-type : SUBROLE (Dog);
    Animal-color: string[5];
    Animal-price: number[5,2];
    Purchaser   : string[10]; );

SUBCLASS Dog OF Animal
   (Breed:            string[10];
    Preferred-food:   string[20];
    Hair-length:      string[8]; );
```

Figure 9-5: SIM Subclass definition

Notice that the subclass of Dog is related to the Animal class by the OF statement. and is related via the SUBROLE called Animal-type.

EVAs

The SIM database allows developers to define specific named relationships between classes and subclasses by creating special attribute definitions that specify the exact relationship. These attributes can be used in one or both of the classes being linked depending upon the relationship being established. The default relationship is to simply point from a class to another with no other constraining criteria.

The creation of these relationships make it possible not only to speed access and increase the navigability of the system, but also to allow developers to eliminate the redundancy of stored data. For example, we might decide that instead of storing the name of the purchaser of an animal twice, once within the animal class and once within the customer class, that we will simply associate the two classes with that name. To do this we would require the above modifications to our schema file definition.

```
CLASS Animal
   (Animal-name string[10];
   Animal-type string[10];
   Animal-color string[5];
   Animal-price number[5,2];
   Purchaser : Customer ;);
CLASS Customer
    (Customer_name string[10];
    Address       string[20];
    Phone         string[8]; );
```

Figure 9-6: SIM referential integrity

By placing the name of the class Customer as an attribute of the Animal class of Purchaser, we have defined a link between the two. This makes it possible for programs and users to find a purchaser record automatically, by simply referring to the Purchaser attribute. (This connection will make more sense when the object manipulation language is explained.)

Types of Attribute Characteristics

The attribute example given here is the simplest kind to make. There are many more complex relationships that can be defined. These are specified by adding keywords to the attribute declaration statement. These keywords include:

- UNIQUE — this guarantees that the attribute value (in our case the Customer-name) is not used more than once.

- REQUIRED — this tells the system to be sure that an attribute value exists.

- READONLY — means that the attribute value (Customer) can only be read, never modified.

- SV (Single-Valued) — by default all attributes are single-valued. but they don't need to be. For example, we might attach several customer records to the same animal record. The SV symbol is appended to the declaration to make the attribute explicitly single-valued.

- MV (Multi-Valued) — when the values can be repeated, it is indicated with the MV symbol.

- MAX (VALUE) — establishes the maximum number of attribute values that can be associated with the class.

- INVERSE IS — (applies to EVA's only) allows the developer to create inverse relationship names, like customer-is (which would name the EVA pointing from the animal to the customer) and animal-owned (which would point from the customer back to the animal). These are inverse relationships.

Of course, understanding how the ODL works to help define complex relationships between classes is meaningless without knowing how the data is going to be accessed. This is done using the SIM-OML (Object Manipulation Language).

OML (Object Manipulation Language)

Navigation through the SIM database is defined solely by the OML. The basic syntax of an OML retrieve command is:

```
FROM class
RETRIEVE attribute names
```

Figure 9-7: SIM OML syntax

To see the name of all of the animals on the system, we would use this command:

```
FROM Animal
RETRIEVE Animal-name
```

Figure 9-8: SIM simple query

To see a specific subset of animals, a WHERE clause is added to the command. For example, to see what color Sammy the Shark is we would query:

```
FROM Animal
RETRIEVE Animal-color
WHERE Animal-name = "Sammy"
```

Figure 9-9: SIM specific query

This simple query shows how a single class can be navigated; but what about cross-class capabilities. To do this, we use the EVAs. Just as the SQL language allows query builders to relate tables with changes to syntax, so does OML. To use a predefined association, the query builder simply refers to the EVA name in the query. For example, to report on the names of each animal, the animal's owner, and address, we could write:

```
FROM Animal
RETRIEVE Customer-name of purchaser,
         Address        of purchaser,
         Animal-name
```

Figure 9-10: SIM Query example 3

The SIM OML has a great deal of flexibility, and unfortunately, it is beyond the scope of this book to consider it in any more detail. For more information about the language, refer to any of the several manuals provided by the manufacturer.

By combining the power of the database constructs created using the ODL and the navigational dexterity of the OML, the user of a SIM database gains access to powerful and useful database management system with a distinctive architecture. The flexibility and intelligence held by this semantic database give it an edge over most other database products on the market.

Architectural Classifications

Our review of hybrid, proprietary, and distinctive applications of architectures concludes our consideration of the navigational and organizational approaches that database manufacturers assume when building a database product.

We defined eight basic architectures, two kinds of hybrids, and the concept of a proprietary architecture and considered their paradigms and organization assumptions. With these concepts in place we can continue with our development of a taxonomy of database profiles with a listing of our findings. You may recall that so far, the architectural taxonomy looks like this:

Architecture Taxonomy

I. Terminology

  1. Terminology for Data Constructs

  2. Data Constructors

    a. Data Definition Language (DDL)

    b. System Generated

    c. Interface Management System Defined

II. Capabilities and Paradigms

  1. Search (full or partial)

  2. Data Cross-Referencing/Mapping

    a. Dynamic

   b. Static
3. Processing Mode
   a. Record at a Time
   b. Set at a Time

We now append to this the actual types of architectures:

III. Types of Architectures
   1. Basic Architectures
      a. Flat-File
      b. XBase
      c. SBase
      d. Inverted List
      e. Hierarchical
      f. Network
      g. Relational
      h. Object-Oriented
   2. Hybrid Architectures
      a. Parallel (architecture1||architecture2)
      b. Superimposed (architecture1//architecture2)
   3. Other Types
      a. Proprietary

Future comparisons of database products will therefore require an additional table entry for the architecture itself. For example:

Summarizing the Navigation Paradigms

For each of the seven architectures considered, we showed how a system could be used to navigate and manage data. We did this by way of explanation and through examples using a product typical of the architecture group. At this stage we will summarize the navigation assumptions typical of each architecture.

Table 9-1: Architectures

Database Architecture	Flat-file XBase Inverted List Hierarchical Network Relational Object-oriented// 2nd architecture Parallel Hybrid arch1||arch2 Superimposed Hybrid arch1//arch2 Proprietary

Flat-File

In the flat-file domain, autonomous files are created through a user interface management system. These files usually have no direct correlation between each other. Navigation is restricted to simple index searches and file scans. Because of this, the flat-file architecture can hardly be considered an architecture at all. However, since this type of arrangement for the relating of constructs is in fact a valid one, and since many products do use it, we include it as one of our basic types of database.

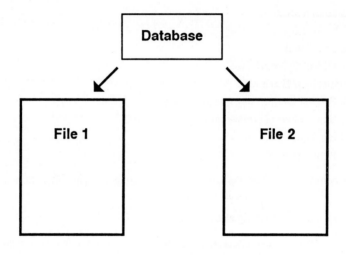

One or the other

Figure 9-11: Flat file database structure

This diagram provides you with a grapical representation of how the flat file database works in terms of cross-file capabilities.

Products that fit into this category:

- BTRIEVE
- My^Advanced Database
- PC-File
- Q&A
- Rapidfile

XBase

With the XBase architecture, autonomous files are created through a programmer interface management system. Single-file access is made through scanning or simple index searches. To associate two files, a field common to both must be identified. The files are then related through the execution of a link or join command, which then keeps the first file (base) and the second file in synch. As the base file is navigated, the second file maintains a parallel position so that both files always have matching linked fields.

File 1   **File 2**

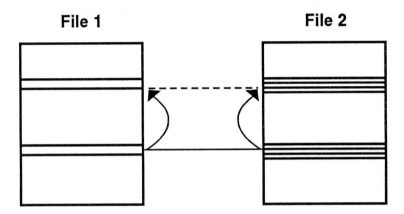

As the pointer moves through File 1, the pointer in File 2 stays in sync.

Figure 9-12: Xbase diagram

This diagram attempts to show the 2 file relationship between XBase files. The main pointer being used for navigation, and the secondary pointer being kept in synch.

The XBase databases were the first and most popular of the PC database products, and they still enjoy a wide number of users today. Many enhancements to the same, basic, but highly functional XBase approach, have led to the creation of not only any number of pure XBase systems, but many hybrid, proprietary, relational and SBase systems.

SBase Databases

The SBase databases allow the user to create autonomous physical files through the use of screens (thus the name SBase or Screen Based systems). It is the relationship of the file to the screen that makes the SBase system unique. (Although in many ways the Flat File and SBase architectures could be considered the same).

The things that distinguish an SBase system from a Flat File system are:

- The SBase system is much more robust in terms of programmability

- The SBase system allows for the creation of sophisticated relationships between files (screens) through the use of a screen.

These databases can be distinguished from all of the other architectures by the way that navigation and access to the data is managed fully by the screens themselves.

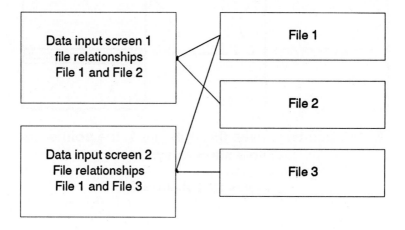

Figure 9-13: SBase architecture

While the Flat File system usually provides only a limited programmability profile, Sbase systems come with fully programmable functionality. These programs actually call and work with screen names and the fields of those screens as opposed to the file names and field definitions underneath. (See Figure 9-13.)

Of all of the architectures listed, the SBase systems are the most loosely defined. They also represent the latest generation of databases to hit the PC market. We can look forward to continued advancements in the sophistication and functionality of these user friendly databases for many years to come.

Inverted List

For the Inverted list database, files are also created autonomously, but special indexes called inverted lists are used to provide search capabilities, along with simple scanning. Two files can be related either dynamically (as with XBase) by using a special command, or statically through the creation of *dataviews* or *coupled* files. When two files are physically coupled, a special inverted list index is created, expediting the process of relating the two. While the XBase architecture *slides pointers* to keep files in synch, the inverted list architecture uses internal processing to relate disparate files more quickly and efficiently.

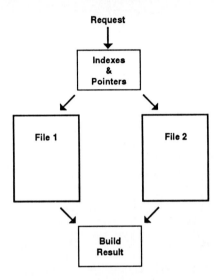

Figure 9-14: Inverted list diagram

This diagram represents the workings of an inverted list architecture, with 2 or more files being related together via the database engine and inverted list indexes.

Examples of inverted list (or formerly inverted list) databases include:

- ADABAS
- DATACOM
- Model 204

and several other products.

Hierarchical

The building of a database using the hierarchical architecture requires that the data be logically grouped into a series of parent-child relationships. Whereas the other architectures provided for the building of autonomous files, the hierarchical database requires all data to be assembled into one large database structure. Access to individual *segments* is made only through the predetermined navigational path. Navigation through a hierarchy is accomplished by moving up and down the *family* of segments. Since the hierarchical segments are not autonomous, there is a big advantage in that matching field values need not exist.

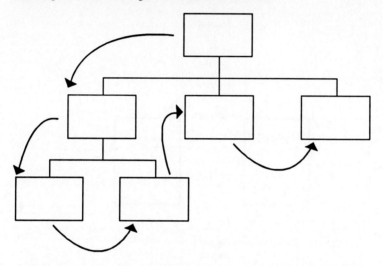

Navigate through the database moving up and down the hierarchy

Figure 9-15: Hierarchical data structures

The hierarchical tree structure, representing parents, children and peer segments. The most famous of the hierarchical databases is the IMS product from IBM, but over time many other versions of this basic operational principle have been built into other data access approaches.

Although having fallen into disfavor by many organizations that prefer the more dynamic capabilities of a network or relational database a large number of existing mainframe applications still drive off of the hierarchical engine.

Network

In a network database, records are grouped into record types. These are then associated with each other through the establishment of pointers, which tell the programmer or user which records are related. Network databases, like hierarchical databases, provide for no autonomous file structures, and therefore require no matching fields to associate two record types. These databases are navigated by *walking the sets*. Sets are the physical linking of two record types.

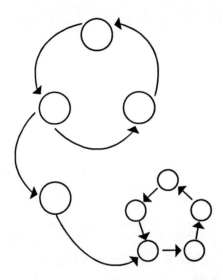

Walking the sets—following chains of pointers
Figure 9-16: Network database structures

The network collection of sets.

The collection of network and network hybrid databases include:

- CA-IDMS
- DMSII
- DMS1100
- Integrated Data Store II
- DBMS
- (HP-)TurboImage

Relational

In a relational database, data is stored in autonomous structures called *tables*, which are made up of columns and rows. Navigation is fully defined by the SQL language for scanning, searching, and cross-file associations. Cross-file mapping is accomplished through the use of SQL JOIN commands, which dynamically *join* any grouping of files at any time, as long as matching columns are indicated.

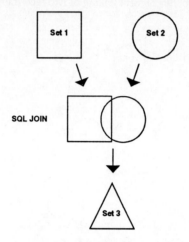

The SQL JOIN command creates a relational
merge of disparate sets of data

Figure 9-17: Relational databases

The relational SQL command and the dynamic relationships between data constructs via the syntax of that language.

The list of relational databases is much too long to include in this section, but a few of the more popular products includes:

- DB2
- Oracle
- Informix
- Allbase/SQL
- SQL/DS
- SQL Windows
- Supra
- SIR/DBMS

Object-Oriented

Object-oriented databases impose a new layer of complexity on the system. In an object-oriented environment, objects are created to manage all I/O and processing functions for a logical entity, called an object. The object-oriented database provides both an object engagement language (for the manipulation of objects, their data, and their processes) and a data manipulation language (which is used by the object to carry out data manipulation operations). The database we considered as an example, Objectivity-DB, provided an overriding object-oriented architecture while capitalizing on a network architecture underneath.

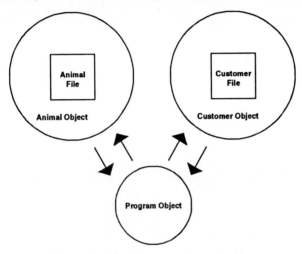

Programs work with object classes (code and data combined). Objects manage data access and merging.

Figure 9-18: Object-oriented data definition

Architecture characteristics recap

Besides these generalized characteristics, these architectures also display some specific ones. These are search capabilities, dynamic or static mapping, and record-at-a-time or set-at-a-time processing.

Search Capabilities

These define whether the database allows users to create search criteria involving any or all fields in the system, or only for a few, predetermined key fields.

Dynamic vs. Static Relationship Mapping

Some databases require that all relationships between data constructs be predetermined and *mapped* into the design of the system. This called static mapping. Others allow this mapping to be done dynamically, on demand.

Record vs. Set Processing

Another difference in architectures is set vs. record processing; this describes whether the database processes data one record at a time, or operates on whole sets of data at the same time.

Intelligence Location

Another aspect that bears significance when examining architectures is consideration of where the intelligence of the system resides. Are the users required to memorize complex commands and learn esoteric languages to retrieve the information they want? Or do the programs hold that intelligence. Or does the database itself?

User Intelligence

Looking back at Pete's Pet Shop, the easiest way for Pete to get business rules into effect is simply to tell his employees about the decisions and trust that they will carry out the orders. This method has advantages and disadvantages. On the positive side, if people carry this intelligence, no demand is placed on the computer system. On the negative side, what if Pete's employees forget or lose track of all of the rules Pete establishes.

Program Intelligence

Another way for these rules to be enforced is for Pete to place them into the programs that handle the sales and inventory of animals. By placing the rules in the programs, Pete can be assured that they will always be enforced.

Unfortunately, there are a few disadvantages to this approach. First, if the rule that Pete wants to enforce requires several programs to be changed, then the cost of puting that rule into place can be quite high. More importantly, as time goes on and rules change, the amount of effort spent programming will be greater and greater. What's worse, for most large systems, people lose track of which rules went into effect when, and for what reason. The result, over a long period of time, is that programs with hundreds of business rules are created, and no one remembers where they came from.

Using the Database to Capture Intelligence

How can the database be used to capture these rules? In one case, the uniqueness of animal names can be enforced by creating a unique index on the name field of the animal file. By placing this index on the file, Pete is guaranteed that the rule will always be enforced, and that this will be true no matter how many more programs are written or modified over time.

In another, the structure of the database (in the case of hierarchical, network, inverted list, relational, and object-oriented databases), assure Pete that many rules rule remain consistent.

In the most robudst situation, relational and obect-oriented systems provide the capture + enforcement of many layers of rules.

As we can see, each database architecture provides the potential for capturing a different degree of system intelligence. Any decision about which one to use depends on the size of the system, the complexity of the applications, the sophistication of the users, the importance of the rule, and how efficiently each of the components will get the job done.

User-Friendly Interfaces and System Intelligence

One of the ways that system developers who depend too heavily on user-friendly interfaces get into trouble, is by making false assumptions about the amount of intelligence the users of the system bring into the profile. Users used to having information spoon-fed to them are often overwhelmed by the complexity involved in running a user-friendly environment. For these users, the more rigid and well-defined their unfriendly applications are, the more they like it.

Confusing the Architecture with the Other Characteristics of a Database

The characteristics that we have considered provide a good understanding of just what an architecture does and does not do. We hope you have noticed that throughout our discussions, we minimized any reference to design, performance, and manageability. There is a good reason for this. In their exuberance to tout the benefits of their products or approaches, many vendors confuse the issues of performance, manageability, and user friendliness with the architecture their database provides.

The fact of the matter is that the architecture of a database product has little to do with the user friendliness, performance or manageability of a system. To say, for example, that relational databases are easier to use than hierarchical ones, or that network databases are faster than XBase databases are oversimplifications of much more complex issues.

It is the combination of a database product's programming, architecture, data storage, and administrative profiles that define these things, not any one of them alone. In fact, you could say that the architecture and data storage profiles define performance; the programming and architecture profiles define ease of use; and the combination of architecture and administrative characteristics define manageability.

Trying to typify databases by their architectures is like trying to describe motor vehicles by their engines. The same size engine may be fast, slow, good, or bad depending on the chassis and body we place it in, the transmission we attach, and the drive train we use.

As we have seen, whether the database is flat-file, XBase, SBase, inverted-list, hierarchical, network, relational or object oriented, or some kind of hybrid, like SIM, CA-DATACOM or the Extended Relational Databases (referenced in Chapter 7), the operational variance between products is pronounced.

In the next few chapters we consider how architectures can be combined with data storage and retrieval techniques and administrative profiles to create fully-functional database products.

Data Storage Management

In this chapter we begin to explore the many ways that databases arrange, store, and retrieve data. To the novice, this preoccupation with keys, indexes, record lengths, and file sizes may seem to be quite complicated and unnecessary. Why is the way data is stored so important anyway? If a person can answer this question, then they understand why so many database products exist, and why there is so much controversy about which database approach is best.

Why are Data Storage Management Techniques Important?

Although the user friendliness, ease of use, or programming interface a database product provides is important, these things alone have little to do with the effectiveness of the products they are associated with. Simply stated, database systems are purchased to help someone manage data. Even though the architecture a database provides helps with management issues in some respects (they organize the data into data constructs and provide a navigation method for accessing that data) this organization in and of itself is only a part of the equation. For all but the smallest and simplest systems, data not only needs to be accessible in an organized way, it must also be made available quickly and efficiently.

As we described in the preceding chapters, the database architecture tells you nothing about how well the database will work, only about how it will function. It is by using different storage management techniques that the database vendors distinguish their products in this regard.

Architectures and Storage Management

By returning to our original diagram of how the four principal database profiles fit together, we can see that the storage management profile of the database defines a separate layer, which is under the control of the architecture profile. The architecture defines the logical organization of the database and the storage management profile defines the physical implementation of that order.

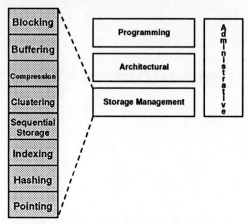

Figure 10-1: Storage management profiles

Different Products use Different Methods

We will see that the majority of the database products available commercially, use eight techniques to help manage the data as efficiently as possible. None of these methods is unique to the database industry *per se*. In fact, most of them have been utilized by applications programmers in the development of systems before databases were ever invented.

It is ironic but true that when you cut through the glamour and hype of the programming interface products and the expounding on architecture theories that underneath them all, lie the same basic nuts and bolts principles of data processing used since the earliest days.

The thing that distinguishes a database environment from a non-database environment is *not* the existence of any truly revolutionary breakthroughs in the mechanics of managing data, but only in the organized exploitation of those things in different ways.

In this chapter, we consider several aspects of the issues of efficient data storage management. We begin with a generalized discussion about the mechanics of computer operations, and the interaction of the three primary components that determine how fast a system will be: the amount of memory, the speed at which the computer works, and the speed at which disk I/Os are performed.

We will then show how each of the principle data storage management techniques (blocking, buffering, compression, clustering, sequential storage, indexing, hashing, and pointing) attempt to increase the speed at which data search operations can be performed. In the process of explaining this, we also consider the trade-offs that each method imposes in exchange for this efficiency.

Finally, we will see how some of the architectures and products apply unique combinations of these methods to create a database product.

Different Products, Different Mixes

One of the more damaging false assumptions many people make about architectures and storage management is that somehow, if you know the database's architecture, you must know how it manages data. This assumption is far from true, except in the case of inverted list databases, which use inverted list indexes.

The most obvious example of this is among the relational database products. Many relational databases work exclusively with B-Tree indexes, while some use hashing, pointing or even plain sequential storage techniques. The architecture defines the way that a programmer or user accesses data, the storage management profile defines how it will be done.

Computer Physics Simplified

Until now we have discussed computer hardware as if it were some kind of magical black box. You write programs, ask it to do something, and wait for an answer.

Although each computer hardware unit has its own unique arrangement of internal components, it is important that we understand at least some of the basics about how these internal components work together. All computer hardware, no matter what its unique approach to the problem of computing, is subject to the same basic laws of computer physics.

Computer power, for the sake of our discussion, can be measured by three criteria:

- How much memory it has
- How quickly it works
- What I/O speed is possible

Memory

Memory serves the same role for the computer that it does for a human. Just as we need our minds to remember when to breath, when to eat and what we should do next, the computer's memory provides the same all-encompassing functionality. Of course, whereas we as human beings remember things automatically and resist the intrusion of instructions from the outside, for the computer, that is the only way that it can work.

Computer memory is used to store the instructions about what the computer is supposed to do, and is also the place where those instructions are carried out. If you examined the memory of a computer system, you would find that it allocates different parts of memory for different purposes.

Computer memory must hold all of the instructions for every layer of software that a system is running at any one time. It usually has a certain area put aside for the operating system and another area for the loading and running of individual programs.

Therefore, the larger the computer's memory is, the more room there is for things to be done. Memory can be used in several ways.

- It can be used to store and run instructions

The more instructions that can be placed in memory at the same time the faster things are accomplished, or the more sets of instructions that can be active concurrently.

- It can be used to hold data that is being used

Memory is used not only to hold instructions (programs), it also holds data itself. By putting aside a certain area of memory as a place for data to be held for future use, the system is able to speed processing tremendously.

The process of tuning a system is the process of balancing these two sets of demands on the system: the need to have memory available for the execution of instructions, against the use of that same memory to hold data for use.

Operating System	Teleprocessing Region		
	Program 1	Program 2	Program 3
Database	User 1	User 3	
	User 2		
I/O Buffers			

Figure 10-2: System memory allocation

Processing Speed

The second measure of a computer's power is its processing speed. This speed determines how quickly the instructions stored in memory will actually be executed. If you load a program that asks the computer to perform 1,000,000 operations and the computer runs at 50,000 instructions per second, then it will take 20 seconds for that program to run. If the speed was up to 1,000,000 instructions per second, then the program will only run for 1 second.

The processing speed and memory alone do not really determine how long it will take a task to be completed. This is because there is another part of this process involved that takes much longer, and that is system input/output.

Input/Output Speed (I/O)

Unfortunately, the speeds at which computers run always have been, and will continue to be, much faster than the speed at which the system is able to retrieve data from a disk storage device. Depending on the computer configuration, the difference between processing speed and I/O speed can be anywhere from 10:1 to more than 100: 1. In other words, at the best, a system able to process one million instructions per second might be able to perform 100,000 or 1/10th as many reads or writes from disk during that same second.

What this means is that as long as a computer must read data from disk, tape, or some other device, the program must wait for the I/O operation to occur before it can continue.

This dependency on I/O to determine the maximum speed at which a system can run means that computer systems are what we call *I/O bound*. That is, the I/O speed establishes the limit of how fast it can do any work.

Why is Physical I/O such a Limiting Factor?

Systems are I/O bound for a very simple reason: physical laws. The speed at which a computer operates within its own memory is set by the speed at which electronic pulses can travel through microchips. This can approach the speed of light in certain laboratory cases.

Physical I/O from disk is determined by the mechanical speed at which physical read/write arms can move across a disk surface and locate the data element being searched for.

So no matter how quickly a computer can handle instructions, and no matter how much memory it has, it will always be slowed down by the time it takes to read and write things from a disk. By the way, we use the disk as our example because reading and writing from a disk is hundreds and even thousands of times faster than from a tape, or in the worst case from a terminal. There is no way a human could type information faster than a computer could process it.

Hardware manufacturers continue trying to improve the ratio between I/O speeds and computer speeds, and they are also trying to develop a computer memory big enough to hold all of the data currently stored on disk. But for the time being, the constraint is one that all database systems must live with.

There are, of course, several ways to manage the input and output of data from the system so that the impact of this constraint is minimized. This is exactly what a database does. Databases attempt to minimize the impact of I/O constraints using several methods:

- Blocking
- Buffering
- Compression
- Clustering
- Sequential storage
- Indexing
- Hashing
- Pointing

These are the methods used by a database to organize things such that the combination of I/O speed, computer speed, and amount of available memory are efficiently balanced. We will consider each of these methods in detail.

The first two of these, blocking and buffering, are things done by all computer systems whenever I/O operations are involved. Depending upon the platform, blocking and buffering can be defined by the operating system (in PCs), defined by the job control language (JCL) that runs the programs, or defined by the program itself. The reason we include them in our discussions of database storage management is that many databases set their own standards, or intervene in the native operating system's treatment of these factors. The level of control a database allows over these factors tells the developer a lot about how well-tuned the database can be.

Blocking

Blocking is the process of putting a lot of little records into one big block. When the system needs to read from disk, it is able to read in as much as possible at one time.

For example, suppose a program must read all of the records from a given file. If the records are 40 bytes (characters) long and there are 1,000,000 records to read, the computer has to do 1,000,000 I/O operations to get them all. This means that the computer ends up waiting a significant amount of time between each read.

If the system runs at 1,000,000 instructions per second, and the disk device is able to provide 100,000 reads per second, it takes more than 10 seconds to do something that could occur in only one second.

By blocking, the system places several of these records into one chunk. Typical blocking factors include 500-byte or 4,000-byte chunks. By using a 4,000 byte block, we can now put 100 records into each block, (4,000 / 40 = 100) and reduce the number of reads to 10,000 (1,000,000 / 100 = 10,000). It will take less than one second to read these 10,000 blocks into memory, and so the speed at which the computer can process records and the speed at which it receives them is much more in synch. The entire process of reading these records takes a little bit more then one second.

(Although our math here is quite simplistic, we use it simply to illustrate the point. Real computer internals are much more complex than this explanation.)

Databases block data in several ways, and the blocking units they work with can be called blocks, blocking units, pages, control intervals, or record groups. No matter what they are called, their objective is to minimize I/O activity and maximize the computer's speed.

All database products enforce some kind of blocking scheme, either explicitly or implicitly, by taking advantage of the platform's own blocking characteristics.

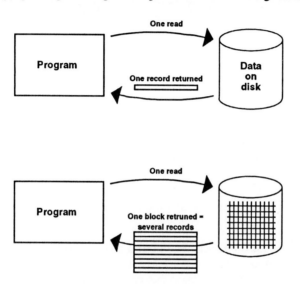

Figure 10-3: Blocking Diagram

Buffering

Blocking helps improve system response time by reducing the number of I/Os that must be conducted to locate the data being requested. This is done by predetermining an optimum arrangement for that data. These techniques can be utilized only under a very limited set of circumstances. You can block data only one way. If the data you are managing must be searched and read according to several criteria, then these approaches will not be all that helpful.

There is another set of efficiencies that databases can provide however, and they have to do with helping the system search through things more quickly.

Buffering is the technique used by most systems to reduce the amount of time the system must wait between I/O operations. It does this by reserving a part of the computer's memory as a data holding area, and preloading it with blocks that the system eventually needs. By placing blocks of data into buffers, the database system is able to establish an I/O queuing discipline and gain more control over the I/O process. A data buffer (and database products use several of these for I/O, logging, and recovery procedures) is like a hopper, where the system can fill the order for data, long before it is actually needed.

Data buffers are measured in the same units as the blocks that are used to fill them, and are usually managed by the database product itself.

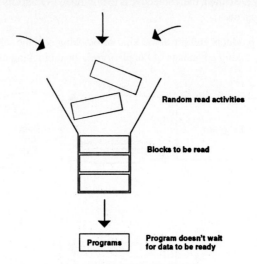

Figure 10-4: Buffering diagram

Different database products use different blocking/buffering combinations to help increase system efficiency. Some set a standard block and buffer size, and then optimize performance based upon that criteria. Others allow the developer to customize block/buffer sizes on a case-by-case basis, making the individual activities perform a little more efficiently, while surrendering the ability to optimize on one size.

When examining database products and their blocking and buffering criteria, it is important to check for several things:

- *Can block sizes be varied or are they standard?* The ability to set the block size based upon the size of a data record allows you to store more data in each block.

- *Is buffering left to the operating system or is it managed by the database?* Operating system-defined buffering is functional, but does not leave the developer with much ability to adjust performance.

- *Can the developer adjust to make more or less memory available for buffering?* A buffer area that is too big keeps the other activities on the system from running well; a buffer area that is too small slows down the database's response time.

Although blocking and buffering are an integral part of any data storage management profile, they function as little more than support structures for the more
active techniques of management. Both of these methods are concerned with how
data is handled once grabbed by the system, but do not consider any of the other
aspects of the operation. The next three methods, compression, clustering, and
sequential storage, are concerned with the way that data is physically stored on the
disk device. These methods define how the data is to be stored as opposed to how
it will be handled.

Compression

One technique that can help make access to data quicker and save disk space at the
same time is called compression. The principle behind compression is quite simple.
Since physical I/O is the limiting factor behind database processing, if we can figure
out how to store more data in a block, then the system can work faster.

Compression works by gathering all of the data ready to be stored, and then
compressing before the storage step. When a block of this compressed data is read,
it is, of course, immediately decompressed.

Compression can be a very effective way to increase a system's performance,
but the effective use of the technique is subtle. Among the factors to consider when
using compression are:

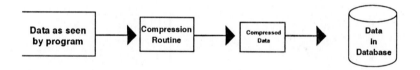

Figure 10-5: A compression diagram

- *What method is being used to perform the compression?* Different compression routines have different ways of accomplishing their objectives. Some
  simple ones strip out all blank spaces from the records being compressed.
  Others employ complex algorithms to encode and decode large strings of
  data. The measure of a compression routine's effectiveness is measured in
  the percentage of compression.

- *Will the CPU expense incurred when compressing and decompressing data be greater than the I/O activity saved by using it?* This criterion can also be difficult to determine. The CPU resources required to compress data may slow down the system more than the additional I/O would. In general, the larger and faster the CPU, and the larger the volume of data being handled, the more effective compression will be. For small or CPU-constrained systems, compression can be a hindrance.

- *Is compression mandatory or optional?* Some manufacturers compress all database data, others give you a choice. Still others make no provision for it at all. In general, having the option to compress or not is the best.

Sequencing

The second technique for storing data while minimizing I/O is to use a technique called *sequencing* or *sequential storage*. Most databases provide at least the option to use this method, although not all of them can. (Data stored with hash keys cannot be sequentially stored.) Under sequencing, data is stored in the same physical order you would want to process it in. By storing the data in this way, I/O is minimized, because every read of a block yields a complete set of data to be processed.

Sequenced Data		Unsequenced Data
Apple / Apple / Banana	Block 1	Watermelon / Grape / Lime
Grape / Kiwi / Lemon	Block 2	Apple / Banana / Kiwi
Lime / Melon / Watermelon	Block 3	Lime / Apple / Lemon

To find all apples, the sequenced file must read only one block; all apples are in that block. The unsequenced file must read two blocks to find all apples.*

Figure 10-6: Sequential storage diagram

For example, if you wanted to store the data from a phone book in a sequenced file, you would read the data from the book into the file in alphabetical order. That way, when you performed a simple database SCAN, GET NEXT, or READ statement, you could follow the alphabet from A to Z, wasting no block-read operation.

The advantage of a sequenced file is that I/O operations for data processed in the same order as the sort is very efficient. The disadvantages include the fact that processing data in any other order is very slow, and we will spend a considerable amount of maintenance time running sort jobs to restore the file's proper order.

Even though the sequencing of database files might be considered to be the most rudimentary form of I/O optimization, it is still quite effective, and is utilized by the majority of database products in one form or another.

Important questions to ask about sequencing are:

- Does the database use it as an option?

- Is it the only option available?

Clustering

The last of the generalized I/O optimization methods is called *clustering*. Clustering is the attempt on the part of a database developer to anticipate the groups, or clusters, of disparate record types that will most likely need to be processed at the same time. If the developer can anticipate this accurately, then the storage of data can be modified to reflect this.

Suppose you knew in advance what arrangement of records into blocks a system was most likely to work on at the same time. Assume for example, you have an employee file holding one record for each employee. Suppose further you know that nine times out of 10, you work on records of employees from the same department at the same time. In other words, most processing is department-based like payroll calculations, benefits analysis, etc.

Different architectures demand different kinds of clustering schemes. A hierarchical database, for example, usually associates each segment with a separate file—one file for the parent and one for each child type. By combining the related records from each segment on the same storage page (storing each parent with all of its children), the cost of reading this family of records is minimized.

For a network database, record types related by different sets can be stored together. Therefore, clustering is the process of predetermining and preblocking data into the order it is most likely to be processed in. Many databases provide different clustering techniques to help gain this kind of efficiency. The difference between clustering and sequencing is that sequencing orders the data from one file and stores it in a sorted order, while clustering combines data from several files into the same physical storage space.

When considering database clustering capabilities, it is important to be sure that if the clustering ability exists that it has been organized in a way that makes it easy to manage. Databases providing clustering can be some of the fastest when the operations being performed against it are of the type anticipated.

On the other hand, if the I/O activity does not mirror the clustering arrangement, then performance is severely degraded. As with everything else, using clustering effectively depends on the ability of the developer to anticipate the processing requirements that will be placed on the system.

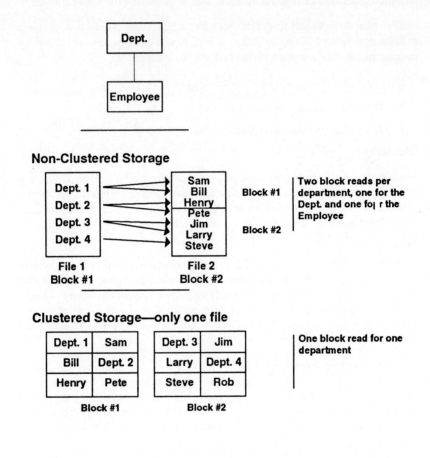

Figure 10-7: Clustering Diagram

Ways of Finding Data

While blocking and buffering help move data in and out of storage quickly, and compression, clustering, and sequencing offer us three ways to physically store the data, the most significant criterion for most database users involves how quickly specific data can be found. This is determined by the next set of three techniques: indexing, hashing, and pointing. We call these the navigation techniques.

Indexes

Perhaps the most frequently utilized form of I/O streamlining is the index.

Buffers, blocks, and clustering all operate indirectly to locate a given record. Indexes work directly to that end. Indexes reduce the time required to find data by giving the system a way to find one record without having to read through all of them. An index works like a small lookup table. It lists all of the values we may be looking for in some kind of alphabetic or numeric order, and provides an address at which the full data record can be found.

For example, a large parking garage that has 15 floors and more than 1,000 parking locations to choose from keeps some kind of lookup list as it accepts each car to be parked. If the blue Ford Fairlane is parked on the seventh floor in spot number 24, this fact is recorded on the list. If the car is moved, the address (floor and spot number) is changed.

With a list like this, anyone can find any car at any time. Without this list, someone would have to check every spot on every floor until the blue Ford Fairlane was found. But this list is an example of only one kind of index.

There are many kinds of indexes that can be utilized by a computer system, but three of these are most often used by database products:

- Binary indexes

- B-Tree indexes

- Inverted list indexes

Binary Indexes

In order to demonstrate how the different indexes work, let's create a simple file that lists cars, their colors, license numbers, model, and parking location (floor and spot number). Notice that this parking lot file has only six cars listed, and that each record in the file has an additional field, an address associated with it. Although we show these addresses here, in a real system, the addresses would be invisible to everyone but the system itself. Internal addresses of this type are often referred to as *pointers*. We use both terms here.

```
(Address)   License   Car      Car     Parking
            Number    Model    Color   Location
- - - - - - - - -  - - - - - - -  - - - - -  - - - - -  - - - - - - - - - -
    1       XY112     Chevy    Blue    F7-S22
    2       ABC123    Ford     Red     F3-S02
    3       A 101     Chevy    Red     F2-S34
    4       SKD001    Subaru   Green   F9-S05
    5       101909    Chevy    Blue    F3-S03
    6       894329    Toyota   Blue    F2-S19
```

Figure 10-8: The parking lot file

Assume that we want an index by car color: a way to find all of cars of the same color quickly. In order to do this we will make a simple color index.(See Figure 10-9).

If you want to find all of the red cars and no index is available, you have to read every record in the file, checking to see which ones are red as you go. You could not stop after finding the first or second one because there would be know way for you to know if the last one was listed or not.

```
Color     (Address)
- - - - -   - - - - - - -
Blue          1
Blue          5
Blue          6
Green         4
Red           2
Red           3
```

Figure 10-9: The parking lot index on color

If we were to use the index to conduct the search, we would save work in three ways. First, we could skip reading records 1, 5, 6, and 4 because the index tells us that these contain some other color. The index also lets us know that all cars of that color have been found as soon as the color changes to something else. Last, you save I/O by reading the index blocks into memory and then reading only those record blocks that hold data you are interested in. Since the index record is so much smaller than the data record (because the index record holds only the color and not the license, model, and parking spot information), more index records can be fit on one block.

Index Search Patterns

Even though an index helps speed access time, by varying the way in which the index is used, you can get it to perform even better.

Simple Index Search Pattern

In a simple index search pattern, the system takes advantage of the index by reading through it from beginning to end until the addresses of all records of interest have been found. Let's replace our Parking Lot List with a Phone List. This list holds the names, addresses, and phone numbers of all the people in a small company. We will store this phone list in a file and create an index that tracks individual names in alphabetical order. Since there are many thousands of names on this phone list, we will block the index alphabetically, keeping all index references to names beginning with the letter A on the first index block, B on the second block, etc. There will be 26 index pages in all. (See Figure 10-10.)

Anderson	101
Abercrombe	102
Alysinski	123
... etc. ...	
B	
C	
D	
E	
F	

W	
X	
Y	
Z	

Figure 10-10: Simple index

If we want to find the pointer that directs us to the record holding information for Mr. Smith, how many reads of the index blocks must we make? The answer is 19. Since the letter S is the 19th letter of the alphabet, we must read 19 blocks before the S records are found.

To find the name Anderson, how many reads will it take ? Just one, of course, because A is the first letter of the alphabet. What about Mr. Zeus? That one will be the worst of all, requiring 26 block reads.

If we assume that the decision to ask for any last name is random, then we can use mathematics to figure out what the *average number of reads* necessary to find a name will be.

We compute this average by simply determining the average block number for the system. In this case it is 26 / 2 = 13. On average, a simple index search requires that half or all index blocks be read every time.

Although the index gains us some efficiency, even when we use this simple search approach, there are ways that we can make it better.

Binary Search Patterns

Another way to search through an index is to use what is called a *binary search*. With a binary search you begin searching in the middle of the index, determine whether the value you are looking for is lower or higher than the place you are at, and then split the difference in the right direction, lower or higher. You continue splitting the difference until zeroing in on the right location. Let's use our Phone List index to illustrate.

To find the name Anderson, the binary search begins by splitting the file in half, at the letter M.

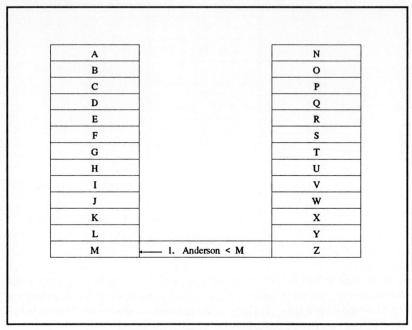

Figure 10-11: Binary search indexes

Since the letter A is lower then M , the search algorithm splits the lower half of the index in half again, at the letter H.

The system will continue to perform this split and search, split and search sequence until the desired record is found.

The following pages show this process, for this particular search in detail.

A		N
B		O
C		P
D		Q
E		R
F		S
G		T
H	← 2. Anderson < H	U
I		V
J		W
K		X
L		Y
M		Z

Figure 10-12: Binary search indexes

Since the letter A is lower then H , the search algorithm splits the lower half of the index in half again, at the letter D.

A		N
B		O
C		P
D	← 3. Anderson < D	Q
E		R
F		S
G		T
H		U
I		V
J		W
K		X
L		Y
M		Z

Figure 10-13: Binary search indexes

Since the letter A is lower then D , the search algorithm splits the lower half of the index in half again, this time at the letter B.

A		N
B	◀── 4. Anderson < B	O
C		P
D		Q
E		R
F		S
G		T
H		U
I		V
J		W
K		X
L		Y
M		Z

Figure 10-14: Binary search indexes

And finally, since the letter A is lower then B, it goes to the A page, and the name Anderson is found.

A	◀── 5. Anderson = A	N
B		O
C		P
D		Q
E		R
F		S
G		T
H		U
I		V
J		W
K		X
L		Y
M		Z

Figure 10-15: Binary search indexes

Coincidentally, the search for this letter is actually be the longest search of any. The most reads necessary to find any value will be 5, in this case, and the average number of I/Os to find a record will probably be 3 or 4. Although this alphabetical case is quite simple, it illustrates the power of the binary search versus the simple index search. In the simple index search the maximum number of reads was 26, and the average was 13. The binary search uses the computer's capabilities much more efficiently with a mazimun of 5 and an average of 3 reads to find the same information.

The B-Tree Index

The binary search algorithm is the most efficient way to use a simple index structure, but there is variation on the simple index, the *B-Tree index*, which can cut down search activity even further.

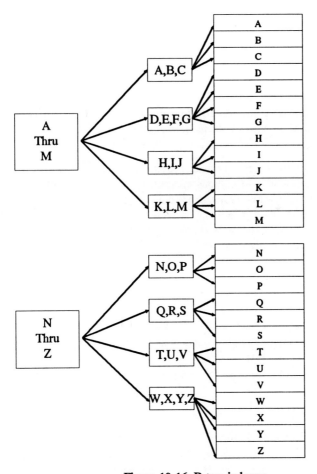

Figure 10-16: B-tree indexes

In a B-Tree index, a simple index serves as the lowest level of a more complex collection of indexes. This collection's lowest level is a normal index. Several layers of indexes refer to the index itself. In other words there are indexes on indexes. This may seem confusing at first but let's see how it might work.

In the following example, the lowest level of the index—the section at the far right—is exactly the same as the simple index was. However, there are two additional levels of indexing, root and intermediate. To locate a record, a program begins by checking the root index. This index tells the program, where to find the intermediate index addresses, (one for the A,B,C pointers, another for the D,E,F pointers, etc.). The program then reads the correct intermediate level index block and gets from it the address for the lowest level block, which in turn provides the pointer to the actual data block.

Although the B-Tree index is more complicated to set up and maintain then the normal index, what does it provide us in terms of reduced I/O?

What is the maximum number of index reads that a program must make to find any letter of the alphabet? The answer is three, one root, one intermediate, and one low-level read. What is the minimum number of reads? The average? The answer is always the same: three.

By using a B-Tree index, we reduced the maximum and average number of reads to a very small number, and only increased the minimum number of reads by a small amount.

Our B-Tree example is very contrived to say the least. B-Tree indexes, in fact, allow you to store pointers to millions of records with only a simple three- or four-level arrangement. That means an average of three or four I/Os to find a pointer, as opposed to the hundreds of reads that a normal binary index would require for that many records. The B-Tree index is the more commonly used form of direct indexing used by database products.

Inverted List Indexes

Another indexing approach is through the use of an inverted list. With an inverted list index, all pointers to records having the same index value are stored on the same index record. This way, the total number of index records is reduced, but the index records become much longer. Following here an example of our Parking Lot File index using the inverted list method.

(Address)	License Number	Car Model	Car Color	Parking Location
1	XY112	Chevy	Blue	F7-S22
2	ABC123	Ford	Red	F3-S02
3	A 101	Chevy	Red	F2-S34
4	SKD001	Subaru	Green	F9-S05
5	101909	Chevy	Blue	F3-S03
6	894329	Toyota	Blue	F2-S19

Figure 10-17: Parking lot database

Assume that we want an index by car color; a way to find all of cars of the same color quickly. Following (Figure 10-18) is an inverted list index that accomplishes this.

The inverted list index provides an even more efficient way of pointing to specific records quickly. To find all blue cars requires only one read, the read of the blue record.

```
Color      (Addresses)
------     -----
BLUE         1,5,6
GREEN        4
RED          2,3
```

Figure 10-18: Parking Lot inverted index

Although the inverted list index is smaller and faster then the other kinds of indexes, it has certain limitations. Unfortunately, because of its compact nature it is difficult to maintain (add or delete index entries) and it can create a lot of problems for a system that requires a lot of concurrent update activity. When several people want to change index records at the same time, someone must wait.Inverted list indexes are most commonly used by inverted list databases where their unique capabilities can be exploited to the fullest.

Although there is an infinite number of subtle var\iations on the building of system indexes, today, almost all databases use some version of the B-Tree index. Even inverted list structures have moved in that direction.

What is important about the use of indexes on the system often has more to do with how actively the system gets involved in the selection of them than in their composition. Many systems have B-Tree indexes, but use them only for their simple lookup capabilities. These systems require that a programmer choose the index to use when making a database call. Some of the more powerful databases (i.e., many relational and inverted list systems) employ powerful optimizer algorithms and database engines, which check statistical records of what indexes are available and how they are built. After checking all available information, these systems apply artificial intelligence algorithms to determine the optimum index selection. This dynamic index selection gives these more sophisticated databases a significant edge in the ability to respond to *ad hoc* queries quickly. On the other hand, the more conservative systems, which run without the overhead of an optimizer, can perform the same I/O operation as the fancier databases in less time. This is because they do not have to go through the extra overhead steps.

So when checking a database for the use of indexes, the important question is not what kind of index it uses, but is instead how the index is used.

Hashing

Another way to store and retrieve data records quickly is through the use of a non-indexing technique known as *hashing*. Hashing eliminates the need to use indexes by creating a special formula that translates the key value of the record directly into a storage address. To utilize a hashing technique, the system takes the key value from a record and hashes it. (This means to derive a storage address based on a hashing algorithm and then store it at that address.) To find the data with that key value, the system uses the same approach. The key being searched for is hashed, and the resultant address is used by the system to locate the data. A simple hashing algorithm might say:

If the key value begins with the letter A store it on page #1, if it begins with the letter B, store it on page #2 etc.

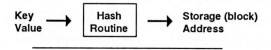

Anderson			Mattison
1	5	9	13
Baker Brown		Jones	
2	6	10	14
Cook			
4	7	11	15
1	8	12	16

A simple hashing algorithm.
Key = Last Name
Hashing Algorithm = Make the storage address the equivalent of the numeric value of the first letter of the last name (i.e., A = 1, B = 2, etc.).

The record for Anderson is stored on block #1, and Mattison is stored on block #13.

Figure 10-19: Hash key algorithm

But more likely than not, the hashing routine is a complex mathematical calculation that attempts to spread the data as widely as possible throughout the available disk storage.

The hashing approach to data storage has some obvious shortcomings. First, what if the hashing algorithm calculates too many records to the same address? Then you end up with too many records to fit at the address the algorithm has assigned. How do you distribute the stored data evenly over the available disk space?

Another big problem with hashing is that you can use a hashing key to identify only one value of your data record, the one you use it to store data with. Any additional pointer arrangements must be built some other way.

Despite its shortcomings, hashing is the best choice for systems where access time and the identification of individual records quickly is at an absolute premium. Examples are an airline reservation system or a bank teller operations application. There is absolutely no faster way available to key, store, and retrieve data than by hashing. This is because you eliminate the extra overhead involved with index lookups.

The last two techniques considered, indexing and hashing, provide the system with a way to locate individual records from among a large population. These methods represent the only ways a database can eliminate the need to read through every record on a file every time a specific record is needed.

Although indexing and hashing tell us how a database can make a single record search as efficient at possible, they do not help us associate two or more files when taking advantage of an architecture's cross-file capabilities. To do this, we have to add yet another level of complexity to our understanding of storage management.

Cross-File Capabilities and Storage Management

There are two approaches to cross-file management that databases can take, and each of these approaches uses indexes, hashing, and pointers (yet to be discussed), to provide this enhanced functionality to the user.

The first approach to cross-file navigation can be called the light overhead or direct approach. Products utilizing this strategy provide the ability to associate two or more files by allowing the programmer or user to specify how that association is supposed to occur. To facilitate this approach, the database provides the programmer with the tools necessary to associate files, and leaves it up to the programmer or user to use the tools. We call this a light overhead approach because it does not require a lot of CPU and other system overhead suffer at the expense of the database. The program accessing data does most of the work. Under this approach the programmer specifies index names, declares associations, and in other ways tells the system how to navigate.

The term *navigational database* is often used to refer to products of this type. Some typical light overhead architectures include flat-file, XBase, hierarchical and network systems. (Please note that not *all* databases of any one architecture fit into these categories by definition. Most of them have been built that way in the past.)

The second, and more powerful approach can be called the heavy overhead or smart database approach. These systems use catalog tables, directories, and other lookup facilities extensively to make navigation decisions for the user. In the process of providing this service, these systems tend to use large buffer pools, temporary disk work areas (which are used by the database itself to create temporary working copies of the data being processed), and many other processing tasks. (Typical of this group are many relational, inverted list, and object-oriented systems.)

Relating Files in a Light Overhead System

Light overhead systems relate files with indexes, hash keys, and a previously undiscussed data management technique called *pointing*. We begin by describing this in detail.

Pointers

The last of the record-finding techniques to consider is known as pointing (or using a pointer). While indexing and hashing require that the programmer or the system become involved in storing, creating, or translating key values, the pointer approach bypasses these intermediary steps and associates one record to another by simply placing the address of the related key on the record itself. A pointer is used to connect two records to each other without using an intervening data construct, and without the use of a common field.

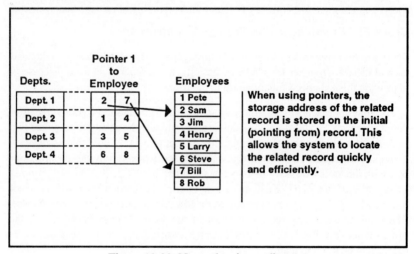

Figure 10-20: Network pointers diagram

If you look at the way the indexes we have been discussing work, you can see that each of the them uses pointers or addresses, which tell the program where the record being searched for is stored. In a system that needs to relate one record to another record, it is always possible to skip the process of using an index to make that correlation, and instead, store the pointer right on the original record.

Just as hashing speeds the process of finding things by bypassing the need to use an index, so does the pointer. Just as hashing limits the flexibility of a system and adds to the complication, so to does the pointer.

The pointer technique is most frequently found on network architecture systems, since physically pointing from one record to the next is conducive to that data arrangement. Many object-oriented systems and the occasional database of another type can use them as well.

The use of pointers to associate records of different types is obvious. Since a pointer can point anywhere, the process is easy. Pointers are not the only way of accomplishing this however. Many systems use indexes or even full file scans to accomplish the same thing.

Using File Scans to Associate Two Files

One way a system can associate two files is by identifying the fields on each that need to be matched, and then letting the database perform the scan necessary to match them. This method, though far from efficient, is certainly effective.

If no indexes, hash keys, or pointers are available, then a database internal scan is the only other way available.

Using Indexes and Hash Keys to Associate Files

Many database systems use indexes and hash keys internally to make the association between two files for the user. In order to use this technique, the system is told which fields to match on, and then uses the appropriate lookup method to carry it out.

These three methods of cross-file association (pointers, internal scanning, and the internal use of indexes and keys) describe the full extent of how the database can accomplish these tasks. Of course, a database product is not usually constrained to using only one of these techniques at a time. Most databases use a combination of these methods to get the job done.

Using These Techniques in the Heavy Overhead Systems

The heavy overhead storage profile systems use the same techniques as the light overhead ones do, with one big distinction. With a heavy overhead database, the database system itself makes most of the decisions about which technique to use. While the programmer using a light overhead system must know what indexes exist, know what their names are, and refer to them explicitly in programs (or have them predefined), the heavy overhead system user needs only to ask for the data and the association requested.

The Internal Makeup of a Heavy Overhead System

The heavy overhead database system has a much more complex arrangement of internal components than the light one. For this kind of system, all requests for data are sent to a special program, which reads the request and interprets it.

In order to help in this interpretation, the system creates a collection of reference files, called catalogs, directories, or some other descriptive name. These reference files provide the interpreter with information about the structure, sizes, and volumes of data to be found in the different data structures on the system. Based upon the interpreter's translation of these facts, a data retrieval execution plan is developed. This plan then is executed by the database and usually involves the invocation of indexes, the copying of data into temporary storage, and the building of a set of data that meets the requirements of the person requesting it. See diagram of DB2 internals in Chapter 7.

Although there is a phenomenal amount of difference between the light and heavy overhead systems in how complicated and expensive they are to run, this difference tends to be missed by many users of the systems. How is it that the difference is so unnoticeable? There are probably several factors.

First, the heavy overhead systems tend to work so well that the differences in performance go unnoticed by most users. In situations where heavy overhead databases are brought in, the additional memory and disk requirements are factored into the decision to use one type of database over another. Because of this, the differences in overhead go unnoticed until the CPU becomes constrained because of the workload placed on it, or until the volume and rate of data manipulation gets so high that the heavy overhead system starts to slow down.

Second, both types of database get the job done; with the heavy overhead systems the database takes more of the burden for processing off of programs and places more on the system itself.

Both types of database management system have a place in the data processing world, and both will continue to grow in popularity and acceptance.

Closure on Access Methods

We have considered eight techniques of storage management optimization that a database can use, and three ways that these can be incorporated into the execution of cross-file capabilities. Each of these techniques has benefits and efficiencies, and each has a reciprocal cost. Let's take a moment to review these tradeoffs.

- **Blocking** —When utilizing blocking factors, the size of the blocks is the key. The block size should be as close as possible to being a multiple of the size of the record. For example, for a record that is 20 bytes long, a blocksize of 2,000 is optimal (20 X 100). The closer the blocksize is to being a multiple of the record size, the less wasted space a given block will have.

Systems with set block sizes take away the developers ability to tune the system in this way.

- **Buffering**—The tradeoff involved with buffering involves the availability of system memory. If the system has available space, then using that space provides a free boost in performance. If the system is pressed for memory, then buffering can actually degrade it.

- **Compression**— Compression helps speed I/O operations when the algorithm used is fast and effective. At some point, the cost of compressing and decompressing data is more expensive than the cost of the extra I/O operations that it replaces.

- **Clustering and sequencing**—Clustering and sequencing techniques antici-pate the most likely order in which data will be processed. If the data is usually accessed in the sequenced order, or if the records that have been clustered are most often accessed at the same time, then these techniques can be quite effective. Access requirements that vary from these patterns, unfortunately, will cause performance degradation.

- **Indexes, hashing, and pointers**—Just as is the case with clustering and sequencing, these three techniques assume that the developer is able to anticipate the most-often requested information. The maintenance of in-dexes, pointers, and hash keys places additional overhead on the system, and this must be offset by the efficiencies gained. Otherwise, the results can be a downgrade in performance.

Database Products and the Combination of these Techniques

We will examine how a few of the database products already considered combine these techniques to produce a distinctive database storage management profile. We will consider the PC File (flat-file),dBASE III (XBase), Adabas (inverted list), IMS (hierarchical), IDMS (network), DB2 (relational), and Objectivity-DB (object-ori-ented) databases as being typical, but not totally representative of their architec-tures.

Storage Management and PC File

You may recall that the PC File database allows users to create simple files and attach several indexes to each of them. The data files created can be located on a PC File system by their name, which ends with the .dbf extension. The data is usually stored in load order, with no internal sequencing.

Indexes are created on the Make A New Index screen. This screen allows the user to specify the field, combination of fields, or calculation involving those fields that will then be used as input to the index building process. After making the selections, the index builder copies all pertinent indexable information out of the file and into a separate index file. This file is then stored in its sorted order. After completing this step, the user can perform requests for data that refer to this index. The index is then used to speed the process.

PC File therefore uses indexes to order the data being processed; a simple storage management profile to say the least.

Because of this limited capability, the PC File system is not very effective for very large systems.

dBASE III and Storage Management

The dBASE III database has a much more complicated set of data management criteria. For the dBASE III system, data is also stored in simple load order, with the ability to create multiple indexes to speed single-file access.

Under dBASE III, different data access commands use different techniques to retrieve data. The FIND and SEEK commands take advantage of indexes to get the record requested, while the LOCATE command simply performs a scan of the entire file to do the same thing.

Cross-file manipulation is handled through the building of an index on the field to be used for cross referencing, and by using the SET RELATION command to tell the system to use it.

```
select 1
use customer index C-custno
select 2
use animal index A-custno
set relation to custno into customer
```

Figure 10-21: Example of dBase III+ relation command

Last, the dBase III system uses B-Tree indexes and scanning to perform its navigation.

SBase Systems and Storage Management

With an SBase system like DataEase, data storage is managed via the definition of screens. The screens define the nature of data constructs, and the relationships between them. Most SBase systems allow the user to define indexes for base constructs and relationships. In general the only method of access optimization is through B-Tree indexes but there is not reason that other techniques could not be utilized (except of course for the fact that this would make the systems more complex and harder for the user to work with).

IMS and Storage Management

IMS, our example hierarchical database, offers the developer nine kinds of database definition syntaxes to use in the generation of the database. Each one of these describes a different storage management profile. These types are HSAM, HISAM, SHSAM, SHISAM, GSAM, HDAM, HIDAM, MSDB, and DEDB. Let's consider a few of these options.

HSAM (Hierarchical Sequential Access Method) stores root segments and all child segments in the same physical proximity. It provides no indexing and all processing is performed sequentially. An HSAM organization is a good example of how a database can use simple clustering to provide database access. A database defined in this way can use only some of the IMS navigational commands.

HISAM (Hierarchical Indexed Sequential Access Method) an index is created allowing for quick access to all parent segments. Stored on this index are the key and as much of the parent and child information as it can hold. Additional child segments are stored in a secondary file in the same area. HISAM is the IMS version of clustering data combined with an index on the parent segment.

HDAM (Hierarchical Direct Access Method) databases use a hash key to locate root segments, and then uses pointers to point from one segment to the next underneath it. HIDAM (Hierarchical Indexed Direct Access Method) uses an index for the location of root segments and then pointers to find its children.

Of particular interest is the MSDB, or Main Storage Database. This construct allows the developer to build a database that resides in memory at all times. An MSDB is obviously quite fast, because there is no I/O to slow it down. Unfortunately, the storage of an entire database in memory can be quite expensive and is utilized infrequently.

The IMS database provides the system builder with many options for optimization.

IDMS and Storage Management

The IDMS database, like the IMS product, gives the developer numerous options for building database structures. Under IDMS, data can be stored using sequential methods, can be accessed with hash keys (called *calc keys*), and can be found with indexes.

The standard method for the association of record types is with pointers, but the system also allows the builder of a structure to cluster related sets of data.

Adabas and Storage Management

The Adabas product takes advantage of inverted list indexes to provide keyed access to all stored records. Additional secondary key indexes can also be defined, and the programmer has the option of scanning an Adabas file sequentially by using the system-assigned record identifier as a key.

Cross-file processing is handled in the same way as it is for DB2, using large buffer areas, temporary disk storage, and a command interpreter to determine an optimum data retrieval plan.

DB2 and Storage Management

The DB2 system stores data in autonomous datasets called tables, which are all simple indexed files. The DB2 developer can then create as many additional B-Tree indexes as necessary to help optimize data access.

Whereas the previously discussed database products were of the light overhead type, and required that programmers know the physical storage structure and use that knowledge to help them navigate he system, the DB2 database is a smart database, which figures out which indexes to use on its own.

DB2 makes no provision for hashing or clustering, but it does make optimal use of its sequential storage capabilities through the creation of clustered indexes, which can be used to speed sequential database access.

Objectivity DB and Storage Management

The Objectivity DB database uses hash keys, indexes, sequential storage, and pointers to help expedite data access. As with the other light overhead systems, the object programmer must know the data storage method used in order to navigate among the stored records. Different commands and techniques are used to access each of the data storage profiles.

Expanding the Taxonomy of Database Systems

We are now ready to add yet another section to our taxonomy of database profiles.

Storage Management Taxonomy

I. Default I/O Techniques
1. Blocking
2. Buffering

II. Ways to Store Data
1. Compression
2. Sequential
3. Clustered

III. Ways to Locate Data
1. Hashing
2. Indexing
3. Pointing

IV. Ways to Perform Cross-File Navigation
1. Light Overhead (programmer controlled)
2. Heavy Overhead (system controlled)

V. Techniques of Cross-File Association
1. Pointers
2. Scanning
3. Indexes
4. Hashing

Based on this taxonomy, we can add the following table to our profiles. (See Table 10-1.)

Database Efficiency

Database manufacturers develop unique products by arranging the way a database uses blocking, buffering, clustering, indexes, hashing, and pointers to deliver data to the program or user in an organized and efficient manner. It is the bundling of these techniques in combination with other functions and capabilities that make database products different from each other.

Obviously, different indexing techniques combined with different buffering and blocking schemes result in a totally different level of system performance. Each unique configuration presented will, by definition and by the simple laws of physics, yield different efficiencies and shortfalls.

Table 10-1 : Storage management table

Storage Management Profile	OS Dependent/Programmable/None
Blocking	
Buffering	
Compression	
Clustering	
Sequenced Storage	
Indexing	
Pointers	
Hashing	

An arrangement optimized for one situation will be inefficient in another. These trade-offs each arrangement provides does not, unfortunately, indicate a stable benchmark against which database products can be judged.

Hardware Improvements and the Impact of Database Configurations

For the selector, user, or evaluator of a database product, the laws of physics for database systems are constantly changing. A database product can be designed so that it operates optimally given a certain platform today, and become far from optimal tomorrow simply because the hardware changed in a way that it cannot exploit.

Take as an example databases written to run on PCs ten years ago. It was not so long ago that the maximum memory in a PC was 64k. In an arrangement like that, a database that is going to perform optimally must deal with that constraint. At that time, it was also considered on leading edge to have a hard disk attached to that machine, and that fixed drive would hold anywhere from 5 to 20 megabytes of data. Floppy disks held 174k.

A database built to run optimally in this environment had very little space for data buffers, used small block sizes, and needed to worry only about processing several thousand rows of data at a time.

What happens to this product with the introduction of 120-megabyte hard drives, 1.2-megabyte floppy disks, and 16-megabyte memory capacities. Simply put, its internal architecture can no longer be optimized for the platform on which it runs.

Of course, for the poor manufacturer, by the time all of the changes are put in to optimize a new environment, yet another set of advances will be made by hardware manufacturers and the process starts over again.

This is not to single out the PC segment of the database market. In fact, all four worlds (PC, workstation, mini, and mainframe) have seen incredible advances in hardware, which force them to constantly retool and remarket their database software products.

There is a constantly shifting equation that balances how much functionality should be assigned to a database product as opposed to programs.

The decision to assign responsibility for a given requirement to a specific component of the database system is determined by the designer at the time the system is built: what the best mix between people, programs, platforms, and database products? As more platform power becomes available at lower costs, the tendency has been to shift more of the burden for system intelligence onto the computer end of the system and away from people.

This shift from people to computer power is the reason for the recent burst in popularity of decision-support systems, artificial intelligence, executive information systems, and other kinds of intelligent computer systems. The fact of the matter is that most of the requirements allocated to programs can be reallocated to database products or people and vice-versa. As hardware continues to become more powerful, this shift will continue.

11

The Administrative Profile

We turn now to the last of the database profiles to be considered, the administrative profile. While the processing, architecture, and storage management profiles of the database each were concerned with some aspect of the delivery of data to end users, the administrative profile consists of database features and functions that overlay the other three, and are concerned more with the management of the inner workings of the database product itself.

These functions are built into the product for a number of good reasons, but all of them focus on making the database easier to manage, more dependable, and more usable to more people more often.

An Overview of Administration

The administrative profile consists of three major components: recovery management, security, and concurrency management. Recovery management consists of those functions and utilities that make it possible for the system to recover in the event of a system failure. Security is the establishment of mechanisms that prevent the wrong people from seeing data. Concurrency management attempts make it possible for as many people as possible to access the same data at the same time.

The administrative profile of a database has nothing to do with its architecture or any other product-related characteristics. But the robustness of the profile does tend to be related to the platform the database runs on. PC databases are the weakest in these areas and mainframe products are the strongest. The reasons for this should be obvious. The larger and more expensive the computer, the more likely it is that there will be more concurrent users, and therefore more need for recovery, concurrency, and security capabilities.

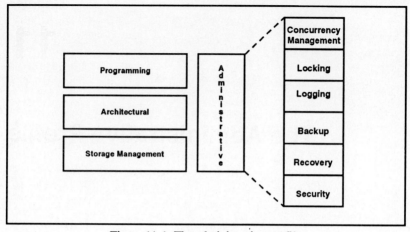

Figure 11-1: The administrative profile

While the administrative profile has little impact on the architecture or usability of a database, it does have a lot to do with the efficiency and manageability of the environment it creates. The security, recovery, and concurrency capabilities of the database are of immense value to the person building a database system because their presence makes it possible to build systems far bigger and more complex than would be possible under normal circumstances.

The Administration Topics we Cover

In this chapter, we discuss these areas of functionality and consider the principles and mechanisms they are based on. We begin by revisiting Pete's Pet Shop and developing an understanding of why Pete might want his database to provide some of these services.

After considering the three fundamental approaches manufacturers can take in the management of database transaction activity (single, data- sharing, and multiple-user), we then take a more in-depth look at recovery management and the three operations that make up a solid recovery profile: backup, logging, and recovery. After that, we consider security in its many forms, including the different levels of security that a database can provide (dataset, access, and internal) and the ways that these can be enforced (catalog vs. data constructor modification).

After recovery and security, we develop some definitions for the ways that databases handle concurrency. This is usually handled through a mechanism known as locking. This locking can occur at several levels (record/row, page/block, data construct, dataset, or database), and that it can be managed automatically (implicit locking) or manually (explicit locking).

Among the issues created by the invocation of a locking strategy are lock types (shared and exclusive) and locking disciplines (the returning of lock codes, lock escalation, and deadlock detection).

Besides the basic locking strategy that a database follows, we also consider the advanced technique known as versioning, which many object-oriented and distributed databases use to make data even more accessible.

Finally, the implementation of these mechanisms as they relate to architectures, and more importantly, platforms are summarized.

The Discretionary Nature of the Administrative Profile

Before proceeding with our discussion, it is important to note that as opposed to the processing, architecture, and storage management profiles of a database, the administrative profile is made up of optional characteristics. A system can run without security, concurrency, or recovery control in place. Because these are discretionary functions, the selector, developer, or assessor of a database system can always include them in their analysis or leave them out, without effecting the baseline performance. However, on the other hand, no system of any formidable size or scope can hope to support significant processing without using at least some of these functions.

Pete's Pet Shop Revisited

Let's go back to our original description of Pete's Pet Shop and the original conditions under which the database decision was being made. When we first introduced Pete and his pet shop, we described a situation where Pete owned and operated the company by himself. Since he was on his own, it was easy for him to decide to buy a PC, pick a database he liked, and simply learn how to use it.

Since Pete worked alone, he had no security problems to speak of, no problems with concurrent system access (he was the only user), and no need to worry about backup and recovery. The amount of data being managed was so small that a simple backup of his hard disk every once in a while was sufficient.

Adding Users to the System

As the company grows however, so does the computer system that supports it. Suppose now the shop expands to the point where three people work in the store at the same time. How does this change Pete's need for an administrative profile?

Assuming that Pete knows and trusts his employees, and that they are of average intelligence, Pete will not develop any problems with security. Assuming also that the business does not increase in volume too much, the existing backup and recovery scheme should still be okay too.

But what if Pete wants all three people to use the system at the same time? With the existing database and hardware this is not possible.

One way to increase the concurrency is to purchase two more PCs, and make copies of the database on each one. This allows the users to work concurrently, but it also makes three different copies of the data over time. No, the best solution is to use a database that allows concurrent access.

Now assume that Pete's business grows even more. Assume also that as the number of employees grows, their dependability becomes more suspect. Now Pete needs not only concurrency control, but some kind of internal database security mechanism that prevents employees from changing their payroll records, and salesmen from giving themselves big commissions.

If Pete's system continues to grow, the amount of data being managed will continue to grow too. Assume that one day, after a staff of 12 people has been entering data for eight hours straight, a disk drive fails and all of the data from the day's transactions are lost. Now Pete has a real problem. He will probably be unable to recover from a disaster like this without paying a lot of overtime and losing a lot of valuable work in the process. At this point, Pete will be ready to hear about system recoverability mechanisms.

The conclusion of this progression is simple. The larger and more complex a system becomes, and the more important the data in that system is to the users, the more critical administrative profiles become.

Administration and Performance

Of course, the administrative functions a database provides are not some kind of magical benefit you get when you buy a system. No, they involve the dedication of disk space, computer memory, and administrative personnel's time to get them to work effectively.

The invocation of administrative functions on a system can increase overhead by 10, 20, or even 30 percent. They also require the dedication of administrative specialists, database administrators, security administrators, and system support personnel to use them.

Because of this, the decision to use administrative functions or not is a big decision, with consequences on the organization's staffing requirements and computer budget.

Administration and Manageability

Although the cost of using these functions may seem high, (large mainframe organizations can have entire departments dedicated to each administrative function), it is simply a fact of life that no large computer system can run effectively without them in place. The amazing organization and harmony that computer systems bring to the operation of a business can be turned into a chaotic free-for-all if the administrative functions are not managed well.

The recovery, security, and concurrency capabilities of a database product offer the system developer several additional options to choose from when determining the optimum arrangement of system components. In this chapter you will become familiar with the concepts and terminology concerned with these functions.

Database Transaction Management

In order to provide recovery, security, and concurrency control, a database product must have a transaction management system in place. Transaction management can take several forms, but we discuss the three generic models, which most databases utilize: simple, shared data, and multiple.

Simple Transaction Management

Another term that can be used to describe the simple transaction management approach is *single-user mode*. These systems manage transactions by simply working with only one user at a time. Multiple requests for data are simply rejected by the system. The current data holder is the only user of interest to the system. Systems built with databases of this type either develop application code to handle security and backup and recovery, or run without. Databases that handle transactions in this way include many flat-file and XBase systems and an assortment of products that can be found on all platforms.

In single-user mode, database activity is reduced to the lowest common denominator. Obviously, this approach is severely limiting, but if only one user is involved with the system, then it is the most efficient way for a product to be built.

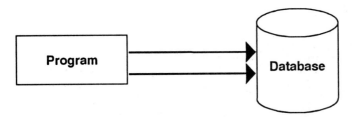

In a simple transaction environment, only one program can access the database at a time. This is the normal mode of operation for many PC products, but many larger systems can be tuned to work in a single-user mode.

Figure 11-2: Single user data approach

Shared Data Approach

Assuming that the user of the database—like Pete with his Pet Shop—finds that the system must support several users simultaneously, then the simple transaction approach will not suffice, and a more robust type of database will need to be found.

One way to provide multiuser access to the same data on a database is to store that data on a common disk area, and then allow multiple versions of the database software to access it. This approach, like the single-user approach, means that each user will be running their own version of the database software. The difference is that all copies of the databases go to the same storage locations to read and write.

When the shared data approach is used, contention for the same data is managed by a simple locking scheme, which allows only one user to access data at the same time. This approach is as much a distributed database solution as it is a multiple user access solution, but it is mentioned here for thoroughness. You are encouraged to skip ahead to the chapter about distributed databases for a more complete discussion of this topic.

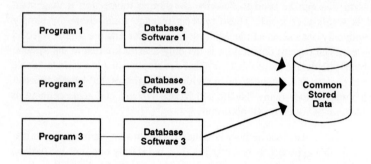

Under the shared data approach, multiple versions of the database code are run, one version for each user. This kind of arrangement takes many forms

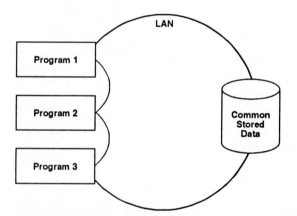

In this case, several PCs, each running a copy of the database software, share a common physical dataset. This differs from a client-server organization in that the common data area has no intelligence or database software associated with it. Each PC manages its own database environment.

Figure 11-3: Shared data approach

Multiple Transaction Management

If the developer of the system decides that neither the simple nor shared data approaches to transaction management will get the job done, then the only choice left is to consider a fully-functional, multiple transaction management system. These systems allow several users to access the same database (the same database code running in computer memory) at the same time. In order to do this, the system must provide for the means to:

- Determine whether a user should be allowed to use the system or not (access security)

- Create a queuing discipline for setting the priority of user tasks (which user is doing what and when)

- Develop a way to identify and manage each user's transaction activity

- Provide the means for the monitoring, control, and overall management of these multiple tasks

Multiple transaction database systems do all of these things and more through the execution of several layers of software control techniques.

Managing Multiple Users

In order to manage several simultaneous users of a database, the system must develop some kind of mechanism for the organization of those users. This is done by the establishment of special areas in the computer's memory called user work areas and through the creation of user identifiers, transaction identifiers, and threads. When a request for database access is received by the database, it immediately allocates an area of computer memory, which is used as that user's work area. This work area is then used by the database as a kind of scratch pad, or reference point, to which all database activity refers.

After creating a work area, the database assigns two identifiers:

- A user identifier, which allows the system to know who is requesting the work

- A transaction identifier, which allows the database to keep one activity request separate from another

After assigning these identifiers, the system performs all of the activities that have been requested, and returns the results to the user. The accumulation of all of the activities performed for the same transaction identifier is referred to as that transaction's *thread*.

Let's walk through a simple case, to help explain exactly how this works. Assume that a user has issued a database call, which requests that the record for Sammy the Shark be returned to the screen. Assume that the user has a logon user ID of XYZ123. When the request is received by the database, it must first be sure that user XYZ123 is authorized to gain entry (access security). If yes, then the database puts aside some of the system's memory for this user and associates user ID XYZ123 with it.

When this is complete, a transaction identifier not currently being used by another user is assigned. Let's assign transaction identifier 1001 for example.

With all of this done, the database is ready to begin work. The system can now check system catalogs, read indexes, buffers, and files and return the requested information to the user. As each of these activities occurs, however, the user ID and transaction ID assigned are kept coupled with the many requests. This way, the system is able to keep track of what work is being done for whom and maintain its own internal organization.

Identifying Individual Users

Systems designed to keep track of many simultaneous users usually work with both user logon identifiers and transaction identifiers. This way, if a user submits several concurrent tasks, the system can keep them separate. The establishment of a unit of work on a computer system is called task initiation, and the full extent of its activities within the database itself is called its thread.

When multiple users are allowed to operate on a system, multiple threads are established.

Although the specific ways that a database product implements transaction management is dependent on the architecture, storage management, and platforms that they work with. Most mainframe, mini, and workstation databases operate using some variation of this basic mode.

The method used to establish and control multiple transactions within the database defines how the other three administrative profile components are to be implemented. Although some standard approaches to the problems created by multiple transaction management have been developed over the years, the specific implementation of them is one of the most product-specific characteristics we have considered thus far.

It is against the backdrop of our understanding of transaction management approaches that we now consider the three administrative characteristics we have highlighted.

Backup, Recovery, and Logging

One way to gain some additional benefits from the use of databases is to take advantage of their ability to restore themselves to the exact state they were in at a previous point in time. This capability, referred to as recoverability, can save hundreds of hours of work and inconvenience when something goes wrong with computer hardware. The ability to recover, although rarely invoked, allows applications developers to simplify their programming efforts. If a programmer or user can assume that if something goes wrong with a disk or other hardware device, that the database will take care of it, then the amount of effort that must be spent making backup copies and checklists is greatly reduced. If this was not the case, then most programs written would need to make backup copies of every step of processing. That way, if anything went wrong, there would be an historical audit file in place that could be used as input to the recovery process.

An example of a typical computer system disaster explains how this works and illustrates how backup/recovery mechanism helps reduce programming maintenance and CPU costs.

Imagine an application program that updates the corporate general ledger database has just finished changing the balance for every account in the system. This program is run every month as part of the regular accounting cycle. The program took several hours to run. It is critical once the accounts are balanced, that a balance sheet be produced. Shortly before the balance sheet can be generated, however, the disk drive, holding this information, fails. The accounting data has all been destroyed.

The first thing the computer operators do is replace the disk drive with a new one. Then the new drive will be restored using the previous night's backup copy of the data. Although a copy of the general ledger is available again, it has only the information on it that was present the previous night. The time and programming effort spent processing the ledger today is lost. In a world without database recovery this means that all of the programs run earlier in the day have to be run again. It will take many hours to resynchronize. Until that happens, all other accounting-related business activity must stop. This will cost the corporation many person-hours. If critical decisions must be postponed until the accounting system can be placed back online the impact could be quite severe.

With database recovery enabled, the database software itself takes care of this. The administrator simply tells the database at what point in time the system should be restored to. No programs need to be rerun and in a short span of time, everything can be put back to normal.

Why does a Database Need to Provide this Ability?

It may seem wasteful for 9 database product to maintain this capability. A lot of time, money, and effort is spent ensuring that the system is protected from these system failures. For the smaller scale system, simple tape backups of the hard disk on a regular basis should take care of most backup, assuming that someone actually does this. There is a difference, however, between *system* backup and recovery and *database* backup and recovery. System-wide and database backup and recovery capabilities can be differentiated by two characteristics; the scope of the recoverability and the precision with which recovery can be performed.

System Backup and Recovery

System backup and recovery schemes are usually based on the principle that the best way to prevent loss of data is to create several copies of it. The approach is very simple. On a regular basis (nightly or weekly) everything on every disk device is copied to tape. By duplicating the data on tape, the programming staff assures that if a disk should fail or the system should lose a large amount of data, they will be able to restore everything to the condition as of the last backup.

For *system* backup and recovery, the scope is usually very large, either the backup of an entire disk device or individual datasets, and the precision is very low, with recoverability to a given day. Most system backups are run in the middle of the night when transaction levels are at their lowest.

Although this gross level of assurance provides a critical fallback position for the organization to maintain, backup/recovery schemes of this kind provide little flexibility. For example, if a programmer accidentally erases a copy of a program in development for several weeks, the system's support staff can copy that program from the previous backup. Although the majority of the work will have been recovered, all of the current day's effort will be lost. The programmer, of course, would prefer that the system restore the program to its condition several minutes ago, not many hours ago.

Database Backup and Recovery

Database backup and recovery allow the system to protect data objects at a much lower level. Both the scope (how much or how little can be recovered at one time) and the precision (to what point in time) of recovery operations are much finer and more adjustable under the DBMS umbrella. By setting the recovery scope, the administrator directs the database to recover a specific file, table, index, page of data, or even a single record or row. This way, the administrator can limit the operation to only that part of the database that needs to be refreshed. The administrator can then set the precision and restore that portion to the way it was last week, last night, or just five minutes ago. This ability to restore the database to a previous state with such pinpoint accuracy makes the recovery mechanism a powerful and helpful component of any database product.

Let us first consider the generic methods utilized by most database systems for backup and recovery and then explore the unique capabilities of some of the individual products.

Recovery capabilities are provided by combining three basic operations. The first, called backup, involves the copying of existing stored data onto some kind of backup device, usually a tape. These backup media are then transported to a safe location, in another room, building, or even to a remote salt mine, where it will be protected from flood, fire, and other kinds of disaster.

Concurrent with backup activities is the maintenance of a system log. A log, which is usually some kind of disk or tape file, keeps track of each transaction as it occurs on the database. If a new row is inserted into the file, a copy of that new row is copied to the log at the same time. If a record is changed on the file, the change is also written to the log. By maintaining this real-time audit trail, the system's log makes it possible for recovery to be done with pinpoint accuracy.

Finally, the recovery activity itself consists of running a utility that combines the backup copies and the system log into an exact duplicate of how the system looked at any point in time.

Recovery: A Three Part Approach

Most database packages provide for recoverability with three different activities:

- Backup—copying datasets (tablespaces, DBspaces, or partitions) to a tape or disk medium

- Logging—maintenance of an online, real-time, step-by-step audit record of every operation performed within the database

- Recovery—usually accomplished by copying the most recent backup into the dataset and then applying the log to those datasets

Backup

All major database products provide the administrator with a backup capability. A backup operation is nothing more than a utility that copies all or parts of the data in a physical dataset to a tape or another disk. All backup facilities are not the same, however. Three features help make the backup process a lot easier for the administrator to manage.

The Database

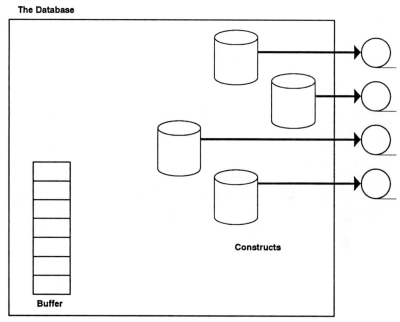

Constructs

Buffer

During the backup process, shared data is copied to a backup medium (tape or disk). A backup copy if a snapshot of how a construct looked at a given point in time.

Figure 11-4: Backup

- **Incremental backups**—Incremental backup features allow the administrator to backup only data that has changed since the last backup copy. With the incremental approach, backups run faster and more efficiently.

- **User concurrent backups**—User concurrent backups are utilities that can run while the user continues to work on the database. Such utilities simply work around the user, backing up whatever is not being worked on at the time. Once the user is done, it backs up anything that was missed.

- **Bulk unload utilities**—A bulk unload utility unloads datasets quickly, bypassing the normal data storage load/unload mechanisms. Although not as safe to use as normal unloads, bulk data movement can be a must for very large systems.

Logging

Logging is often referred to as system journaling, depending on the product. Logging mechanisms keep track of changes to the database as they occur. In a simple logging scenario, changes to parts of a database's physical record (block, page, etc.) are recorded twice. First, a change is made to the actual database record and, second, the exact nature of that change is written to some kind of log record.

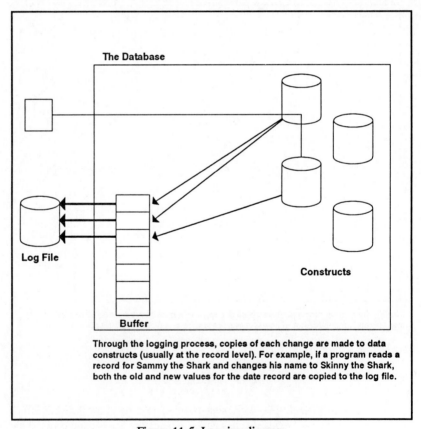

Through the logging process, copies of each change are made to data constructs (usually at the record level). For example, if a program reads a record for Sammy the Shark and changes his name to Skinny the Shark, both the old and new values for the date record are copied to the log file.

Figure 11-5: Logging diagram

The way a database manufacturer organizes logging operations has a lot to do with how well and how quickly the system can be recovered in the event of a failure. Logging activity complicates the database's internal architecture. Not only must the thread activity of each user be kept separate, but in addition, log records for each user's activity must be written.

Some databases create log records by simply writing the log or journal information to an independent log file, but most use a log buffer to allow more logging more quickly. When log buffers are involved, the system simply writes log records to that buffer until it is full. At that time the buffer is externalized, that is, the log records in the buffer are written to a file. Remember, all computers are I/O bound; any mechanism that allows the system to avoid physical reads and writes as long as possible helps speed up the system.

In the most comprehensive case, the system provides backups of the log files by backing up these to tape. These tape files are usually called archive or extended history records.

The unique combination of backup, logging, and recovery mechanisms define the individual database product's recovery profile. Obviously, depending upon the sophistication of the product being considered and the needs of the system developers, all, some, or none of these features can be capitalized. The important thing for the selector and evaluator of a database product is to be aware of how well or poorly the database can meet their specific recoverability needs.

Recoverability and Database Products

Let's examine a few of our previously discussed database products to illustrate the ways that a recoverability profile can be defined.

PC Databases and Recoverability

For the most part, databases that run on PCs provide little or no recoverability. This may be due to several factors, but the biggest is that since the volumes of data being managed on these computers is low, and the control that the individual user has is high, there is less reason for the execution of sophisticated recovery techniques. For these systems (like PC File and DBase III), backup and recovery is managed by the creation of system backups (making copies of database physical files to disk). In these cases, recovery is accomplished by copying the data on disk, back to the hard drive.

Although this method works, the biggest problem is that few users are willing to spend the time making backup copies on a regular basis. This reluctance can lead to the loss of significant amounts of data.

Full-Fledged Recoverability

While the PC databases rely on system backup and recovery schemes, most other products provide a unique combination of backup, logging, and recovery utilities to make system integrity easier to maintain. Of the database products we have considered Adabas, IMS, IDMS, DB2, Informix, and Objectivity-DB all provide complete logging capabilities, the creation of backup copies, and the provision of a recovery utility.

The physical arrangement of recovery mechanisms within the DB2 database is perhaps the most illustrative of a typical recoverability profile.

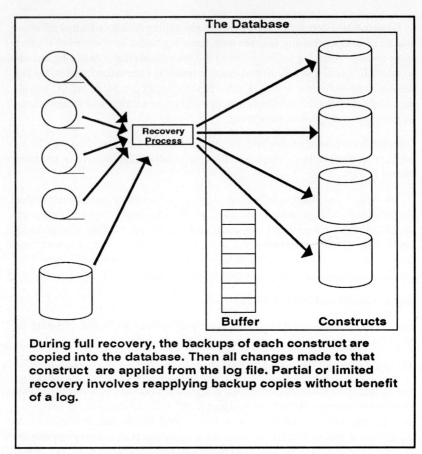

During full recovery, the backups of each construct are copied into the database. Then all changes made to that construct are applied from the log file. Partial or limited recovery involves reapplying backup copies without benefit of a log.

Figure 11-6: Recovery diagram

DB2 Backup Capabilities

The DB2 database provides database administrators with three types of backup utility. The full, incremental, and user-concurrent modes can all be used. When these utilities are run, data is not only backed up to tape, but entries are made in the system catalogs. These entries specify the name of the table being backed up, the date and time at which the backup is made, and the name of the dataset holding the data.

DB2 Logging Capabilities

DB2 provides logging through a log buffer, log files, and log archives. Log buffers hold log information as soon as it is available, Log files are what log buffers are written to on a regular basis. Log archives are tape copies of log files themselves.

This three-tiered approach to the establishment of a log data trail is tuned so that logging can be performed with a minimal impact on overall system performance.

DB2 Recovery

When the database administrator needs to recover a DB2 system, the Recover utility is executed. This utility accepts as input the name or section of the tables to be recovered and the date and time to which they should be restored. Given this information, the utility is able to check the catalog tables for information about which backup copies to use, and then combine these with the log information stored in the archive tapes and log files. These are both applied to the database with the result being a restoration to the time and date requested.

Database recoverability is an extremely complex and sophisticated operation. It gives the users of a database system a level of assurance that they could never attain with a nondatabase-controlled environment.

While recoverability defines how safe system data will be from natural disaster and accidents, the next topic, security, is concerned with making the data safe from intentional and accidental abuse of a more subtle nature. This can occur when people want to change or see things beyond their privilege.

Security

Security is another area that can benefit from databases. Before databases existed, the only way a company could control who got to see what data was by building security checks into the application programs themselves. In a world where dozens of programs are used to access the same file, it becomes extremely difficult to make sure that all of the programs are enforcing these security rules consistently. Even more troublesome is the expense incurred when security rules change. In these cases, when the rules of access change for a given file, all programs accessing that file must be changed as well.

Database security, on the other hand, places muchall responsibility for security access rules on the database software itself. The database, not the program, decides who gets to see what information. Again, the work required of the application programs is reduced and the ability to manage the system is enhanced.

The security profile of a database product consists of several levels. In the broadest category is the requirement that the database not allow programs or users access to the stored data itself (dataset security). On the next level we define whether the database product screens the individuals allowed to access the database or not (access security), and on the lowest level is security of activities that occur within the database (internal security).

Dataset Security

No matter what specific database software is chosen, all packages store data in some kind of physical dataset. DB2, IMS, Oracle, and many others use a virtual storage access method (VSAM) structure. XBase databases use the .dbf format, and most other products use a proprietary file arrangement. In all cases the data is physically offloaded to some disk storage area. Unless an encryption routine is included in the software, that physically stored data is decipherable by an expert system intruder. The most sophisticated database security is useless if an intruder can gain access to the native data files and read them.

Fortunately, this window of vulnerability is usually quite narrow. All major mainframe, Unix, and minicomputer products allow the native operating system or a resident security software (i.e., ACF2, Top Secret, or RACF) to secure their datasets just as they do any other critical data files. PCs, on the other hand, must use the more sophisticated operating systems or must count on the security of the physical machine itself. This means that PCs should be physically locked when not in use, and diskette copies of data must be correspondingly secured.

We will assume here, that the appropriate security of the native files themselves is being managed appropriately with security packages or security procedures.

Access or Attachment Security

The next type of security is attachment security. This capability allows the administrator or security director to determine in advance who will and will not be allowed into the system at all. This type of security, like dataset security, offers a very high-level but necessary defense against illegal system access. Most database products can use one of four options to keep unwanted users from gaining access to the system.

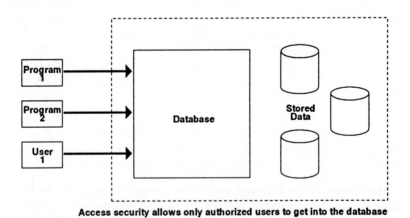

Access security allows only authorized users to get into the database

Figure 11-7: Access/ Attachment security

1. **No security**— Some PC products have no logon screening process at all. These systems are open to entry by anyone who can turn on the system. Most other products allow you to leave access security disabled, allowing anyone to access the

database. In this case, you are trusting the lower levels of security to catch invaders before any damage can be done.

2. Autonomous security—Under this security arrangement, the database itself requires that all users enter a special database logon ID and password. This logon/password combination is separate from any operating system or security package that may be running at the same location. Autonomous access security is often built into PC products, though larger platform systems also use it.

Although autonomous access security is sufficient when no other security mechanism is in place, it can be quite cumbersome when installed on a system where there is already a security package. In these cases, users can get quite frustrated with the need to logon to the system twice, once for the operating system, and once for the database.

3. Security mingling—The most common approach is to tie in the database software with an existing security package. This allows the regularly assigned security administrator to handle access permissions to the database along with all other system access privileges. This solution is most often used in the mainframe and large-scale mini-computer environments.

No matter which of the access security mechanisms is used, the utilization of the facility accomplishes at least two things for the system. First, the integrity of the system itself is protected. No unauthorized person will be given the opportunity to change or view sensitive data unless the appropriate password is provided. Second, by establishing who a person is before allowing them entry to the system, the database is able to establish its user identifier for the tagging of transactions and threads. Access security provides a vital link in the building of a production-oriented database environment.

One area where this kind of access security can break down is within systems that link autonomous teleprocessing systems with the database. Many times, the security mechanism of the teleprocessing system takes precedence over that of the database system causing security gaps to appear. If the TUI (text-based user interface) or GUI (graphical user interface) is not a part of the database's own product offering (when you pair up CICS and DB2 or tuxedo and informix for example), then the resident security software may not be able to guarantee that only authorized individuals are using the teleprocessing gateway to the database.

The easiest way to plug this gap is to rely on the teleprocessing system's own security scheme to cover the database vulnerability. Although this is easily done, it does make the job of maintaining a secure environment just a little bit harder for the security administrator.

Having considered this second line of defense against violation—the database's interface with the outside world—we can now consider the internal layers of database security.

Securing Access to the Data Itself

Assuming that the potential violator has been allowed through the gauntlet established by the dataset and access security mechanisms, they still must deal with the database's internal security profile.

Internal security is the database's own mechanism for deciding which files, records, and data elements an individual user or programmer is allowed to see or change. It is through this facility that the bulk of database security is enforced.

Under a given security approach, system administrators or security personnel define which data elements each individual is allowed to operate on. After determining these rules, they are loaded into the system using a variety of means. Since the access security mechanism guarantees that anybody using the system must have a valid user identifier, the security administrator's job is simply to identify which things can be done by which user IDs. After loading these associations, the database software itself can check its own internal security list whenever a user requests that some activity be performed.

There are three techniques for loading security information into the database. The one used depends upon the database, the operating system, and the existence of security package interfaces.

In the simplest case, the administrator enters security rules with a security package's own interface management system. If the database and the security package can work together, this technique will be the fastest and easiest to use. If the security package and the database are not tied together, then the administrator must use one of the other two techniques, either issue security commands to the database or modify the data constructors in some way to include the security information.

An example of constuctor driven security can be found with focus. The Focus database allows administrators to append a list of authorized users and their access rights to the data constructor statement file.

By centrally defining and loading security requirements, the database product makes it possible for the integrity of system data to be maintained with a minimum of inconvenience to everyone.

These two methods for loading security rules have associated with them two mechanisms for storing those rules. When rules are entered into the system with a data control language (DCL), there is usually a catalog table or internal database audit file that permanently stores the specifications. We refer to this as the catalog-driven approach to internal security.

If, on the other hand, security rules can be entered only by the modification or extension of data constructors, we define this as the constructor-driven approach.

Catalog-Driven Security

This approach, most typically used with relational and inverted list databases, stores security information within a set of system catalog tables. These tables inform the system which users can see what table, view, or column and whether they can insert, update, or delete items. Users can be authorized to do almost anything an administrator can do, or they can be prevented from doing anything but reading tables. Even if users have access and transaction authorization, they are still unable to access data if this final level of authority has not been granted.

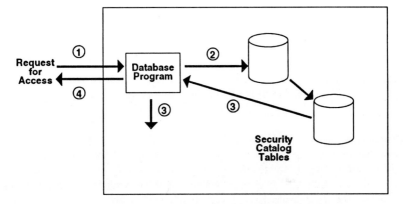

Under the Informix database security arrangement:

① A user requests that database activity be performed

② The database program checks the security tables to see if the user is authorized

③ If the user is authorized, the work is performed

④ If not, a security error message is returned

Figure 11-8: Informix Security (Table Driven)

Constructor-Driven Security

With this method only certain predetermined navigation paths, segments, or keys are made accessible to a specific user. These security rules must be built into the construction of the database itself. This can mean that changes to those security rules require the regeneration of the entire database, a costly and time-consuming option. Although the technique is effective, it can be difficult to administer and

modify. *Ad hoc* access, for example, can be accomplished only when the administrative staff is able to predetermine what navigational calls a user is likely to request.

```
FILENAME=ANICUST,SUFFIX=FOC,$
SEGMENT=ANIMAL,SEGTYPE=S1,$
   FIELD=NAME     ,FORMAT=A12
   FIELD=TYPE     ,FORMAT=A10
   FIELD=COLOR    ,FORMAT=A5
SEGMENT=CUSTOMER,PARENT=ANIMAL,SEGTYPE=S11,$
   FIELD=NAME     ,FORMAT=A20
   FIELD=ADDRESS ,FORMAT=A20
   FIELD=PHONE    ,FORMAT=A9
END
DBA=MSMITH, $
USER=TOM ,ACCESS=RW, $
USER=BILL,ACCESS=R, $
USER=SUE ,ACCESS=W,RESTRICT=SEGMENT,NAME=CUSTOMER,$
USER=MARY,ACCESS=R,RESTRICT=FIELD,NAME=ADDRESS,$
```

Figure 11-9: FOCUS (constructor driven security)

The establishment of an internal security profile makes the database easier for
everyone to use. Not only is the individual's data secure from violation, but the
user need not worry about ruining things for somebody else. In an unsecured
environment anybody can change anything. In this environment, it is impossible
to delete, modify, or insert data unless you are authorized to do so. Database security
makes it easier for everyone; users, programmers, and administrators to function
effectively.

Security Profiles and Database Products

Just as with the recoverability profile, the security profiles of database packages
tend to be the weakest for the PC products, and strongest for mainframe systems.
A lot of PC database products have no security mechanisms at all, and those that
do utilize the simple logon or password. Since PCs are single-user platforms, they
also have no need for the establishment of user IDs.

The more robust database products, however, normally use access and internal
security to varying degrees.

Security, like recoverability, is an optional database feature, but it is unlikely that
any system of size could function without the supporting mechanisms in place.

Concurrence

Database concurrency refers to the way that a database product manages those
situations where more then one individual (user or program) wants to access the

same piece of data at the same time. Although each database product may develop certain idiosyncratic features to its own management of this capability, in general, all databases must work with the same kinds of things to be managed (files, blocks, records, and fields) and are subject to the same constraints (memory, speed, buffering, and disk space). Because of this, we will discuss the issues surrounding concurrency from a generic perspective. Individual differences between database products will be highlighted when appropriate.

Why is Concurrency Management Important?

No matter how effective or efficient a database happens to be, if it is unable to manage several people trying to access the same data at the same time and resolve the conflict, then it will end up being able to support only a very low number of users. The more concurrent users a system has, the more important the database product's concurrency management organization.

Not all database products provide concurrency. Many PC-based products were designed to work with only one user at a time. In this case, concurrency is not present at all. Most databases allow the option of making the database available to only one user. Although this option is only used in rare cases, when it is invoked, the database runs with no concurrent capabilities.

A Description of the Concurrency Problem

To better understand concurrency issues, let's consider a situation where no database is present. Assume that Pete's Pet Shop was keeping track of animals by writing the information about each animal on a separate 3" x 5" card. These cards could be organized with one animal per card (a row or record), all animals of the same type kept in the same card box (a page or block), and all boxes kept in the same cabinet (a database). Whenever one of Pete's employees wants to change information about a particular animal, they must find the card, pull it out, make the change to the information, and put it back.

Assume however, that two of Pete's employees want to make a change to the card at the same time. What happens now ? The only thing that can happen is that one person will get to use it (will receive a lock), while the other will be forced to wait.

How is Concurrency Established?

In order to manage concurrent access to the database, a database system must have built into its architecture certain key elements.

The first element is the establishment of ownership for a certain activity. Each request for data must be attributable to a unique source. There are several ways that task ownership can be managed by a system.

Either the system must keep track of a user's identity, with a logon ID, user ID, or some other identifier. In this case, every request for an operation is then tagged with this unique identifier.

Another way to tag requests for data is by assigning a unique identifier to each transaction as it is started. This technique generates identifiers called task IDs, transaction IDs, or execution IDs.

Most databases are actually set up to track both the user ID of the person initiating the activity, and a transaction ID assigned to that task.

In the least sophisticated case, ownership is established by the simple rule of possession. If you can get at it, it must not be locked. If you can't, then someone else must have it. This simple first in, first out discipline fully describes the locking strategy for many of the databases with less powerful administrative profiles. In all cases, the data being operated on is somehow flagged as being unavailable to all but the current possessor.

Levels of Locking

The process of making data unavailable to certain programs or users while leaving it available to others, is called locking. Locking can be done on several levels.

The highest level of locking is accomplished when the entire database system is available to only one user. A database working in this manner is said to be in single-user mode. The single-user mode is useful for database maintenance and repair, and can also be used to help make extremely resource-intensive database applications run more quickly. This is akin to saying that when one person is using Pete's card file, no one else can use it.

A lower level of locking is accomplished when only one file, dataset, or table, is locked. In this mode of operation, other tables or files can be accessed by system users, but the object being locked is available only to the person holding the lock.

Depending on the architecture of the database, there is another level of locking, whereby the logical data storage constructs are locked, as opposed to the physical ones. For example, DB2 allows you to lock tablespaces (which are physical data constructs) or tables (which are logical constructs).

The next lower level occurs when the actual physical storage blocks that hold the data, are held exclusively. This kind of lock is comparable to saying that the employee holding the box full of Fish index cards has exclusive control over those cards until done.

Some databases allow even lower locking to occur, and individual rows or records of the database are held. This type of locking brings us back to our original example. The person holding the index card first gets to finish with it before someone else can change it.

The lowest level of locking possible, though not now provided by any of the popular database products, would be to lock the individual data elements themselves, the fields, columns, or attributes.

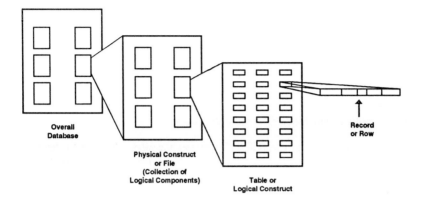

Overall
Database

Physical Construct
or File
(Collection of
Logical Components)

Table or
Logical Construct

Record
or Row

Figure 11-10: Locking levels

Types of Locks

In the situations described thus far, we have talked about locks and index cards as if that was to only way to manage concurrent access. It is not. Remember, with a computer system, you can allow several hundred people to see the same thing at the same time. So the system is able to enforce a rule that says *although the first person grabbing the data is the one that gets to change it first, there is no reason that someone else can't simply look at the data at the same time.*

Not only can locks be issued against different levels, there are usually several kinds of locks a database system will enforce. Each product may call them different things, but in general there are two categories of locks—shared and exclusive—and several variations within each category.

A *shared* or *read only* lock allows the lock holder to read the data being locked, but allows other users to read it, too. An *exclusive* or *update* lock, which is placed on data when it is being changed, makes sure that the task holding the lock makes all changes before anyone else is allowed to change it.

By using both shared and exclusive locking mechanisms, the system provides the maximum amount of information to the greatest number of people, with a minimum of contention for individual data elements.

Implicit vs. Explicit Locks

Locks can be obtained in two ways. For most normal operations, a database product itself issues locks to guarantee the integrity of the system. For example, a command to read, locate, find, fetch, or get a record for examination, automatically issues a share lock as part of normal execution. A command to modify, change, update, or alter a data value, carries with it a corresponding exclusive lock command. Locks of this type—that the database places automatically—are called *implicit* locks.

In most databases, the programmer or administrator is allowed to override the normal locking mechanisms with an *explicit* lock command. Explicit lock commands allow programs to optimize performance and minimize the chances of the system slowdown by a lot of unnecessary lock management activity. The explicit lock command makes it possible for users to tune the database's performance to meet their own specific needs.

For example, assume that a program that needs to update a very large, heavily-accessed file cannot run because it is always locked out. This can be remedied with an explicit lock, which overrides all of the implicit ones.

Another way explicit locks find their way into the picture is for those databases that have no implicit locking at all. In these cases, explicit locking is the only locking available.

How Is Locking Executed?

Assuming that a database handles locking automatically, and that a programmer chooses not to explicitly lock anything, how would anyone know that locking is occurring at all? The answer lies in the codes that databases return when a program asks for data and doesn't get any back.

Just because a program or user asks the database for data doesn't mean that they are going to get it. Every requestor of data has the potential of finding that their data is currently unavailable. In the simplest case, a request for unavailable data results in either a database return code, which the program must recognize as a lock condition, or a message returned to the user's screen informing them of the condition.

This simple approach to lock management, however, can be quite costly for many large systems. The length of time that a program or user holds their lock on a particular piece of data could be anywhere from 5 milliseconds to several hours. In those cases where the duration of the lock is short, it is very inefficient and inconvenient for the system simply to send back the locking return code to a program that is waiting for the same data immediately. What these more sophisticated systems do when a lock suspensioon occurs is wait for a specified period of time, and then try to access the record again. This attempt to reaccess the data is repeated a certain number of times this is called *(automatic lock retry)* If after all of these attempts the data is still unavailable, then and only then is the locking return code sent. When this code is received by the program, the program itself must back out all other related transactions and notify the user that the work requested must be completed at some other time. This is known as a lock timeout condition.

Obviously, the ability to keep track of the transactions running against the database at a given point in time combined with requests attempted several times before sending back a lock condition return code can put a lot of additional strain on a database system. Despite this fact, the ability to manage concurrent access to data in this way is a requirement for most database products on the market today.

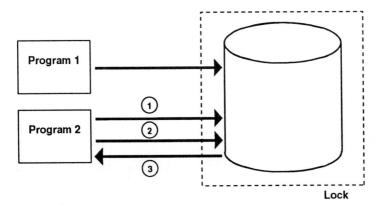

In an environment where Program 1 has established a lock on a construct, Program 2 will:

① Request access and not be allowed because of the other lock

② The system will retry a certain number of times automatically

③ After a certain number of retries, the system will "time out" the transaction and send back a lock-out return code

Figure 11-11: Locking retry scheme

Lock Escalation

Some databases have built in a feature known as *lock escalation*. In these cases, when the system places locks on pages or rows of data, the database system has some limits as to how many locks it can keep track of. When the database is created, or when a particular data storage structure is created, several limits on the number of allowable locks are included in the creation parameters. When the number of locks the system can track is exceeded, the system has a built-in mechanism called *lock escalation* that protects it from becoming overwhelmed.

There are two lock escalation criteria of special interest.

• The number of locks allowed on any one data structure

• The number of locks any one user can hold

As the system locks up more and more rows, records, blocks, or pages, it can quickly have too much to keep track of. When its limit is exceeded, the system *escalates*; it overrides whatever *level* of locks users asked for and enforces a higher level of locking (from a record to a page lock, or from a page to dataset lock, etc.).

Obviously, in order to change from a record lock to a block level lock, the system has to do something with all the locks currently established.

What the system does is kick out all users except for the one that first established a lock. The unlucky latecomers have all of their current work rolled back, and are sent a return code informing them of their misfortune.

The lucky user who got in first will has the lock level automatically escalated, and processing continues totally as if nothing happened.

Just as in the previous case, each user ID is allowed a certain number of locks overall. If that user exceeds the limit, the transaction is canceled and treated like any other lockout situation.

When lock escalation occurs, all but one user of the data construct being escalated are kicked out of the system. All other users must deal with the lockout return code received. The lucky user who got to stay in the database is then allowed to complete tasks normally.

Deadlock Detection and Polling

The Database as a Traffic Cop

What if two people want to read a the same page and one of them wants to update it? How does the database handle this case?

Without getting into too much detail, the database grants a lock to whomever asks first and makes all others wait. If someone obtains an exclusive lock, no one else is allowed a shared lock until the exclusive lock is released. Conversely, if someone has a shared lock, the person requesting an exclusive lock has to wait.

Unfortunately, situations are not always this simple. Oftentimes, several levels of contention for locks occur simultaneously and the system must be able to arbitrate when those cases arise.

The most common example of contention problems is called the *dreaded deadlock scenario.*

What is the Dreaded Deadlock Scenario?

In the dreaded deadlock scenario, there are two tables with data necessary for the processing of several transactions. For our purposes, let's call these Table1 and Table 2. By the nature of the data in these tables, in order to update to one, we must check for information contained on the other.

We now introduce two users, User 1 and User 2, each running a program that updates records on these tables. User 1 runs a program, and checks Table1 for some information about the row he or she wants to update in Table 2. User 1 now has a share lock on Table1.

User 2 now logs on, runs a program, and begins by checking values in Table 2 for some information he or she needs to update Table1. User 2 now holds a share lock on Table 2.

User 1's program now tries to get an exclusive lock on Table 2, but cannot because it is locked out by the share lock held by User 2. User 1 now waits for the lock to be released.

User 2 now tries to get an exclusive lock on Table1, but cannot because User 1 has a share lock on the data he or she wants. So he or she waits also.

The dreaded deadlock has now occurred, because neither program lets go until the other one does.

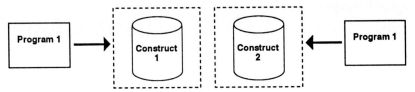

In a deadlock scenario, Program 1 locks Construct 1 and Program 2 locks Construct 2

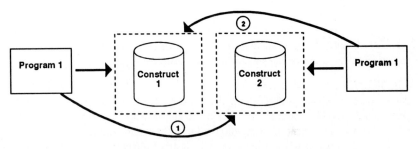

① Program 1 atempts to gain access to Construct 2

② Program 2 attempts to gain access to Construct 1

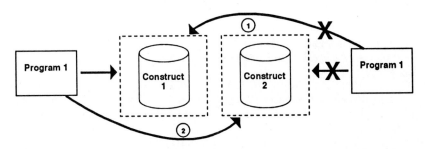

With deadlock contention-handling, the database decides to:

① Cancel Program 2's access

② Allow Program 1 to proceed

Figure 11-12: Deadlock

How does the System Handle Deadlocks?

What the system does in order to prevent deadlocks is establish *intent locks*. An intent lock informs the database that someone is waiting to put a certain type of lock on a section of data. In deadlock scenario, User 1 would not only wait, will establish and intent exclusive lock on Table 2. Conversely, User 2 will get an intent exclusive lock on Table 1.

The system now knows not only what locks are current, but what each user ID's future intentions are. By having this information, the system can detect deadlocks and resolve them as they occur.

When a deadlock is detected, the system simply kicks out one person with a lock error return code, leaving the other user all resources necessary to complete the processing. As with other lock-handling situations, programs must be written to detect and react when forced off the system by lock contention.

Commit and Rollback Work Commands

To make transactions as concurrent as possible, most database products provide the ability to commit and roll back work being done on the system. By allowing users and programs to change data elements temporarily, without *committing* the transactions until they are sure that everything is alright, databases allow programs to perform concurrent updates to several files simultaneously.

In the default case, where no commit or rollback capabilities are possible, the database automatically assumes that every change made to a database should be permanently recorded immediately upon execution of the command. In a commit/rollback arrangement, the execution of these commands results in a temporary change to the data, but is not made permanent until a *commit work* command is issued.

If for some reason it is decided that a mistake has been made and that the changes should not be made, a *rollback work* command undoes all of the changes made.

The ability to commit and rollback work, though useful in a single database environment, is critical for the successful operation of a distributed environment. In these cases, a special kind of commit processing, called *two-phase commit* is used.

Under two-phase commit, no change is made unless all of the databases involved in a given transaction have verified that the requested change can be made without interruption.

Advanced Lock Management: Versioning

In response to some of the more complex processing involved with distributed or object-oriented databases, several manufacturers have built in a kind of super-locking mechanism call *versioning*.

To help explain versioning, we return once again to our cardfile example. Assume that the need for animal index cards was so great that Pete decided employees could not afford to wait until somebody else was finished with a card. In this case, he might decide that it makes sense to have copies of the cards available to anyone that needed them. Every copy of the card that is passed out is called a version.

So let's say that Pete gives a version of the Sammy the Shark index card to Employee 1. After working on it, Employee 1 makes a copy of the card and gives it to Employee 2. Employee 2 then changes it some more and passes it back to Pete for return to the file. In this case, which version of the card is the right one? It is the job of versioning control mechanisms track this passing of data, and to make it possible for the user to access all versions with impunity.

Whereas normal locking criteria try to guarantee that only one person at a time can make changes to the same data, versioning control allows several users to make modifications to different versions of the same data at the same time.

In order to manage several versions of the same data, a database product must do several things:

- It must store each of the multiple versions of the data.

- It must assign unique keys to each version so that they can be distinguished.

- It must keep track of the progression of the versions over time to record when each new version was cloned from an old version.

- It must keep track of who creates each version.

- It must have an internal set of rules allowing it to decide what the *real* version of the data is.

- It must allow users to access and review these versions.

Most of the databases that provide versioning control do so by using special data storage areas (internal files) and special versioning control commands (like check-in and check-out).

Versioning definitely represents one of the latest in database concurrency control techniques and is still in its early stages of development. Despite the excessive overhead costs associated with versioning, for the right kind of application, it represents a significant improvement over simple lock management techniques.

Locking Mechanisms and Database Products

Consistent with the other examples cited thus far, the completeness of the database product's locking mechanisms is a function of the size of the systems it is built to manage. The dBASE III database provides a simple locking strategy, including no implicit locking, no lock escalation and simple enforcement of first in-first out read or write locks on data. The Informix database, on the other hand, provides lock escalation; row, page, and dataset level locks; and sophisticated lock management algorithms.

The extent of locking that individual products provide is a function of the manufacturer's commitment to the most efficient database environment possible.

Database Transaction Management and the Platform

Two things should be made apparent by this brief examination of database transaction management. First, transaction management as provided by the database product is optional. The system designer can choose to go without certain functions, or can choose to have the programming or people components of the system enforce the requirement. Whether to take advantage of the options is strictly a matter of environment, requirements, and available resources.

Second, in providing these transaction management capabilities, the database product adds significantly to its complication and its system overhead demand. The memory, speed, and disk space required to provide security, recovery, and concurrency services in a manner that does not slow the system down is a challenge for any product. Because of the extra demands these capabilities place on the system, usually only the larger and more solid database products even bother to provide the functionalities. Conversely, the large system databases (those associated with large mainframe applications) usually apply a lot of their resources to these functionalities.

Working without Administrative Functions

As we have already noted, it is possible, though not always desirable, for a database system to run without the benefit of administrative functions. Since these functions are optional, how does the system developer decide when to use them and when not to. The key to this decision-making process, is for the developer to generate a good understanding of what the system requirements and to determine whether any more effective or less expensive methods can be found for accomplishing the objectives.

Recoverability Options

Database recoverability is a good example of an optional functionality. Although the maintenance of full backup copies, log records, and recoverability to the split second is an attractive capability for any database to have, this level of commitment may be overkill in many situations.

If a database is created primarily for only a handful of users, or if it is utilized to provide reporting data only with no online insert/update or delete activity, then the maintenance of sophisticated and resource-intensive recoverability is a waste of money, time, and effort.

One of the most expensive aspects of system overhead can be the maintenance of system log files. Remember, to make use of a logging capability, every physical write to the database is really two writes, one to the database and the other to the log. When you combine this with the fact that database systems are usually I/O bound, you begin to see just how expensive a feature like logging can be.

If, on the other hand, a large number of users are involved, or the transactions being managed are critical to the operation of the business, then the most robust recoverability profile possible should be maintained.

Alternatives to Database Recoverability

We have considered several alternatives to database recoverability. One of them is simply to rely on the backup/recover capabilities of the system itself. In many situations a nightly backup copy of data is more than enough.

Another approach, used by most application systems before database recoverability came on the scene, was to modify application programs to create their own backup files and audit trails.

A Hybrid Approach

Often, the best organization of a database environment is to rely on neither approach completely, but to have applications, systems, and databases share the responsibility for recoverability. This hybrid approach can result in an environment that is much more responsive to user needs, faster, more efficient, and less expensive than a solely database-driven environment.

Security Options

Security issues also present the system developer with options and alternatives. Whether a database has built-in security capabilities or not does not mean that it can't be used to develop secure applications. In cases such as this, it is simply a matter of being sure that the application programs developed to work with the database have within them all of the security mechanisms necessary to protect the data from violation.

On the opposite side of the spectrum are those situations where a product provides security enforcement, and it is decided that these capabilities are not desired. All databases allow the developer to disable security. In fact, disabling security is one of the first things done in the creation of a training environment for programmers or users.

Except for convenience or manageability, however, security overhead is the least expensive of the three administrative profiles we have been considering.

Locking and Concurrency Options

Unfortunately, there is little that the developer can do about turning system concurrency on or off. If you need concurrent access, then the database product provides the best possible means for enforcing it.

The way that locking criteria can be modified, however, does allow the developer to adjust the profile to an optimum arrangement. The lower the lock level (row vs. page vs. construct vs. file), the more expensive the maintenance of the locks. On the other hand, the higher the locking level, the less concurrent the system will be, because more people must wait longer to do their work.

The Administrative Profile Taxonomy

Having completed our discussion the administrative profile, we can conclude with a summarization in taxonomic form.

V. Administrative Taxonomy

  I. Transaction Management Approach

    1. Simple (single user mode)

    2. Data Sharing

    3. Multiple Use

  II. Backup, Logging, and Recovery

    1. Backup Types

      a. Full Backup

      b. Incremental Backup

      c. User Concurrent Backup

      d. Bulk Backup

    2. Logging Options

      a. Log Buffers

    3. Recovery Options

      a. None (use system backups)

      b. Recover Backups Only

      c. Combine Backups with Logs to Recover

  III. Security

    1. Dataset Security

    2. Access Security

      a. None

      b. Autonomous (database logon and password)

      c. Integrated (database and security or operating system)

    3. Internal Security

      a. Using Security Package

      b. Using Data Control Language (DCL) and Catalogs

      c. Using Data Constructor Modification

  IV. Concurrency

    1. Lock Levels

      a. The Entire Database (highest level)

      b. The Dataset

      c. The Data Construct

      d. Tte Page or Block (most common)

      e. The Row or Record (lowest level)

    2. Types of Locks

      a. Read Only

      b. Write and Read

        c. Intent Lock
    3. Lock Invocation
        a. Implicit
        b. Explicit
    4. Lock Disciplines
        a. First In-First out
        b. Lock Timeout Detection
        c. Lock Escalation
        d. Deadlock Detection
    5. Versioning
        a. Multiple Copies of the Same Record/Row
        b. Track Copies, Changes, and Times

Database Profiles Conclusion

With the completion of the definitions for the databases' administrative profile, we complete our discussion of the four profiles that make up a database management system. For each profile we have defined a taxonomy. This provides a vocabulary and scope for the profile and a table, which can be used to help quickly and easily determine the exact characteristics of database products. We have considered these profiles by applying them to some specific database products that best represent the concepts being discussed.

Although the profiles and taxonomies we have developed are far from exhaustive, they do provide the database evaluator with information key to understanding what a database product really is and what it can or cannot do in a given situation.

In Appendix A, you will find a collection of the detailed profile table information for more than 75 database products. These tables, coupled with a short narrative description, make it possible for you to evaluate any database product, its usability, and applicability in a relatively short time.

We continue now, in the next chapter, to consider distributed database capabilities and some of the other future approaches and directions being taken by database vendors.

12

Distribution

In this, our last chapter on the construction and organization of database products, we consider some of the leading edge directions in which these products seem to be heading. This direction has very little to do with advancements in architectures and data storage techniques, but instead, concerns the incorporation of multiple databases, on multiple platforms, into large homogenous *database environments*. This move toward system distribution has been a dream of system developers for some time. Recently, these dreams have started to become a reality as a direct result of the improvements in hardware, telecommunications, and software management.

We begin this chapter by considering several of the reasons, from both a technical and business perspective, for this increased desire to distribute systems. We then consider several of the general industry trends, which support these ends. Given this introduction, we proceed to analyze three approaches to the creation of a distributed database environment, the development of distributed database systems, the use of database machines, and the new generation of macro system architectures (repositories and cross-platform management systems), which tie multiple systems through using a common operation umbrella.

After reviewing the terminology, principles of operation, and some of the product implementations of each of these approaches, we conclude with the development of a taxonomy of distributed database systems and consider some of the strategic implications of these technologies.

Why does Everyone want to Distribute their Systems?

There are many reasons for the great push to distribute database systems. Some of them have to do with trends in organization and economic pressures. Others concenn a desire to decentralize the large MIS organization structures, and a desire to integrate information like it has never been integrated before.

Business Organization and Reasons to Distribute Systems

The last 20 years have seen the birth of entirely new classes of computer power with an ensuing impact on business organization. On the low end of the computer hardware spectrum—PCs—computer power has definitely arrived at the desktop. Almost every major organization is flooded with laptop, desktop, and notebook computer systems. These systems have spread to every corner of most companies, and are continuing to expand their spheres of influence. This overwhelming support for PCs has not been without its drawbacks, however. In the rapidly expanding, easily alterable world of PCs, centralized management and security are weak or nonexistent. The result of this unchecked growth has been to create another whole MIS organization not subject to the same integrity checks that the other traditional MIS organization must adhere to. Although this free-wheeling expansion has its advantages, it makes the coordination, verification, and sharing of data extremely difficult.

The Overburdening of Traditional Systems

At the same time that the PC and workstation platforms have spread, mini and mainframe systems have also continued to grow. Unfortunately, these systems, though managed well, suffer from their own problems. Large, unwieldy systems can become extremely difficult to maintain over time. What's worse, as these systems get larger and older, they become less suitable to change. The result is that organizations pay more and more money to get less and less new productivity out of existing systems.

The obvious method to resolve the problems of both smaller and larger systems, is to integrate them, taking advantage of the strengths that each brings. Small systems bring their versatility, low cost, and ease of use, and large systems bring their ability to handle big volumes of data and manage complex environments well.

Economic Reasons to Distribute Databases

In addition to this organizational imperative to take better advantage of both small and large computer platforms come some significant economic trends.

In the final analysis, the cost of maintaining large centralized data processing centers is constantly increasing. This increase in cost is *not due* to the costs for hardware and software. These costs continue to go down. The real expense incurred is in maintaining and enhancing large older systems. Unfortunately, it is not possible for most companies to simply scrap older systems and start over. Too much depends on their continued operation. No, the only way to control these expenses is to gradually move to more fluid environments.

On the other hand, PCs and workstations continue to grow in their raw computing power. When power is measured in dollars per CPU, these smaller platforms come up with much better profiles than the larger systems. More importantly, the processing speed of these machines continues to increase exponentially. In theory at least, large mainframe and minicomputer systems could be replaced by several dozen workstations producing an equivalent amount of processing power for a fraction of the cost. Of course, there are many reasons why a direct conversion of large centralized systems to smaller distributed ones cannot be done automatically. These issues are being addressed by the builder of distributed database systems.

Not only is computer power getting less expensive, but the telecommunications costs necessary to make distributed systems work are also becoming more affordable. The old days of large computer-driven telecommunications backbones are being replaced by smaller, easier to use, more autonomous local area networks with names like *ethernet* and *token ring*.

Better price/performance ratios for smaller platforms combined with faster, easier to implement, and less expensive network facilities is all of the encouragement most organizations need to tackle the problems associated with distributing systems.

The Bigger Picture: The Development of a Data Warehouse

Although the innovations in the areas of computer power and telecommunications certainly serve as catalysts for the development of these systems, an even stronger push is generated by the desire of managers of large systems to create large, homogenous superdatabases. In the minds of these visionaries, every computer that a company owns, whether it is a PC, workstation, mini or mainframe, would be connected in the formation of one incredibly large data bank. In this world, all users, no matter what type of computer or terminal they happen to be using, could access data from anywhere else in the company with the simple execution of a data request. In the ultimate execution of this dream, that user could make such requests without any knowledge of where the data actually physically resides. The system would take care of it all.

The distributed database approaches that we will discuss, both the traditionally-defined distributive techniques, and the more radical database machine and global repository approaches, all have the attainment of this long-term goal on their horizons. As we shall see, each contributes something to the possibility of creating this fully-integrated world, and yet none of them alone provides all of the answers.

So Why Distribute Systems?

So why does anyone want to distribute their systems? There are many answers to this question, and all of them will be true for certain situations. Let's examine some of the bigger reasons.

1. *The cost of computer hardware*

Mainframe and minicomputers have continued to be numbered among the most expensive acquisitions organizations make. The amount of computer power that a mainframe provides per dollar spent continues to be much higher than the power per dollar from the smaller workstation and PC products. If 100 workstations, at a cost of $10,000 a piece (100 x $10,000 = $1,000,000) can provide the same CPU, memory, and disk storage space as one mainframe costing $5,000,000, then getting the work done with the workstations makes more sense. Of course, this is possible only if those 100 workstations can operate in harmony.

2. *The versatility vs. performance trade-off*

On several occasions, we have cited situations where a system developer must choose between the versatility provided by one solution against the efficiencies of scale that large megasystems can produce. These trade-offs must be faced when selecting a database architecture, when determining a programming environment, and when deciding on a platform configuration. When system builders open up the possibilities provided by distributed systems, many, if not all of these trade-off decisions can be avoided.

With a distributed system, developers can eat their cake and have it too. By mixing and matching the efficiencies and programming interfaces of mainframe, mini, workstation, and PC solutions, many systems can be developed using a heterogeneous approach that is both cost effective and robust.

3. *The sophistication of users*

Many users in large organizations are no longer satisfied with the simple transaction processing and process management applications currently provided. These users want to take advantage of word processing packages, desktop publishing software, and spreadsheets to enhance their performance capabilities. Only a hybrid platform solution, a *distributed database system* can allow them this capability.

4. *The nature of new technologies*

The newer technologies require extensive management of screen displays. Graphical user interfaces, *What-if* query managers, and statistical and graphical management packages must have a computer dedicated to the management of these graphical displays. A sophisticated graphical display terminal can have as much as 16 megabytes of memory dedicated to the management of the screen alone. *That's more memory than mainframe computers had not too many years ago.*

These new technologies require distributed system configurations to make optimum use of the capabilities that they have.

By distributing systems, developers take advantage of the inherent strengths and weaknesses of different hardware alternatives and put those processes that are better managed at the local level into the hands of those individuals.

Terminology and Symbols

To assist us in our discussions about distributive approaches we employ the following sets of terminology and symbols. This helps show in a graphical way how these approaches differ.

When discussing the distribution process in general, we will use simple boxes and lines.

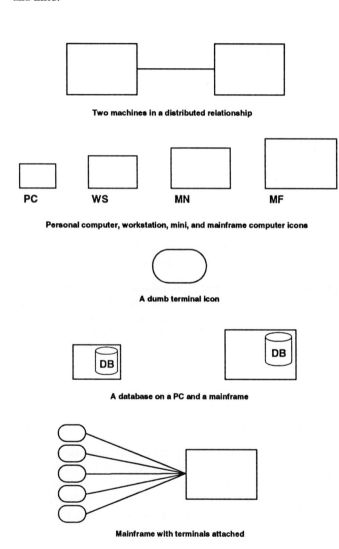

Two machines in a distributed relationship

Personal computer, workstation, mini, and mainframe computer icons

A dumb terminal icon

A database on a PC and a mainframe

Mainframe with terminals attached

Figure 12-1: Diagram symbols

To describe configurations that use different size platforms, we use boxes of different sizes and a short abbreviation for the platform type. PCs are represented by the smallest boxes. Workstations are identified with a slightly larger box and the letters WS. Minis and mainframes are correspondingly larger, and use MINI and MF as abbreviations.

When referring to *dumb* terminals—user terminals with no processing power of their own—the box is shown with rounded corners.

The place where the database software resides is indicated by a small box with the letters DB enclosed. The physical location of stored data—the machine to which disk space is attached—is signified by the cylinder symbol.

The preceding symbols help us show the topology (physical arrangement of components) of a distributed system. They do not however, help us display the different ways that work is distributed throughout the system. In order to do this, we refer to both the system's database profiles (previously discussed) and the location of that profile's processing and the systems programming functionalities. Specifically these are presentation of data, processing of data, enforcement of business rules, and management of data access, and the places where these are executed.

Distributed Databases Overview

Before considering the many ways that database systems can be distributed, let's consider just exactly what a distributed database is and what it is not.

A distributed database approach involves a multiple-platform application development environment. This splits the traditionally platform-bound database profile and application development functions across those platforms in a way that seems transparent to end users. In other words, a distributed database approach uses databases to split operations across different machines but doesn't let the user know that it's been done.

Before delving more deeply into the area of distributed *database* systems, let's consider some distributed *data* configurations and see how these differ.

Distributed Data Approaches

Assuming that a developer desires to share data between different devices, the first decision that should be made is exactly how that sharing needs to be done. There are several options to choose from, none of which has anything to do with databases. Assuming the appropriate telecommunications software is in place, the developer can take advantage of file movement, download/upload capabilities, shared files, and virtual disks.

File Movement

The first and most obvious way to move data from one device to another is to create a file holding the data, and write that file to a tape or floppy disk. The tape or disk can then be carried to the target machine and loaded. This solution is humorously called *sneakernet*, a reference to shoes. Although simple and cumbersome, this method has been used for years and is often a sufficient solution to the problem.

Download/Upload

The second way to arrange sharing is to upload or download physical files from one device to the other. In this operation, a temporary telecommunications link is established between the two machines, and a file is physically passed from one device to the other.

Shared Files (Virtual Disks)

The virtual disk method allows one device to act as if a second device's disk drives are its own. For example, it is possible to make a user's UNIX logon ID and its data appear as the D: drive of a PC. The PC operator can then write to, read from, create, and delete files on this D: drive, just as if the drive was on the PC. In reality, the data being manipulated is physically attached to the mainframe.

These three methods can be used to share data between machines. They are limited, of course, because they are all based on the movement and manipulation of files. Of course, these techniques require the user to know where data is coming from, and where it is going. In addition to this, none of these operations involve the kinds of functionalities that databases provide. Many organizations demand that data sharing be at a much lower level than this. In other words, the objective is to share access to a database, not simply to data.

The data sharing approaches have several positive characteristics:

- They are inexpensive
- They are simple
- They can be easy to manage

Unfortunately, the functionality they provide is limited.

Distributed Database Approaches

There are almost an infinite number of ways for a manufacturer to distribute database functionalities across platforms. Luckily, there are four main configurations that most vendors adhere to, with several distinct variations. We will consider these four: common physical data, client-server configurations, fully-distributed, and data replication systems.

The Common Physical Data Approach to Distribution

You may recall from the last chapter, *The Administrative Profile*, we discussed locking capabilities and multiuser PC systems. This arrangement defines the simplest distributed database configuration we will discuss. Under this arrangement, multiple versions of the database code run on different PCs. All of these computers, however, share the same physical data stored on a common disk device.

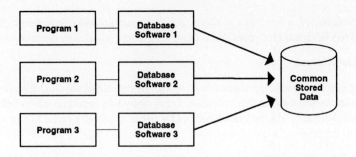

Under the shared data approach, multiple versions of the database code are run, one version for each user. This kind of arrangement takes many forms

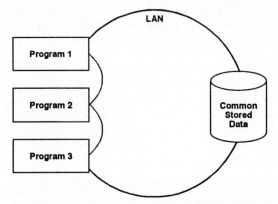

In this case, several PCs, each running a copy of the database software, share a common physical dataset. This differs from a client-server organization in that the common data area has no intelligence or database software associated with it. Each PC manages its own database environment.

Figure 12-2: Common physical data distribution

Since each PC sees the same physical disk as a virtual disk, multiple versions of the database are able to use the same data.

To guarantee the integrity and concurrency of individual transactions, however, the system must provide some kind of locking mechanism. In most situations, the database is able to maintain simple locking services through native operating system or network data locking mechanisms. These mechanisms provide for locking files or individual records with internal lock tables and record offset addresses.

The common data approach has several limitations. First, the amount of concurrency possible when locks are managed in this manner is much lower than for systems with memory-managed locking. More importantly, the overall administrative profile for a system of this kind is very weak. Each program running against the database must enforce its own locking, security, and recoverability profiles since there really is no one copy of the database software responsible for these services.

Client-Server Configurations

The client-server configuration provides a much more usable distributive arrangement of database processing. In the client-server arrangement, each pair of machines involved in the system has a special, predefined relationship. One is defined as the client, or the system that requires database services. The other is called the server, or the database services provider.

Let's begin by considering some of the more generic ways that this split of functionality can be accomplished.

The Traditional Client-Server Arrangement

In the traditional client-server arrangement, the client machine maintains full responsibility for the processing requirements (profile) of the system. All programs are written and run on the client. The other three database profiles, administration, architecture, and storage management are managed by the server machine.

Application functionalities, presentation, processing, and rules enforcement are controlled by client processes, while data access work is done by the server machine.

In other words, in the traditional client-server arrangement, programs are written to run on client machines. These programs make database calls that are transported over the network to the server machine, which then retrieves the data and sends it back to the client.

Modifying the Relationship between Client and Server

Of course, with the new and more powerful relational databases that have appeared on the distributed market, this simple client-server model can be modified significantly. By adding the features of database programmability to the mix, the balance of power and the performance expense incurred by clients and servers can be adjusted to place more work on the server and take work away from the client.

The ability to perform this shift can have a great impact on the development of a client-server-based system, and makes client-server arrangements some of the easiest to tune. In a single-platform database environment, if the processing load on the platform becomes too great, there is very little that the developer can do about it other then to retune the database or rewrite the programs. With the variable client-server arrangements, it is possible actually to shift the processing load from the client to the server when necessary. This can be particularly helpful when the client machines, which tend to be smaller and less expensive than servers, become overworked by the processing load.

Using Structurally-Defined Business Rules Enforcement

If the developer of a client-server system uses the structurally-defined rules enforcement capabilities (like referential integrity and constraint enforcement), a

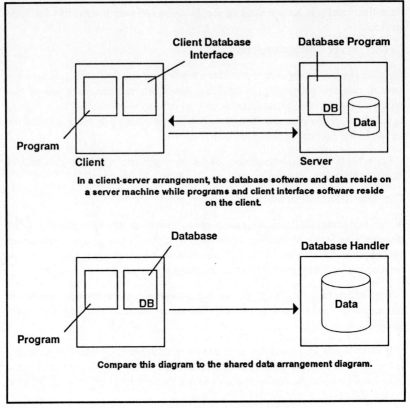

In a client-server arrangement, the database software and data reside on
a server machine while programs and client interface software reside
on the client.

Compare this diagram to the shared data arrangement diagram.

Figure 12-3: The client-server arrangement

significant portion of the programming load is shifted from the client to the server
machine.

Another way to look at it is to say that the business rules enforcement functionality has been shifted from the processing machine (client) to the database platform
(server).

It is important to note that the net processing power to perform the work has not
been alleviated, only shifted from one platform to the other. This is true in all cases
of shifts of this kind.

Command-Driven Stored Procedures

By extensively using command-driven stored procedures, the system developer
shifts even more processing requirements from the client to the server.

Making as Much of a Shift as Possible

Of course, if triggers, stored procedures, and business rules enforcement all are invoked on the server side, then only the task of data presentation is left for programmers to worry about.

On the other hand, the work load on the server machine will be significantly greater than originally envisioned, and the management of that machine will be made correspondingly complex.

Administrative Considerations and Simple Client-Server Arrangements

In the simple client-server situations just described, the administrative complications remain relatively stagnant. Since the one server machine is managing all of the database activity itself, it can manage the security, concurrency, and recovery mechanisms in a manner similar to that of a single-platform environment.

Of course, things are never quite that simple. What happens when the client-server model is expanded to include more than one server at a time? Suppose for example that one client wants to perform an operation involving data from two different servers. What needs to be modified in order to make this possible?

Administrative Profiles for Complex Client-Server Systems

In order to manage a complex client-server environment effectively, the database system must provide the means for the logging, backup, recovery, and concurrency assurance of transactions over which they have only partial control. There are two ways that this can be managed.

One way is to assign one database as the *master*, which keeps track of all requests for data operations between different systems, and makes sure that concurrency and recoverability are maintained. The Objectivity-DB object-oriented database is a good example of a product that takes this approach to distributed environment management. You may recall that under Objectivity-DB, a special type of object, called the *federated object*, took responsibility for the traffic of distributed activities across several database objects, which could reside on different platforms.

The other way to manage distribution is to establish protocols and rules of conduct that all databases in the environment adhere to. Under this organization, each database has the potential to act as the master for those transactions that are initiated from its work area. The Sybase, Informix, and Interbase relational database products are good examples of products that use this approach.

One rule of conduct standard for most client-server database configurations is called the *two-phase commit* arrangement. Under two-phase commit, the normal decision to commit a portion of database work or to roll it back is postponed until the client requesting the operation receives a validation message from each of the server databases it is working with. If the client receives all commit messages, it

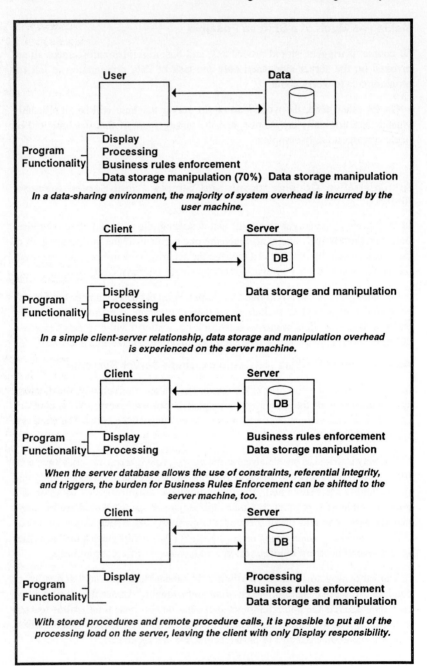

Figure 12-4: Shift of processing responsibility

knows that the data has been successfully inserted, deleted, or altered. If the follow-up commit message is missed, then it knows that something is wrong.

The Different Client-Server Arrangements

Before adding any more complication to our model of how client-server systems can work, let's stop to consider some specific database products and hardware topologies that utilize this approach.

When most people think of client-server computing, they usually envision an environment where PCs work as the clients, and either a workstation, mini or, mainframe is the server.

The workstation/PC combination is probably the most popular arrangement in recent years, and many products, like Informix, Interbase, Oracle, and Sybase have built the majority of their business on these configurations. Under this arrangement, several PCs are connected to each other through a local area network (LAN), like Ethernet or Token Ring, and then the entire network is hooked into a workstation server machine. Application programs are then written on the PC platforms, and any need for commonly-defined data is accessed through the LAN client-server connection.

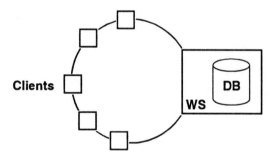

Figure 12-5: A PC-LAN client-server arrangement

Another popular configuration combines PCs and mainframes. These arrangements, like the workstation-based ones, attempt to leverage the convenience of the PC with the power of mainframe database systems into an optimum sharing of work loads.

Of course, in reality, any two hardware platforms, even two computers that are exactly the same, can be set up in a client-server relationship; workstation-to-workstation, mainframe-to-mainframe, or any combination of different machines. If the machines can be connected with a telecommunications line, there is a good chance that there is a database vendor who can provide a complementary client-server offering.

Up until this point, we have spent most of our time talking about client-server arrangements as if they were simple two- or three-platform organizations. In reality,

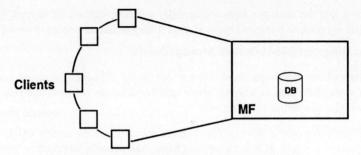

Figure 12-6: A PC-mainframe client-server relation

the size and complexity of a client-server relationship is limited only by the physical
limitations of network hardware and software.

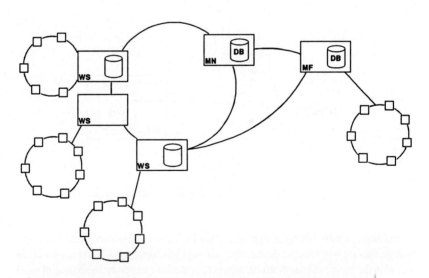

In this environment, each user has access to all databases on the network through several
client-server relationships.

Figure 12-7: A full-blown client-server arrangement

It is quite common to find dozens, or even sometimes hundreds of computers linked into a massive maze of client-server functionalities.

The following section addresses four ways of categorizing client-server arrangements.

Simple Client-Server Relationships: Read-Only

The client-server method of distribution involves placing two separate physical devices into a specific relationship to each other. The machine requiring information is called the client machine. The one providing information is called the server. The client machine sends a data access request (a database call like an SQL command) to a second machine set up to receive these calls, gather up the data requested, and send it back to the requestor. In the this configuration, the client can request data from only one server at a time, and cannot write any data to the server database.

Simple Client-Server Relationships: Read/Write

In the read/write arrangement, the client not only reads data on the server, but can actually make changes to it. This additional functionality forces the server machine to be much more sophisticated. All of the issues involving logical units of work, change control, and security must be addressed. The server must be prepared to handle those situations where it or its client may fail in the middle of an operation.

Complex Client-Server Relationships: Read-Only

In some situations, the ability to work with one server at a time is not sufficient. By using the SQL language, it is possible for a client machine to request a join of data between two tables in different physical locations. The database software necessary to support this kind of sophistication must therefore accomplish an additional level of functionality.

Complex Client-Server Relationships: Read/Write

The most complex capability to require of a client-server relationship is to allow writing to these disparate servers at the same time.

The client-server approach is only one way of addressing database distribution, however. There are two other major approaches worth considering.

Fully-Distributed Systems

What would happen if a large network of client-server relationships was modified so that each machine was both a potential client of the other machines and a potential server at the same time. This would come pretty close to defining what is meant by a *fully-distributed* database system. This is the deluxe method of database distribution. With full distribution, the concept of client-server is carried to its ultimate extreme. In the fully distributed environment every database is considered to be both a potential client and server to any other machine. In addition to this, the actual location of data is considered to be irrelevant. In the fully distributed

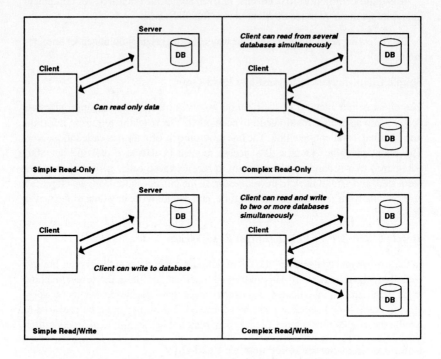

Figure 12-8: Read-only and read/write arrangements

environment, a data request (an SQL command in most cases) is submitted to the
network without regard for where the data may happen to be located. Under normal
client-server processing, the client must know where the data being requested
resides. Each node knows whether it has the information the client has requested
or not, and if it does not it passes the request from one node to the next until one
of them provides an answer. This type of distribution is both the most powerful and
the most expensive of the distributed database options. The Oracle, Ingres, Datacom, and Interbase products are representative of this type of database.

Data Replication Services

In conjunction with the other distributed database approaches, many vendors are
beginning to offer another kind of distribution called *data replication*. In a data
replication environment, full or partial copies of the physical database are made on
each of the machines involved. In the distributed arrangements discussed so far,
the user on one machine issues commands that work against the databases located
on other machines. With this arrangement, the user works only with a local *copy*
of the data, but the local database being accessed remains synchronized with the
databases on other platforms through a background synchronization mechanism.

In this way, each database can service the data requests it receives immediately and efficiently without needing to poll the other machines on the network. The thing that distinguishes replication services from the simple copying of data from one machine to the next is that multiple copies of the same database are kept in synch by the database software itself.

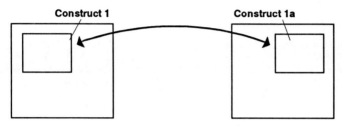

With full replication services, an exact copy of a construct is kept on a separate platform. Any changes made to one copy are applied to the other automatically.

Figure 12-9: Database replication

If there are two systems (system A and B) each with a fully-replicated copy of a database, and a change is made to data on system A, the distributed database system makes the same change to the data on system B and vice versa.

There are three ways replication services are executed depending on what the developer is trying to accomplish and the available system resources.

In a full implementation, the data constructs are duplicated in full on both systems. So if system A holds a table called Animal with 100,000 rows of animal data and 10 columns of information, a duplicate animal table could be found on system B, which would also have 10 columns and 100,000 rows.

In a *horizontal* distribution, the rows of the table are split between machines. For example, imagine all of the fish records are kept on system A and all dog records on system B.

In a *vertical* distribution, certain columns reside on system A while others are on B. For example, customer name and address go to system A, while customer payment records and credit history go to B. In this case, both tables have 100,000 rows, but each has half of the complete set of columns.

Partial distribution (horizontal and vertical) allows the system developer to optimize performance based on the concept of putting data where it is most needed.

Efficiency and Replication Services

While the replication of data can be very expensive for organizations, especially regarding the cost of disk space (which is doubled), the differences in user response time are significant. A system that doesn't require the user to wait while data requests cross platform boundaries definitely looks better to those users. On the other hand, the additional cost in CPU and system complication can be offsetting conditions. For those situations where access time and cross-platform synchronicity is of paramount importance, replication can provide an optimum solution.

Trade-Offs Involved in Using Each Method

Assuming that all databases working on all platforms could provide all of the distribution methods considered (which they *cannot* do), what are the benefits and liabilities that an organization can expect by using each method?

Several issues must be considered in order to make this determination. Each distribution arrangement provides trade-offs of the following costs and benefits:

- *Hardware cost*—Is it necessary to buy additional or more powerful hardware devices (disk drives or CPUs) to support this approach?

- *Telecommunication cost*—How much additional expense will be involved in the purchase of telecommunications facilities?

- *Software cost*—Must additional software be purchased?

- *Development cost—What additional programming efforts are required?*

- *Ease of use*—How manageable is the environment created by this approach?

- *Concurrency*—How well will the distributed data be kept synchronized?

- *Security*—How secure will the data be?

- *Timeliness*—How quickly will changes to data be propagated throughout the system?

- *Redundancy— How many additional copies of the same data must be kept?*

- *Administrative cost—What is the administrative burden of this solution?*

Database Products and Distributed Systems

Different database products take different approaches to managing the distribution of database services. Some products, like Sybase, were originally designed with distribution in mind. Others, like DB2, are being retrofitted to support distributed functionalities. No matter what the origin of the product or its current organization, the list of distributed database capabilities and concerns involving distribution must be added to the list that we have already developed.

Host or *server* databases are products that function as free-standing, fully-functional databases in and of themselves. In addition, they also serve as the source of data management for a distributed system. The client, or user of a host database, can be either a programming product or another database. For a programming product to be considered the client component of a client-server system, it must be a program that resides on a physical platform other than the one that the host system resides on. The presence of client-server database technology has led to the creation of a new program support product called *database client* software. This software is not a database, but allows programs and users on remote platforms to access host databases through their pre-established gateway.

Multiplatform Database Products

There are several ways that database distribution can be established. One way is to simply allow two versions of the same database product, running on two physically separate but compatible machines, to operate as one distributed system. For example, IBM's DB2 allows two DB2 systems, operating on distinct MVS-based 3090 mainframes, to communicate and work together. This is called *homogenous distribution*.

Another, more challenging arrangement, induces two versions of the same database, running on two different platforms, to work in harmony. For example, the Oracle database allows distributed systems to be established between Unix and DEC platforms. This is referred to as *heterogeneous hardware* distribution arrangements.

The most challenging distribution approach of all is accomplished when two different database products, running on two different platforms, work together as one distributed system. These are called *fully heterogeneous* systems.

A list of products that provide both fully-distributed capabilities over several platforms would include Oracle, Ingres Star, Datacom, and Interbase.

Products providing client-server capabilities include Informix, Sybase, XDB, and SQLBase.

Upsizing and Downsizing Database Products

Of course, developing products that work in a cooperative, distributed manner is only one way that manufacturers attempt to expand their customer base and broaden their control over the computer systems market. Many manufacturers are in the process of *upsizing* or *downsizing* their products in order to sell their products in other vendors' markets. The term downsizing refers to the creation of versions of database software that originally runs on a large platform, such as a mainframe, and creating a version of that product that runs on a smaller platform, like a PC. Upsizing is the opposite.

For example, the dBASE products, a giant in the PC database market, has begun marketing versions for Unix, mini, and mainframe computers. The large mainframe database vendors of products like IDMS, Datacom, ADABAS, and Supra are in the process of developing and marketing mini, Unix, and PC versions of their products.

This upsizing or downsizing can be done for several reasons. First, it is a simple attempt to extend market share; to take some business away from competitors. Second, many system developers are demanding the versatility to do develop on one platform while running production on another. This is especially true in the case of large mainframe-driven organizations that cannot afford to allow their expensive mainframe CPUs to be used for system development. For these organizations, using a downsized version of the mainframe database on a mini or PC allows them to develop applications more cost effectively. Third, and probably the most important, is that many companies are attempting to move their products in the direction of distributed systems. But they can do that, they need to have products that run well in all of the different environments before they can tie them together.

The IBM Distributed Database Strategy

As opposed to database upsizing or downsizing, IBM has developed a comprehensive distributed database strategy using its existing relational database products:

- DB2—for the large mainframes (MVS operating system)

- SQL/DS—for small and midsize mainframes (VM and DOS/VSE)

- SQL400—for the AS/400 minicomputer

- OS2/EE-DM—for the PS/2 and PC/AT and XT platforms

This strategy has already seen some integration of this disparate platforms (DB2 and SQL/DS specifically), and is scheduled to continue rolling out improved connectivity.

The DEC Distributed Database Strategy

Digital Equipment Corporation has taken a different approach to posturing for a distributed database world. Under the DEC strategy, the RDB relational database is considered to be central to the capability. DEC provides several products for the binding of disparate DEC hardware and software to a command RDB database, and then ties that database to the non-DEC world through DECnet and the RDBAccess gateway.

Although single-vendor solutions to multiplatform distribution offer one approach to the problem, these solutions tend to favor the hardware of the vendor sponsoring the initiative. There are of course other ways to go about this task.

Distributed Strategies and Partnerships

Yet another factor in the ongoing struggle to accomplish distributed database capabilities is the current trend between the sellers of computer hardware and software to establishment of alliances or partnerships. There are several kinds of partnerships to be aware of.

Hardware/Software Partnerships

Some hardware manufacturers are joining with database software vendors to develop joint strategies that benefit both parties. These partnerships establish common research and development budgets, which offer staffing agreements in exchange for information and joint marketing activities that better address the needs of their customers.

Hardware/Hardware Partnerships

There are also partnerships being established between hardware manufacturers, the most notable one between IBM and Apple. In this case, both hardware and database capabilities could become integrated at a very basic level.

Software/Software Partnerships

Last, but not least, are the pairings of software development companies. One of the best examples of this is the partnering of IBM with several relational database manufacturers to help develop a joint heterogeneous database strategy.

Acquisitions and Take-Overs

Although not to be considered partnerships in the truest sense of the word, software company acquisitions are another way that database product integration can occur. Some of the larger software manufacturers have developed reputations for buying up competitive or complementary companies. When these buy outs occur, the vendor is better able to control the compatibility of products.

Standards Committees

Several standard-setting bodies, including ANSI and several open systems advocacy groups, are working diligently in an attempt to create a body of common standards which the sellers of both hardware and software products can adhere to. As these alliances and integration efforts continue, more and more progress should be evident as time goes on. Of particular import is SAG(the SQL Access Group) which is trying to develop standard rules for the deployment of distributed SQL access between vendors products.

As all of this activity continues, however, the burden will fall upon the individual practitioner and the vendors to stay informed as to the capabilities and limitations of each approach. It is not uncommon for a new product, which does exactly what you need, to be a complete mystery to you, simply because it was released recently. There is no way for all products to get equal publicity everywhere in a short amount of time. In the meantime, the understanding and exploitation of database technologies and especially distributed database capabilities will remain a moving target.

Database Machines

Database machines represent a slightly different approach to the development of a distributed environment. The database machine itself is nothing more than a piece of computer hardware dedicated to the delivery of database services to anyone that requests them. By dedicating these functions to a hardware platform, the manufacturer is able to build a machine finely tuned, and completely dedicated to, the providing of database architectural, storage management,and administrative functions. This means that a database machine can perform the same work as a software-based database, but more efficiently and economically. Remember, database software must share computer resources with an operating system, multiple users, multiple programs, and myriad other resource demanders. By isolating database functions to a single machine, it is possible to take advantage of hardware features that a software-based database cannot. A database machine concentrates solely on the storage and retrieval of data as quickly as possible.

In order to be usable, the database machine must be connected to a conventional computer—be it a PC, workstation, mini or mainframe—and provide a mechanism for the passing back and forth of data requests and data results. This is usually done in the same manner as client-server systems. In fact, one way to look at a database machine is to consider it a dedicated server in a client-server arrangement.

The programming functions of presentation, processing and business rules enforcement are handled by the clients, while database functionalities are handled by the database machine.

One of the more popular database machines is the Teradata DBC1012. This database can be linked to DEC, IBM, or any of a number of other LAN- or network-based systems. The database product itself provides a relational architecture with its own unique storage management profile. Refer to Appendix A for a description of the Teradata product.

Under the Teradata storage management scheme, the data for a table is stored using a hashing algorithm, which spreads data across several disk areas. The machine then takes advantage of multiple dedicated data-search CPUs to locate and process those rows of data. While a conventional computer must queue up database I/O operations using the same CPU, a database machine is able to spread the work across several CPUs and therefore get the data back a lot faster.

Secondary indexes are also provided using the same basic hashing and distribution approach.

Database machines have found their way into many different data processing organizations. Their history of successfully serving many different processing needs indicates that they should continue to find niches where their solutions provide an optimum combination of hardware, software, and database functionalities.

Global System-Management Solutions

While distributed databases and database machines represent approaches to the fundamental mechanics of how to integrate disparate systems, they do not address many of the issues necessary to make an environment like that practical.

The ability to distribute databases is one thing, the ability to make the power that distribution implies available to all users is another. In order to make large, multiplatform, multidatabase environments truly manageable and transparent to users requires that some additional resources be allocated. It is in an attempt to fill this role that the global system-management solutions position themselves.

Making Megasystems Work

Stop for a moment and imagine an environment made up of hundreds of PC databases and dozens of workstation, mini, and mainframe systems. By logging onto any of these systems, the user is able to access all of them with a simple data request.

How usable would a system like that be? How would a single user be able to locate anything, with literally thousands of tables and files to choose from? Even if the data could be found, how could one user possibly be familiar with all of the peculiarities the individual database products require? A technically elegant solution to the problem of distributing databases is not especially a functional one. .

What *is* required in order to implement a system of this kind is an organization scheme that makes it all manageable.

There are three approaches to the development of a heterogeneous, megadatabase environment we will consider. None is a fully-developed solution yet, but all of them attempt to address the underlying issues. These methods are the hardware vendor-sponsored solutions, software vendor solutions, and industry standards-setting solutions.

The real key to making systems like this work, is the provision of a dictionary or repository, which keeps track of the locations, nature, and rules for the management of the many different data constructs being managed. Although many of these solutions involve a repository of some kind, most of them are in the early stages of development. It should be several years before a mature, dependable repository manager becomes available.

In the meantime, the repository manager will continue to be the hot new topic of discussion. Although we only mention repository management systems here, we will consider the more theoretical aspects of their design in the chapter about design and modelling.

Hardware Vendor-Sponsored Solutions

Of the three types of solutions to the physical building of a global system-management environment, the most comprehensive are proposed by the hardware vendors themselves. It is in the self interest of most major hardware builders to develop products that can be plugged into a large, homogenous application development supersystem like the one we have described.

The vendor who can provide an assortment of products that all can be integrated will have a strategic advantage over the vendors who cannot. More importantly, the manufacturer that can show customers how its products can be used to manage other manufacturers' products will create the opportunity to gain even more sales.

In an effort to position themselves as *the platforms* on which to build these systems, each of the major vendors has published its own strategic direction statements and implemented unique integration approaches. We consider three of these directions, those proposed by DEC, IBM, and Unisys.

The DEC Solution

Digital Equipment Corporation has announced the creation of an integrated CASE (computer-aided software engineering) application development environment called Cohesion. Cohesion, in conjunction with the DEC distributed database strategy, will define a fully-operational, integrated, megadatabase environment that incorporates DEC, OS2, Macintosh, and MS-DOS platforms.

Included with the Cohesion is the definition for the DEC CDD/Repository, which will serve as both data dictionary and repository manager for the systems being created. The DEC strategy is based on a strong commitment to object-oriented principles of design and implementation.

The IBM Solution

IBM's attempt to define a fully-integrated database world is made up of three separate strategy directions. SAA, or the Systems Application Architecture, defines a set of standards for the consistent definition of interfaces and protocols between application development, user interface, telecommunication, and other hardware and software components. AD/Cycle provides a blueprint for building integrated application development environments using multiple modeling, design, and CASE products. To top off the strategy is the MVS/Repository, a product designed to serve as the overall system manager and component integrator. Under the IBM solution, entity-relationship modelling provides the theoretical foundation.

The Unisys Solution

In its attempts to integrate multiple platform systems, Unisys has developed the Infoexec initiative. Infoexec provides the developer with an integrated data dictionary facility and tools allowing users to build, manipulate, and manage databases at different locations using one common set of reporting, accessing, and administrative procedures. The Unisys model is based on fundamental semantic data modeling principles.

Although the hardware vendor-sponsored proposals provide one approach to the development of integrated system solutions, these solutions are still far from comprehensive or economical. Because of this, and the generally immature nature of the approaches, many organizations are turning to the software vendor-sponsored solutions instead.

Software Vendor-Sponsored Solutions

While the hardware vendors struggle with the many physical, logical, and operation issues that the comprehensive integration of their systems require, software vendors have been able to integrate systems at a much higher level. Although far from being elegant or highly-efficient solutions in some cases, these solutions do provide the ease of use and functionality that many organizations need.

Many large software vendors (like Computer Associates and Borland) have taken an approach similar to that of the hardware vendors, publishing strategy documents and attempting to build the fully-integrated world by migrating existing products in that direction.

Others have modified their architectures and internal organization to work as superclient systems, which can serve as the client to several different database servers. Under this arrangement the database product itself functions as the intermediary between the user and the foreign databases.

The easiest way to create an almost transparent interface to multiple database servers is for the vendor to build foreign database calls and call converters into their own 4GLs. Typical of this approach is the Focus database's user language, which allows users to access the data from dozens of different databases with a standard set of database calls.

Although hardware and software vendor-solutions can help the developer build a customized solution, a truly long-range solution would be able to work with any hardware, any software, and any telecommunications environment at any time. In order to do this, however, a set of standards and policies would need to exist. These would cross all vendor lines. The development of these kinds of standards is being spearheaded by many standards-setting committees, the most prominent of which is the OSF (Open Systems Foundation). OSF has attempted to define physical and logical interface standards that all products can adhere to.

Conclusion

In the preceding pages, we have considered from a very cursory perspective the approaches that hardware, software, and standards-setting organizations are taking to define megadatabase environments. Only the future will tell us which of these approaches, if any, will finally claim dominance in the marketplace.

Of all the issues discussed in this chapter, it is clear that whether we are talking about distributed databases, database machines, or the integrated multiplatform multidatabase, that the level of complication and frustration when working with a single-platform database is increased exponentially.

In the multiple database environment, the normally critical issues of performance, tuning, and overall system manageability are made hundreds of times more complex. This is because the developer must learn not only to deal with the idiosyncrasies of each product, but must also take into account the networks, client-server relationships, and other paradigms that make the distributed database world something entirely different from the single database world. For better or worse, distributed databases and their related complexities are here to stay and will continue to grow across organizations as the needs for better and more integrated information increase.

This chapter concludes our discussions about database products and physical functionalities. In the next chapters we turn to the investigation of the conceptual, logical, and organization issues of actually building an effective database system.

Chapter

13

Database Design: Introduction

Throughout our investigation of database systems, we have concentrated solely on the operation, mechanical, and managerial aspects of databases. We have purposely minimized any discussion about how actually to build these systems for several reasons.

First, a good understanding of what is involved in the development of a solid design is dependent, to a large degree, on having a good understanding of how the database system works. Second, all design techniques are not equally effective for each kind of database. In fact, the art of effective database design is impossible without a good understanding of the architecture paradigms with which you will be working. Third, although the first phase of the design process—modeling—can be conducted without knowing which database product is being used, the second and third phases are impossible without an intimate knowledge of the product itself.

Like so many other areas of database technology, the definition of design, how it should be performed, and how to tell a good one from a bad one are subject to a lot of controversy, inconsistencies, theories, approaches, disciplines and paradigms.

We attempt to develop a definition and a taxonomy that combines most of the approaches and perspectives on the design process into a comprehensive, consistent model of what design is, and how it is done.

What is the Design Process?

We define the overall database design process as that collection of processes, disciplines, and guidelines whose principal functions are to help in the development of an efficient, effective, manageable, stable, and usable physical database implementation. In other words, design is the process of building database systems, and the objective of the design process is to turn the developer's ideas about what the system needs to do into a real working system that does those things, and does them well.

The Subjectivity of Design

Obviously, this definition of the design process is very open-ended. How do you define efficient? How are usable, stable, and manageable defined? It is people's interpretations of those terms that make design the most controversial part of any systems development project.

The fact of the matter is, different people have different perspectives on what a good design should deliver. Depending on the experience and prejudices of the person reviewing the design, their assessment can be quite different. To some people, a design might look great, while the same design could be shunned as terrible by another.

Criteria by which Designs can be Judged

The objective of the design process can be many, often contradictory, things. A design can be judged based on how well the system performs, by how manageable the system is, by how friendly it is to end users, or by how dependably it performs. Ultimately, the database designer must somehow include all of these criteria into the actual database implementation.

Informal Design

The first concept to clear up in everyone's mind is that, like it or not, all systems are built using some kind of design. It is impossible to build anything without beginning with some picture of how it should look and act. Unfortunately or fortunately, depending on your perspective, the vast majority of database design decisions are made without the benefit of very much formal design at all. Depending on the nature of the system being built, its size and scope, and the experience of the designer, it will more often than not be an informal undertaking.

The Value of Experience in Designing

In many ways, design is much more of an art than a science. Even though there are formally-defined techniques that can help people make good design decisions, the acid test of any system is not how elegant the design is, but how well it works. One of the quickest ways to sabotage a database project is to rely too heavily on formally-defined techniques and guidelines during the design phase. Design and modeling are helpful starting points for the beginning of a design endeavor, but they are not panaceas or cookbooks to be followed with impunity. There is no such thing as a best design. There are good designs, which are identified by the good systems they support. There are also bad designs, which seem to make the work of administrators, programmers, users, and managers harder. *There is no substitute for practical experience and common sense in the development of database designs!*

For the rigid formalist, we discuss the formal modeling, construct design, and tuning techniques as a road map to the design process. We do this with the understanding that these disciplines must be applied with discretion and flexibility. For the old salt practitioner, who has no time for such wasteful activities, we provide the same analysis, with the hope that even the experienced designer can see value in reviewing some of the basics.

Design and Paradigms

Throughout this book, we have referred to paradigms and the fact that different database products provide a unique combination of programming, architecture, storage management, and administrative profiles. These create for that product a unique operation paradigm.

The most seriously-botched design jobs are those engineered by people who go into the process with incorrect assumptions about the appropriate paradigms to use with a given product. It is the people who think they know how to design a system using database A because they have a lot of experience with product B that make false assumptions about access, storage, and system tuning. They wind up with a disastrous end product.

How then can anyone but a person experienced with a particular database know how to do an effective job of designing? It's very simple; they can't unless they begin at the outset by admitting their own lack of familiarity and seek help for those areas.

For example, a person with a lot of experience building large mainframe, 3GL- and 4GL-programmed, relational DB2 databases cannot simply step over to a PC and begin designing databases for an RBase system. In this case, the mainframe designer who does have experience with relational databases but has no experience with PCs, the RBase product, or the programming environment, is in danger of carrying over too many assumptions from the previous environment. The DB2 designer would probably have a much easier time designing another mainframe database system like IDMS or Datacom, where the architecture profile has shifted, but the others remain consistent.

Our discussions so far have been about the general nature of design and the design process. We begin now with our formal introduction.

The Three Phases of the Design Process

Whether done formally or informally, the designer of a database system must go through three phases to develop a complete, effective system. These phases are:

- The logical or conceptual phase

- The architecture mapping or construct design phase (also sometimes referred to as logical design)*

- The physical implementation or performance tuning phase.

Figure 13-1: Three phases of the design process

A good designer with previous experience may be able to conduct all three phases in a split second by simply reviewing the material and making off-the-cuff recommendations. Do not be misled by this nonchalance. It is definitely possible for a good designer to develop layouts that quickly, provided the system is simple enough. But this is true only if they have gone through the processes described enough so that for them, it is second nature to think that way. We consider these phases in sequential order.

* The term logical can and often is applied to the definition of all three phases of the design process. For this reason we will avoid its use as much as possible. In general we will equate the term logical design to the conceptual phase of design, but the term will also be found refering to the construct design phase.

Conceptual or Logical Design (Data Modeling)

The first thing that must happen before trying to build a database system, is to develop a mental or oftentimes physical picture of what the system will do and how it will do it. The development of a formal picture of this kind is called *modeling* or conceptualizing the system.

Through conceptual or logical modeling the designer attempts to tie down as many of the abstract and higher-level aspects of the system as possible. In order to assist the designer in the building of this picture, several logical modeling techniques have been developed.

The output of the conceptualization phase is some kind of formal document, such as a collection of data models, which are formalized descriptions of all of the data to be stored by the system. They can also be simple written statements about the nature and scope of the system with handwritten lists of data elements scratched on a napkin. No matter what the medium, the conceptual phase is complete when the designer knows what data the database will be holding.

In this chapter we consider three of the formal techniques for data modeling: entity-relationship modeling (known as ER modeling), semantic data modeling (SDM) and object-oriented modeling (OOM). Although each of these techniques is distinctive in its execution, they also share some common underlying principles. Some of these principles include:

- **Abstraction**—viewing real, point-in-time events in light of their abstract, theoretical meaning

- **Formalization**—the development of a discipline with a vocabulary and rules for right and wrong decisions

- **Documentation**—the development of a technique for capturing the models in a permanent form.

By utilizing abstraction, formalization, and documentation techniques, the modeler is able not only to develop a good understanding of the systems themselves, but can turn that understanding into something that database administrators, programmers, and even end-users can refer to and interpret.

While considering models, we include a brief discussion of the data administration, data dictionary, CASE, and repository approaches to design and see how these modeling techniques can be used with or without their assistance.

The Architectural Mapping or Construct Design Phase

Construct design is the process of developing names and identities for the data constructs that make up the system. These constructs (tables, files, segments, etc.) become the substance of what is known as the database system. As a part of the process of naming and identifying constructs, the designer actually determines the names, sizes, and locations for every field of data that will reside on the database.

We call this the *mapping process*, because during this phase, the designer turns the logically-defined relationships between entities and objects into the physically-dictated mappings required by a particular architecture. The output of the construct design phase is a collection of data constructors and data elements that the system will hold.

In other words, when mapping is done, all data elements are assigned to a data construct, and all logical relationships between those constructors are defined.

In the next chapter, which covers data construct and physical design, we consider how to develop a database model, or what is commonly known as a *database design* (*as* opposed to a *data* model or logical design).. We discuss the many ways to derive this design and discover that the decision to use one technique over another depends on the environment and the nature of the system be.ing built.

The formal method of database construct design requires that designers transform data models (ER, SDM, or OOM) into construct models of how a particular architecture is actually implemented. This transformation process is pretty straightforward and is fully dependent on the architecture of the database being built. In cases where no formal conceptual model has been prepared, the construct designer has two other methods available to help: normalization and transformation.

Normalization, which was developed in conjunction with relational database theory, has become a standard process for building constructs when little or no formal model is available.

When a system is being converted from one architecture to another (for example, replacing a DB2 relational system with a hierarchical IMS system, *direct transformation* techniques are available. These allow the designer to convert the data from one form to another.

In reality, experienced designers usually apply some of each of these transformation processes to building database constructs. The decision to use one, both, or all three depends on how quickly, efficiently, and effectively the design is to be conducted.

The Physical Design Phase

The final phase of the design process involves the physical implementation of the system. The output of the this process is a fully-functional database system loaded with data and supporting production activities. During this phase, the actual performance of the system and the programs that run against it are considered. It is here that the assumptions made during conceptual design are tested for validity. The tuning phase provides the developer with the last opportunity to adjust the construction of the system to help it perform better.

While the modeling phase is concerned with deriving abstract business issues and data relationships, and the construct design process stays focused on the database's programming and architecture profiles, it is during physical design that the storage management and administrative concerns are addressed.

Although the formal model of the design process tries to organize the otherwise chaotic world of database building, it is far from being comprehensive. Database systems are extremely complex, from the business, programming, and internal perspectives and the development of a good design for the system is a serious challenge for anyone.

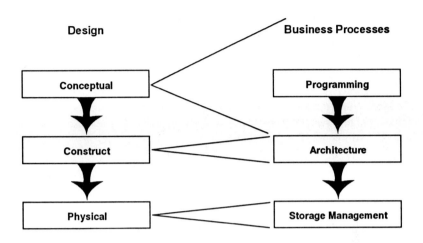

Figure 13-2: Three phases and related profiles

Summary

Before delving into our more detailed descriptions of these three phases, it is helpful to consider yet another aspect of design: the design process is an iterative one. Although our formal description of these phases and their sequencing might seem to imply that it's common for people to follow this process in a rigid and disciplined way. That is far from reality in most situations. Although it is common for people to try and finalize the complete design of the system before beginning to build it, more often than not, the system builders end up revisiting and revising design decisions, over and over again.

The design process is clearly a demanding one, requiring extensive knowledge of the business organizations involved and the business processes being captured, along with the database's own programming, architecture, storage management, and administrative profiles. To be a good designer, a person must know a little bit about everything.

Although a significantly larger amount of space could rightfully have been attributed to these design phases in this book, it is more important that you develop a good understanding of the basic processes and the principal disciplines involved. As we have stated, the key to good design is experience and theory, not one or the other.

What is a Model?

Webster's dictionary defines a model as "a structural design, an imitation or an example for duplication." In the case of data processing and the development of database systems, the term model is normally used to refer to the *an example for duplication* part of the definition.

For the data processing professional, the term model refers to a group of theories, disciplines, and techniques that help simplify and explain the construction and behavior of human/computer systems and document in a way that can be used as input to the system building process.

Why Use Models at All?

Database models are important because in the complex world of large-scale computer operations, it is almost impossible to develop an understanding of what a system is going to do or how it is going to work without writing it all down. Models provide developers with a road map, which allows them to determine the best way to build a system. For the database designer, modeling provides the discipline that can be used to help create a database.

Where do Models Come from?

Models are a relatively new addition to the world of systems development. As systems become more complex, it is obvious that some criteria for deciding whether a system is good or bad must be developed.

Data processing models traditionally have come from the academic community. The Association for Computing Machinery and its special interest groups have been serving as the unofficial clearinghouse for computer science theory for several years. These special interest groups concentrate on several areas of expertise including the management of data. More recently computer hardware and software manufacturers have been credited with some significant contributions in this area. Some sources of models and computer science theories are the IBM labs at San Jose, AT&T Bell Labs, Wang Laboratories and other manufacturer's research and development facilities as well as several educational institutions.

It is important for the developer to keep in mind the sources of models when trying to apply them. A theory and its related models are much more like the theories and models of the economist than those of the chemist or physicist.

When are Data Models Used?

Formal data models and other design techniques will undoubtedly be found whenever the scope of the system is big enough to justify their existence. In the very large organization, models of this type are required as a part of the development process for any system, no matter how big or small. In smaller companies, data models usually appear only when the system being built has reached a level of complexity that defies intuitive design solutions. For smaller systems and the smaller business organization, data modeling probably be done only in the simplest sense.

For those situations that do not require models, for whatever reason, it is more likely that the database administrator or programmer will simply develop an unwritten conceptual model and implement it on the fly. If the system is too large for this kind of quick-fix design, then data elements' names might be written down.

In the full-blown modeling case, all data elements are identified and cataloged for reference by users, programmers, and system administrators.

User Interviews: The First Step Toward Development of a Model

Whether the design procedures for a system are informal or extremely formal, the first step in their development is always conducting interviews with the ultimate users of the system. Only the users of the system (or the people commissioning the system to be built), can tell the modeler what it is the system is supposed to do and what data will be required to do it. Remember, business computer systems are built to do real work for real people. They are not built for abstract reasons.

The user interview process may involve a short one-hour meeting, during which everything that the system must do is discussed. It could also involve dozens of meetings with hundreds of users over an extended period of time while the details are worked out. Either way, the user is encouraged to reveal how the business is conducted and how the system is expected to help in that process.

Although this cursory description of modeling and the user interviewing process may seem trivial or obvious, it is by no means an optional or simple task. Business users and computer specialists have different ways of looking at the world. The data processing professional tends to think along structured, ordered, and logically rigid lines that are foreign to the typical system user. Users often have only a vague notion about what they want the system to do and how they want it organized.

A Typical User Interview

Let us take a look at a short excerpt from a typical user interview. Pete, the owner of the pet shop, is being interviewed by a programmer who is about to design a new database.

Designer: Okay Pete, what I'd like you to do is to tell me about the system and how you want it built. Let's start with a list of the kinds of information you want the system to provide you with.

Pete: Well, I'm not exactly sure. I need to keep the names of all of the animals in the store...and I want to know if it's a fish or a cat that was sold, and of course the new owner's phone number.

Designer: What about the owner's name and address?

Pete: Yes, that would be nice too.

Designer: Anything else?

Pete: No, that's everything, I'm sure.

Of course, four weeks later, when the system is done, the designer finds out that Pete forgot to mention a whole lot that now must be added to the system after the fact. Rabies shot records, whether the fish is salt- or fresh-water, and a lot of other things. It is the objective of the design process to uncover all of the little things that users forget until after the system is built.

More Users, More Complications

The simple example given here involved the participation of one user and one designer. Imagine how much more complicated and frustrating it can be when hundreds of users and dozens of designers must all work together on the development of a system. Without formal methods of system design, it would be impossible.

Organizing the User Interviewing Process

In order to help structure the user interviewing process, several approaches have been used with considerable success. When working with a large group of users, a technique know as JAD (Joint Application Development/Design) is utilized. Under the JAD discipline, key users are identified and enlisted. These volunteers are shuttled into a closed room where a series of highly structured question and answer sessions are held. These sessions are designed to elicit clear, concise design information from a group of people who have probably never worked together before. JAD has proved to be a highly successful method for the development of models and system specifications in a short amount of time.

Although the interviewing of smaller groups of users or individual users need not conform to the rigidity of the JAD discipline, a similar kind of structured approach to the development of designs is always helpful. A typical design meeting elicits information from users by getting them to describe the business functionality that they expect from the system. This description, if thorough and accurate provides the modeler with plenty of material upon which to base the development of a data model.

Here is an example of a poor business description of a system, taken from the files of a JAD session conducted at a large corporation.

User: We need a system that reads the accounts payable file, provides us with payable values that can be compared to the receivables and purchase order system, and then turned into a report.

Although this user has provided a lot of information about expectations of the system, nothing has been said about what the system is actually supposed to do in business terms. Let's look at another example. This time, it's the solid description of a system given by Pete for his store.

Pete: I need a system that helps me keep track of all of the different animals that I sell and the customers who buy them. I want to use this system to create mailing labels, animal status reports, and to keep track of which customers buy what kinds of animals.

Contained in this description is most of the information that a modeler needs in order to develop a pretty solid data model. If the system was small enough, the system builder could sit down and sketch out a quick conceptual model of the system right then and there. In this case, it might look like Figure 13-3.

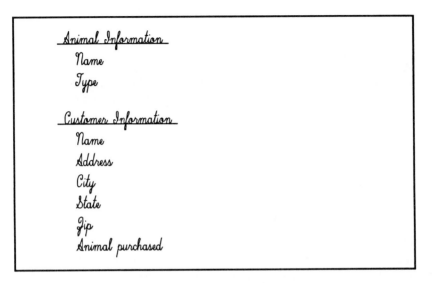

Animal Information
    Name
    Type

Customer Information
    Name
    Address
    City
    State
    Zip
    Animal purchased

Figure 13-3: A quickie design list

The designer could then review this sketchy model with Pete and fill in the rest in short order.

No matter what design discipline is used—formal or informal—it is always assumed that the design is based on good quality information provided by the appropriate user. User interviewing is both prerequisite to and a critical part of the design process.

Next, we consider the formal processes of data modeling, which are commonly used for the larger and more complex systems. These include the entity-relationship, Semantic data modeling, and object-oriented modeling approaches.

The Entity-Relationship Model

Entity-relationship modeling, also known as ER, is perhaps the simplest and most popular of the modeling techniques. Using ER, the designer is able to reduce the complexities of a very large system to a simple, manageable form. The output of the process is a collection of ER diagrams, which communicate to the observer at a glance what all of the major collections of data within the system will be.

The entity-relationship methodology was first introduced by Dr. Peter Pin-Shan Chen from the Massachusetts Institute of Technology. Dr. Chen submitted a paper called "The Entity-Relationship Model—Toward a Unified View of Data." This was subsequently published by the Association for Computing Machinery in the

Transactions on Database Systems in March 1976. In this paper, the entity-relationship model was developed. This model is designed to help conceptually define the data, and to define it in such a way that the definition is independent of the architecture and storage management profiles of the targeted database product. In other words, an ER model is equally effective for the building of relational, hierarchical, network, XBase, and flat file systems. (At the time of its publication, the paper did not address object-oriented databases.)

The ER model provides a method that can simplify the definition of complex data relationships. This model, like all conceptual modeling techniques, is based on the premise that computer systems are themselves electronic models of reality. For example, for a shop-floor control system to be effective, it must simulate the critical activities of an idealized shop floor through computer code. Based upon this assumption, the ER approach requires the modeler to first identify all of the things (entities) about which a system will be capturing information. In the Pete's Pet Shop example, animals and customers are the only relevant entities. In the case of a banking application, customers, checking accounts, savings accounts, and tellers might be the entities. In a small manufacturing concern, the entities might include machinery, employees, and supplies.

After defining the entities, the designer then determines how these entities relate to each other. For example, when building a system that keeps track of students and teachers for a semester, there are two entities, *students* and *teachers*, and one relationship, *class-assignment*. The student construct holds all information unique to the individual student, the teacher construct does the same for teachers and the class-assignment construct holds information about the relationship between teachers and students, naming the classes taught by the teacher and attended by the student.

There are three types of dependencies between entities.

- 1:1—meaning that there is a one-to-one correspondence between entities. For any occurrence in the first entity there is only one matching occurrence in the other.

- 1:m—the one-to-many relationship. For one occurrence in the first entity there are many occurrences in the second.

- m:n—representing the many-to-many relationship. Many occurrences in the first set have many matching occurrences in the second.

After defining entities and relationships, the designer can assign attributes (data values) to each entity or relationship. For the concept designer, the problem of grouping hundreds or even thousands of diverse data elements is reduced to the simple process of:

1. Identifying all of the entities that the system must keep track of

2. Identifying the relationships between those entities

3. Assigning each of the individual data elements to one of these entities or relationships

The ER model is simple and quite useful for logical design. It's clear-cut, top-down approach often helps make the designer's task easier.

A Example Student Enrollment System

This approach supports a top-down view of design. You begin by looking at the system you are designing from a general perspective, and then, break it down to its smallest, most basic pieces: the data elements. The following steps illustrate how a generalized ER analysis might be done. For our example let's assume we are building a reporting system for a school. This system will keep track of students, the classes they are taking, and the teachers of those classes.

Step 1. Identify the entities—In this example, we could identify teachers, students, classes, and classrooms.

Step 2. Identify the relationships and dependencies between those entities. In this example there are three relationships of interest.

- class/teacher—*Since one teacher can teach several students at the same time, they have a one-to-many relationship; one teacher has many students.*

- class/student—*Since one student can take several classes, they have a one-to-many relationship.*

- class/classroom—*Since several classes can occur in the same classroom this is a one-to-many relationship as well.*

Notice that we did not specify a teacher/-student relationship. This is because students and teachers have no direct relationship; they relate only through the classes they share.

Step 3. *Diagram the entities and relationships—This is done using boxes, diamonds and lines.*

Step 4. *Identify the attributes of each entity—Attributes are those data elements that pertain to the entity. For example, teacher-name is an attribute of teacher and number of seats is an attribute of classrooms.*

Of course, the practice of the ER methodology is much more complex and systematic than this. There are some very large user groups devoted to nothing but applying ER theory to real world situations. Luckily, even at this level of simplicity, it can be very useful. To aid in the dissection of complex table design problems, ER comes complete with its own diagramming representations: an entity is represented by a box, a relationship by a diamond. The designer uses these symbols to draw a picture of the elements.

To use the diagramming scheme we would:

1. Determine the entities

2. Determine the relationships

3. Draw the entities (in boxes), connecting them with a solid line to any other entity they may be related to. It might take several attempts at rearranging the

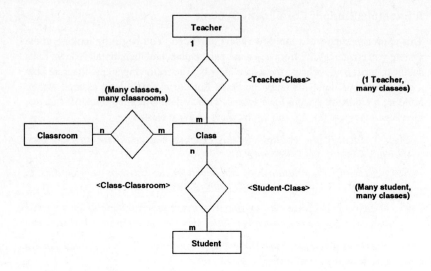

Figure 13-4: An ER diagram for the school example

boxes before the diagram can hold all of the information in a simple, easy-to-understand manner.

4. Insert the relationship diamonds, one for each relationship line drawn.

5. Determine the dependencies between entities and include the mappings (1:1, 1:n, m:n) on the diagram.

As is illustrated by the diagrams, all of the entities and relationships can be captured for an entire system within one compact diagram.

Of course, an ER diagram in and of itself is not too useful. Its usefulness becomes apparent when it is transformed into a construct model, something we consider in the next chapter.

Obviously ER has its strengths and weaknesses as a conceptual modeling tool. Included in its list of strengths are that it reduces complexities to simple, atomic forms, is easy to do, and is easy to understand (making it especially helpful for communication with users and other non-technical personnel). On the other hand, because of this simplicity, the designer often runs into situations where the model is unable to capture the full extent of the system's subtleties. For situations like this, we must turn to the more robust data modeling techniques, semantic and object-oriented modeling.

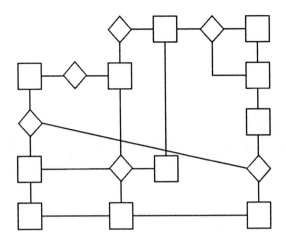

Figure 13-5: A large ER diagram

Semantic Data Modeling

Semantic data modeling (SDM) provides a high-level semantic (word-based as opposed to diagram-based) approach to the definition of conceptual database design. In many ways ER is restrictive. It often fails to fully capture the true nature of the relationships between data elements.

Under ER, only very simple constructs can be built. With SDM, the modeler can develop a more realistic and richer understanding of just what exactly it is that the database must accomplish.

SDM, like ER, was first introduced as a paper published in the *Transactions on Database Systems*. This paper, called "Database Description with SDM: A Semantic Database Model" was written by Michael Hammer of the Massachusetts Institute of Technology and Dennis McLeod of the University of Southern California.

In this paper, the authors describe a modeling technique that captures a lot more of the nuance that goes into building a real database system. SDM is semantic-based, which means that it derives its power from the use of language as opposed to physical abstractions.

This use of semantics to drive the design allows the semantic data modeler to use all of the richness of the written word to describe how data elements relate to each other.

SDM Specifications

Under SDM, the following general principles are applied to the design process:

1. A database is viewed as a collection of entities.

2. Entities are organized into classes.

3. Classes are logically related to each other by interclass connections.

4. Entities, classes, and interclass connections can all be assigned attributes that help describe their character.

So like the ER methodology, the SDM approach builds on the entity foundation. Also like ER, SDM defines relationships between entities. Where SDM differs is in the way it allows for building hierarchies of entities (classes) and relationships between those classes.

Defining the Elements of an SDM Model

SDM begins the definition of a database by designating the entities that will make it up. These entities are defined in a way similar to that of the ER model. Entities are computerized representations of real world things of interest to the users of the system.

After defining the system's entities, the SDM modeler defines the many classes to which they may belong. Using the school system example, both students and teachers represent an entity that can be called *people*. Those who teach, belong to the *teacher* class, while those who are taught belong to the *student* class.

STUDENTS
description: all persons who have ever been and are currently, or intend to enroll at the university.

　Name
　　value class: PEOPLE_NAMES
　Sex
　　value class: SEX_TYPES
　Status
　　value class: STUDENT_STATUS
　　.
　　.
　　.

and for the STUDENT_STATUS class

STUDENT _STATUS
description: the different ways that a student can be catoegorized.
Can consist of CURRENT, ALUMNI, CANDIDATE, or EXPELLED.

Figure 13-6: SDM class description

To define a class, the modeler must give it a name, a textual description, a collection of attributes that help define it (data elements), and a list of its members (those entities that belong to the class).

After creating classes, the modeler can then define the interclass connection—these describe the ways that classes relate to each other. There are two principal interclass connections: subclasses, which create a hierarchy of classes; and groups, which define classes that relate to each other in a peer-to-peer relationship. Interclass connections can also have names, descriptions, and attributes of their own.

EXPELLED_STUDENTS
description: student asked to leave the university for failure to meet disciplinary or scholastic standards.
interclass connection: subclass of STUDENTS where STUDENT_STATUS = "EXPELLED"

Figure 13-7: SDM interclass description

After defining entities, classes, and interclass relationships and their subsequent descriptors, individual entities can be tied-in wherever they belong.

An accurately-defined SDM can serve as the conceptual model for any type of system, but its best applications are found for the creation of semantic databases (like the Unisys SIM database) or for object-oriented databases.

SDM, though not as easy to use as the ER methodology, provides the designer with a much more inclusive set of tools for the definition of data elements and their relationships.

In order to develop an SDM, the practitioner:

1. Defines the entities for the system.

2. Begins by defining the high level *classes* of data the system will work with.

3. After defining these classes (i.e., people, places, things, etc.) the population of entities belonging to that class are categorized. For example, for a baseball database, the class of *people* would be made up of the *player*, *manager*, and *owner* entities.

4. The relationships between these classes and entities is then documented. The fact that a group of nine players works for one manager might be one relationship the designer would capture.

5. The attributes (data elements) belonging to each entity grouping are identified.

6. Descriptions are assigned to each class, entity, interdependency, and attribute.

The SDM, though voluminous and complex, captures a much truer picture of the real world represented by the database.

An Example Baseball Database

To show how an SDM might be developed, let's define a database that keeps track of statistics about different teams in baseball's National League. This database is to be created for Martha "Stats" Riley the famous newspaper sports columnist.

In order to develop an SDM model we must proceed with the following steps:

1. Name all entities involved with this system

2. Organize the entities into classes of data

3. Document the dependencies

4. Assign simple attributes

5. Assign derived attributes

6. Assign descriptions

```
PERSONS
description: all individuals belonging to, owning or managing
a baseball team.

    Name
      value class: PERSON_NAMES
    Role
      value class: ORGANIZATIONAL_ROLES
    Age
      values class: AGES
      .
      .
      .

ORG_NAMES
description: The names of all major league baseball teams.
```

Figure 13-8: A sample baseball schema

1. **Entities**—Based on interviews with "Stats" we can determine that the following list of entities will accurately capture the information she requires:

Teams
Players
Owners
Games
Cities
Dates
Managers
Scores

2. Classes of entities—Along with this information, we can determine that these entities all have to do with the following classes.

Organizations—teams, leagues, unions

Persons—players, managers, owners, umpires

Events—games, press conferences, results

Places—cities, ballparks

3. Interclass dependencies—Armed with the list of classes and entities, we can begin to define, in semantics, the nature of the relationships between them.

Teams:

have personnel

are scheduled to participate in events

are based in cities/ballparks

create results

Persons:

belong to teams

participate in events

must be certain places at certain times

create results

Events:

occur when teams interact at certain places

create results

Places:

are where events occur

4. Attributes— Given this information, we can begin to assign attributes (data elements) to the different entities, classes, and interclass relationships.

Teams—name, address, city, phone, owner, manager, players, statistics

Persons—names, statistics

Events—time, place, results

Places—address, city, state, zip, name, phone, seats

5. Derived data elements— Derived data values are those values that can be calculated using data that has already been stored somewhere else in the database. For example, a commission amount is equal to the sales multiplied by the commission rate. When derived data elements occur, it is usually better to not store them as a separate calculation because this increases the amount of data that must be stored. This requires a program that changes one of the values to recalculate the

```
ORGANIZATIONS
      Description: all groups of individuals that have identified
themselves as being associated together in order to
accomplish some common objectives.


member attributes:
      Name
              value class: ORG_NAMES
      Type
              Description: nature or identity of the organization
              value class: ORG_TYPE
      City_Based_In
              value class     : CITY
              inverse : organizations based here
MANAGER
      Description: the manager of a ball club
member attributes:
      Name
              value class     : PERSONS
              match    : MANAGER to TEAM
      Games_Won
              value class     : OUTCOMES WHERE TEAM WON
              .           .
              .

PERSONS
      Description: all individuals belonging to owning or
managing a baseball team.
      Type : ......

CITY
      Description : the municipality where a team is based.

ORG_NAMES
      Description : the name of the organization, valid values
are (the name of a ball club).

ORG_TYPE
      Description  : whether the organization is a corporation
      or not
  .
  .
  .
  .
  .
```

Figure 13-9: A semantic data model schema

derived value as well. By noting the presence of derived values in the SDM schema, the model captures the fact that the derivation exists, and allows the developer to be aware of it. Derived data values are noted in the SDM with a separate entry in the schema.

6. Description definition— After defining all of the data elements and relationships within the system, the modeler then includes descriptions for each of them.

After full expansion of the obvious relationships between these elements, and the creation of all derivations and descriptions, we are able to develop a full semantic data model schema (see Figure 13-9).

A typical semantic data model is quite an extensive document involving dozens or even hundreds of pages for a large system. Although it is thorough and informative, for this reason it can also be overwhelming. The technique is extremely useful for the specification of systems that use semantic or object-oriented databases, and can be helpful in the development of systems using relational and prerelational architectures, but in a limited fashion. For many, the SDM still falls short of a conceptual model which communicates enough about the system being built. For these individuals, there is the object-oriented modeling approach.

Object-Oriented Modeling

The last data modeling approach that we consider is used for the development of object-oriented database systems. Since object-oriented systems are so radically different in concept and design than any of the other types of databases that a special modeling technique is warranted. That is not to say that an object-oriented model could not be used to effectively define any kind of database system. To the contrary, an object-oriented model can serve as the perfect conceptual modeling devise for any type of system.

Object-oriented modeling, like the object-oriented systems they are meant to model, are built on the basic premise that systems can best be modeled through the definition of objects and their relationships to each other. Objects, unlike the entities of ER and SDM techniques, embody not only the data characteristics of a real world thing, but the processing ones as well.

One of the more applicable publications that addresses object-oriented data modeling is a paper called "Data Modeling Issues for Object-Oriented Applications" written by Jay Banerje, Hong-Tai Chou, Jorge F. Garza, Won Kim, Darnell Woelk, Nat Ballou, and Hyoung-Joo Kim. This paper also was published in the *Transaction on Database Systems*, in 1987.

In this paper, the authors considered a prototype object-oriented database called Orion and the many data modeling issues that had to be addressed in its development. They cited many of the shortcomings and inconsistencies that can be found in many object-oriented approaches and attempted to address some of the more perplexing inadequacies.

Along with this paper, which addressed many of the more technical aspects of object-oriented modeling, another good reference for the modeling of these systems is "Object-Oriented Modeling and Design," written by James Rumbaugh, Michael Blaha, William Premerlani, Frederick Eddy, and William Lorensen (Prentice-Hall 1991). In this, the authors propose a graphical modeling scheme for object-oriented design, similar, in spirit at least, to that used for the ER methodology. This technique, called *object diagramming* or the *object modeling technique* provides the designer with a series of symbols, conventions, and notation techniques that make it possible to document and symbolize large, complex systems in easy-to-interpret graphical form.

Beginning the Object-Oriented Modeling Process

Object-oriented systems are based on the premise that a system is made up of objects. So the process of building an object-oriented model proceeds in pretty much the same way as the other techniques do. Key users are identified and interviewed to derive the correct impressions about how the system must ultimately work. The users are asked to begin by defining the object classes the system will be modeled after. After these object classes are defined, they are assigned attribute lists (field values). Of course, since object-oriented principles declare that an object is defined not only by the data elements that describe it, but the processes it participates in as well, these processes (called operations) are then added to the description list.

A typical object class definition list for Pete's Pet Shop might look like this:

Object: Animals
Data attributes:

Name

Size

Color

Operations:

Eat food

Are purchased

Object: Customers
Data attributes:

Name

Address

City

Phone number

Operations:

Buy animals

Pay money

This simple object definition list is only the beginning of the development of an object-oriented model however. There are many other relationships that we must have information about. We need to understand about:

- How these object relate to each other? (their 1:1, 1:m, and m:m relationships, called links or associations)

- How many objects can be related at the same time? (their multiplicity)

- What are the characteristics and attributes of that relationships. (the associative attributes)

- What special names can be used to relate one object to another? (the use of roles and aliases)

- How is an association defined. (the associative qualifiers)

- How do objects relate to each other as a part of a whole. (the aggregation relationships)

- The existence of superclasses that define some of the characteristics for many subordinate classes. (generalization)

- What are the ways that one class's attributes or operations can be applied to others? (inheritance)

Through comprehensive, and usually iterative meetings with the end users of the system, the designer is able to develop a full-blown object model diagram, which can then be used as data in the logical modeling process. To help keep these object data models easy to understand, the object diagraming methodology is often used. By using this technique, the modeler can build a picture of the system that designers, programmers, and users can understand.

A short explanation for each of these concepts is provided, simultaneously showing how object diagramming can be used to demonstrate them graphically.

The Object Diagramming Methodology

We begin the development of our model by defining each of the objects that the system will manage. Objects are graphically represented by small rectangular boxes that have three sections within them. The first is filled with the name of the object, the second with the data attributes that apply to it, and the third holds the names of the operations that the object will be concerned with.

To relate two objects, they are connected with a line. A straight line with no other markings drawn between two objects indicates a one-to-one relationship between the two. This relationship is called an *association* or a *linkage*. Each linkage can be given a unique name, which helps the person reading the diagram understand what the nature of that relationship is.

To show a one-to-many relationship, the modeler places a solid ball at the end of the line that connects itself to the many occurrences object.

A many-to-many relationship is shown with the placement of solid balls at both ends of the line.

A complex, three-way relationship is called ternary. These are represented with a diamond through which all three of the objects connect.

In the one-to-many and many-to-many relationships, if the number of occurrences on one side or another of the link is known, then that number is included on the diagram. This is referred to as documenting the multiplicity of the relationship. For example, if we wanted to link the *week* object with the *day* object, we would know that they have a one-to-many relationship: one week has seven days.

On the other hand, if an association is not always valid, we can define a special link. For example, there is a relationship between persons and cars, but not everybody owns a car. The optional side of the association is indicated by a hollow ball.

When the association or linkage has characteristics of its own, for example, in the *Animal/purchased-by/Customer* relationship, the price paid for the animal is an attribute of the *purchased-by* association, not of the *Animal* or *Customer* that participated in the sale. In fact, the *purchased-by* association could include information about the price, terms, and the date of the purchase.

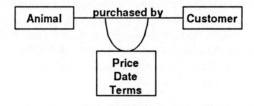

A relationship with its own attributes.

Figure 13-10: A relationship with attributes

Part of the object-oriented approach to programming allows programmers to assign aliases or role names to define the relationship between objects. For example,

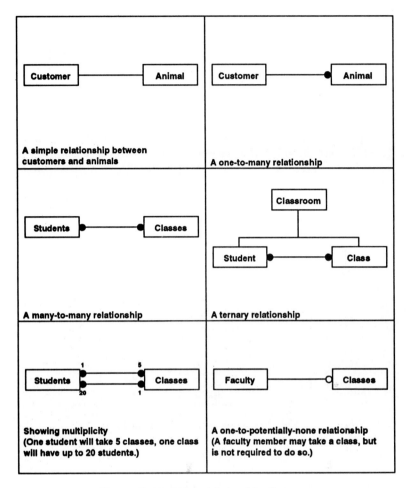

Figure 13-11: Object relationship diagrams

you are a person and your parents are also people. Your relationship is that you call one of them Mother and the other Father. The role names help make object-oriented programs more indicative of the way that people really refer to things. To define these relationship names in the object-oriented model they are simply placed at the appropriate ends of the association line.

When associations are not always valid, but only when certain conditions exist, the conditions are cited and used to qualify the association.

Aggregation notation allows the modeler to show how numerous smaller components can become aggregated into higher ones, which create an entire assembly of some kind. For example, a group of soldiers make up a squadron, a collection of squadrons make up a platoon, and a lot of platoons will make an army.

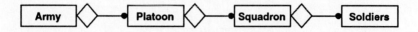

Figure 13-12: An aggregation diagram

Aggregation is demonstrated by using diamond to indicate the object being aggregated to and the solid ball to indicate the objects begin aggregated.

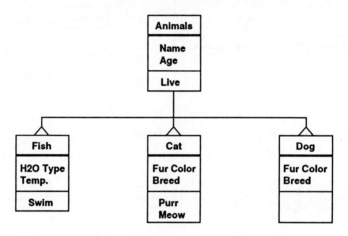

Figure 13-13: A generalization diagram

Generalization, as opposed to aggregation, defines hierarchical relationships between objects. For example a biological taxonomy defines a generalization. Animals are divided up into mammals, reptiles, and fish. Mammals are divided up into bovines, canines, and felines. Dogs can be segregated into collies, poodles and German shepherds.

The big difference between aggregation and generalization is that under aggregation, the attributes of the lower-level items all go into making the larger aggregate object. Under generalization, the lower-level objects inherit characteristics, operations, and attributes from their superior objects.

Generalization is demonstrated graphically, by the building of hierarchy trees, similar to those used to model hierarchical databases. In a generalization model, the subordinate objects inherit the properties of their superior objects.

We have illustrated the object-oriented model for a small system, which keeps track of the animals in Pete's Pet Shop.

The object-oriented diagramming technique shown here can communicate a lot about a large system, using only a small amount of space. The graphical nature of the technique makes it ideal to use in many different situations.

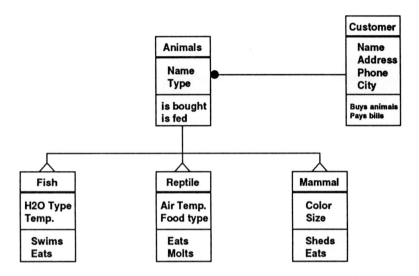

Figure 13-14: An OOM for Pete's Pet Shop

Data Modeling Summarized

The three data modeling techniques shown here certainly are not the only ones being used today. Several other methods have been successfully applied to the challenges of conceptually modeling what a system should do and how it can be put together. These three techniques, however, are certainly indicative of them all and are the most commonly used methodologies.

A Taxonomy of Conceptual Design Techniques

As in other sections, we include a short taxonomy that should help you understand and mentally organize the modeling of databases.

Conceptual Design Techniques
  I. Informal design (entity/element lists)
  II. Formal Design
    A. Entity-Relationship Modeling (ER)
      1. Define Entities
      2. Define Relationships
      3. Define Multiplicities (1:1,1:m,m:n)
      4. Develop Graphical Model
        a. Boxes for entities

        b. Diamonds for relationships
        c. Lines to show inter-relationships
   B. Semantic Data Modeling (SDM)
     1. Define Entities
     2. Organize Entities into Classes
     3. Document Interdependencies (interclass connections)
     4. Assign Attributes to Entities, Classes and Connections
     5. Determine Derived Attributes
     6. Create the SDM schema for the database
   C. Object-oriented Modeling (OOM)
     1. Define Object Classes (box)
       a. Name
       b. Attributes
       c. Operations
     2. Define Associations (1:1,1:m,m:n;ternary)
     3. Define Multiplicity (1:n,m:n,ternary)
     4. Assign and Define Associative Links
     5. Assign Roles and Aliases
     6. Derive Associative Qualifiers
     7. Develop Aggregations
     8. Develop Generalizations and Inheritance

Data Administration and Data Administrators

Throughout our discussions of the different modeling techniques, we have referred to the modeler as a person with a title and function all their own. In fact, modeling can be done by the programmer, the systems analyst, the user, or even the database administrator. For large organizations, a specialized job is created for the persons who spend most of their time determining the nature and rules that go into building large, enterprise-wide models. These people often referred to as data administrators.

The data administrator usually spends a considerable amount of time modeling the many aspects of systems for which they have responsibility. After defining these models, they work with developers helping them transform those models into a system. But the development of models is only one part of the data administrators job. A much bigger part of it is determined by the computer-assisted development and maintenance systems the organization may have.

There are many ways that models can be used to aid in the development of database systems. Most often, models like these are used as input into the next phase of the design process.

What is perhaps more interesting about conceptual models, however, is some of the other ways that they are being used. Several organizations, in an attempt to streamline the process of building and maintaining large systems, are turning to powerful software engineering tools like CASE, data dictionaries, and data repositories. These tools all use conceptual models in one form or another to help drive the automated system generation and maintenance process.

An Introduction to Computer-Assisted System Management and Development

CASE, data dictionaries, and repositories all fall under a category of software tools that have been developed to assist organizations in building and maintaining large computer systems. Although each of them attempts to tackle the problem from a different perspective, all use conceptual models as the foundation for their operations.

CASE Tools

CASE (Computer Aided Software Engineering) products represent an assortment of tools that make it possible for developers to enter high-level descriptions of business processes and data models and turn out physically executable database descriptions and programming code.

Since CASE tools address both the data/database issues as well as programming logic issues, they use conceptual models from both the database (ER, SDM, OOM) and processing (Gane-Sarson, data-flow diagramming, etc.) fields. These products allow the developer to enter data and process models into a menu- and screen-driven interface management system, which in turn transforms those models into executable programs and database constructs.

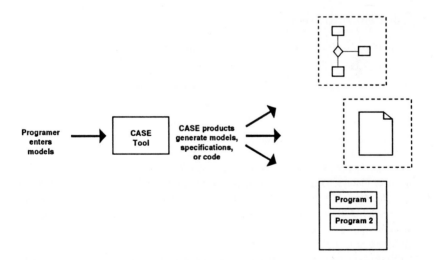

Figure 13-15: CASE tool functions

Different CASE tools take on different aspects of the systems development process. Some attempt to automate only a small part of the process of deriving a physical system from the model. There are products dedicated simply to the creation of a conceptual model. Others that transform these models into logical designs and yet others that carry the model all the way to a physical implementation.

Those systems specifically built to perform the total transformation of a conceptual model into a physical implementation are called I-CASE, or Integrated CASE tools.

For users of these systems, the development of a conceptual model is—theoretically at least—the full extent of participation that anyone must have in the building of a system. Logical and physical modeling are performed by the software tool itself.

Of course, things are seldom that simple. More often than not, the users of I-CASE products end up manually assisting the software product throughout the system development lifecycle.

CASE products have been receiving reserved acceptance at most large computer sites. Although there are some success stories on which to base confidence in the CASE approach, there are also some not-so-successful projects to be considered.

Naturally. CASE is only one approach to helping people build systems better and faster. We consider some of the other approaches that products of this type use.

Data Dictionaries

While the CASE approach deals directly with the generation of systems, the data dictionary products take a less proactive stance.

A data dictionary is a software product designed to store and manage a collection of the organization's data models. It allows the data administrator to enter all of these models, categorize and manipulate them, and then use them in several ways.

What can a Data Dictionary do?

Throughout our discussions of the design process and our detailed explanations of the user interviewing and modeling cycle, we have operated under the assumption that the models being developed must be generated each time a new system is conceived. Although conceptual design can, and often is, done in this manner, this assumes that the conceptualizing done for one project is totally unrelated to other systems. In fact, this is far from accurate. The more likely scenario is that as more and more conceptual models are developed for the organization, they will have more and more overlap. If it was possible to save all of the conceptual models and catalog them someplace, they could be reused again and again. This is one of the efficiencies that data dictionaries try to address. By placing data models into a data dictionary, the development cycle can be speeded up, because there is no need to wait for a model to be generated each time a new project is conceived. Besides that benefit, if all of the systems built draw their conceptual models from the same common pool, there is a great likelihood that they will be more consistent, more compatible, and less redundant.

With a data dictionary, designers can develop enterprise models of the business, store them in the dictionary, and then use them to expedite the rest of the development process.

There are actually two kinds of data dictionary: passive and active. A passive dictionary has no connection to any other software products or tools. These dictionaries serve as the common storage area for models. Active dictionaries, on the other hand, are connected to databases, CASE tools, and repositories to make them even more effective. An active dictionary not only provides the same services as a passive one, it also actively monitors ongoing development and operation activities. It also guarantees that the business rules and relationships it defines are followed by the system's users and builders.

Data dictionaries usually use some kind of internal database that stores the specifications fed into it. The cataloging of entities, objects, data elements, and business rules is facilitated by the presence of an interface management system that structures the process for the user and makes it as easy as possible to get things into or out of the system. After entering these basic elements, the dictionary usually requires the modeler to include detailed narrative, which defines the nature and application of each of these elements so that the casual user can determine immediately what data elements really mean.

It is at this point that the passive and active dictionaries diverge. Here, the user of the passive dictionary is done. All that remains is to generate reports showing the dependencies between entities and elements and to help the developers understand exactly what they are dealing with.

Active dictionaries, on the other hand, work with attached database and CASE products to actively enforce those rules even after the system is built. It is in support and anticipation of active data dictionaries that many database vendors have added so many referential integrity, constraint enforcement, and trigger-type mechanisms. A fully-active dictionary is able to use these database programmability functions to guarantee that business rules are adhered to

Data dictionaries, both active and passive, have had mixed reviews from those organizations using them. They are, in reality, still relatively new and immature products, and there is still a lot to be learned about how to use their potential effectively.

Based on the current condition of many large data processing environments, however, it is highly probable that work using data dictionaries will continue.

Repositories

The most recent additions to the ranks of computer-assisted system development and management are the repositories. Repositories are products usually marketed by hardware vendors. They attempt to create an entire meta-environment, which is

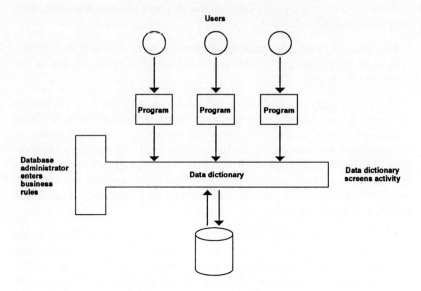

Figure 13-16: An active dictionary

a globally-controlled, multiplatform, integrated computer system. This allows the system's builders to integrate several different platforms, databases, and applications under the control of one software package.

The repository incorporates into its structure several characteristics including:

- An overall strategy and implementation for the integration of diverse platforms

- An overall strategy for the integration of diverse database products

- A series of standardized interface declarations (protocols), which allow the builders of CASE, database, and data dictionary products to plug their products into the system with a minimum of customization

- A control mechanism of some kind allowing the repository to monitor transaction-level activity, and intervene when appropriate.

By building and using repository environments, organizations hope to gain a level of control over their diverse computer systems never before imagined.

Conceptual modeling plays a key role in the development of a truly integrated repository environment for several reasons. Conceptual models, and especially data models, are able to dictate:

- The nature of the relationship to be established between distributed databases. An ER-based model requires less interdependency between databases than an object-oriented one, which includes data and operation constraints.

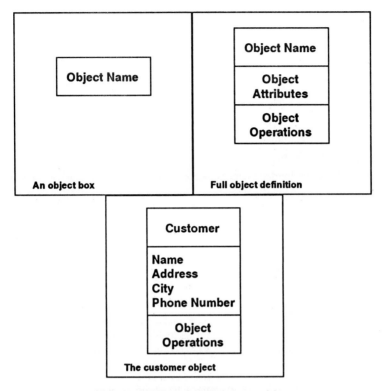

Different ways of showing an object
Figure 13-17: Object boxes

• The construction of dictionary and CASE tools that will work in conjunction with the repository.

The conceptual modeling techniques on which a repository is based define at the outset what the ultimate strengths and weaknesses of that repository will be.

Currently, many of the bigger hardware vendors are developing and publishing information about their own repository products. IBM's Repository Manager is based on ER modeling, the Unisys Repository Initiative focuses on the SDM, and DEC continues to develop its repository along object-oriented lines.

Repository approaches are currently in an embryonic stage of development. The ultimate depth and completeness of these products will be a function of not only the product's development itself, but of the yet-to-be realized advancements in the areas of distributed databases, CASE, data dictionaries, and telecommunications technology. All of these approaches to the management of large, heterogeneous metacomputer systems will continue to advance as the ever-increasing demand for their services continues to skyrocket.

Computer-Assisted Management and Development Tools: Summary

We have considered three principal groups of products that are designed to attack the problems of large systems building and integration.

- CASE tools, which consist of products designed to use conceptual models as input, and which generate programs and other kinds of executable code.

- Data dictionaries, both passive and active, which serve as reference libraries for the storage and retrieval of data models and to enforce those definitions dynamically.

- Repositories (metasystem management software), which allow the developer to couple disparate systems into an integrated environment, and which use a conceptual model as the basis for the ways that databases, CASE tools, and dictionaries can relate to each other.

All of these are based, in one form or another on conceptual models.

Conclusion: Conceptual Design

The conceptual design phase is by far the most important part of the database design process. It is at the conceptual design phase that the real nature of the system being built and the business-related reasons for its creation are uncovered, explored, and defined. The output of the process is a collection of entity or object descriptions, the data elements that support them, and all of the other rules that apply to them.

If a conceptual design is flawed, you can be assured that the subsequent logical and physical models will be too. Only by doing a good job in this phase can the designer hope to create a truly effective database system.

In the next chapter, we consider the other two phases of the design process, the construct and physical design phases, and see how conceptual models can be turned into an operational database system.

14

Mapping and Performance Tuning

In the previous chapter, we introduced the overall design process. We said that the database design process could be viewed as consisting of three major phases: the conceptual phase, where the relationships between entities and objects could be defined in abstract terms; the construct design phase, where these abstract relationships are mapped to a physical arrangement based on the architecture; and the physical design or performance tuning phase, where the performance of the database is considered and its design modified to enhance or optimize that performance.

By the end of the last chapter we considered several of the more popular conceptual design techniques, referred to as data modeling methodologies. We saw how each of the three (ER, SDM, and OOM) are used to create abstract views of business processes.

In this chapter, we complete our discussions of the design process by investigating how construct design and physical design are usually carried out.

Objectives of Construct Design

While conceptual design is primarily concerned with the development of abstract pictures of the organizational operations it is meant to model, construct design (which is also referred to as the mapping process) has a much less esoteric, and more tangible objective. The objective of construct design is to develop a working blueprint of how the database will actually look and work.

Construct design involves two processes: the definition of base constructs, and the mapping of relationships between them. In order to perform construct design, the designer must know the architecture of the database being built, but at this point doesn't need to know which database product will be used. Construct design turns conceptual models into architectural solutions.

We begin the process by defining base constructs, which are the data constructs (tables, files, segments, etc.) upon which the system is based. We then proceed by assigning data elements to those constructs. Then, a primary key, or logical identifier, is assigned to each.

After defining all of the base constructs, the mapping process is invoked. Mapping is the process whereby the designer determines how the relationships between constructs (the links, associations, relationships, etc.) will be captured and controlled by the database itself.

For example, if a data model shows that two entities, *animals* and *customers*, have a logical relationship of one-to-many (one customer buys many animals), how will the database be used to guarantee that users are aware of that relationship and can store and retrieve information based upon that relationship? Obviously, in order to perform this mapping process, the designers must be very familiar with the architecture to which they are mapping. The process of construct design is where the designer actually begins to build the database as it will ultimately look.

Many studies of the design process stop at this point and say that once construct design is complete, the designer's task is over. This, in reality, is not true. The designer should be concerned not only about whether the logical model of the system is mapped accurately to the architecture, but should also be concerned about whether the ultimate database system will actually be able to perform well. This is where the physical design, or tuning process, comes in.

Physical Design

The physical designer takes the output of construct design, a collection of constructs, and determines exactly how the database will be physically implemented. In other words, the construct designer is most concerned with the architecture profile of a database, but the physical designer concentrates on the implementation of those constructs taking the database product's storage management profile into account. In order to conduct the physical design, the designer must know which database product will be used to build the system.

It is during the process of physical design that the majority of the indexes, hashing key algorithms, and other database physical configuration issues are considered and folded into the design.

One of the more frustrating aspects of the physical design process is that often the physical designer must modify the logical and construct designers' work to accomplish the performance objectives set up for the system. This can make the physical designer a less-than-popular member of a database design team.

How does the Physical Designer Work?

While the logical and construct designers are concerned with making sure that the system reflects the way it is supposed to look to the programmer and user, they are usually not too concerned with the performance of the system. It is the physical designer who must take this into account.

A critical input to the physical design process, in addition to the logical and construct designs provided, is a collection of statistical and performance information. The physical designer needs to know things like how many records each construct will hold, how often each construct will be accessed, and how many people will be using the system at the same time?

Because of the extremely technical nature of physical design, the work is usually done by database administrators and systems programmers as opposed to business analyst who perform the other kinds of design.

Only when all three phases of the design process have been completed is the database actually ready to be used.

Construct Design and Mapping

Assuming that the designers have developed or been provided with an accurate, comprehensive conceptual model of the system they are ready to begin the construct design phase . The first thing that the designer must do is be sure that the architecture of the target database for this system is known and understood. With these two pieces of information, the designer can begin the process of transformation.

Transforming Models

The transformation of models into constructs is really a multi-part process. The first step is to turn the logically-defined entities and objects into base construct definitions. We refer to this as base construct assignment. These are called base constructs because they are the more permanent, stable parts of the database design. During this time, the final disposition of most of the data elements is decided and the primary keys (those data elements that will be used to uniquely define each construct) are assigned.

The second step is to determine how the relationships that the model shows are going to be captured within the structure of the database. We refer to this as relationship assignment. (See Figure 14-1.)

Base Construct Assignment

Although there are eight major architectures with which the designer might ultimately need to work, the base construct assignment process is usually the same for all. Unless some conditions that are only visible during the physical design phase are uncovered, the designer can assume that each major entity or object defined during logical design will be transformed into a base physical construct. Base constructs define the real-world things about which the database stores information, and these constructs tend to be the most substantial components of any system.

Starting with an ER model, the designer knows that each box of the diagram (each entity) is to be transformed into a base construct. Using the SDM approach,

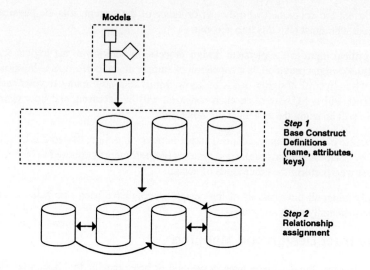

Figure 14-1: Model transformation

each class, superclass or entity defined within the SDM schema becomes a base construct. Using the object-oriented modeling technique, the designer can transform each object box into a base construct.

Along with creating base constructs out of each entity or object that a system has modeled, the modeler must also assign all of the data elements associated with that entity or model to the base construct. For each of the modeling techniques that we have discussed, this is a trivial process. Each of the techniques (ER, SDM, and OOM) lists data elements as a part of the entity, class, or object descriptions. These elements become the actual fields or columns of the targeted database.

After defining the base constructs and the data elements they hold, a primary key—or logical identifier—is assigned or created. This key is used by the designer to complete the design process, and is often turned into the physical key of the completed database. In order to determine which element of a construct should become the primary key, the designer must consider which of the elements associated with it are able to uniquely identify each occurrence. For example, for a student construct, some kind of student ID number should be used. For an animal construct, the animal's name, license number, or some other element can be enlisted. When one of the data elements stored within a construct is utilized as the primary key, it is called a natural key.

If no single data element uniquely identifies occurrences within the construct, then the designer can look for combinations of elements that accomplish the same thing. For example, maybe the name of an animal is not unique, but the combination of its name, age, and color does. Combining multiple elements to create a unique identifier for the construct is called creating a compound key.

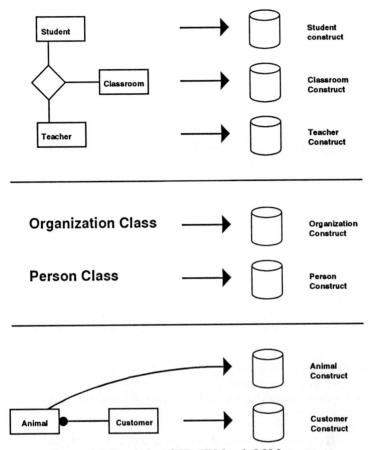

Figure 14-2: Examples of ER, SDM and, OOM constructs

If no obvious key—either stand-alone or compound—is available, the last resort is to simply create a key. For example, if the animals in the Pete's Pet Shop database have no unique identifiers, we can decide to simply number them from 1 to 100, assigning a unique number to each one. This is known as developing an artificial key. (See Figure 14-3.)

Upon completion of the base construct identification, definition, and keying, the designer can move to the second part of the process: mapping. Before discussing mapping, however, let's review the first step of the process with some examples.

Base Construct Assignment Based on ER Models

If we have an ER model that defines all of the entities necessary to run the system, the designer is safe in assuming that each entity box on the diagram will be converted to a base construct. For example, the student enrollment model from the previous chapter used several entities (students, teachers, classes, and classrooms) and three relationships (student-class, teacher-class, and class-classroom). At this time, we are concerned only with the entity definitions.

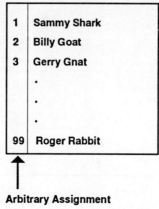

1	Sammy Shark
2	Billy Goat
3	Gerry Gnat
.	
.	
.	
99	Roger Rabbit

Arbitrary Assignment
Figure 14-3: Key assignment

For each of these entities (students, teachers, classes and classrooms) let's discuss the data constructs to be built based upon their descriptions. In addition, remember that not only will the constructs be defined, but the data elements that make them up and a primary logical key will be assigned to each. In the case of the student, teacher class, and classroom constructs, we assume that the logical keys will be teacher-ID, student-ID, class-ID, and classroom-number (all natural keys).

Under the flat-file, XBase, SBase and inverted list architectures, each of these entities will be transformed into physical (base) files. Under the network architecture, each will become a record type. For a hierarchical database, each base entity becomes a segment, and in the case of relational databases, entities become individual base tables.

The object-oriented databases present us with a special problem. You may recall that we said object-oriented databases are really hybrid products, combining a higher-level object-oriented view of reality, while at the same time utilizing a lower-level data management architecture (usually network or relational). Because of this, the designer needs to know not only whether a database is object-oriented or not, but also whether it is an object-oriented//network, or object-oriented//relational system. The lower-level architecture that the object-oriented database uses determines how entities are transformed. If it is object-oriented//network, then it converts entities into record types. If it is object-oriented//relational, then it converts them into tables.

In all cases, the list of data elements associated with each entity becomes the data elements that are stored within it.

Base Construct Assignment Using SDM

For a semantic data model, which has defined the system in terms of entities, classes and their attributes, we can use the same rules. Every entity or class defined within the SDM schema is transformed into a base construct using the same one-to-one correspondence as was used in the ER transformation. The attributes assigned to each of the entities or classes become the data elements belonging to that construct. The same rules for the assignment of primary keys apply.

Base Construct Assignment Using Object-Oriented Modeling

The object-oriented model, too, uses the same direct one-to-one approach during this part of the transformation process. Each object box converts into a base construct all its own. The data attributes within the box become the data elements that belong to the construct and a principal identifier selected as the logical key.

Relationship Assignment (Mapping)

While the creation of base constructs is a relatively simple and straightforward process, the development of relationship assignments is much more complex. To start with, let's consider how each of the modeling techniques discussed show us these relationships.

Models and Mapping

Under the ER model, the relationships between entities are indicated with connecting lines. Each line represents a relationship. In addition, those relationships involving many-to-many multiplicity, are shown with a diamond that has a relationship name inside. Under ER, each line (for the one-to-one and one-to-many cases) and each diamond (for the many-to-many cases) must be mapped to the database itself.

Under the SDM approach, the relationships between classes, superclasses, and entities are shown by several entries. The most commonly-defined relationship indicated by the *interclass connection* categories is the subclass. A subclass, is a class that has a one-to-many relationship with its subordinate classes. The second type of interclass connection is the *grouping category*. Entities belonging to the same group share common data elements. Grouping relationships can be one-to-one, one-to-many, or many-to-many, depending on their nature. Only by reading the schema can the designer determine which is which.

Under object-oriented modeling, we saw that objects are linked with a line. Either a solid or hollow ball at the end of the line indicates one-to-one, one-to-many, or many-to-many relationships. In addition to these simple associations, we must also be concerned with the aggregation and generalization criteria defined by the object-oriented model. Both of these represent a special kind of one-to-many relationship.

The Application of Models to Mapping

It is certainly possible to use any of the logical design methods to design any type of database. However, different modeling techniques become associated with different architectures. Informal modeling techniques are usually associated with the design of flat-file and XBase databases; ER modeling is used to design inverted list, hierarchical, network, and relational databases; and the SDM and OOM are used to assist in the development of semantic and object-oriented systems. We will continue to apply all three modeling techniques to the development of databases using each of the architectures. But it is important to realize that SDM and OOM capture much more information about the nature of the data being modeled than the non-object-oriented databases can handle. In these cases, the additional information must used as input to the application development process.

Mapping Relationships to Architectures

At first glance it might seem like quite a task to figure out how to map the one-to-one, one-to-many, and many-to-many relationships to eight different architectures. Luckily, as regards the actual method for developing the constructs for doing this, we can reduce these eight architectures to two: those that use logical mapping and those that use physical mapping.

Logical and Physical Mapping

If you were to examine closely the architectures we have considered you would find that each of them uses one of these techniques for capturing the relationships between constructs. Under the category of logically-mapped architectures we include the flat-file (for those flat-file databases capable of cross-file association), XBase, SBase, inverted list, relational, and object-oriented. These architectures require that the relationship between two constructs be mapped, with matching data elements on each. Specifically, this is a logical linkage, instead of a physical one.

Physically-mapped architectures include the network, hierarchical and some object-oriented databases. For these architectures, the relationships between constructs are physically determined with pointers or other architecture devices. The presence of matching data elements has no effect on these databases; it is the physical construction of the database itself that maps relationships.

Transforming Logically Mapped Architectures

In a logically-mapped architecture, the system is able to keep track of the relationships between disparate constructs only with a logical linkage between the two. In other words, to relate two logically-associated constructs, we must have a data element on one of the constructs that matches the data elements on the other constructs.

To transform the relationships of a logical model into relationship assignments using the logically-mapped architectures, the designer must be sure that every logical relationship indicated by a model has been duplicated in the construct design. This must be in the form of a matching data element or additional data construct.

Logical Relationship Mapping from an ER Model

Going back to our entity-relationship model example, remember that we transformed entities into base constructs, but failed to do anything with the relationships. (student-class, teacher-class and class-classroom). These relationships had different characteristics: the teacher-class relationship was of the one-to-many type; and the student-class and classroom-class relationships were of the many-to-many type.

One-to-one relationships are captured in one of two ways. Either the two constructs they represent can be combined into one large construct or the logical key of one can be duplicated and stored on the other. (See Figure 14-4.)

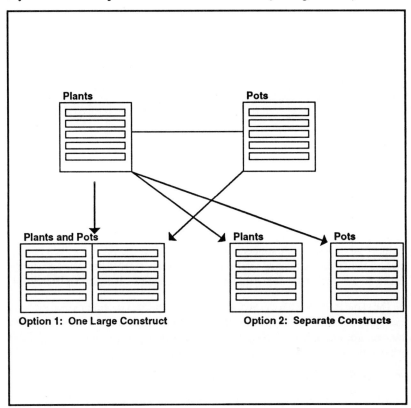

Figure 14-4: One-to-one relationship mapping

One-to-Many Relationships

In a logically-mapped system, one-to-many relationships are captured by placing the primary key of the entity on the *one* side of a one-to-many relationship as a secondary identifier key on the construct on the *many* part of the relationship.

For example, the teacher-class relationship is one-to-many. One teacher teaches many classes. To capture this relationship logically, we take the teacher construct's primary key (teacher-ID) and make it an additional data element of the class table as well.

This means that every class record has a teacher-ID field. (See Figure 14-5.)

One-to-Many Relationships and Architectures

Let's see how this transformation rule can help each of the logically-mapped architectures capture the one-to-many relationship.

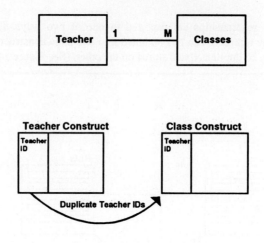

Figure 14-5: One-to-many relationship mapping

In the case of the XBase database, we change the class file to include a teacher-ID field. Now, when a programmer wants to write a report about teachers and the classes they teach, a pointer can be set between the teacher and class constructs based on the teacher-ID field, and the sliding pointer relationship can be utilized.

The same is true for SBase, inverted list, relational, and object-oriented systems. Matching columns make it possible to use the one-to-many relationship whenever needed. For example, with the teacher-ID column on a class table, an SQL JOIN command can be used to capture the relationship.

Many-to-Many Relationships

In the case of our ER model, however, we still have not determined what to do with the many-to-many relationships. In these cases, it is necessary to turn each of the relationship diamonds from our diagram (student-class and class-classroom) into separate data constructs called *bridge constructs* or *relationship constructs*. These constructs represent no particular entity or object that the system monitors, but instead hold information about the relationship that two constructs share.

To build a relationship construct, the designer must first name the construct using the relationship name and then assign a primary key to it. In this case, the primary key is a two-part key. The first part is the primary key of one of the base tables that it relates, and the second part is the primary key of the other table.

For example, in order to capture the student-class relationship where one student takes many classes but each class also has many students, a separate construct, called student-class can be created. This construct is made up of several records, each representing one occurrence of a student registering for a class. Each record has a two-part key, one being the student's ID, the other being the class number. Whether the database is an XBase, inverted list, relational, or object-oriented architecture, the designer creates exactly the same kind of bridge construct to

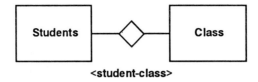

<student-class>

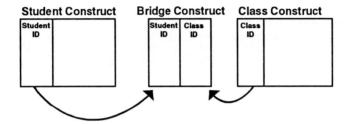

To map a many-to-many relationship, an additional
bridge construct is built

Figure 14-6: Many-to-many relationship mapping

capture the information. It is not uncommon to find a system that has several bridge constructs, all of which have only two fields: the two keys from the two base constructs being related.

Transforming a Physically-Mapped Architecture

The creation of databases containing information about the relationships between constructs in a physically-mapped database is a little more straightforward than it is for the logically-mapped ones.

When working with hierarchical databases it is possible to capture as many one-to-many relationships as you want, but it is almost impossible to capture the many-to-many relationships. In cases like this, the designer must decide which relationship is the most important to capture and then resort to logical mapping or the duplication of data records to capture the inverse relationship.

One-to-Many Relationships in a Hierarchical Database

To capture one-to-many relationships, the designer places the *one* part of the base construct's relationship as the parent segment and the *many* part as the child segment. For example, in the teacher-class relationship, the teacher segment becomes the parent and the class segment becomes the child. Obviously, it is not necessary to create and propagate foreign keys across a system like this, since the presence of the class segment defines which teacher is teaching it.

Many-to-Many Relationships in a Hierarchical Database

As we said, the many-to-many relationships are not captured very well within a hierarchical database. To capture a relationship of this type, we must decide which part of the relationship is the most important and then use logical mappings to capture the inverse.

In the example of our student database, we might want to include the relationship of classes and students in the construct design. To do these we would make the student segment a child of the class segment (capturing the one class has many students relationship) and then store duplicate student records, one for each class the student takes.

It is this shortcoming of the hierarchical architecture that makes it one of the most confining of the database approaches.

One-to-Many Relationships in a Network Database

We can capture the one-to-many relationship under a network architecture similar to the way used for hierarchical. Remember, under the network architecture constructs are related through the creation of pointers. The one end of the relationship becomes the anchor record of the network's set and the many records are attached along the networks chain of records. In this way, the program following the relationships can walk the set.

Many-to-Many Relationships

To capture a many-to-many relationship under the network architecture, we simply establish another set of pointers (create another set), which walks the set in the other direction.

To capture the many-to-many relationship of students and classes, we simply set up one set of pointers going from a class to each student in the chain and another set, pointing from each student, to all of the classes they are taking.

Using SDM and OOM To Map Relationships

Luckily, although the syntax and display characteristics used by SDM and OOM are different than for ER modeling, the logical relationships they display are basically the same. Because of this, the method of transformation is the same.

SDM uses the interclass connection statements and OOM uses the association line, with solid and hollow balls to indicate multiplicity. In both cases, the relationships boil down to one-to-one, one-to-many, and many-to-many. The mapping of these to each of the architectures remains the same.

Data Construct Layouts

The output of the construct design phase should follow a formal construct layout document. Among the forms that this layout can take are:

1. Simple lists of constructs and their elements.

2. Formal documents defined by the DBA or Data Administration group.

3. The output of a CASE product.

4. The STUDER diagram.

5. Architecture or product specific modeling techniques.

6. Database product DDL (data definition language) or constructor syntax.

We will discuss only a few of these options, the Studer diagram, hierarchy charts, network diagrams and SQL-DDL. The decision to use any of these techniques is dependent upon the conventions of the organization for which modeling is being done. Remember, the ultimate objective is the creation of a real functioning database system. Whatever convention is decided upon for the output of this phase, it should support that ultimate objective.

STUDER DIAGRAMS

One method, which defines constructs generically, is called the Studer Diagram. Studer diagrams provide the designer with the ability to describe all of the constructs and elements that will be contained within a database system in a way that is database product independent.

The Studer Diagram consists of 2 basic parts, an element layout section, which names each of the elements that the construct will contain, and defines their major characteristics. The second section contains a textual definition of those elements.

The element layout selection, which appears at the top of the diagram, is nothing more then a 4 tiered matrix.

See Figure 14-7.

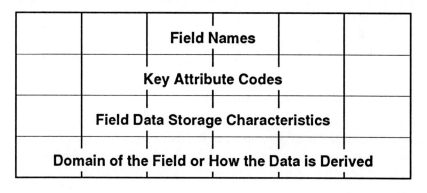

Figure 14-7: The Studer diagram layout

Each column of the matrix represents a data element, and each row of the matrix is used to describe a different set of characteristics about those elements.

The first row will hold the name of each element, the second, a series of key attribute codes, the third, field storage requirements and finally, a description of the domain of the field, and a reference to the textual definition to be found later in the document.

Field names— Field names can be from one to 18 characters. Underscores and numbers can be included, but not as the first character. The names given to fields in these boxes should correspond with the ultimate physical names of those fields in the database.

Key attribute identity codes—These codes allow the designer to communicate the nature of the element at a glance.

PK = Primary Key   UN = Unique to table

FK = Foreign key   DA = Data Attribute

IA = Identity Attribute DD = Derived data

DK= Derived data   MK = Multiple key

Field Data storage characteristics—Any valid storage value. These define the nature and size of the element. Example of field types would include:

1. Integer   4. Float

2. Decimal   5. Small Int.

3. Character   6. Varchar.

Domain of the field—A description of what values will be valid for this field (i.e., key from some other table, integer only, etc.). Along with a short textual definition of domain to be found within the diagrammatic box itself, the designer will assign a reference letter to each element, which refers to the much larger textual area below.

The following example shows how the top half of a Studer diagram might look for a typical system. The bottom half would, of course, contain a more detailed explanation of the field. (See Figure 14-8.)

Architecture/product specific techniques

For certain database technologies, conventions for the building of data constructors have been devised. With relational databases, the database DDL (data definition language) is used to convey the information. For the hierarchical database, the hierarchy tree is used, and for network databases, the network box layouts.

Hierarchy trees

The hierarchy tree provides the DBA with the means to communicate quickly and effectively the logical organization that a system will have. Under this technique, the parent or root segments of the database are shown as existing within a box at the top of the tree. Segments which are immediate children of the root, are

student id_num	student name	student addr	student sex	student state	student age
pk, u	ia	ia	ia	ia	ia
int	char 30	char 30	char 1	char 6	dec 3,0
a.	b.	c.	d.	e.	f.

Figure 14-8: The Studer diagram in use

displayed on the next layer down, and the children of those children are shown below these as well. Many hierarchical databases include facilities which will create and maintain these hierarchy trees on demand.

Network layout diagrams

For network databases, the network record representation diagram has been used extensively. Under this technique, important information about each record (name, id, length, storage mode, key or set name and storage area name) are recorded within the record box. These individual boxes are then related to each other via arrows, indicating the networked relationship that they have to each other.

SQL-DDL

For many databases the database DDL or constructor syntax is simply generated and used as a reference to the layout of constructs. Although this method is certainly efficient (since the database in now ready to be created), it has a serious shortcoming.

Why not use constructor syntax to model the system ?

When construct layouts are generated at this phase of the design process two things will occur:

1. It gives everyone a false sense of "being done" with the design process. Design will in fact not be done until indexes, cross construct relationships and many other physical constraints have been taken into account. The DDL generated at this phase of design will most certainly have to be modified before the database is ready to be built.

2. When the construct design of a system is documented via constructor syntax, it can become very difficult to develop an appreciation for the "big picture" of how these constructs must relate to each other. CASE product output or hierarchy trees and network record representations do not suffer from this same shortcoming.

For most logically-based architectures, the database
DDL (data definition language) can serve as full construct documentation:

```
Create Table Students
   (Name          CHAR(15)
    Address       CHAR(25)
    Age           NUM(3)
    Student_ID    Num(5));
```

Hierarchical database constructs are usually documented with a
hierarchy diagram:

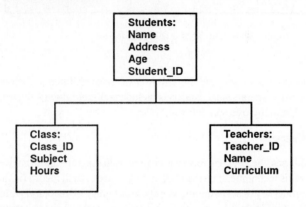

Network databases sometimes use the Record Represented diagram
in conjunctionn with network diagrams

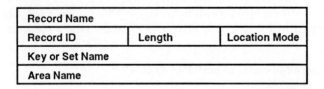

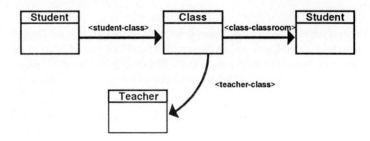

Figure 14-9: DDL, Hierarchy Tree and Network Models

Summary of Construct Design Using Models

For the designer with the benefit of a conceptual model upon which to base the design of the system, the next step is to transform that model into a collection of physical constructs. We have seen that construct development is a two-step process, the creation of base constructs (including their associated data elements and keys) and the mapping of inter-entity relationships.

Base construct development is a straightforward process involving the identification of base entities, classes, or objects within the models provided and then adding their data elements and unique identifiers. The process of mapping however, depends on the architecture of the database being built. If the architecture is logically mapped (using common data elements), the model is transformed through the duplication of key values on targeted constructs or through the creation of bridge constructs. If the architecture is physically mapped, then the architecture's own techniques for mapping are used.

In all cases, the output of this part of design should be a collection of construct definitions that the physical designer can then use to build the final DDL or database generation code ultimately used to create the database.

Normalization

Unfortunately, not all designers of databases are lucky enough to have the time or facilities for the development of good logical models. In cases where this is not possible, there are some other techniques available for the development of constructs. One of the most popular of these techniques is referred to as *normalization*.

Normalization techniques were first proposed by Dr. Codd as an adjunct to his discussions of relational theory and design techniques. The technique has proved so useful and effective, it has become something of an industry standard for the development—or at least validation of the effectiveness-of designs for all types of databases.

The Objective of Normalization

The objective of the normalization process is to develop the identities of all of the base constructs a database will be working with. It is also to identify all the data elements each construct will contain, and does so with only limited information from the users. In fact, normalization is a method for deriving the nature of database constructs based on the identity of the data itself. Although normalization can be applied to any architecture, it is the most appropriate for logically-mapped systems (XBase, SBase, inverted list, relational and object-oriented).

Methods of Normalization

Normalization begins by assembling all of the data elements to be stored by a database system and establishing rules for how they are to be stored and grouped. As the data is conformed to a given set of rules, it is said to be promoted to a higher normal form. The objective is to get the data in the database to be of the highest normal form possible without undermining the system's performance. The higher the normal form a relation has, the better it is. In this case, better means less data redundancy and more flexibility. In normalization terminology, data elements are said to be grouped into *relations*, which are logically related groups of elements.

Zero-th Normal Form (0NF)

Any arrangement of data, no matter what elements are in it, can be said to be normalized to *zeroth normal form* (0NF) simply because it is associated with some relation. Under 0NF, the designer groups logically-related data elements into proposed constructs, also known as *candidate relations*. When this data is grouped into relationships, primary keys are assigned to them (just as they were under base construct design).

Non-normalized Data (0NF)

```
Customer SSN
Customer Name     (made up of lastname, firstname and middle initial)
Customer Address  (made up of street, city, state and zip)
Customer Phone Number
Customer Purchases (Purchases #1  through #3)
Customer Relative Information (Name, phone, animal preferences)
Animal Info (Name, Type, Color, Weight)
```

Figure 14-10: An example of 0NF

First Normal Form (1NF)

A relation with atomic values only (data elements that cannot be broken down into smaller meaningful data elements) are said to be in first normal form (1NF). The breakdown of compound data elements is important, because a logically-linked system cannot perform mapping operations if the elements are hidden within compound fields. A good example of a compound field is a name field, which holds the last name, first name, and middle initial of a person.

This field is compound and not optimally defined. With a field of this kind, a lot of extra programming intervention is required to manipulate the data. For example, to list the first names of all the people in database the programmer must read each name field, locate the comma separating last name from first name, and then extract the first name. By eliminating all compound fields by breaking them down to atomic level, the designer completes the first step to the normalization process. (See Figure 14-11.)

```
First normal form data (1NF)
(All data is atomic)

Customer SSN
Customer Lastname
Customer Firstname
Customer Middle Initial
Customer Street Address
Customer City
Customer State
Customer Zip
Customer Phone Number
Customer Purchase #1
Customer Purchase #2
Customer Purchase #3
Customer Relative Name
Customer Relative Phone
Customer Relative Animal Preference
Animal Name
Animal Type
Animal Color
Animal Weight
```

Figure 14-11: An example of 1NF

Second Normal Form (2NF)

A relation is in second normal form (2NF) if all attributes are atomic (1NF), and all non-key attributes are dependent upon the primary key. In other words, now the designer looks at the meaning of each element stored within a relation and determines if they all belong with the assigned primary key. If an element is dependent on the key, the key is what gives it meaning. For example, a relation made up of social security numbers, first name, population of the person's home state, and age has a key (social security number) and four dependent attributes (the remaining information). Without the social security number, the values for name, name of home state, population of home state and age would be meaningless. By moving our data to 2NF, we eliminate the storage of any unrelated data elements from the base construct descriptions. In this case, the relation is in 2NF. (See Figure 14-12.)

But what happens when we remove an element from the relation? Where does it go? The data element was present for a reason when it was originally created, but we can't just make it disappear. As we carry data through the normalization process, data elements that we originally thought belonged in one place actually land up

```
Second normal form data (2NF)
  (All data dependent upon keys)

Customer Table
- - - - - - - - - - - - - - - - - - - - - -
Customer SSN
Customer Lastname
Customer Firstname
Customer Middle Initial
Customer Street Address
Customer City
Customer State
Customer Zip
Customer Phone Number
Customer Purchase #1
Customer Purchase #2
Customer Purchase #3
Customer Relative Name
Customer Relative Phone
Customer Relative Animal Preference

Animal Table
- - - - - - - - - - - - - - - - - -
Animal Name
Animal Type
Animal Color
Animal Weight
```

Figure 14-12: An example of 2NF

someplace else. If we remove a data element from one relation, it is usually because it must be placed into another relation or create a new one.

Third Normal Form (3NF)

A relation is in third normal form (3NF) if it is in 2NF and none of the attributes associated with it are transitively dependent upon the key. Another way to look at it is to say that its primary key identifies some entity, and all attributes describe some aspect of that entity.

What is Transitive Dependence?

A data element that is transitively dependent upon a key is one which, though uniquely defined by the key, is really defined by something else, and that thing is defined by the key. For example, in the case of our <social security number, first name, home state name, population of person's home state, and age> relation, <population of home state> is really dependent on <home state name>, while <home state name> is dependent on <social security number>. This is called *transitive dependence*.

```
Third normal form data (3NF)
(No transitive dependency)

Relative and purchase information is only transitively
dependent upon customer, they in fact relate to purchase and
relative tables.

Customer Table
- - - - - - - - - - - - - - - - - - - - - -
Customer SSN
Customer Lastname
Customer Firstname
Customer Middle Initial
Customer Street Address
Customer City
Customer State
Customer Zip
Customer Phone Number


Customer Purchases Table    (Repeated 3 times per customer)
- - - - - - - - - - - - - - - - - - - - - - - - - - - - - - - - - - -
Customer SSN
Customer Purchase

Customer Relative Table
- - - - - - - - - - - - - - - - - - - - - - - - - - - - - - - - - -
Customer SSN
Customer Relative Name
Customer Relative Phone
Customer Relative Animal Preference


Animal Table
- - - - - - - - - - - - - - - - - -
Animal Name
Animal Type
Animal Color
```

Figure 14-13: An example of 3NF

To eliminate a transitive dependency, the designer creates a new relation, in this case probably a <state> relation. This holds the name and population of each state. Then the population of home state field could be removed from each of the <social security number> relations.

By making relations 3NF, the designer has accomplished a significant improvement in the basic design. The list of normal forms goes on, and a detailed examination of it goes beyond the scope of this study. In practice, 3NF proves very useful for most applications, and not coincidentally, it also yields roughly the same table design as an ER analysis. (See Figure 14-13.)

As we said earlier, normalization can be used to develop designs for all types of databases, and more importantly, is often used to validate the design of existing or proposed constructs.

Denormalization

Although normalization proposes a way to develop an optimum design from a logical perspective, it often yields constructs that are less than optimum from a performance perspective. In these cases, the physical designer performs a process called *denormalization*, which is the reverse of normalization decisions for the sake of performance.

In fact, the term denormalization is used generically to refer to the process of moving away from a logically-defined construct arrangement to one that is more performance-oriented.

Physical Design (Construct Tuning)

Having completed logical and construct design, we are ready to begin the final phase, physical design, or construct tuning. Up until this point, no aspect of the design process has been concerned with the real capacity or performance expectations of the system. In fact, the procedures we have followed until now would be equally valid for any size, shape, or depth of database system. At some point, however, someone must begin taking the performance characteristics of the system into account, and begin to modify the design to support that performance.

Physical design can be a trivial and straightforward process, or it can be an incredibly complex undertaking, depending on several things. Among these things are the complexity of the system, the volume of data that the system must manage, and the transaction rate at which it must work.

Doing Informal Physical Design

It is not uncommon to find situations where a person speaks with users or programmers for a few minutes, and then turns around and immediately creates a collection of database constructs, seemingly without effort. Although this is not especially the best way to do physical design, it is certainly optimal if certain conditions are right. Those conditions are:

- The person doing the database construction is very familiar with the database product itself and has experience using it.

- The person is familiar with the users and has a basic understanding of the business processing being captured.

- The system is not too complex or too large.

If, however, any of these three conditions are not met, then the database builder must become a physical database designer and gather information to used as input to the process. These three sets of information define the first three steps of the physical design process. The steps are:

- The collection of information about the logical and construct design of the system (the logical and construct design steps described earlier)

- The collection of information about the database product's storage management and administrative profiles

- The collection of information about the performance requirements of the system (details about the size, speed, and complexity of the system)

Gathering Information about the Logical and Construct Design

In most situations, the physical designers of a database system have participated in the process of developing the logical design or at least the construct design. For these persons, the process of preparing to do physical design is easy. They simply take the formally prepared design documents and continue to the next step.

However, if they were not privy to these processes, then they must obtain the supporting documentation and take some time to become familiar with it.

In the worst case, where no supporting documentation is available, then the physical designer simply conducts the logical and construct design phases.

In all cases, physical design cannot proceed unless some kind of construct layout document or Studer diagram is available.

Gathering Information about the Database Product

It should be obvious at this point that if the physical designer is a database administrator or programmer who has worked with the database in the past, then the process of gathering information about the database product is trivial. Simply locating the DBA manuals and dusting them of is often sufficient.

On the other hand, if the physical designer is not that familiar or comfortable, then it is imperative for that person to take the time to become better acquainted with it. More database designs are botched by the improper development of a physical plan of construct implementation than anything else.

Too often, designers who excel in the process of logical and construct design fail to realize how critical and complicated the physical design phase is. An elegant design that runs poorly can be worse than no design at all.

How is it that physical designs become sullied? How can a person working so well with logical and construct design make decisions about the database's ultimate physical implementation that are so far off the mark? There are several contributing factors, but more often than not it related to a problem with paradigms.

Someone working with one database product develops a complete set of assumptions about how a database physically works, regardless of its environment. If, when these people move to a new database product, they fail to reeducate themselves as to the new programming, architecture, storage management, and administrative paradigms of the new system, then they will use the old ones instead.

We have reviewed hundreds of database designs where the system builder was obviously crossing paradigm boundaries, but failing to make the shift. This has resulted in relational databases built into hierarchies, network databases operating like flat-files, and dozens of other combinations. We reemphasize paradigm shift so strongly at this point because it is when the constructs are converted into physical databases that failure to make the paradigm transition costs the system's performance.

If the physical designer is unfamiliar with the database product's profiles, then time must be spent gaining that familiarity. This process may entail taking database design and implementation classes for the particular product; it could involve building test systems to become familiar the idiosyncrasies of the system; or it could involve nothing more than a few hours of pouring over vendor-supplied manuals and tutorials.

As a minimum familiarity check, the physical designer should be able to complete one of the database product-profile characteristics sheet we have developed throughout the course of this book. Of particular interest is the designer's ability to complete the storage management and administrative profile sections.

Gathering Information about System Requirements

Assuming that the designer knows the product and the constructs that need to be built, there is still one additional set of information that must be gathered. That is information about the system and the capacity at which it can run. System requirements information can be collected in three sets:

- The complexity of the system

- The volume of data that the system must manage

- The rate at which the system will run

System Complexity Analysis

How do we determine how complex a system really is? This is obviously a subjective question, since that complexity must be measured in comparison to something. To help determine just how complex a particular system is, however, the designer can use a simple table.

Since complexity to the database designer includes all issues having to do with the number of constructs a system will hold and the amount of cross-construct activity the system must perform, the designer can form an appreciation for complexity by developing a two-dimensional table. Along the vertical axis of this table is the name of every program that the system will run. Along the horizontal axis is the name of each data construct. This table can then be completed noting each construct access, from each program, with an X in the intersection square. (See Figure 14-14.)

Construct Names

Program Names	Animal	Customer	Relative
Animal Control	X		
Customer List		X	
Phone List		X	X
Owner Report	X	X	

Figure 14-14: Construct vs. program

If the system is user-driven as opposed to program-driven (i.e., users gain most of their access through a user-interface management system) then a table replacing the program names with user names will be more informative.

Either way, the result is a graphical representation of what kinds of access the designer can expect for each construct. (See Figure 14-15.)

Data Constructs

User	Animal	Customer	Relative
Alice Accountant	X	X	
Harry Handler			
Sam Salesperson			X
Sandy Salesperson		X	X
Pete	X	X	X

Figure 14-15: User vs. construct

For a more detailed picture of how each construct will be used, we add several more columns. These columns represent the number of times that:

- A key search is executed (looking for one record)

- A scan of the construct is performed (reading several or all of the records)

- A nonkey search (looking for one record without a key).

Under each column, the number of times the access is performed by each program is listed. (See Figure 14-16.)

Construct Names

Program Names	Animal			Customer			Relative		
	Key	Scan	Non-Key	Key	Scan	Non-Key	Key	Scan	Non-Key
Animal Control	4	52	32	35	2	151	5	39	135
Customer List	76	3	4	12	131	64	45	85	32
Phone List	31	46	93	56	78	23	138	157	8
Owner Report	6	8	10	112	7	9	11	4	115

Figure 14-16: A key, scan, and nonkey example

In cases where relating two or more constructs is an issue, the designer can develop a short table naming each construct, as well as all of the other constructs associated with it.

Between these three sets of information, a basic understanding of how complex and how large the system will be can be derived.

Gathering Volume Statistics

Of course, the simplest system in the world—the one with a single construct—can be a performance failure if the amount of data it must hold is not taken into account. Developing an appreciation for what the volume characteristics will be is a two-step process. First, we must determine how many rows or records of data each construct will hold. We refer to this as defining the *depth* of the construct. Second, we must determine how wide a given row or record will be. This is known as the *width* of the construct. Why do we need to know the width of a database record? Because we need to determine how many of those rows or records will fit on one I/O block or data page. Why figure out how many will fit in a block or page? Because database performance is in most cases I/O-bound, not bound by the number of records. The true measure of how much work the database must do to read through a construct is based on how many blocks it must read, not how many rows it must read.

For example, a construct with 100,000 rows, each 10 bytes long results in 1,000,000 bytes of data. A system using 1,000-byte blocks (1K) results in 1,000 pages of data. On the other hand, a construct with 1,000 rows, each row being 1,000 bytes, also results in 1,000,000 bytes or 1,000 pages.

In other words, one construct with 100,000 rows and another construct with 1,000 rows can actually be the same physical size as far as the database and I/O activity is concerned.

Calculating the Volumes for Constructs

The first step in developing volume statistics, is to create a two-column table, column 1 holding the name of each construct, and column 2 holding the number of records.

Customer Name	Number of Records	Width	Block Size	Number of Blocks
Animal	1,255	75	4,000	24
Customer	10,001	125	4,000	313
Relative	75,000	110	4,000	2,084

Figure 14-17: Constructs and block estimates

After completing this table, an additional column can be added for the width of each of these rows.

We now add two more columns to the table, one for the size of a block or data page for the given database, and another for our result.

Finally we can multiply the depth times the width and divide by the blocksize to give us the real size of the table from the database's perspective.

This simple method can, of course, be modified depending on the database product being used. Some databases provide for tight packing of data, as in the previous example. Others require that the data being stored use extra space for the storage of keys, extra space for the insertion of extra data, or simply wasted space.

The example provided can be modified by adding more columns to include this in the calculations.

Gathering Information about Transaction Rates

While volume statistics and complexity analysis certainly give the designer valuable information, the analysis is not complete without some information about how often each construct will be used.

In order to assemble this information, the designer often has to develop several rough estimates for the values desired. Very few people can definitively state exactly how much activity a new system will experience, but it is possible to develop some useful approximations.

As in previous cases, we will develop a table which will hold the transaction rate information that we are interested in collecting.

If the system is 2GL-, 3GL-, or 4GL-driven (in other words, if the main user access is defined by applications programs), then programs and their transaction rates can be listed in columns 1 and 2.

After doing this, we must translate all of these rates to a common unit of measurement (i.e., number of executions per hour). We do this by adding a third column to the table.

After computing these values, we can add one more column, this one listing the constructs that each program will access. This information can be found on one of the tables developed under the previous section about system complexities.

Although the information that this provides is far from 100 percent accurate, (because it doesn't indicate how many times a program will access a construct), it does provide a snapshot of what the busiest constructs will be. For those who require a more precise measure of these values, several techniques are available. These include using simulation models, artificial intelligence, and extensive user surveys. If the system is extremely important, then these more drastic measures might be called for. For a typical application development environment, estimates should suffice.

In those cases where a user-interface management system will provide the primary database accesses, then a list of user names and corresponding construct accesses can be used instead of program names.

If the number of users happens to be high, thus making the table cumbersome or too detailed, we should be able to lump several users into some common activity groups (i.e., controllers, analysts, salespeople, clerks, etc.) and assign approximate transaction rates for these groups.

The purpose of developing this table is to get a feel for how often each construct will be accessed. To complete the analysis we simply add up the transaction rates listed for each construct resulting in a final table, which should tell us how many times the construct will be accessed for a given time period.

Program	Rate	Trans/Hr	Animal	Customer	Relative
Animal Control	100/day	12.5/hr	X		
Customer List	10/day	10/hr		X	
Phone List	200.day	25/hr		X	X
Owner Report	once/week	0.025/hr	X	X	

Assume an 8-hour day and 5-day week

Animal construct	= (12.5 + 0.025) = 12.525 access per hour
Customer construct	= (10 + 25 + 0.025) = 35.025 access per hour
Relative construct	= (25) = 25 access per hour

Figure 14-18: A complete program/construct/rates table

The Physical Design Process

With these three sets of preliminary information in place (database product, construct design, and system performance characteristics) we is ready to begin the formal physical design process and to build data constructors.

We conduct physical design by working with each construct on an individual basis, and then carrying them all through seven steps. During each step, the proposed constructor makeup is questioned and modified, if necessary, to meet the new criteria. At times, these decisions are easy; at others they require judgement calls forcing the designer to make a guess as to what the best arrangement is. Sometimes, changing the physical design requires a change to the construct design itself. When this happens, the physical designer has to be sure that the appropriate parties (construct designers and application programmers) are notified of the change.

The seven steps required to turn database constructs into database constructors (a process which we refer to as *physical mapping*, are all concerned with defining an optimum physical implementation. These steps involve modifying our assumptions based upon:

1. General database configuration characteristics (blocking, buffering, and compression)

2. Simple direct keyed access (hashing and indexing)

3. Scanning access (sequencing)

4. Nonkey search capabilities (indexes)

5. Cross-construct relationships (pointers, indexes, and clustering)

6. Building groups of constructs that work together (architecture)

7. Overall system performance capabilities

Overview of the Seven Steps

As the designer carries the design and redesign of constructs through these seven steps, the concern is with determining how precisely to best meet performance requirements based on what the database product can provide in storage management capabilities.

During the first step, general configuration, we consider the databases blocking, buffering, and compression capabilities and see how the designer can modify the construct or the database to help overall system performance.

During the second step, direct access mapping, a keying scheme is devised for each construct. This scheme ultimately entails using hash keys or indexes to provide fast access to records being searched for most often by users.

In the third step, the design is again reexamined to consider the scanning capabilities required. In order to assist programs or users in the scanning process, the database products sequencing capabilities are invoked.

Step four involves considering those situations where the nonkey access of individual records is important. In this case, secondary indexes (those indexes not used to access the primary key of the construct) are built.

Step five, usually the most challenging of all the physical design steps, is where the designer considers the sticky questions of cross-construct access. It is during this step that hierarchies and networks begin to be assembled, and when the designer often has to back off from earlier decisions in order to optimize cross-construct activity.

Steps six and seven provide the designer with the opportunity to consider some of the broader performance issues. In step six, the designer begins to look for patterns and flows of access, and attempts to develop logical groupings or families of constructs, which are to be optimized to work together. Finally in step seven, the administrative profile and system-wide performance criteria are worked into the final design.

Throughout the process of physical design, the designer constantly creates proposed physical implementations, and then alters or discards them based on the optimum construction of a database that meets all performance demands as well as possible.

Although the physical design process may seem arduous, for the experienced database administrator or programmer, it becomes second nature. We detail the process here for those unfamiliar with the discipline.

Step 1: General Characteristics

The general characteristics that influence the way constructs are built have to do with those default storage management profile settings that have an effect on all database I/O activity. Specifically, this covers the blocking/buffering and compression settings.

Blocking and Constructs

To consider how to handle blocking for each of our constructs, we must consider two cases. The first case is those databases with a set block size, in which case we try to fit the data to the blocks. The second case is those databases that allow the developer to modify the block size to fit the data.

Although there is little that can be done for those products that do not allow the adjustment of blocking, one thing we can do is determine the number of records that will fit on a block, and see if there is any obvious waste occurring. For example, a database using a 2,000-byte block size can hold a maximum of only two 1,000-byte records on it. If the record is 1,001 bytes long, then only one record will fit in a block. (A very inefficient ratio). In cases like this, we should consider breaking the construct down into two smaller constructs, by reducing the construct width. Even though doing this requires the duplication of a primary key in two places, the net gain in saved disk space and reduced I/O is significant.

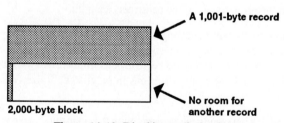

Figure 14-19: Blocking optimization

If, on the other hand, the block parameters can be changed, then we can calculate optimum block sizes for each construct. The optimum block size is some multiple of the record size. For example, for a 20-byte record an optimum size might be 2,000 bytes (20 x 100) or 100 records per block. (Detailed information about blocking optimization is available through database vendors.)

As for using compression, it really depends on whether that compression is optional or not for individual constructs. Some databases compress all data. Others compress none. Sometimes it is possible to purchase compression software as an optional package. When compression can be done on a construct basis, it should be utilized whenever constructs are extremely large, wide, or infrequently accessed.

Setting Priorities

The determinations made during step 1 of the physical design process can be made regardless of the performance characteristics of the system. No matter what you are trying to get the system to do, tightening up the blocking, buffering, and compression characteristics always makes that performance better.

During the rest of physical design however, it is not that simple. For the remainder of the process, we have to use a lot of judgement in making decisions. This is because it is not possible to tune a system to do *everything* well. Not every construct can be optimized for primary key, sequenced and secondary indexes of all shapes and sizes. Therefore, the operative words for the physical designer is discretion and sound judgement.

In order to help us decide when to create an extra index, decide on the sequencing order, or any other physical tuning operation, the statistical information gathered earlier in the process is of extreme value.

Culling Down the Field

For a system of any depth or complexity, we are going to have to come up with a way to set priorities for the decision-making process. Some of this is provided in step 6, but a lot of it must be done before that is possible.

To help focus the designer's activity, a simple 90/10 rule can be used. In deciding which constructs to design and optimize first, we should pick the top 10 percent of all constructs. This decision should be based on information provided by the complexity, volume, and transaction rate statistics. For a system with 100 constructs, the 10 biggest constructs, the 10 most frequently accessed constructs, and the 10 most complicated constructs should be addressed first. Usually, there is considerable overlap between these three groups. In fact, it is likely that the same 10 will appear at the top of the list each time.

Having selected the primary targets of design activity, we must now decide on a priority for the tuning of each. This priority, too, should be set using a 90/10 rule. In this case, the top 10 percent of the access requirements (key search, scan, nonkey search and cross-construct access) should be attacked. This also can be determined by the statistics that were gathered.

It is important for you to be aware that many old-salt designers consider the tuning of a system based on real performance requirements somewhat less than effective. There are those who feel that physical design should somehow be a mechanical and precise process, with plenty of black and white situations and right and wrong answers.

Although it is possible at times to apply some precision to the physical design process, more often then not it is judgement, not precision, that proves the most cost-effective. With these caveats in mind, we can continue with our review of the steps of physical design.

Step 2: Optimizing Direct Key Access

Earlier, we developed a table that included information about how many direct access, scan, and nonkey accesses would be performed against each construct within our system. It is during the next few steps of the physical design process that we take this information into account. For each of the next few design steps, the designer's decision about what to do depends on how often the specified action will occur, and whether there are any more demanding actions that take precedence.

After setting the general characteristics, we are ready to begin the real physical mapping process. Based on the statistical information available and the database product being used, we can use one of two methods for speeding direct key access. These methods are by using hash keys or indexes.

For optimum system performance, the absolutely fastest way to gain access to specific data is through the *hash key*. A hash key mechanism requires no indexes and no intermediary I/O to locate a record. It simply hashes the key and finds it. If the database allows hashed access and we are sure that no other access requirements will be too great (nonkey access, scan, or cross-file), then hashing should be the choice.

If, however, any of these conditions is not true, then hashing should be used with caution. Unfortunately, hashing makes sequencing, secondary indexing, and clustering impossible. If the database does not allow hashing, or it has been decided that using hash keys is too restrictive, then the only other option is indexing. In either case, the hashing or indexed access method selected must be built into the database constructor. This is, of course, a product-dependent feature.

If no primary access key is assigned to a construct, then it must be for one of two reasons:

- Either the construct will be a part of a hierarchy or network, and its position has already been determined (therefore no key is necessary).

- No indexing capability is available, which is highly unlikely.

Step 3: Optimizing for Scanning Access

Optimizing the system so that individual records can be found is only one kind of database access that must be considered, although it is probably the most common form. The second most-invoked type of access is scanning access. These are situations where the program or user reads through all, or a large part, of the construct from beginning to end.

To optimize for scanning access, we can use a database product's sequencing capabilities, which is the ability to load and store data in a certain order. We can also create a secondary index, which is an index used to drive accesses other than primary key access. Unfortunately, there are usually several different kinds of scanning sequences in demand. In these cases a determination must be made as to which scanning sequence is more important. It is an unfortunate rule of databases that you can optimize for only one thing. If the first scanning access for a construct is based on one field, and a second access uses another, then the system must be built to favor one or the other. The larger and more complex a system becomes, the more often the designer must face decisions like this.

The optimum way to scan is using a sequencing order and an index, which work together to make that particular order the fastest. Any other secondary indexes help improve running those scan processes as well, but not as much as for the first one.

To aid in determining which sequencing order to use, we can:

- Choose the one that makes the most sense (the fast way)

- Make a decision based on the performance statistics collected (the safe way)

- Wait and hope that one of the next design steps forces the decision one way or the other (the lazy way)

In any case, all constructs should have a sequencing order associated with them, unless some other processing requirement overrides it.

Step 4: Optimizing for Nonkey Searches

At this point we have created a primary access key (using hashing or a primary index), a sequencing order, and secondary indexes (for scanning access to the system). We also need to consider are those situations where users or programs need to access individual records based on values other then primary key values (i.e., the animal construct is keyed by animal-ID and the user wants to find the animal named Fred.)

Depending on the database product, we have the option of either creating an additional secondary index, which facilitates access by the alternate value (i.e., an index on the animal name), or just letting programmers and users know that those kinds of accesses will not be optimized.

Some Perspective on the Addition of Indexes to a System

Earlier, we stated that a system could only tolerate so much tuning activity and that at some point, the designer's discretion would be critical. It is in the area of secondary indexes that this discretion becomes obvious.

System performance, measured by the speed at which it will run and the resources it will take to get work completed, is based on several factors. For database performance, this can be how long it takes to retrieve requested data for a user (make searching fast), or how much time and energy it takes to insert, update, or delete database records (make modification fast). In the case of secondary indexes, these are contradictory performance criteria.

Assuming that a construct is very large and that lots of users require access using different fields at different times, it makes perfect sense for us to add as many secondary indexes as possible. This makes all of those accesses as fast as possible: more indexes, faster response.

Unfortunately, by speeding up the system on the retrieval side, we inadvertently make the system less efficient on the modification side. The more indexes that exist for a given construct, the longer it will take to load. Several indexes can make the load process two to six times longer because the system must also build and load each index. It will also greatly lengthen the amount of time necessary to insert, update, or delete rows. This is because, for a construct with 10 indexes, an insertion or deletion of one record actually requires the insertion or deletion of 11, not just one record. One record of the construct itself is added or dropped, but one row of each index also must be added or dropped. A costly operation to say the least.

So the addition of an index to the system speeds access times, but slows modification times. This is why secondary indexes must be added with care. Obviously, for a system that is read-only and loaded infrequently, these concerns do not apply and we can add as many indexes as desired. For updatable constructs, however, the reverse is true; secondary indexes should be added only when absolutely necessary.

Assuming that we have taken these facts into account, our system should now have a primary index, from zero to many secondary indexes, and some kind of sequencing order.

Step 5: Cross-Construct Relationships

Unfortunately, as difficult as the development of optimal arrangements for the individual constructs was, we are not yet through with the process of re-evaluating those decisions. At this time, we must go back and evaluate how the construct arrangements help support cross-construct relationship access (joins, navigational calls, etc.).

You may recall that during the construct design phase we developed a mapping for this, either through logical relationships or physical relationships. What we did not discuss was how these logical relationships would be physically executed.

Cross-Construct Capabilities for Logically-Related Constructs

For those architectures that support the logical relationship of constructs, the database product usually facilitates the joining of two constructs through underlying indexes.

Remember, that for the XBase database, a secondary index on the joined table is created prior to execution of the SET command. The same kind of joining indexes are created for inverted list and relational systems. These indexes, which may already exist as the primary index of the construct being joined to, are used by the database product internally to assist it in relating the two otherwise unrelated constructs.

Cross-Construct Capabilities for Physically-Related Constructs

Those products relying upon physical pointers or associations for affiliating disparate constructs (hierarchical and network) have standard procedures for creating these links (via pointers or indexes) and can be taken as default physical criteria.

Optimizing Cross-Construct Access

Depending on the database product considered, there are several ways that execution of cross-construct accesses can be optimized. These involve using sequencing or clustering.

To use sequencing to enhance cross-construct access, we can often arrange the database so that the two constructs being associated are loaded in the same sequencing order. If the database is sensitive to this order, then relating these two files is greatly enhanced. This is because every time the program or user moves forward in one construct, the complementary move in the other construct retrieves all of the matching records with a minimum of I/O activity. This is referred to as *synchronized sequencing*.

Student Construct

Student-Class Construct

NAME	AGE	STUDENT ID		STUDENT ID	CLASS ID
Jim	18	1		1	Math101
Mary	25	2		1	Comp102
Brigitte	16	3		1	Engl023
Laura	25	4		2	Math101
James	19	5.		2	Comp102
				2	Engl024
				3	Math101
				3	Span200
				4	Comp102
				4	Math399

Figure 14-20: Synchronized sequencing

The other way to optimize cross-construct access is through clustering. Under clustering, related constructs are stored physically adjacent to each other on the same storage page. This means that when one of the related group is requested, all associated records are accessed automatically and without additional I/O activity. Several of the large database management systems have built-in clustering capabilities.

Of course, as is always the case when a designer decides to cluster data constructs or to use sequencing to enhance cross-construct access, the result is that other kinds of access may be penalized.

The decision about whether to cluster or sequence or not must be made based on all of the system performance requirements information available. If accessing these two constructs together occurs more often than any other kind of access, then clustering or sequencing should be done.

Step 6: Evaluating Groups of Constructs

Step 1 of physical design concentrated on the global settings that constructs would deal with. Steps 2 through 4 are concerned with the process of accessing individual constructs one at a time, and step 5 looked at how to synchronize two constructs. During step 6 we address the issues of how to work on systems where constructs relate more than two at a time, which is how the majority of them relate.

If we had to deal with the physical mapping of constructs one or two at a time, it would be a relatively easy process. Unfortunately the ultimate value of a system is based not on how the individual pieces work, but on how the system operates as a whole.

Luckily for the typical business system, there are several ways that this overall flow of the system can be addressed. It is assumed when we begin this kind of analysis that:

- All single-construct access issues have been addressed

- All pairs of related constructs have been addressed

- We are now ready to begin considering how to get the overall performance of the system optimized as well

To perform this kind of analysis, it is advantageous to resort to one of the graphical forms of database layout (like ER or object diagrams), since these help in the process of visualizing the flow.

A typical system is made up of dozens or even hundreds of individual constructs all assembled in support of some major business objective. Let's look at a typical ER diagram and see how the business purpose can be derived from the model.

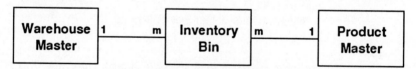

Figure 14-21: A simple ER diagram

This diagram obviously represents a set of three constructs for an inventory management system. Notice how the main construct, the inventory bin construct, is related to both a product-master and a warehouse-master construct. Notice also that one warehouse has many inventory bins, and one product can be found in many warehouse bins. (Each bin holds an inventory of the same product).

Establishing Priorities for the Optimization of Several Constructs

How can our designer decide which construct relationship should be optimized. Should it be the warehouse-inventory relationship, or the product-inventory relationship?

One way to decide is to find out who the system is being built for and what they want it to do. If the system is sponsored by the product management department, and they are most interested in reporting on different products, then the product-inventory relationship will be favored. If on the other hand, the system is sponsored by Warehouse Management, then the warehouse-inventory relationship will take precedence.

This business-driven approach to setting the priorities of design may seem somehow non-technical, but what is system building about if not to satisfy the needs of the people sponsoring it.

Statistics-Based Priorities

Another way to decide which of the two relationships to optimize is to consider the transaction rates each relationship expects. If product-inventory is accessed 1,000 times a day and warehouse-inventory is invoked only 10 times a day, then obviously the former relationship should be optimized.

Volume-Based Priorities

Yet another way to analyze this relationship is to use some kind of volume-based method. With this method, we determine which of the constructs has the largest volume, and then optimize its relationship with the next biggest construct. For example, if the warehouse construct has five records, inventory has 2,000 and product has 400, the inventory-warehouse relationship is optimized.

This method is also called *cardinality based optimization* criteria. The term cardinality refers to the number of values in a given mathematical set. To perform cardinality-based analysis, we can develop an ER diagram and replace the (m) and (n) symbols with the real numbers.

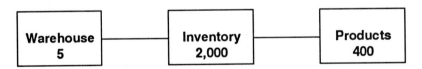

Figure 14-22: An expanded ER diagram

This allows us to develop cardinality ratios. The cardinality ratio is made up of the lower number over the higher number. For this example, the product-inventory cardinality ratio will be 1/5(400/2000 = 1/5). For warehouse-inventory it will be 1/400(5/2000 = 1/400). (See Figure 14-23.)

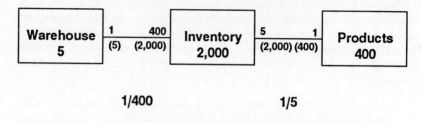

1/400   1/5

Figure 14-23: Cardinality with ER

The ratio closest to 1 (1/5 in this case) is the relationship that should be preferred. in other words we want to optimize the product-inventory relationship because it requires the most work to access. (See Figure 14-24.)

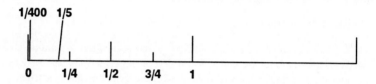

The closer the cardinality ratio is to the number 1, the higher the cardinality ratio.

Figure 14-24: The cardinality ratio

Whether gut-feel, statistics, business preferences, or cardinality guidelines are used, we should be able to view a collection of constructs and see a flow in the relationships between the constructs.

We can help explain the process of flow by looking at a larger expansion of the previously developed ER diagram for the warehouse inventory system.

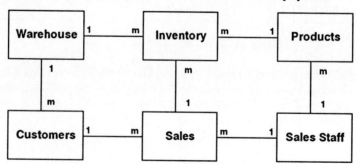

Figure 14-25: An expanded warehouse ER diagram

In this system, we have many more relationships to work with than in the previous example. We have address, salespersons, customers, and sales to add to the model. What we now have is a system that tracks not only the product inventory for the company, but also tracks salespersons, the products they sell, the sales they have made, and the warehouse through which customers are provided with products.

How can a System like this be Optimized?

Again, we can use statistics or gut feel, but business or cardinality analysis will probably prove more beneficial.

Business analysis might dictate that sales, the objective of salespersons and the company itself, probably deserves the preferred physical design treatment. In order to determine where the preference should go, the designer should answer this question, "What information is the most important?" Or, "What data should be made available the most quickly?" If knowing about sales, how they are going, and the product's availability to meet those sales, then we optimize the sales construct and build everything else around it. When we make a decision like this, we begin the process of defining a flow for the construct relationships.

Families of Constructs

When the number of constructs is especially high it can be useful for the designer to anticipate the different construct grouping that users will require most frequently and optimize these groups. Luckily, these groupings usually occur naturally. For example, accounting data is often separate from shop-floor control data.

Grouping constructs in this way can make the process of designing a large system easier by allowing the designer to establish interim priorities for performance and the integration of constructs. After optimizing the performance of the individual constructs with a construct group or family, the designer can then turn to the tuning of intergroup relationships.

When Analysis Isn't Enough

Sometimes, all of the configuring and reconfiguring in the world fails to result in a design that meets both the performance requirements of the system and the logical requirements as defined by the logical designers. When this happens, the physical designer has several less-than-appealing options, which will make it possible for the database to be built to meet both sets of demands. These solutions are referred to as design *kludges*. The term kludge refers to those situations where the developer of a system builds things into a system that violate the basic principles of structured, logical, theoretically-sound system design. Most systems have kludges built into them. It is not a matter of having kludges or not, it is more a matter of minimizing them as much as possible.

Denormalization

Denormalization, one of the most common forms of kludging, is the process of combining two or more logically distinct constructs to improve system performance. Of course, when two or more separate constructs are combined (unless they have a one-to-one relationship), the result is that several records from the smaller set of data, are duplicated within the new larger set.

The denormalization solution solves a performance problem but creates new problems as well. By combining two constructs into one, the duplicated records from the smaller of the two sets are disconnected from each other. This means that when one of them must be changed or deleted, the program doing the modification must locate not just one, but all copies of that duplicated information. This replication of data makes a lot of extra work for the programs using the system and makes it possible for data to get out of synch, or even lost in the system. Denormalization should therefore be used sparingly.

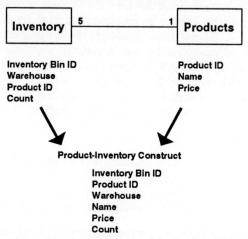

Figure 14-26: An example of denormalization

In general, the higher the cardinality ratio between the two constructs being merged (the closer the number is to one), the easier and less costly denormalization is.

Construct Replication

In cases where even denormalization cannot get system performance up to requirements, the designer's last resort is actually to make partial or complete copies of the constructs. This makes different kinds of processing possible by running them in parallel. Let's consider a case where this might happen. Take the customer/sales/salesperson constructs.

Assume that the designer is told that both the customer/sales and the salesperson/sales relationships must be optimized. Since it is not physically possible to optimize both of these relationships at the same time, the only choice left is to replicate the sales construct optimizing one version for each relationship.

Of course, in this case the designer has once again created new problems in exchange for the one solved. With two copies of the same data, how can anyone ever know which copy is the real copy?

This can be addressed in several ways:

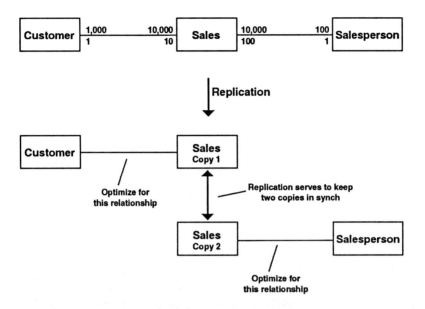

Figure 14-27: An example of replication

- If the system is read-only, then it doesn't matter. No updating is being done so the constructs will not change.

- One copy of the construct can be made read-only, while the other is made updatable. That way, everyone knows which is the good copy.

- Database replication services can be used to keep the two constructs in synch automatically.

Although the different methods of kludging (denormalization and replication) are far from optimal solutions, they are ultimately the last resort solutions the developer can count on to improve system performance.

Step 7: Global Administrative Considerations

After all of the constructs have been physically mapped and the designer is relatively sure that things have been arranged in the best way possible, there is still one more level of checking that must be done before the design can be considered complete. It is very important for the designer to validate that the overall performance level expected of the system is possible. Remember, not only must every transaction and I/O operation be supported by the hardware, network, and operating system, but so must the security, logging, recovery, and concurrency mechanisms as well as any other programming or development being done on the system. The accurate estimation of these kinds of parameters is well beyond the scope of this book, but a good thumbnail sketch of the global activity level can be obtained by adding all of the system performance statistics gathered and multiplying them by

2 or 3. This gives the designer a decent approximation of what the ultimate load on the hardware will be.

With hope, this kind of scrutiny was provided long before the physical design of the database was considered. But you might be surprised at how many projects are carried on to near completion before anyone asks the simple question "Can this hardware handle it?" When no one asks the question, more often than not, it results in a failed or seriously botched system.

Validation

Even if the designer has carried the design through all of these phases (conceptual/logical, construct design, and physical) and all of the physical design steps are executed meticulously, there is still no absolute assurance the system will be able to deliver what is required.

In order to develop systems and really have that assurance, the designer must either be very good, or some kind of validation of operating assumptions must be made.

To help hedge the physical design as much as possible, it is a sound and often used approach to build prototype and test databases. With these, the designer can validate the assumptions made throughout the design process.

Indeed, large data processing organizations usually maintain two or three parallel copies of their computer systems in order to facilitate the process of validation. These copies usually run on separate hardware so that developer experimentation has no impact on production performance.

The best kind of validation plan to build usually involves duplicating the production environment in a test environment. All databases, data, and programs are run on the test machine to assure performance before users are allowed to access it.

Unfortunately, this is a very expensive and time-consuming alternative. In other situations, only a small portion of the ultimate system is developed and tested in advance.

In all cases, the following tests should always be performed when the environment being worked on is less then 100 percent familiar to the developers:

1. **Volume testing**—In volume testing, designers build versions of all the largest constructs in the system, load them with full data record counts, and then run critical programs against them. Volume tests are critical for many kinds of data processing, but are not optional for database-intensive applications. Too many people have discovered too late that a database performs differently using different volumes of data. A database may fly through the processing of 100,000 records and then when the count reaches 100,001, performance degrades by 60 percent. Only testing of volumes higher then the maximum anticipated level tell the designer for certain whether a database can handle the job or not.

2. Pressure testing—In pressure testing, a series of test programs that simulate the expected activity level are run against a test database. Whereas volume testing checks the database's ability to handle lots of data, pressure testing allows the designer to gauge how it handles high transaction rates.

3. Prototyping—Prototyping involves the development of a scaled down version of the fully-functional system. Prototyping validates the logical design of the system and all of the business assumptions upon which it was based.

4. Benchmarking—Benchmark tests are kind of generic pressure or volume tests. They allow the developer to gauge how well a database performs based on some industry-defined standard of activity.

The decision to use any or all of these testing techniques is dependent on how much experience the system builders have with the products and business procedures they are dealing with. In a mature environment these techniques may not be necessary. In an environment where the products have never been used or the system covers a new business area, this kind of testing is mandatory. Too many database systems have failed for lack of solid testing.

Product Capabilities and Requirements

Throughout our discussion of database products and design, we have purposely avoided any discussion about the capabilities of the individual database products. Information about what one product can do versus another is best left to individuals to determine based upon their environments and experience with the products.

In general, database product's performance is a function of more than the product itself. Specifically, it is a function of how it is built and the storage management techniques it uses, how good the design is, and how appropriate the platform is. It is the interaction of these things that determine database performance, not any one of them working alone. Therefore, to answer the question of which database offers better performance requires that you provide information about platforms, design and volumes.

Vendor Claims

Database users should be wary of exaggerated performance claims and incredible volume capacities that most vendors advertise for their products. A database product's ability to handle these things is not the same as its ability to handle them easily and efficiently.

It should be intuitively obvious to someone that a PC database's claim of being able to handle one million records is a very different kind of million than the *millions* of records that a mainframe database can handle. They are totally different worlds.

When it comes to performance claims, let the buyer beware. And more importantly, let the developer test before committing large resources to projects.

A Taxonomy for Design

We conclude our discussion of database design by providing the last of our subject area taxonomies.

I. Conceptual Design
  A. Input-User Interviews
    1. Informal
    2. JAD
    3. Surveys
  B. Output-Data Models
    1. Informal (element lists)
    2. Entity/Relationship
    3. Semantic Data Modeling
    4. Object-Oriented Modeling
  C. Other Uses
    1. Data Administration
    2. CASE
    3. Repositories
II. Construct Design
  A. Inputs
    1. Conceptual Design Documents (see conceptual design)
    2. Database Architecture Information
  B. Process
    1. Transforming Models into Constructs
    2. Define Base Constructs (assignment)
      a. Names
      b. Elements
      c. Primary Keys
    3. Define Mapping Relationships
      a. Logical Mapping (XBase, inverted list, relational)
        -1:m—Foreign key assignment
        - m:n—Bridge constructs
      b. Physical Mapping (hierarchical, network)
        - Hierarchy diagrams
        - Network diagrams
    4. Normalization
      a. Atomicity
      b. 0th, 1st, 2nd, 3rd normal forms
  C. Outputs (produce a construct layout document)
    1. Studer Diagram
    2. Hierarchy Diagram

3. Network Diagram
III. Physical Design
 A. Informal
 B. Inputs
  1. Construct Layouts
  2. Database Product Information
  3. Performance Statistics
   a. Complexity
   b. Volume
   c. Transactions
 C. Processes
  1. General Configuration (buffers, blocks, compression)
  2. Direct Access Optimization
  3. Scan Access Optimization
  4. Nonkey Search Access Optimization
  5. Cross-Construct Optimization
  6. Grouping of Constructs
   a. Intuitive
   b. Statistic-based
   c. Cardinality analysis
   d. Business needs-driven
  7. Overall System Optimization
 D. Validation
  1. Benchmarks
  2. Volume testing
  3. Pressure testing
  4. Prototyping

Database Design Topics - Conclusion

The process of database design is a rich, complex, and demanding discipline. There are few challenges in the data processing world that can equal the that of developing an effective database design. We encourage you to refer to any of the several publications listed in the bibliography to find detailed sources of information about many of the aspects of database design. It was not our intention to provide a comprehensive investigation of database design; that would require volumes. Instead, it was our intention to provide you with an overview of the discipline and its many facets, and to provide a common vocabulary for the understanding of these processes as they relate to so many different organizations.

15

Conclusion

Congratulations

Assuming that you have just completed reading this book from the beginning, some congratulations are definitely in order. Even though it was our intention from the outset to present as much information about the different database systems as possible, from within a format that was both informative and yet easy to understand, the subject matter is so incredibly complicated and intricate that a large amount of patience and perseverance is necessary to really grasp the many different aspects of database management systems that are important.

A Brief Recap

In order to help the reader develop some closure on the many different areas that we have covered, we will take a moment to review the material as presented.

We started with a brief description of the discipline and principles upon which the writing of this book were based. The assumption was that there were a lot of database products on the market today, and that although many similarities between them could be detected, that there was a serious lack of consistency between the different sources of information about databases.

This lack of consistency is most easily detected in the areas of architectures, system design and system performance discussions.

Scholastic journals, trade publications, published books and vendor provided manuals all seemed to attack the problem of trying to understanding databases from a different perspective and yet no source could really provide a global sense of what the world of databases was really about. It was our objective to try to provide a first step in this area.

For a work like this to be meaningful, the author and researchers had to skirt a thin line between including so much detailed information so as to further exacerbate the situation by making things even more complicated and contradictory then they already are, or by being so generalized so as to make the work meaningless. We have attempted to measure this compromise carefully.

By starting with the most comprehensive list of products that we could muster, and then "triaging" that list down to the 70+ products included in the Appendix and the dozen or so products that were highlighted within the chapters about architectures, we have tried to give the reader a real sense of the depth and scope of the many different database products that are available today, without showing bias towards any group of products or approaches.

Review

In Chapter 1 we considered the most generalized database issues. Simple questions like "What is a database ?" , "What is a database management system ?", and "What are the different ways that they can be used ?" were covered.

We introduced the concept of the 4 database "worlds", four different environments (all hardware based),from which different styles of database systems have evolved over the years. We saw that the personal computer, scientific workstation, mini and mainframe environments all spawned their own unique approach to database management. Not coincidentally, these approaches were effected by:

• The needs of the people using their type of machine

• The hardware capabilities specific to the environment

• The administrative environment required

As time has gone on, and the business, hardware, telecommunications and performance requirements for each of these types of system have changed however, the organization of the database products have adjusted accordingly.

As a result of the migratory nature of database products, we are left with the ambiguous and contradictory jumble of theory, approach and terminology that floods the database market today.

In Chapter 2 we considered the different ways that database products are built and the challenges that people face when trying to understand and make use of them. We considered several of the ways that people can be *blind sided* when learning new database technologies. Specifically, the problems of myopia, anxiety and technical tunnelvision; all ways that people can inadvertently try to fill the gap in their understanding of database technologies with erroneous information.

We also considered the *expert* solutions, database gurus and the search for the *perfect* product. If this book is to accomplish anything, it should be to resolve in peoples minds that there are no *best* databases, only different approaches to solving the same problems.

The concept of the database *paradigm* was defined, and the critical importance of understanding different hardware, telecommunications, software and database paradigms when working with these technologies.

Finally, in this chapter, we considered the three ways that people can approach the use of a database, as a selector, as a system builder or user and finally as a system evaluator.

The key concept behind Chapter 2 was the introduction of the concept of the database profiles; programming, architecture, data storage management and administrative. It is proposed that the best way to understand and compare different products, is to segregate their functionalities into these four major areas. In this manner, it is possible to compare *apples to apples* across the vast array of differences between products.

We began our definition of the database profiles with the programming profile in Chapter 3. We defined both internal and external programming characteristics, and considered the different ways that:

- Programs and users can manipulate database data directly (the program data manipulation language (PDML or Calls), the user data manipulation languages (SQL or others), and the direct access facility(for products with no other available interface).

- Ways that programming could be done outside of the database itself through the use of user or programming languages and the user or programming interface management systems.

- The ways that the database itself could be used to provide programming, via stored procedures, triggers, structurally defined business rule enforcement and rules interface management systems.

Chapter 4 began the formal definition of the architecture profile. The architecture layer of a database system defines the way that data will be logically organized within the system. Unfortunately, too much time and energy has been spent on simply trying to decipher exactly what an architecture is, how important it is, and what its true impact on system performance is.

In Chapter 4 we introduced some generic terminology to help explain database system performance from an architectural perspective. Included are the concepts of the data construct (the building blocks of a database system), database constructors (the devices used to build database constructs) and some of the capabilities that database architectures provide including:

- Search capabilities

- The ability to cross reference data between constructs

- The ways that data can be cross referenced (static and dynamic)

- The way that data is accessed (record vs. set processing)

With the formal, generic definition of architectures established in Chapter 4 we considered the specific architectures in more detail within Chapters 5,6,7,8 and 9.

In Chapter 5 we investigated the Personal Computer based architectures. These architectures, the Flat File, XBase and SBase approaches to data management were all conceived based upon the principles that databases needed to be user friendly and capitalized upon the unique capabilities of a personal computer to do that. The nature of the platforms upon which they run is exemplified in the way that personal computer databases:

- Take advantage of high quality graphics

- Exploit GUI and GLUI functionality

- Take advantage of the efficiencies of a single user mode

Because of this disposition however, personal computer systems tend to:

- Be weak in the areas of multi-user support, backup and recovery and other administrative functions

We formally defined these three architectures as having certain organizational and performance characteristics but, of course, each product conforms to them in their own unique ways.

In Chapter 6 we considered the traditional architectures, the inverted list, hierarchical and network approaches to data management. These architectures can be found on most of the pre-relational mainframe and mini environments and are based upon the concept that databases must:

- concentrate on the minimization of i/o activity

- provide a database environment that includes a significant amount of administrative capabilities

- be flexible enough to work for many different kinds of applications

Chapter 7 reviews, in some detail, the make up and theories behind relational databases. No database architecture has received as much attention as the relational approach, and a large number of products in use today capitalize on relational principles to some extent.

The controversy surrounding relational databases, "What makes a database relational?" and "Is your database 'truly' relational?" may often times serve to more confuse then inform the database user as to what the real issues are. The issue is NOT whether a database is relational or not, it is "How well does the database in question help meet the business objectives at hand ?".

To help illuminate the controversy we spent a significant amount of time discussing the foundations of the relational database theory, as well as illustrating two physical manifestations of its principles in a tangible form via the DB2 and Informix databases.

Perhaps even more interesting then the relational databases themselves, are the additional capabilities that they make possible. Database programmability and interconnectivity have opened a whole new world of distributed processing and databases, and the relational databases have played a critical role.

After considering the relational systems, Chapter 8 discusses the Object Oriented systems. These are the newest and the most sophisticated of the database management system offerings to become commercially available. Although the understanding of different paradigms is critical throughout the database world, nowhere is it more critical then in the area of object oriented systems.

The object oriented paradigms, though powerful and productive, require an incredibly sophisticated approach to system management and the organization of data.

Chapter 9 concluded the discussion of architectures by considering the hybrid architectures and those products which use them. The hybridization of architectures allows the database manufacturer to build a product which capitalizes on the strengths of two otherwise oppositional architectures, and blend them into one product.

We sighted several ways that hybridization can come about including attempts by a manufacturer to re-engineer their product into a more advanced version, or to built an entirely new product based upon these principles.

In addition to the hybrid architectures, are the proprietary ones. Those products build using unique and vendor enforced architectures. Among the most notable of these was the SIM database with its Semantic Data Model approach.

Chapter 10 reviewed the operational principles underlying the data storage profile of a database system. We considered several different data storage techniques and saw that the minimization of physical input/output was the major objective for any storage mechanism. Since any system will eventually become I/O bound (since I/O is the most resource and time intensive operation within the computer), strategies that make data available to programs and users more quickly will make the database perform more effectively.

We saw several ways that data storage in general could be optimized including:

- The use of blocking or paging

- The creation of buffers or caches

- The use of compression routines (which also save disk storage space) and then saw how storage could be organized to help speed different kinds of search processing using:

- Indexes
- Hash keys
- Clustering
- Sequencing

and concluded with a view of cross file access optimization:

- Pointers
- Indexes

After highlighted each of these techniques we showed how each architecture could tend to use or not use any or all of them.

Chapter 11, which covers the administrative profile, discussed the many different aspects of a database system which have to do with managing many users who want to work simultaneously. Included were the topics of:

- Concurrency management
- Locking strategies
- Logging
- System backup
- System recovery
- System security

We saw that there was a dazzling array of different combinations of these functions that a vendor could provide.

Chapter 12 discussed the area of databases receiving increasing interest and popularity, the problems of running distributed database systems. We saw that there were several ways for data and databases to distribute operations:

- Data sharing
- Client server
- Fully distributed

and that these approaches, too, had their nuances including data replication services, which can be horizontal or vertical.

In Chapters 13 and 14 we investigated the principles of database design and implementation. Throughout these chapters we saw that design was in fact a three step process:

- Logical or conceptual design
- Mapping or construct design
- Physical design or system tuning

Whether the person designing the system has had formal training or not, and whether they are aware of it or not, all database designs must pass through these three phases.

During conceptual design, the business principles upon which the design of the system will be based are uncovered. This allows the database designer to understand exactly what it is that is supposed to be built.

Under the mapping or construct design phase , these logical business principles are turned into a reality. The designer maps logical objects (people, places, things and events) into the database constructs that will eventually hold the data that will drive the system.

After mapping the constructs, and determining where all data elements will reside, the designer must decide upon the optimum physical arrangement of the storage components in order to provide a system that will perform will.

Finally, the Appendixes at the back of this book provide the reader with an analysis of some 70+ database products in common use today. These appendix entries can be considered to be the opportunity for the reader to make the theory and conceptualizing that occurred throughout the book, tangible.

By comparing your own knowledge of some of the database products listed, to the content of this book, you should be able to develop a real appreciation for the make up of all of these products.

Benefits

The reader should come away from this book with certain clear cut principles which will hopefully change the way that databases are used, selected and evaluated in the future. Among the principles that should be very clear are:

The Dangers of Myopia

This discussion of all database products should help make it clear that no one set of database operating principles can be used to evaluate all products in all situations. A myopic or product prejudiced evaluation of any situation will leave a person short if the full range of possibilities is not considered. It is incredibly easy to believe that if you understand one database product, you understand them all. While in a very general sense this is true, in reality, this false sense of security can lead to very bad decisions.

The solution to this dilemma is to be sure that you fully understand the technology BEFORE making decisions, not after or during a project.

You Can't Oversimplify

It should also be blatantly obvious from our discussions that a database product is in no way a simple or trivial product. There are layers upon layers of issues, complications and inter-relationships which make databases some of the most sophisticated pieces of software running on computers today.

The oversimplification that many people try to enforce on these systems is only natural. We must try to simplify things to the point where we can understand them. However, in the case of database products, this can be difficult undertaking.

Understand the Business Objectives First

The real key to building effective database systems, is to start with the source of your problems of concerned. Too often, people tend to learn what the capabilities of a database system are, and then try to build a system around those functionalities. This is a backwards approach.

The objective of business database systems, is to provide services to business people, in order to help them to accomplish real work objectives. Computer systems can and often do enhance that ability dramatically.

Unfortunately, in our world of sophistication, specialization and focus, systems are often built seeing the business objectives as being secondary to the needs of the technology.

Fitting System Characteristics to Business Needs

The manager of a large data processing organization has heard a lot about client-server technology. It is said that these systems are faster, better, more economical and easier to use then existing mainframe systems. So, based upon this information, a large client-server project is conceptualized, proposed and approved.

It is only after the project is half done that the manager begins to understand the other consequences of this decision.

- *Development is NOT faster if the programmers do not understand how to code for the new technology.*

- *It is NOT less expensive to use client-server technology if the end users are so physically dispersed that the cabling costs are astronomical.*

- *Performance is worse, not better, then that of existing mainframes if the telecommunications environment is not stable and well managed.*

This is a good example of how NOT UNDERSTANDING the prerequisite paradigms and environmental characteristics can set up a database project for imminent failure.

Only by understanding how the technology works, the environment it must be in and the business needs to be addressed can database solutions be effectively applied.

Let's Consider Another Case

A manager has been told by the president of the corporation that the organization will be converting from a centralized organizational structure, to a decentralized one. The current corporate headquarters will be disbanded, and the corporate functions will be distributed to local offices. The manager must determine the best way to reconfigure computer systems to keep them in synch with the business plan.

In this case a client-server solution, or some kind of distributed database approach will make sense. Not because its newer or better, but because the organization of a client-server environment fits well with the new organizational structure that will be put into place.

Decisions driven by business needs, and that use those needs as their anchor points, will always succeed better then those using some other criteria.

The True Meaning of Architecture

Along with driving home some obvious points about how to use database technology, it is hoped that our in depth discussion of the different architectures has helped to make the term more understandable.

The architecture of a database tells the reader or user, something very important about the way that it is logically organized, and about how it will provide the user or programmer with access to the data that it stores.

What an Architecture does NOT Tell Anyone

- How effectively the system will run
- How well organized data will be
- How easy the system will be to use
- How much less expensive it will be to work with or any other of a number of factors.

These are characteristics of database PRODUCTS not database architectures. Different vendors implement architectures differently, and only by examining a particular product in all of its facets, can an evaluation be made.

The True Meaning of Database Efficiency

Along with desimplifying peoples spontaneous assessments of database architectures comes the even more fundamental question of "How does one assess how efficient a database really is ?"

Clearly, our investigation here shows that this question, like so many others, is not easily answered.

Since a database is made up of so many different parts and components, it is impossible to say how efficiently it runs or how well it is working without taking all of its aspects into account.

The efficiency of a database system is the net effect that all of its component parts have on the overall usability of the system that it supports.

The Database Juggling Act—(blending program, architecture, storage management and administration)

To understand database systems, and use them effectively, the designer must keep in mind and juggle all of the profiles that the product may have. A system with a limited programming profile does not do you much good if you are trying to build systems for a large organizations with many different needs.

On the other hand, to build a single application that requires some specific programming functionality that one product may have makes perfect sense.

The Future Of Database Products

Among the trends that are apparent in the development of database products are: Certain trends in the way that the architectures for these products are being developed :

- A continued mutation of products as the telecommunications world becomes more sophisticated

- A continued push-pull toward consistency between products, in order to enable cross product compatibility, while trying to maintain product distinctiveness

Architectural Migrations

Examining the existing products, and some of their history has indicated that there is a definite trend in the construction of database products by vendors.

Flat-File and XBase to SBase

The Flat File and XBase systems are being modified in order to capitalize on the newer and more user friendly SBase approach to architecture. Some of the Flat File products are not that far away from a full blown SBase approach, and most of the

XBase product manufacturers have aggressively pursued the building of SBase front ends to their systems.

Inverted List, Hierarchical and Network to Relationa

There has been a pronounced effort on the part of several manufacturers of the more traditional architectures to make their products more relational in construction. This is most clearly seen in the development of hybrid architectures that combine the existing products characteristics with relational enhancements.

Relational to Object-Oriented

In the same way, the extended relational systems herald the beginning of a new migration path, from relational systems towards object-oriented approaches.

Related Breakthroughs in Data Processing

Since it is in the self interest of every database manufacturer to capitalize on the new strengths that come available as overall computer technology continues to expand, it should come as no surprise that any new breakthroughs in database systems will probably be the direct result of some of the newer hardware related breakthroughs.

SMP Machines

One of the most exciting areas of system expansion will probably come from the area of SMP or symmetric multi-processor machines. These computers have been developed with a totally different internal organization from those of micro, workstation, mini or mainframe systems.

SMP machines break the processor barrier that has throttled back the ability of system designers to get more then one processor to work on the same task at the same time.

Under the SMP approach, many parallel processors can be dedicated to working on the same task at the same time, thereby changing all kinds of heretofore accepted standards of system performance predictability.

SMP and I/O

It is as of yet unclear, as to whether SMP machines will actually BREAK the I/O barrier of database systems or not. By being able to assign several processors to the task of expediting I/O operations, it is possible that the database systems of the future will be able to function without this constraint.

RISC Machines

Another, equally pronounced change in the makeup of computer systems can be found in the scientific workstations marketplace. The vast majority of machines being made for this market now make use of what are called RISC or Restricted Instruction Set Chips. These RISC chips, which are built to work with a smaller set of instructions are able to speed operations astronomically because they can execute these few instructions much more quickly.

Although RISC machines must still remain I/O bound, their increased speeds and power do make them attractive alternatives to mini and personal computer solutions.

Virtual Memory Explosion

The micro, mini and mainframe hardware worlds are not without their own memory and speed revolutions going on.

The personal computer 486 chip, with faster speeds and the availability of dozens of megabytes of memory, bring the personal computer ever closer in power and speed to the other computer platforms. This increased personal computer power will most likely start off another round of expansion of personal computer products which will boast more speed, more flexibility and more GUI type interfacing.

The mini and mainframe markets are also defying speed and memory barriers with new and effective means of creating virtual memory management systems that give them powers never before thought possible.

While the other platforms go for speed and fancy front ends, these workhorse systems are concentrating on improving their ability to manage more users, faster and with higher volumes of data.

Telecommunications Breakthroughs

As if all of this additional power were not enough to keep vendors busy, changes in the speed, flexibility and compatibility of heretofore unconnectable systems, means that distributed systems will become more and more of a reality with each passing year.

Future Works

So the user and student of database management systems will find that the understanding of today's technologies and approaches is necessary, not simply for the purposes of survival in the current environment, but as the only means possible to mastering the next generation of data management systems that will inadvertently arise.

Farewell

I hope that the reading of this book was as informative and enjoyable for you as the writing of it was for us.

APPENDIX A

Database Products

The following pages are provided to help the reader understand exactly what criteria were used to develop the values reported within each of the table entries for the products listed in this appendix. Each table entry is referened with an alphabetic character (a..z) and the text below explains the criteria.

Product Global Information

A._____

Architecture	: b.
Manufacturer	: c.
Platform	: d.

A. The name of the database product.

b. Architecture (see Chapters 5,6,7 or 8).

This will indicate the most closely definable architectural categorization based upon the characteristics of these architectures as identified with this book. (Please be aware that the categorizations given to products here, are based upon the characteristics described, and represent the authors assessment of the product. Vendor evaluations may differ. This does not make one or the other evaluation valid, it simply represents a different view of the evaluator.)

Values for this entry can be:

Flat File, XBase, SBase (Chapter 5-PC Architectures): Inverted List, Network, Hierarchical (Chapter 6-Traditional Architectures) Relational (Chapter 6); Extended Relational (Chapter 9-Hybrid Architectures) Object-Oriented (Chapter 7-Object Oriented Architectures) Proprietary or Hybrid (indicated by the // or || notation) (Chapter 9-Hybrid Architectures).

c. Manufacturer.

The full name of the product manufacturer or main distributor.

d. Platform.

This describes the hardware, operating system or combined hardware/operating system environment upon which the database runs. Values will be used which best communicate the environment in the simplest notation (i.e., PC-DOS will refer to all computers running with the MS-DOS or PC-DOS operating systems, UNIX will be used to refer to those systems which run on a large number of UNIX-based platforms).

Database Access Information

Database Access Method	
Program Data-Manipulation Language (PDML)	e
User Data-Manipulation Language (UDML)	f
Direct Access Facility (User interface system)	g

Database access method refers to that layer of the databases operational makeup which has to do with the direct manipulation of stored data. (This is as opposed to the programming languages which access the database and perform other procedural logic as well). (Refer to the first section of Chapter 3 for detailed information.)

e. Program data manipulation languages.

Database access methods can be independently defined access languages which are embedded into programs (i.e., IMS, IDMS, etc., parameterized calls), or that subset of a database products programming language which performs database I/O operations [i.e. The FOCUS, dBASEIII or Objectivity DB database call commands (find, lookup etc). Although these calls are only a subset of the programming language itself, we identify that subset as DIRECT database access languages, as opposed to the rest of the language, which is dedicated to processing the data retrieved.

f. User data manipulation languages.

The user data manipulation languages are those database access commands which perform database I/O operations, but are executed in such a way that they can be used by end-users or programmers without the benefit of a programming languages. The most popular user data manipulation language is SQL (Structured Query Language) but several database manufacturers have created similar types of nonstandard access methods (the INGRES QUEL or UNIFY GDML).

A user data manipulation language is usually, by default, also a programming data manipulation language since the user language can be embedded into application programs. The distinction is that a user can use an UDML but cannot use a PDML.

g. Direct access facilities.

This category of database access facilities is reserved for those products which have NO OTHER database access method available (no UDML or GDML). Products that have a UDML or GDML may have a database access facility built in too, but these will make use of the existing languages to make database access possible.

Databases without these languages, however, provide access to stored data, ONLY through the interface management system built into the product. Only personal computer based products (usually Flat File databases) will work with a Database Access Facility.

Languages and Interface Management Systems

Languages and Interface Management Systems	
User Programming Languages	h
Programmer Programming Languages	i
User Interface Management Systems	j
Programming Interface Management Systems	k

Languages and Interface Management Systems define the different ways that database systems allow programmatic access to the database. The languages and interface management systems listed here, make use of the database access methods (DAM) referenced within the previous box, in order to build an application system. (See the second section of Chapter 3.) Languages and Interface Management Systems are categorized as either USER- or PROGRAMMING-based. This distinction indicates whether the apparent intent of the products manufacturer is to provide the facility for the developement of application programs which are then run by end users (the Programming languages and Interface Management Systems) or for direct use by end users in the creation of queries and reports (the User Languages and Interface Management Systems). Obviously, programmers can take advantage of user tools, and users can write application programs, but most products are engineered to favor one group of the other. In general the terms user, executive, query or report in the name of the product indicates a user based product while terms like application development or programer indicate a programmer based tool.

Languages

Languages and Interface Management Systems are made available through several channels. Manufacturers can build it into the database (bundled) sell it as a separate product (packaged) or provide the facilities through a different vendor (3rd party).

Languages can be one of three types—2nd , 3rd or 4th generation.

h. User languages.

Included among user languages are products like the FOCUS or NOMAD products. User languages are always 4th generation languages.

i. Programming languages.

This includes the "traditional" 2nd- and 3rd-generation languages (Assembler, Cobol, C, Basic, Fortran, C++, PL1, Pascal, etc.), or several fourth generation languages (dBASE languages, Informix 4GL, etc.)

Interface Management Systems

Interface Management Systems define any kind of product or functionality provided to the database which involves the "management" of the database environment through screens, menus or other kinds of graphical representations. These systems can be GUI's (graphical user interfaces), GLUI's (Graphic Like User Interfaces) or TUI's (Text based user interfaces).

j. User Interface Management Systems (UIMS).

These systems include any facility for accessing databases which allow end users to manipulate the database directly. User Interface Management Systems occasionally require the user to make use of a User Data Manipulation Language (UDML) or even a User Programming Language(UPL), in order to develop the queries and reports desired. UIMS's can be spreadsheets, word processing packages, query to ls, report generators or any of several other kinds of access methods.

k. Programmer Interface Management Systems (PIMS).

These systems are designed to make it easier for programmers to develop applications. There are several kinds of PIMS including Code Generators or Application Generators (APGENS). These products accept programmer input from any of several kinds of forms or menus and generate compilable or executable code. PIMS's often require programmers to make use of a programming language as part of the generation process. The difference between a PIMS and a programming language is that PIMS's may use languages as part of their input, while a language is ussually written using some kind of text editor and then compiled and run separately.

Architecture Profile Information

Architectural Characteristics	
Data Constructs	l
Data Constructors	m
Search Capability	n
Data Cross-Referencing (Mapping)	o
Processing Mode	p

Architectural Characteristics describe those things about a database product which tell the developer something about how it manages data. While the architecture of a database product itself indicates how data is logically organized, the architectural characteristics define how that organization is implemented. (Information about architectural characteristics can be found in Chapter 4, Introduction to Architectures and in Chapters 5,6,7 and 8 about the individual architectures.)

l. Data constructs.

These describe the terms used by the database manufacturer to explain how data is physically organized within a file. Listed here will be the data construct hierarchy (i.e., a group of fields make a record, a group of records makes a file and a group of files makes a database). Common data construct terminology includes the terms field, occurance, attribute, or column (for the field level), row, record, tuple or instance (for logical records), tables, files, segments, object classes or record types (for the data constructs themselves) and logical databases, containers, tablespaces etc. (for large groupings of constructs).

m. Data Constructors.

These are the commands, utilities and methods used to build data constructs. Data constructors ussually consist of some kind of data definition language (DDL), database generation syntax, or database schema.

n. Search Capability.

The search capability tells the developer to what extent single construct query capabilities are possible. Search capability is either full or partial. [partial search capabiltiy means that only certain fields can be used as search criteria (key searches) while full search capability means that any field can be searched for.]

o. Data cross referencing (mapping).

In this box we will define the different ways that a database will provide for the mapping of related records in separate constructs to each other. Data cross referencing can be static or dynamic, logical or physical.

Static mapping refers to the databases ability to relate cross construct records only through the creation of a predefined relationship. Static mapping is provided by pointers, cross construct indexes or clustering techniques. Dynamic mapping means that the database does not require the developer to predefine the relationship between constructs, but allows the user or programmer to dynamically relate constructs at any time.

Logical mapping is accomplished when two constructs are related to each other via a shared common data field. (i.e., to relate animal and customer records, the animal record must have a customer id number as one of its fields).

Physical mapping occurs when the database developer establishes a physical relationship between two constructs (pointers or clustering).

(It is possible for a database product to optionally provide all four types of mapping capabilities.)

p. Processing Mode.

The processing mode describes how the database returns requested data to the user or programmer. Record at a time processing means that the database retrieves and returns only one record of data at a time. Set at a time means that the database returns whole blocks of data at the same time.

Database Programmability Information

Database Programability	
Command-Based Stored Procedures	q
Event-Driven Stored Prodedures (Triggers)	r
Structurally-Defined Business Rule Enforcement	s
Rules Interface Management System	t

Database programmability describes those capabilties of the database to allow programmers or database administrators to store programming logic or business rule enforcement in the make up of the database itself. (Information about database programmability can be found in the last section of Chapter 3). Database programmability is usually characteristic of only the newer database products (relational, object-oriented and some personal computer based systems).

Stored procedures are programs (written in 2nd- 3rd- or 4th-generation languages) which reside and are executed within the database itself.

q. Command based stored procedures.

These are stored procedures that are executed by the issuance of some kind of execution command.

r. Triggers.

These are stored procedures that are executed whenever the database itself detects that some event of interest has occurred. (i.e., a value in a certain field has been changed).

s. Structurally defined business rule enforcement.

This defines those situations where the database products provide for the enforcement of logical rules without the creation of programs. Field level constraints (defining what values can belong in a given field) and referential integrity are the two most common executions of this characteristic.

t. Rules Interface Management System.

Although rare, the rules interface management system will probably become an increasingly popular form of database programmabiltiy. Through this capability, the database provides system administrators with a series of screens, which allow them to define constraints, referential integrity and other kinds of business rules through the use of menus and forms. These rules are then stored within the database and enforced automatically. The repository and active data dictionary products provide this kind of functionality, but some databases include it as part of their construction.

Storage Management Information

Storage Management Profile	
Blocking	u
Buffering	v
Compression	w
Clustering	x
Sequenced Storage	y
Indexing	z
Pointers	aa
Scattering/Hashing	bb

The storage management profile of the database tells the developer what physical means of storing and retrieving data can be used by the database. Most databases have more then one option in this regard. The more options available, the more robust the storage management profile is said to be. The most robust group of database products in this regard are the classical object-oriented databases, which ussually provide all of them. (Detail on these characteristics can be found in Chapter 10.)

u. Blocking.

This box will indicate the default blocking size for the database (in bytes) or will state "Customizable" meaning that the developers can set their own block sizes or OS Dependent meaning that the database has none and uses the operating systems defaults.

v. Buffering.

This box indicates the buffering capabilties that the sytem has. It will either be OS dependent, customizable or of a set size.

w. Compression.

This is the databases capability for compressing strings of data before storage and decompressing it again on retrieval. Compression can be default (always compressed), optional (the developer can choose to compress or not) or none.

x. Clustering.

This is the databases ability to allow the developer to store related construct occurances in the same physically adjacent area (storing customer records with all purchased animal records).

y. Sequenced Storage.

This is the ability of the developer to store data in a presorted load order, and to make it possible for the database to take advantage of this fact.

z. Indexing.

This box indicates the presence and utilization of indexes by the database. Where possible, the type(s) of indexes used will be sighted, though this is not always possible.

aa. Pointing.

This indicates whether the database allows for generation of explicit physical pointers between data constructs.

bb. Scattering/Hashing.

Scattering is a storage optimization technique which attempts to spread stored data across as many physical disk devices as possible, thereby minimizing the chances for access contention. Hashing is the most popular scattering technique, which makes use of a hashing algorithm to predetermine storage addresses in a relative random fashion.

Administration Information

Administrative Profile	
Security	cc
Concurrency	dd
Backup/Recovery-Logging	ee

The administrative profile characteristics define the ways in which a database products make it easier to manage the ongoing database environment. (Details on these characteristics can be found in Chapter 11.)

cc. Security.

Defines the level and complexity of the security capabilties of the database product. Security is always at least as good as the operating system setting (OS Dependent) but can also be partial (securing some of the data within the database) or full (providing most of the database security characteristics considered).

dd. Concurrency.

Describes the ways in which the database allows for multi-user access to the same data constructs. Concurrency is described in terms of lock levels, versioning capabilties and may be called Full or Limited.

ee. Backup, Recovery and Logging.

Backup will be described in terms of how granular the facility is:

None—No database defined backup (OS Dependent backups only)

Partial—Backups of the entire database only

Full—Backups of individual constructs is possible

Incremental—Backups of only changed data records can be made

Logging will be described in terms of how much logging is done:

Full—Means that roll forward and roll back of all transactions at any time is possible

Limited—Means that logs are only kept for the life of a transaction

None—No database controlled logging at all

Recovery will be dependent upon the Backup and Logging capabilities.

ADABAS

Architecture	: Inverted List || Relational
Manufacturer	: Software AG
Platform	: MVS, DOS, VM, Fujitsu, Siemens,
	: BS2000, WANG, UNIX , VAX/VMS

Database Access Method	
Program Data Manipulation Language (PDML)	ADABAS direct calls (Add, Find, Update, Delete, Find-couple, Read(Sequential, Physical and Logical) and SQL
User Data Manipulation Language (UDML)	SQL
Direct Access Facility	None

Languages and Interface Management Systems	
User Languages	Natural Language (4GL)
Programming Languages	COBOL, C, FORTRAN, PL1, ASSEMBLER, RPG(3GL)
User Interface Management Systems	SUPERNATURAL
Programming Interface Management Systems	CON-STRUCT (program generator) and Natural (Interactive)

Architectural Characteristics	
Data Constructs	Fields, records, files, databases
Data Constructors	Utilities (DB generation) , PREDICT, ADABAS on-line services of SQL (DDL)
Search Capability	Full dynamic search
Data Cross Referencing (Mapping)	Logical or physical and dynamic
Processing Mode	Set and record at a time

Database Programmability	
Command Based Stored Procedures	No
Event Driven Stored Procedures (Triggers)	Yes
Structurally Defined Business Rule Enforcement	Yes, Constraints and referential integrity
Rules Interface Management System	Yes (Predict)

Storage Management Profile	
Blocking	Customizable (4k default)
Buffering	Customizable
Compression	Automatic but can be overridden (Decompression is at the field level)
Clustering	Yes
Sequenced Storage	Yes (smart buffering)
Indexing	Yes (Inverted list, modified B-Tree)
Pointers	Yes (Optional - physical/logical level)
Scattering/Hashing	Yes (in addition to above indexing)

Administrative Profile	
Security	Full transaction, field and table security
Concurrency	Locking at row and table level
Backup/Recovery-Logging	Full Backup/Recovery including incremental backups and full roll forward and roll back

Many database systems involve extremely complex data structures and data handling procedures which require a high degree of knowledge and extensive experience to design and use the system.

ADABAS, in comparison, has a remarkably simple structure, yet provides unique advantages for operation efficiency, ease of design, definition and database evolution.

The basis of the ADABAS storage module is the complete separation of the data and access structures. This separation allows ADABAS to manage the data and the access structure independently.

This simplified database model makes database planning and designing easier and more efficient. ADABAS's storage structure provides the following advantages:

°   Data retrieval/update is field oriented.
°   New fields may be added to existing files.
°   Keys (descriptors) can be created and removed without file reloading.
°   File size and update activity do not affect access efficiency.
°   Reorganization for space reclamation is not necessary.

These capabilities enable ADABAS to provide a level of flexibility unmatched by other systems.

(HP) ALLBASE/SQL

Architecture	: Relational
Manufacturer	: Hewlett Packard
Platform	: HP 9000 HP-UX, HP3000

Database Access Method	
Program Data-Manipulation Language (PDML)	ANSI SQL1 Level 2 with SQL2 extensions
User Data-Manipulation Language (UDML)	ANSI SQL1 Level 2 with SQL2 extensions
Direct Access Facility	None

Languages and Interface Management Systems	
User Languages	Powerhouse (Cognos), Speedware (Infocentre), FOCUS (Information Builders), Powerbuilder (Powersoft), Uniface (Uniface), SQLWindows (Gupta), ALLBASE/4GL (Hewlett-Packard)
Programming Languages	C, COBOL, FORTRAN, PASCAL
User Interface Management Systems	ISQL (Interactive SQL), ALLBASE/Query (Hewlett-Packard)
Programming Interface Management Systems	PowerCase (Cognos), Maestro II (Softlab), PacLan (CGI)

Architectural Characteristics	
Data Constructs	Columns, rows, tables, databases, database environments (DBEs)
Data Constructors	Data definition language (DDL) commands based on ANSI SQL
Search Capability	Full search on any construct
Data Cross-Referencing (Mapping)	Full logical or physical mapping
Processing Mode	Set and record-oriented processing

Database Programmability	
Command-Based Stored Procedures	Yes
Event-Driven Stored Procedures (Triggers)	Yes
Structurally-Defined Business Rule Enforcement	Yes
Rules Interface Management System	No

Storage Management Profile	
Blocking	Customizable
Buffering	Customizable
Compression	No
Clustering	Yes - on index structure
Sequenced Storage	Yes
Indexing	B-tree
Pointers	No
Scattering/Hashing	Yes

Administrative Profile	
Security	Grantable read/write/delete authority on columns, tables and views. Grantable run authority on stored queries and procedures. Grantable DBA and resource authorities
Concurrency	Configurable, automatically enforced record or page level locking. Table level locking per user request
Backup/Recovery-Logging	Full; roll backs and roll forwards, dual logs, online backup

The HP ALLBASE/SQL relational database management system provides a full range of information management components for mission-critical OLTP and decision support applications. The HP ALLBASE/SQL RDBMS provides extremely high performance and leading cost of ownership on all Hewlett-Packard computers: the HP 3000 family of MPE/iX systems, and the HP 9000 family of HP-UX systems. It allows fast development and deployment of 3GL and 4GL applications using a broad range of client/server and host-based tools, and provides industry-leading features like stored procedures, business rules and two-phase commit.

The HP ALLBASE/SQL product line provides the following high-performance, high-reliability products to address today's information processing needs:

HP ALLBASE/SQL, the relational database engine for all HP computer systems. The engine is available as a full development version for MPE/iX systems and as both a full development version and as a runtime version on HP-UX systems. The development version includes the language preproccesors (COBOL, C, FORTRAN, Pascal); the runtime version does not. Scalable performance is provided on all of HP's HP 3000 uniprocessor and multiprocessor systems.

HP ALLBASE/TurboConnect, the interface which provides an SQL "shell" for HP's TurboIMAGE network model database.

HP ALLBASE/DB2 CONNECT, a networking component which provides client/server read-write access from MPE/iX systems to DB2 data on IBM mainframes. The LU6.2 protocol is used for message transfer and DB2 can be accessed under CICS or VTAM.

Alpha Four

Architecture	: XBase
Manufacturer	: Alpha Software
Platform	: PC/DOS

Database Access Method	
Program Data-Manipulation Language (PDML)	None
User Data-Manipulation Language (UDML)	None
Direct Access Facility	Alpha Four (part of system)

Languages and Interface Management Systems	
User Languages	Alpha Four scripting language[1]
Programming Languages	None
User Interface Management Systems	Alpha Four (part of system)
Programming Interface Management Systems	None

Architectural Characteristics	
Data Constructs	Fields, records, databases, sets[2]
Data Constructors	Interactive data definition screens
Search Capability	Full, dynamic searches
Data Cross-Referencing (Mapping)	Dynamic
Processing Mode	Single record processing

Database Programmability	
Command-Based Stored Procedures	No
Event-Driven Stored Procedures (Triggers)	Calculated fields and autolookup[3]
Structurally-Defined Business Rule Enforcement	Field templates and validation[3]
Rules Interface Management System	No

1. The Alpha Four Scripting language is actually part of the keystroke macroing language. This brief set of commands allows user/programmers to enhance Alpha Four macros, to include certain logical constructs.

2. A Set in Alpha Four is a group of related database files. With the interactive interface of Alpha Four, a user/programmer can specify exactly how files in a set should be related, with the set design tool. Once a set is defined, the user only needs to choose a set to open, and all the related database files will be open, with the relations made.

3. The Alpha Four data definition process, unlike other XBase systems, provides users with an interactive interface for defining field values, calculations, lookups, and templates. This information is not stored in the actual .DBF file, but is maintained in a proprietary file format that Alpha Four uses whenever an Alpha Four database file is opened. Field Rules specified in Alpha Four are only maintained with the data in the Alpha Four environment. Any external access to an Alpha Four .DBF files will provide the data, but not the rules.

Storage Management Profile	
Blocking	OS dependent
Buffering	OS dependent
Compression	No
Clustering	No
Sequenced Storage	No
Indexing	Dynamic, B-Tree
Pointers	No
Hashing	No

Administrative Profile	
Security	Partial
Concurrency	Partial
Backup/Recovery-Logging	OS Dependent

Alpha Four, By Alpha Software, Inc., is an XBase compatible database system for nonprogrammers. The system offers an menu driven user/programmer interface. With the Alpha Four menus, a user can choose to open, or define database files, format screens, reports, or sets. Other tasks like defining a printer for the reports, specifying the screen colors, and importing and exporting data, are also accessed from the menus.

Intended as a "user becomes programmer" tool, Alpha Four provides quick, easy-to-understand methods, and assistance in the data definition, and system development processes. First the user can create a database, this process is all handled through menus, and easy to understand prompts. The next step is to define SETS, in this case, the program provides screens showing the names of the files, and arrows from the parent to children files. This way of displaying data relations is quick to learn and easy to understand.

Programming in Alpha Four is also an easy process. First, the user creates keyboard macros, opening database sets, accessing the appropriate data input screens, and creating the most common report forms. After the Macros are defined, the programmer can use the custom menuing capabilities to create menus for other users. After a fully automated system has been designed, the last step is to assign the main trigger macro to the configuration file. Now, whenever Alpha Four is started, the main macro starts, and a fully functioning database system with custom menus, custom input screens, and custom reports is running with no additional user input.

BTRIEVE

Architecture	: Flat File
Manufacturer	: Novell Inc.
Platform	: DOS, XENIX, OS/2

Database Access Method	
Program Data-Manipulation Language (PDML)	CALL BTRIEVE (Opcode, Fileno,...Status) Including Open, Get_First, Get_Next, etc.
User Data-Manipulation Language (UDML)	None
Direct Access Facility	None

Languages and Interface Management Systems	
User Languages	None
Programming Languages	C, COBOL, BASIC, PASCAL
User Interface Management Systems	None
Programming Interface Management Systems	None

Architectural Characteristics	
Data Constructs	File, header page, data page, index page
Data Constructors	BUTL.EXEC, through program callls
Search Capability	Limited (keys only)
Data Cross-Referencing (Mapping)	None
Processing Mode	Record at a time processing

Database Programmability	
Command-Based Stored Procedures	No
Event-Driven Stored Procedures (Triggers)	No
Structurally-Defined Business Rule Enforcement	No
Rules Interface Management System	No

Storage Management Profile	
Blocking	Customizable by operating system
Buffering	Variable cache
Compression	Yes
Clustering	No
Sequenced Storage	No
Indexing	B-Tree
Pointers	No
Hashing	No

Administrative Profile	
Security	Owner name, encryption, decryption
Concurrency	Lock at row level only
Backup/Recovery-Logging	Pre-image/Postimage (duration of transaction only)

Btrieve is a key-indexed record management system that provides high-performance file handling and improves programming productivity. Btrieve functions allow applications to retrieve, insert, update or delete records by key value, using sequential or random access methods.

The product was first released in 1983 and because of its association with NOVELL, the makers of one of the most popular collections of LAN software for personal computers, the database can be found in use supporting distributed applications throughout the U.S. and the world.

Because of its simple file structure, the Btrieve product boasts good performance on I/O type activities and provides developers with several toolkits that make it easy to work in the DOS, OS/2 and Windows environments.

The product is distributed with NetWare 2.x and 3.x LAN products and comes complete with language interfaces, developer utilities and supporting manuals. The applications developed to work with this product are portable between different environments (assuming of course they are using the NOVELL network software).

Btrieves record level locking and encryption/decryption services make it usable for many types of production applications and transaction integrity is preserved throughout the life of each logical unit of work.

Clarion Professional Developer

Architecture	: Proprietary
Manufacturer	: Clarion Software Corp.
Platform	: PC/DOS

Database Access Method	
Program Data Manipulation Language (PDML)	Clarion 4GL (data access subset)[1]
User Data Manipulation Language (UDML)	None
Direct Access Facility	None

Languages and Interface Management Systems	
User Languages	None
Programming Languages	Clarion 4GL
User Interface Management Systems	Clarion report writer (bundled)
Programming Interface Management Systems	Several programming tools included. Clarion Application Developer [2](Bundled)

Architectural Characteristics	
Data Constructs	Fields, records, files
Data Constructors	Clarion 4GL
Search Capability	Full dynamic searches
Data Cross-Referencing (Mapping)	Dynamic, Clarion 4GL
Processing Mode	Record processing

Database Programmability	
Command Based Stored Procedures	No
Event Driven Stored Procedures (Triggers)	No
Structurally-Defined Business Rule Enforcement	No
Rules Interface Management System	No

1. The Clarion 4GL Data Access Subset includes OPEN, CLOSE, SET, NEXT, PREVIOUS, SKIP, GET, PUT, ADD, APPEND, DELETE, and PACK.

2. Other tools provided with the Clarion Professional Developer, include:
   1. The Filer, an interactive data definition tool, (which eliminates the need to emmbed Data Definition in a program).
   2. The Editor, which allows programmers to edit source code, and generate database forms, and reprorts.
   3. The Compiler, which allows developers to compile applications in an interactive environment.
   4. The Helper, an interactive tool for creating Context Sensative help screens inside Clarion applications.

The Total list of available utilities provided with the Clarion Professional Developer is extensive.

Storage Management Profile	
Blocking	Clarion 4GL (By 1k segments or Record)
Buffering	Clarion 4GL (By 1k segments or Record)
Compression	No
Clustering	No
Sequenced Storage	ISAM
Indexing	Dynamic (B-Tree indexing)
Pointers	No
Hashing	No

Administrative Profile	
Security	OS dependent
Concurrency	File and record locking
Backup/Recovery-Logging	OS dependent-full roll-forward logging

The Clarion Professional Developer is an application development system. The system includes a very fast and flexible 4GL, with several user tools to simplify the task of programming.

Designed as an application developer first, the Clarion programming language offers some of the full featured commands found in 4GLs, but it also provides some lower level commands provided by 3GLs. This mix of language types makes Clarion programs faster than 4GLs, but easier to write code in, than 3GLs.

Data definition with Clarion is done with the language, or with the interactive "Filer" utility. One of the unique features in Clarion is the ability to specify "Key" fields during the Data Definition process. (This coincides with "Indexed Sequential Access Method" ISAM data tables.) But Clarion also provides programmers the ability to create index files, which can be defined dynamically, and only used when appropriate.

(CA-)DATACOM

Architecture	: Inverted List || Relational
Manufacturer	: Computer Associates Inc.
Platform	: MVS, VM, VSE, PC ,UNIX,
	: VAX, OS2, AS400

Database Access Method	
Program Data-Manipulation Language (PDML)	Call DBNTRY(ADDIT, DELET, GETIT, SELFR(SELECT), etc) and SQL
User Data-Manipulation Language (UDML)	SQL
Direct Access Facility	None

Languages and Interface Management Systems	
User Languages	None
Programming Languages	COBOL, ASSEMBLER, PL1, FORTRAN and C
User Interface Management Systems	CA-Data-Query (packaged)
Programming Interface Management Systems	CA-Ideal and CA-MetaCOBOL (packaged)

Architectural Characteristics	
Data Constructs	Fields, records, tables, data areas and databases (relational) elements, dataviews (Non-relational)
Data Constructors	SQL-DDL or CA-datacom schema definition or CA-data dictionary
Search Capability	Partial (inverted list)||Full (relational)
Data Cross Referencing (Mapping)	Static (inverted list)||Dynamic (Relational)
Processing Mode	Record or set

Database Programmability	
Command-Based Stored Procedures	None
Event-Driven Stored Procedures (Triggers)	None
Structurally-Defined Business Rule Enforcement	Yes, referential integrity and domain constraints
Rules Interface Management System	None

Storage Management Profile	
Blocking	From 512 to 16k (4k preferred)
Buffering	Customizable
Compression	Optional
Clustering	Yes
Sequenced Storage	Yes
Indexing	Yes
Pointers	No
Scattering/Hashing	No

Administrative Profile	
Security	Full transaction and table security
Concurrency	Locking at record, page and table level
Backup/Recovery-Logging	Full Backup/Recovery

The CA-DATACOM product is marketed by software giant Computer Associates and has a significant following especially in the mid-range to large IBM mainframe environments. Prior to 1990 the product was solely an inverted list architecture, but with release 8.0, it includes full ANSI SQL support in parallel to the inverted list functionality. This includes support for full SQL-DDL, DML and DCL. The personal computer version of the product provides the user with all of the functionality of the mainframe product in the PC-DOS environment.

Also included in the CA-DATACOM product line is CA-IDEAL, a complete lifecycle support development tool, which allows programmers to build applications while working interactively with the databases data dictionary capabilities.

For end users, the CA_DATAQUERY tool, allows them to work interactively with the database by filling defined screens. The product works in three modes, NOVICE, Intermediary and EXPERT. The NOVICE mode presents lists for the user to select to construct a query. The Intermediary mode provides the user with helpful prompts and fill -in-the-blank capabilities to make query building easier, while the EXPERT mode allows the more proficient end user to bypass these features and get right to the job of generating information.

The other product of particular importance to the user of the DATACOM collection of products is the CA-DB:STAR offering. This product makes it possible to establish communications between several different databases, on different kinds of platforms, and makes it possible for them to work together as a single, distributed database system.

The CA-DATACOM database, like all parallel hybrid architectures, provides the system developer with the ability to take advantage of the strengths of both architectures (relational and inverted list) while minimizing the detriment.

DataEase

Architecture	: SBase
Manufacturer	: DataEase International
Platform	: PC/DOS

Database Access Method	
Program Data-Manipulation Language (PDML)	None
User Data-Manipulation Language (UDML)	DQL Language (database access commands) including list, delete, enter, output and modify records
Direct Access Facility	None

Languages and Interface Management Systems	
User Languages	None
Programming Languages	DQL (the DataEase Application Programming Language)
User Interface Management Systems	Record entry, query by example and DataEase menus
Programming Interface Management Systems	Forms definition and relationships, DQL avanced processing and menu definition screens, GrafTalk (packaged)

Architectural Characteristics	
Data Constructs	Database, form, records, fields (under DataEase a file corresponds to a form)
Data Constructors	Form definition menu
Search Capability	Full
Data Cross Referencing (Mapping)	Static defined in form relationships or ad-hoc
Processing Mode	Set processing

Database Programmability	
Command-Based Stored Procedures	No
Event-Driven Stored Procedures (Triggers)	No
Structurally-Defined Business Rule Enforcement	Referential Integrity via multiform match/key fields and constraint definitions
Rules Interface Management System	No

Storage Management Profile	
Blocking	Customized by operating system
Buffering	Customized by operating system
Compression	No
Clustering	No
Sequenced Storage	No
Indexing	Yes
Pointers	No
Hashing	No

Administrative Profile	
Security	Yes, Field, database, different levels, menus,users
Concurrency	Lock on Multiform, database, files, records
Backup/Recovery-Logging	Limited (full refresh of backup copies only)

This product is DataEase International's "relational" database application development system and flagship product for single- and multi-user environments. DataEase's intuitve menu system and query-by-example (QBE) reporting enable novice users to build, maintain and run database applications, while expert users can quickly build sophisticated applications using the power of DataEase's DQL, the DataEase Query Language. DataEase's selective use of Object-oriented techniques replaces hundreds of lines of code with a few keystrokes. It allows applications to address from 1 to 16MBytes of extended memory.

DataEase permits conversion of single-user applications to network file-server environments via one key stroke. DataEase offers the LAN user transparent access to the data they need wherever it resides on the network including automatic screen refresh, user conflict messages, and automatic safeguards to protect the security and integrity of the data.

With its powerful form-based approach to application development DataEase makes it possible for nontechnical users to develop intuitively pleasing systems with a minimum effort.

Release 4.5 of DataEase also provides SQL database connectivity through the addition of DataEase SQL Connect drivers. By adding DataEase SQL Connect PRISM Drivers to the 4.5 environment, users can simultaneously and transparently access: Microsoft/Sybase SQL Server, Oracle Server, Micro Decisionware's Database Gateway for DB2, and IBM OS2 Extended Edition Database Manager. (Access to Information Builders EDA/SQL, IBM's DRDA and Netware SQL are currently under development.)

DataPerfect

Architecture	: SBase[1]
Manufacturer	: WordPerfect Corp.
Platform	: PC/DOS

Database Access Method	
Program Data Manipulation Language (PDML)	None
User Data Manipulation Language (UDML)	None
Direct Access Facility	DataPerfect (part of System)

Languages and Interface Management Systems	
User Languages	None
Programming Languages	None
User Interface Management Systems	DataPerfect (part of System)
Programming Interface Management Systems	DataPerfect (part of System)[2]

Architectural Characteristics	
Data Constructs	Fields, records, panels, databases
Data Constructors	Interactive panel definition screen
Search Capability	Full dynamic searches
Data Cross Referencing (Mapping)	Dynamic[1]
Processing Mode	Record processing

Database Programmability	
Command-Based Stored Procedures	None
Event-Driven Stored Procedures (Triggers)	Field calculation and lookups
Structurally-Defined Business Rule Enforcement	Field templates and defaults
Rules Interface Management System	None

1. Although DataPerfect is referred to as network, the database engine handles each data file (panel) as a separate entity, and cross referencing is done with logical (index key) links. This does not coincide with the strict definition of network, but the most efficient use of DataPerfect is to define the data panels in hierarchical structures.

2. Database programming in DataPerfect is handled through the interactive programmers interface, provided within the DataPerfect environment.

Storage Management Profile	
Blocking	OS dependent
Buffering	OS dependent
Compression	No
Clustering	No
Sequenced Storage	No
Indexing	Static
Pointers	No
Hashing	No

Administrative Profile	
Security	Partial
Concurrency	No
Backup/Recovery-Logging	No

DataPerfect, by WordPerfect Corporation is more than just a good tool for WordPefect mailmerge. DataPerfect offers an intuitive user/programmer tool for quick data definition and entry.

The main work area for DataPerfect is the panel window screen. A panel is a collection of fields, stored in a single DOS window, relations between panels are defined through index key links. The child records for any data panel must have a unique index key for a relation to succeed. The ability to dynamically link data panels, allows users to create sophisticated hierarchies, and networks of data with no previous programming ability.

As mentioned above, the DataPerfect interface is a user/programmer tool. Most of the DataPerfect features are Function key driven, like the manufacturers staple product, and are therefore quite easy to learn for anybody proficient with WordPerfect.

Panel definition is done interactively with the panel definition mode. Panels can be defined, and redefined by simply pressing the appropriate function key. A user/programmer can specify a password to limit access to the panel definition screen, but once accessed, all facets of data definition can me changed from the same screen as the data entry and management is performed.

DataPerfect field types offer the normal set of; characier, numeric, date, and logical, but the unique feature is that character field types can be defined as static (i.e., No more than 20 characters) or as variable length fields, which are only limited to the amount of storage space on the computer.

The report abilities include a feature to output selected fields to a file written in WordPerfect merge format, this ability makes DataPerfect a good tool for sophisticated database/word processing jobs.

DB2

Architecture	: Relational
Manufacturer	: IBM
Platform	: MVS

Database Access Method	
Program Data-Manipulation Language (PDML)	SQL
User Data-Manipulation Language (UDML)	SQL
Direct Access Facility	None

Languages and Interface Management Systems	
User Languages	None
Programming Languages	2nd,-3rd-and 4th-GLs (including COBOL, C, FORTRAN, ASSEMBLER, PL/1 and others)
User Interface Management Systems	QMF(packaged)
Programming Interface Management Systems	CSP(packaged)

Architectural Characteristics	
Data Constructs	Stogroup, tablespace, table , row, column
Data Constructors	DDL-SQL
Search Capability	Dynamic
Data Cross-Referencing (Mapping)	Full
Processing Mode	Set processing

Database Programmability	
Command-Based Stored Procedures	No
Event-Driven Stored Procedures (Triggers)	Edit procs and valid procs
Structurally-Defined Business Rule Enforcement	Referential integrity
Rules Interface Management System	MVS repository manager (packaged)

Storage Management Profile	
Blocking	Yes, (4k page size)
Buffering	Buffer pools (variable)
Compression	No
Clustering	No
Sequenced Storage	Yes, (refered to by IBM as "relational clustering")
Indexing	B-tree
Pointers	No
Scattering/Hashing	No

Administrative Profile	
Security	Full SQL-DCL (Grant/Revoke) for columns, rows, tables and databases
Concurrency	Locking at the page or tablespace level
Backup/Recovery-Logging	Full backup and recovery including incremental backups and full roll forward and roll back

The DB2 database is considered by many to be "the" database that put relational systems "on the map." Through the combination of an aggressive marketing program by IBM over the past several years, and an equally aggressive commitment by IBM to the continued enhancement of the DB2 product, DB2 has become a shining example of how effective relational systems can be in the large scale, high-volume database processing environment.

With it companion product QMF (Query Management Facility), IBM has been able to provide customers with a database environment that meets the needs of many large organizations for very large relational databases.

DB2 is one of the two direct descendents of IBM's System R, the original prototype relational database management system (along with its "sister" product SQL/DS), which is IBM's mainframe relational database for the VM and DOS/VSE environments.

DB2 has definitely been "the hot database product" of the 1980's and continues to experience continued acceptance among large IBM mainframe organizations.

DB2 is a critical component of IBM's SAA (Systems Application Architecture), and AD-CYCLE (Application Development Cycle) initiatives as well as the DRDBMS (Distributed Relational Database Management System) and the MVS-Repository Manager products and should therefore continue to be a major force in the definiton of database management systems for many years to come.

dBase III+

Architecture   : XBase
Manufacturer : Borland International
Platform   : PC/DOS

Database Access Method	
Program Data Manipulation Language (PDML)	dBase 4GL (data access subset)[1]
User Data Manipulation Language (UDML)	None
Direct Access Facility	None

Languages and Interface Management Systems	
User Languages	None
Programming Languages	dBase 4GL
User Interface Management Systems	dBase assistant (bundled)
Programming Interface Management Systems	Report and screen generators,[2] (part of system). dBase Apgen[3] (bundled). Several 3rd party Apgens.

Architectural Characteristics	
Data Constructs	Fields, records, databases (files)
Data Constructors	Interactive data definition. File structure copy commands
Search Capability	Full dynamic searching
Data Cross-Referencing (Mapping)	Dynamic
Processing Mode	Single record processing only

Database Programmability	
Command-Based Stored Procedures	No
Event-Driven Stored Procedures (Triggers)	No
Structurally-Defined Business Rule Enforcement	No
Rules Interface Management System	No

1. The dBase language data management subset includes the commands USE (*filename*), INDEX ON (*fieldname*), FIND (*keyvalue*) EDIT, ERASE, REPLACE, etc.

2. The dBase III+ environment includes a screen format generator, a report generator, and a query generator. These three, pull-down menu, interactive utilities are designed for nonprogrammers to create sophisticated applications without prior programming capabilities.

3. The dBase III+ Apgen (Application Generator), is a pull-down menu interface that allows users to define simple applications. Along with predefined queries, custom data input forms, and custom report definitions created with the above utilities. The Apgen creates the dBase 4GL program code, so that no user knowledge of programming or programming languages is necessary.

Storage Management Profile	
Blocking	OS dependent
Buffering	OS dependent
Compression	No
Clustering	No
Sequenced Storage	No
Indexing	Dynamic indexing capabilities (B-Tree)
Pointers	No
Hashing	No

Administrative Profile	
Security	Partial
Concurrency	Limited
Backup/Recovery-Logging	OS dependent

dBase III+, recently acquired from Ashton Tate, is the father of the XBase database management systems. The predecessor, dBase II, is the grandfather, each of the dBase products, offers the combination of a user friendly interface, with the powerful dBase 4GL.

Requiring only 384k of DOS memory, and operating with dual floppy disk drive systems, dBase III+ runs on the range of hardware configurations found in most organizations, from limited capacity 8088--based PCs, to todays most powerful new workstations

The dBase III+ environment has the capability to maintain up to 10 open database files, and up to 15 files can be open at one time, including index, format, and query files. Among it's strongest features, dBase III+ includes an automatic catalog system for programmers to maintain a list of all files in a system, with descriptive text. Another useful feature is the "dBase assistant," the "assistant" is a pull-down menu interface, that offers users the ability to create, index, append, edit, and modify database files.

The dBase III+ programming language is an interpreted 4GL, any programs written can be run and debugged on the fly without the compile step. The language offers programmers the ability to define program menus, interactive data management screens, and macro capabilities to provide access to MEMO fields.

Optional dBRUN, dB-CODE, and dB-LINKER module permit source code protection and linking, once application development is completed.

The system provides immediate LAN connectivity for the single user, with file, and record locking, and up to eight levels of password protection which can be applied to groups, users, files, or fields. Four forms of access can be specified at each level, UPDATE, EXTEND, READ, and DELETE, and with the dBase III+ LAN pack, (supplied optionally by Borland) a system can be installed at a low per-user cost.

dBase IV

Architecture	: XBase
Manufacturer	: Borland International.
Platform	: PC/DOS, UNIX, Sun/OS,
	: AIX, MVS, VM

Database Access Method	
Program Data-Manipulation Language (PDML)	dBase 4GL (Data management subset)[1]; SQL[2]
User Data-Manipulation Language (UDML)	SQL
Direct Access Facility	None

Languages and Interface Management Systems	
User Languages	None
Programming Languages	dBase 4GL
User Interface Management Systems	dBase assistant (part of system)
Programming Interface Management Systems	Format, report, and query generators (part of system) dBase Apgen[3] (bundled),

Architectural Characteristics	
Data Constructs	Fields, records, databases (files)
Data Constructors	Interactive data definition SQL
Search Capability	Full dynamic searching
Data Cross-Referencing (Mapping)	Dynamic
Processing Mode	Single-record processing only

Database Programmability	
Command-Based Stored Procedures	No
Event-Driven Stored Procedures (Triggers)	No
Structurally-Defined Business Rule Enforcement	No
Rules Interface Management System	No

1. The dBase language data management subset includes the commands USE (*filename*), INDEX ON (*fieldname*), FIND (*keyvalue*) EDIT, ERASE, REPLACE, GET, etc.

2. Although dBase IV is an XBase system, the sytem offers two processing modes, dBase 4GL, Commonly referred to as the Dot Prompt Mode, and an interactive SQL Mode, which uses the ANSI syntax of SQL to manage dBase files.

3. The dBase IV Apgen (Application Generator), is a pull-down menu interface that allows users to define simple applications.

Storage Management Profile	
Blocking	The dynamic memory management system
Buffering	The dynamic memory management system
Compression	No
Clustering	No
Sequenced Storage	No
Indexing	Dynamic indexing capabilities. B-Tree, multiple index files.
Pointers	None
Hashing	None

Administrative Profile	
Security	Full, up to 8 levels of password protection
Concurrency	File and record locking on networks
Backup/Recovery-Logging	Full backup, and logging

The dBase IV family of products offers a full range of database capabilities on several computer platforms. The UNIX versions of dBase IV offer full transparent portability between the UNIX and DOS systems, Most program code, data, and indexes can be ported between platforms with no conversion required, except for operating system-specific differences. Among the several enhancement gained with the faster UNIX operating system, the dBase IV UNIX products automatically apply UNIX security procedures to access, and supply automatic data encryption.

For the dBase IV 3270-MVS and VM versions, the additional ability to access DB2, IMS, FOCUS, TSO, and CMS data makes it a powerful tool for all ranges of data processing needs.

Among the enhancements to the dBase III+ programming language, dBase IV provides a pseudo compiler, several different language enhancements for easier interface creation, and the ability to add UDFs (user defined functions) to programs, and data input screens, for field validation. dBase IV also provides programmers with the option of using embedded SQL, or the dBase data access commands to manage data.

The system also provides programmers and users multiple index files. The multiple index file stores all index definitions for a particular database in a single *filename*.MDX file, reducing the programmers index maintenance resposabilities to simply making sure the .MDX file is open.

DBC/1012

Architecture	: Relational - Database Machine
Manufacturer	: Teradata Corp.
Platform	: Provides its own platform but
	: can be connected to LAN'S and
	: IBM, UNISYS, AMDAHL and
	: SIEMENS platforms

Database Access Method	
Program Data-Manipulation Language (PDML)	DBC/SQL
User Data-Manipulation Language (UDML)	DBC/SQL
Direct Access Facility	None

Languages and Interface Management Systems	
User Languages	None bundled, third party(NOMAD2, FOCUS, INGRESS interfaces)
Programming Languages	COBOL, C and PL/I
User Interface Management Systems	ITEQ (Interactive Teradata query)
Programming Interface Management Systems	Batch/Basic Teradata query (BTEQ)

Architectural Characteristics	Name or Names
Data Constructs	Database, table, columns and rows
Data Constructors	DDL-DBC/SQL
Search Capability	Full
Data Cross Referencing (Mapping)	Dynamic
Processing Mode	Set processing

Database Programmability	
Command-Based Stored Procedures	No
Event-Driven Stored Procedures (Triggers)	No
Structurally-Defined Business Rule Enforcement	Referential integrity
Rules Interface Management System	No

Storage Management Profile	
Blocking	System controlled
Buffering	Depends upon the number of CPUs
Compression	No
Clustering	No
Sequenced Storage	No
Indexing	Yes
Pointers	No
Scattering/Hashing	Yes

Administrative Profile	
Security	Full SQL(like) DCL
Concurrency	Database, table and row level locks (exclusive,) read, write and access)
Backup/Recovery-Logging	Full capabilities using journals

The DBC/1012 DataBase computer is one of that special class of database products called a database machine. Because it is a database machine and not simply a software product which runs on some kind of a "host" system, the Teradata DBC/1012 system is able to take advanatage of the full resources of its hardware platform in the singular task of executing database functions quickly and efficiently.

The database is basically relational in architecture, supporting a full implementation of an ANSI-SQL-like DML, DDL and DCL. This means that programmers and database administrators are able to capitalize on SQL compliance, while taking advantage of its dedicated hardware functionalities. As a complete database management system on its own platform, the DBC/1012 attaches directly to the high-speed I/O channels of mainframe computers, as well as to minicomputers and intelligent workstations via local area networks(LANs).

The Teradata DBC/1012 employs a unique architecture of multiple processors, software, and direct-access storage devices. The DBC/1012 is distinguished as the first system to provide high performance, full-function relational database management capabilities on a dedicated machine. In fact, the DBC/1012 DataBase Computer breaks the central processing unit bottleneck by harnessing the cost-efficient power of multiple microprocessors operating in parallel.

Internally, DBC/1012 makes extensive use of internal buffers, sophisticated indexing and hashing schemes and a scattered data storage approach in order to make SQL response time as fast as possible.

dBFast

Architecture	: XBase
Manufacturer	: Computer Associates
Platform	: MS/Windows

Database Access Method	
Program Data Manipulation Language (PDML)	XBase 4GL (data access subset)[1]
User Data Manipulation Language (UDML)	None
Direct Access Facility	None

Languages and Interface Management Systems	
User Languages	None
Programming Languages	XBase 4GL
User Interface Management Systems	dBFast[2] (part of system)
Programming Interface Management Systems	dBFast[3] (part of system)

Architectural Characteristics	
Data Constructs	Fields, records, files
Data Constructors	Interactive data definition screen
Search Capability	Full dynamic searches
Data Cross-Referencing (Mapping)	Dynamic, Xbase 4GL
Processing Mode	Record

Database Programmability	
Command-Based Stored Procedures	No
Event-Driven Stored Procedures (Triggers)	No
Structurally-Defined Business Rule Enforcement	No
Rules Interface Management System	No

1. The XBase Data Access Subset includes the commands; (FIND, SEEK, USE, EDIT, REPLACE, BROWSE, DELETE, etc.).

2. The dBFast interface include the tools for users to open databases, edit records, view, and create reports. All from an interactive, windows, interface.

3. The dBFast system also provides programmers with the tools to edit, and compile their XBase applications, directly from DbaseIII+, or Clipper source code, with little or no debugging. The dBFast compiler can translate most standard XBase commands to the DBfast equivelent, and create a sophisticated windows application, including windows menus, and control corners, with only slight modifications.

Storage Management Profile	
Blocking	OS dependent
Buffering	OS dependent
Compression	No
Clustering	No
Sequenced Storage	No
Indexing	Dynamic, B-tree
Pointers	No
Hashing	No

Administrative Profile	
Security	OS dependent
Concurrency	Full network support
Backup/Recovery-Logging	OS dependent

dBFast is the XBase compiler for MS/Windows. The system is made for, and best used for creating windows applications from existing XBase programs. Once the transition is made to windows, the programmer can use dBFast's enhancements to the XBase 4GL to take advantage of the windows GUI.

dBFast provides a degree of compatability with other XBase languages. dBase III+ applications usually require only minutes of work to move into dBFast. Most Clipper applications move quickly to dBFast by utilizing support of Clipper (Summer 87) extensions such as FOPEN(), and ACOPY() commands. FoxBase applications can be Readily moved into the Windows environment with dBFast, and even dBase IV applications can be altered to run with dBFast.

One of the most amazing features, is the ability of dBFast to share data, and program files with dBase III+, in a DOS/Windows network, with both dBase III+, and dBFast running, it is possible for users to access Data, Indexes, Report forms, Query files, and Program files, from either the Windows environment, with dBFast, or from DOS, with dBase III+.

dBFast provides many powerful extensions to the XBase language which allows developers to capitalize on the Windows development environment, while taking advantage of the XBase language conventions.

Among the Programming enhancements, is the ability to apply Pushbuttons, and picture buttons to XBase applications. Becoming a requirement in Windows Programming, the Button Bar is a feature that dBFast provides the tools for, including the integration of graphical objects, making attractive, and easy-to-understand user interfaces.

dBFast also provides programmers all of the necessary tools for creating Windows pull-down menus, including the ability to create nested menu groups, menu check items, and menu activated triggers.

DBMS

Architecture	: Network
Manufacturer	: Digital Equipment Corp.
Platform	: VMS

Database Access Method	
Program Data-Manipulation Language (PDML)	The DBMS DML
User Data-Manipulation Language (UDML)	None
Direct Access Facility	None

Languages and Interface Management Systems	
User Languages	None
Programming Languages	COBOL, FORTRAN, ADA, BASIC, BLISS, C, DIBOL, PASCAL, and PL/I
User Interface Management Systems	DATATRIEVE, DBQ
Programming Interface Management Systems	None

Architectural Characteristics	
Data Constructs	Schema (logical database, record, set and areas), subschema (user view), storage schema (physical description), security schema (access to areas, records, items and sets)
Data Constructors	DDL compiles the schema from CDD/PLUS, DMU via input text
Search Capability	Partiial
Data Cross-Referencing (Mapping)	Static
Processing Mode	Record processing

Database Programmability	
Command-Based Stored Procedures	No
Event-Driven Stored Procedures (Triggers)	No
Structurally-Defined Business Rule Enforcement	Constraint enforcement
Rules Interface Management System	CDD/PLUS repository

Storage Management Profile	
Blocking	Yes, customizable
Buffering	Yes, customizable
Compression	No
Clustering	Yes, via areas
Sequenced Storage	FIFO, LIFO and sorted
Indexing	B-tree
Pointers	Yes, DBKEYS
Hashing	Yes

Administrative Profile	
Security	Full defined in the security schema
Concurrency	Full
Backup/Recovery-Logging	Two-phase commit, full logging

Digital's VAX DBMS (Database Management System) is designed to effectively manage high-volume applications in which data relationships are complex, the ability to tune the database for performance is important, and the information requests are predictable and will remain fairly constant over the long term.

VAX DBMS gives you the tools to manage and control access to this data, protect its integrity, and significantly reduce application development and maintenance costs.

VAX DBMS is a full-scale CODASYL-compliant database mangement system that runs under the control of Digital's VMS operating systems on the VAX family of computer haardware systems. VAX DBMS provides the software to define, create, and mange data in simple or complex databases. You can use VAX DBMS in single VAX systems or in a VAXcluster environment.

For large applications, including transaction processing systems, VAX DBMS provides multiuser support with data security and performance advantages. VAX DBMS users with VMS symmetric multiprocessing capabilities reap further benefits of optimal multistream performance.

DATA BASE-PLUS

Architecture	: Hierarchical || SBase *
Manufacturer	: Tominy Inc.
Platform	: IBM Mainframe, Series 1, UNIX,
	: System 36, PC-DOS, Xenix,
	: VAX/VMS, DG-AOS, Novell

Database Access Method	
Program Data-Manipulation Language (PDML)	DML messages **
User Data-Manipulation Language (UDML)	None
Direct Access Facility	None

Languages and Interface Management Systems	
User Languages	None
Programming Languages	COBOL, PL1, C, FORTRAN (3GL) ASSEMBLER (2GL) Logic, DB+PL(4GL)
User Interface Management Systems	Data base-plus (query and report writer)
Programming Interface Management Systems	Data base-plus screen handler and Mach1

Architectural Characteristics	
Data Constructs	Field, group, logical (Line, record, file) and database **
Data Constructors	Data definition language source statements (a database gen)
Search Capability	Limited
Data Cross-Referencing (Mapping)	Logical
Processing Mode	Record at a time

Database Programmability	
Command-Based Stored Procedures	No
Event-Driven Stored Procedures (Triggers)	No
Structurally-Defined Business Rule Enforcement	No
Rules Interface Management System	No

* The Data Base-Plus product enforces a hierarchical relationship on the stored data. This hierarchy, however, is limited in its depth and navigational capacity.

** See the description section of the next page for details.

Storage Management Profile	
Blocking	OS dependent
Buffering	OS dependent
Compression	No
Clustering	Yes, default storage
Sequenced Storage	Yes
Indexing	No
Pointers	No
Scattering/Hashing	Yes, default access

Administrative Profile	
Security	No
Concurrency	Yes, logical record locking
Backup/Recovery-Logging	Backup/Recovery only

The DATA BASE-PLUS database product provides a unique and effective database management system environment for developers on many different platforms. Database direct access commands include Read Forward and Backward, Key, Add Record (Before or After) and Write (Sequential or by Key).

The smallest unit of data storage is the field. Several fields can be repeated to make up a group, and several groups can be combined to make a logical line. (A logical line is equivalent to a detail record or child record in a traditional hierarchy.) A logical record consists of a collection of logical lines and a logical file is a collection of records. The combination of all logical files makes up the database.

The DATA BASE-PLUS data storage structure forces a clustered hierarchical organization on the data (parents and related children are stored contiguously), and provides for a fast, intuitively obvious access for many kinds of applications.

The DML message is a parameterized database "call" which identifies to the database which file, key, key value and line item number (position in the hierarchy) to operate upon next.

The product offering includes the database itself, a screen handler, a print handler and a Query/Report Writer, all of which work together to form a cohesive database environment. Also marketed as a separate product is the Mach1 application generator.

(CA-)DB/VAX

Architecture   : Relational
Manufacturer   : Computer Associates International, Inc
Platform   : VMS, VAX, UNIX

Database Access Method	
Program Data-Manipulation Language (PDML)	SQL
User Data-Manipulation Language (UDML)	SQL
Direct Access Facility	None

Languages and Interface Management Systems	
User Languages	None
Programming Languages	C, COBOL, FORTRAN
User Interface Management Systems	None
Programming Interface Management Systems	None

Architectural Characteristics	
Data Constructs	Fields, tables, tablespaces, databases, Indexes
Data Constructors	Data definition language
Search Capability	Full search
Data Cross-Referencing (Mapping)	Dynamic
Processing Mode	Set

Database Programmability	
Command-Based Stored Procedures	Yes, data integrity with data dictionary
Event Driven Stored Procedures (Triggers)	No
Structurally-Defined Business Rule Enforcement	Referential integrity, domain integrity
Rules Interface Management System	No

Storage Management Profile	
Blocking	OS dependent
Buffering	OS dependent
Compression	No
Clustering	No
Sequenced Storage	No
Indexing	Binary
Pointers	No
Hashing	Exists

Administrative Profile	
Security	Yes
Concurrency	Yes
Backup/Recovery-Logging	Yes

CA-DB/VAX is a database management system that lets you organize your data into one or more relational databases and gives you tools for accessing and managing that data.

You define, access, and manipulate a database and its tables by using the commands of a data-manipulation language called SQL (Structured Query Language). Although the CA-DB/VAX version of SQL is almost identical with that of the industry-standard SQL, it contains many enhancements to make it more powerful and easier to use.

With this product, the developer working with most of the more popular DEC platform products is able to enjoy the full capabilities of a relational database management systems, while capitalizing on the enhanced interconnectivity afforded by the broad spectrum of products offered by Computer Associates.

The CA-DB/VAX product provides the administrator with a complete suite of database monitoring and tuning tools including the ability to customize both data management buffers (page buffers) and the log buffers.

Tuning capabilities include the provision of a performance monitor that tracks active sessions, wait states and I/O activities.

dB_VISTA III

Architecture   : Proprietery
Manufacturer : RAIMA Corporation
Platform   : UNIX, OS/2, VMS, DOS, Windows

Database Access Method	
Program Data-Manipulation Language (PDML)	dal (C functions)*
User Data-Manipulation Language (UDML)	None
Direct Access Facility	None

Languages and Interface Management Systems	
User Languages	None
Programming Languages	C', C++
User Interface Management Systems	db_QUERY
Programming Interface Management Systems	None

Architectural Characteristics	
Data Constructs	Fields, records, pages, files, databases
Data Constructors	Database definition language processor
Search Capability	Full search
Data Cross-Referencing (Mapping)	Static
Processing Mode	Record

Database Programmability	
Command-Based Stored Procedures	None
Event-Driven Stored Procedures (Triggers)	None
Structurally-Defined Business Rule Enforcement	None
Rules Interface Management System	None

Storage Management Profile	
Blocking	OS dependent, 512 default
Buffering	OS dependent, 512 default
Compression	No
Clustering	Exists
Sequenced Storage	Exists
Indexing	Exists
Pointers	Exists
Hashing	No

Administrative Profile	
Security	No
Concurrency	Yes
Backup/Recovery-Logging	Yes

The Raima data manager (dB_VISTA III) has been designed to provide powerful, high-performance database management capabilities for your C language application development. By combining the network and relational model technologies in a single system, db_VISTA lets you efficiently organize and access information, regardless of the complexity of your data. The combined technology gives you tremendous speed advantages and allows you to minimize data redundancy.

The proprietery Raima architecture is assembled in order to provide the functionality of hierarchical, network and relational operations all from within the same programming environment. Although the architecture might best be described as NETWORK in its basic underlying assumptions, the data structure and manipulation languages and rules make it a truly multi-architectural product.

With its C language based programming profile, and the consequential performance enhancements, the Raima database can be counted upon to perform exceedingly well in high transaction rate types of systems.

The complexity of the architecture and its unique paradigm set require the programmer or user to invest in a non-trivial learning curve in order to make the product "friendly."

DMS 1100

Architecture	: Network
Manufacturer	: Unisys Corporation
Platform	: Unisys 1100 and 2200, OS/1100

Database Access Method	
Program Data-Manipulation Language (PDML)	CODASYL based DML
User Data-Manipulation Language (UDML)	QLP
Direct Access Facility	None

Languages and Interface Management Systems	
User Languages	None
Programming Languages	COBOL, FORTRAN
User Interface Management Systems	QLP
Programming Interface Management Systems	None

Architectural Characteristics	
Data Constructs	Data items, subitems, databases, indexes, Sets, Datasets
Data Constructors	Database definition language
Search Capability	Full search (via QLP)
Data Cross Referencing (Mapping)	Static (Logial and Physical)
Processing Mode	Record

Database Programmability	
Command-Based Stored Procedures	Yes
Event-Driven Stored Procedures (Triggers)	No
Structurally-Defined Business Rule Enforcement	Value constraints
Rules Interface Management System	No

Storage Management Profile	
Blocking	Customizable (Dataset Level)
Buffering	Customizable (Dataset Level)
Compression	Yes
Clustering	Yes
Sequenced Storage	Yes
Indexing	Binary
Pointers	Yes
Hashing	Yes

Administrative Profile	
Security	Yes
Concurrency	Yes
Backup/Recovery-Logging	Yes

DMS 1100 is based upon the old tried-and-true CODASYL network DBMS structure. This database is well-suited for use in a highly batch-oriented environment or for systems that require high rate transaction processing capabilities and all the required integrated components.

The DMS1100 product which has been in use for several years, is one of that early second generation of database products (network, hierarchical and inverted list). As such, the user of the product can be guaranteed of a system with:

- A mature data storage management profile
- The availability of time tested utility and administration procedures
- The availability of skilled data base administrators and programmers
- Good memory management and logging capabilities
- Sophisticated lock management and concurrency control

In tandem with a companion product UDS RDMS 1100 which is a relational system that works on the same platforms, this UNISYS database "family" can provide both network-based and table-based processing on the same physical platform. RDMS 1100 can execute SQL commands and supports SQL interfaces to standard programming languages such as COBOL and FORTRAN. The developer can combine network and relational processing in one application. Through the Unisys MAPPER application development language, programs can also access the MAPPER Relational Interface (MRI) which supports a user-friendly, menu-driven SQL command builder which can be used to access local and remote RDMS databases, along with Oracle (UNIX), DB2 and CA- databases.

The presence of these products on the UNISYS platforms, means that the developer working in a UNISYS environment can take advantage of all of the benefits that relational databases have to offer, while being assured of an easy migration path for their existing proprietary UNISYS database applications.

DMS II

Architecture	: Network
Manufacturer	: Unisys Corporation
Platform	: Unisys 1100 and 2200

Database Access Method	
Program Data-Manipulation Language (PDML)	DM interface
User Data-Manipulation Language (UDML)	EGRO (Component of IQF interface)
Direct Access Facility	None

Languages and Interface Management Systems	
User Languages	LINC II
Programming Languages	ALGOL, COBOL, RPG, PL/1, EGRO, IQF
User Interface Management Systems	TUI, OCFM, APRS (components of InfoExec)
Programming Interface Management Systems	Some third party products

Architectural Characteristics	
Data Constructs	Data items, subsets, sets, datasets
Data Constructors	DASDL Language
Search Capability	Full with some performance impact
Data Cross-Referencing (Mapping)	Static (Logical - Physical)
Processing Mode	Record

Database Programmability	
Command-Based Stored Procedures	None
Event-Driven Stored Procedures (Triggers)	None
Structurally-Defined Business Rule Enforcement	Limited - Field Level Contraints
Rules Interface Management System	(ADDS) UREP/A

Storage Management Profile	
Blocking	Customizable
Buffering	Customizable
Compression	Optional
Clustering	Optional
Sequenced Storage	Yes
Indexing	Yes(5 of the 6 main organization types)
Pointers	Yes
Hashing	None

Administrative Profile	
Security	Full
Concurrency	Yes
Backup/Recovery-Logging	Yes

DMS II is a full-scale, production quality, network data model DBMS that runs on Unisys A Series computers. DMS II enjoys a very high penetration in the A Series installed base, to the extent that virtually all A Series recorded-oriented databases are managed by DMSII. The reasons for DMS II's high penetration include high transaction performance, robust recovery capabilities, and close integration with the A Series operating system (MCP/AS). These characteristics of DMS II made it the ideal choice as the physical data engine underlying both the SIM and SQLDB databases which also run on Unisys Series A machines. A full suite of development and decision support tools and utility programs is available for DMS II databases.

The database represents a network type database management system with interfaces to several different 3GL's.

DMSII has a long history of providing efficient and flexible database management services in the support of every kind of business data processing requirements. Because of the inherent flexibility of the network architecture, DMS II databases are used to model network, hierarchical and even relationally based applications.

Inherent in the makeup of DMS II is a highly sophisticated set of system generation facilities (referred to as DASDL - The Data and Structure Definition Language). Through DASDL, the database administrator is able to define the sets and subsets (data constructs and their relationships) within a database, and to additionally specify the access paths which will be provided for navigation.

DMS II provides the physical database designer with a unique set of options for the building of database structures. By the strategic combination of different access parameters (defining the way in which a physical dataset is used) the DBA can combine the benefits of clustering, sequencing, indexing and pointing in any number of unique ways.

Double Helix

Architecture	: SBase
Manufacturer	: NorthCon Technologies
Platform	: MAC

Database Access Method	
Program Data-Manipulation Language (PDML)	None
User Data-Manipulation Language (UDML)	None
Direct Access Facility	Double helix, built into the system

Languages and Interface Management Systems	
User Languages	None
Programming Languages	None
User Interface Management Systems	Double helix, built into the system
Programming Interface Management Systems	Double helix, built into the system

Architectural Characteristics	
Data Constructs	Fields, records, relations, databases
Data Constructors	Relation Icons, field Icons, data definition Icons.
Search Capability	Full dynamic searching avaialable
Data Cross-Referencing (Mapping)	Dynamic (part of user object)
Processing Mode	Single record processing

Database Programmability	
Command-Based Stored Procedures	Stored in relation objects
Event-Driven Stored Procedures (Triggers)	Stored in relation objects
Structurally-Defined Business Rule Enforcement	Stored in relation object
Rules Interface Management System	Part of relation object programming

Storage Management Profile	
Blocking	OS dependent
Buffering	OS dependent
Compression	No
Clustering	No
Sequenced Storage	No
Indexing	Index object, a subobject of relation object
Pointers	No
Hashing	No

Administrative Profile	
Security	Partial, defined in user objects
Concurrency	No
Backup/Recovery-Logging	No

Double Helix, by Odesta Corporation, is a fully functioning DBMS for the Apple Macintosh computer system. All programming is managed from the object-oriented interface. The programmer can define the data, the business rules, and the data input screens, all from within the interface. After a system is designed, a programmer can create user specific icons, each granting and restricting different levels of user acces. Data format screens, table relations, and security controls can be attached to each user icon, making powerful network applications.

Double Helix applications can be shared on mutiuser Macintosh/VAX networks, and the system comes with report and application generators, and also provides a compiler for completed applications.

The Double Helix interface offers several levels of programming, each represented by a graphical object on the screen. At the highest level, the system offers control over environmental conditions, user objects, relation objects (the individual data tables), and full control over the database configuration. Due to the graphic icon-driven interface, it is easy for nonprogrammers to learn and create sophisticated databases in a few sessions, and with some time, fully functioning database management systems can be developed.

Data definition in Double Helix is unique. The system allows scanned image graphics to be assigned to fields, along with character, date, boolean, and several numerical field types. The data definition object (Create Relation Screen) provides an interface to place icons representing fields into the relation. After a field is defined through the menu, the user/programmer can attach the abacus (field calculations and values) icon to the field, offering a large variety of field programmabilty.

FOCUS

```
Architecture    : Hierarchical
Manufacturer    : Information Builders Inc.
Platform        : MVS, VM, VSE, DEC/VAX, WANG,
                : HP, TANDEM, BULL, UNIX, AS400,
                : OS2 and others
```

Database Access Method	
Program Data-Manipulation Language (PDML)	The FOCUS 4GL (data access subset) which includes calls to relational, hierarchical, network and inverted list databases
User Data-Manipulation Language (UDML)	Same as PDML. FOCUS provides a programming language which both users and programmers can take advantage of
Direct Access Facility	None

Languages and Interface Management Systems	
User Languages	The FOCUS 4GL
Programming Languages	The FOCUS 4GL can be considered both a programmer and user language. HLI, embedded call into FORTRAN, COBOL, etc.
User Interface Management Systems	The FOCUS environment itself
Programming Interface Management Systems	LEVEL5, EDA/SQL and LEVEL5 OBJECT (application development environments for the creation of FOCUS applications)

Architectural Characteristics	
Data Constructs	Fields, records, segments and files
Data Constructors	The FOCUS master file description
Search Capability	Full
Data Cross-Referencing (Mapping)	Dynamic
Processing Mode	Record at a time

Database Programmability	
Command-Based Stored Procedures	No
Event-Driven Stored Procedures (Triggers)	No
Structurally-Defined Business Rule Enforcement	Yes, domain constraints
Rules Interface Management System	No

Storage Management Profile	
Blocking	OS dependent
Buffering	OS dependent
Compression	No
Clustering	Yes
Sequenced Storage	Yes
Indexing	Yes
Pointers	Yes
Scattering/Hashing	No

Administrative Profile	
Security	Full field-level security (optional)
Concurrency	Locking at record and file level
Backup/Recovery-Logging	OS Dependent

The FOCUS database and its related family of products represent an approach to database management systems quite different than most. While the majority of the DBMS vendors concentrate on creating products which will function as the main source of data for an entire business organization, IBI has concentrated on creating a database, and supporting products, which make it easier for the system end-user to access and manipulate the data that is stored elsewhere.

It is in this spirit that the FOCUS product has been developed. A FOCUS database is really much more than simply a data storage area. It represents a place where end-users can make use of a common access method (namely the FOCUS 4GL) in order to satisfy their own reporting needs. The FOCUS database and programming language allow end-users to gain access to dozens of other database products via its database front-end services. The end-user can access DB2, IMS, IDMS and many other kinds of databases, and process their own reports using the FOCUS access language. This makes FOCUS a very popular product within organizations where the users data tends to be spread across many different platforms and database systems.

In addition to serving as a "front end" to other DBMS's, FOCUS, with its own built in hierarchical database capabilties, it is able to serve as a data holding area for users that wish to build their own mini-dbms environments. With its pre-established proficiency as a cross-database/cross-platform expert system, the Information Builders' family of products has expanded to include EDA/SQL or (Enterprise Data Access/SQL). It consists of a family of client/server products that work together to provide SQL-based access to relational and nonrelational data on interconnected, multivendor networks. The LEVEL5 and LEVEL5 OBJECT environments complete the set with application developement tools of the traditional (LEVEL5) and object-oriented (LEVEL5 OBJECT) slant.

Formbase

Architecture	: Hierarchical || SBase
Manufacturer	: Columbia Software Inc.
Platform	: MS/Windows

Database Access Method	
Program Data-Manipulation Language (PDML)	None
User Data-Manipulation Language (UDML)	None
Direct Access Facility	Formbase (part of system)[1]

Languages and Interface Management Systems	
User Languages	None
Programming Languages	None
User Interface Management Systems	Formbase (part of system)
Programming Interface Management Systems	Macroing facility (part of system)

Architectural Characteristics	
Data Constructs	Fields, subforms/subtables, tables/forms
Data Constructors	Interactive (part of system)[2]
Search Capability	Full dynamic searches available
Data Cross-Referencing (Mapping)	Static, part of form creation (data definition)
Processing Mode	Both record and set processing

Database Programmability	
Command-Based Stored Procedures	No
Event-Driven Stored Procedures (Triggers)	Calculated fields and lookup fields[3]
Structurally-Defined Business Rule Enforcement	Field templates
Rules Interface Management System	No

1. Formbase is designed to be a user tool. The main menus, and screen, are the only access provided within the program.

2. Data definition is done through the Formbase screen. The user/programmer chooses whether to work in design or update-only mode. IN design mode, the user/programmer can modify the structure and input data at the same time.

3. A relational aspect of Formbase, the ability to define static cross-file lookups for field validation is part of the system. The cross-file lookup capabilities can access formbase data files, or can use Dbase .DBF file types.

Storage Management Profile	
Blocking	OS dependent
Buffering	OS dependent
Compression	No
Clustering	No
Sequenced Storage	No
Indexing	Static
Pointers	Physical
Hashing	No

Administrative Profile	
Security	No
Concurrency	No
Backup/Recovery-Logging	No

Formbase, by Columbia Software, is exactly what the name implies. The program offers an intuitive interface for forms based data management. If your company uses a standard form for manually filing data, than Formbase can electronically store that same information.

Formbase uses an easy-to-learn, user interface to help users get acquainted with the system. Once data is entered on the screen, a form, or table is created, and the user simply needs to specify where and how different elements of the form are to be shown and stored.

Subforms, and subtables are defined in the main form, or users can create several views (forms) of different elements of the database. As users learn to create links between main forms, and subforms, the ability to quickly create additional views becomes a matter of simply selecting NEW from the views menu.

FoxPro

Architecture	: XBase
Manufacturer	: Fox Holdings Inc.
Platform	: PC/DOS, Windows, UNIX, MacIntosh

Database Access Method	
Program Data-Manipulation Language (PDML)	XBase 4GL[1] (data management subset); SQL[2]
User Data-Manipulation Language (UDML)	SQL
Direct Access Facility	None

Languages and Interface Management Systems	
User Languages	None
Programming Languages	XBase 4GL
User Interface Management Systems	FoxPro user interface (part of system)
Programming Interface Management Systems	Forms, menus, projects, queries, and reports, (part of system) FoxPro Apgen

Architectural Characteristics	
Data Constructs	Fields, Records, Files
Data Constructors	Interactive data definition; FoxPro DDL[3]
Search Capability	Full dynamic searches
Data Cross-Referencing (Mapping)	Dynamic, XBase 4GL
Processing Mode	Set and record processing available—Rushmore Technology"

Database Programmability	
Command-Based Stored Procedures	No
Event-Driven Stored Procedures (Triggers)	No
Structurally-Defined Business Rule Enforcement	No
Rules Interface Management System	No

1. The XBase language data management subset includes the commands USE (*filename*), INDEX ON (*fieldname*), FIND (*keyvalue*) EDIT, ERASE, REPLACE, GET, etc.

2. Although FoxPro is an XBase system, the sytem offers an interactive SQL Mode, RQBE, which uses a superset syntax of SQL to manage files.

3. FoxPro offers interactive, menu-driven, report, format, and query file definition tools (part of the system). These tools create the files that can later be used by a user or programmer for system configuration.

4. Along with interactive file creation, FoxPro offers an SQL like DDL. The syntax is CREATE TABLE *filename* ; (*fieldname fieldtype(fieldsize)*).

Storage Management Profile	
Blocking	OS dependent
Buffering	OS dependent
Compression	No
Clustering	No
Sequenced Storage	No
Indexing	Dynamic, B-tree, multi-index files
Pointers	No
Hashing	No

Administrative Profile	
Security	Partial
Concurrency	File and record locking ability
Backup/Recovery-Logging	OS dependent

FoxPro is a GLUI system, all interfaces are mouse/keyboard-driven, and the system has an flexible interactive environment that allows users to use the 4GL directly, or the menus interactively without changing modes. The "Rushmore Technology" (named for the film North by Northwest, which part of the crew watched the night before starting the project) is an enhancement to the XBase engine, which allows set processes to be performed at a speed relatively equal to single record processing. FoxPro SQL is actually an enhanced SQL. Two features clearly show that FoxPro SQL is a superset.

°   The use of both XBase and user-defined functions in an SQL query.

°   FoxPro SQL does not include the SQL-DDL. (Although FoxPro does use a CREATE TABLE command, the command syntax is not SQL syntax.)

The enhancements to the XBase 4GL, added to FoxPro, allow programmers to create, and document an application all from within the GLUI environment. The Apgen, along with a bundled program called FoxDoc allow a programmer to create sophisticated systems, run FoxDoc to create a developer's documentation of the application, and run the pseudo-compiler to create the object module that the system will use. Programmers have full control of where and how windows, data elements, help, and user information screens will appear; additionally, users have the ability to move the windows around to their taste.

FoxPro also provides space for expansion with the ability to call "C" language subroutines. With the addition of BLOB field types, and direct, interactive editing of MEMO field within a window, FoxPro has crossed the limits of XBase capabilities. All other XBase systems require the user to open the interactive menu driven interface, or choose the command line mode, but they do not allow both to be active simultaneously.

Integrated Data Store II

Architecture	: Network (CODASYL)
Manufacturer	: Bull Information Systems Inc.
Platform	: GCOS 6/7/8

Database Access Method	
Program Data-Manipulation Language (PDML)	Embedded DML (including FIND, GET, STORE MODIFY and ERASE) and SQL interface via Bull's INTEREL RDBMS
User Data-Manipulation Language (UDML)	CODASYL DML and SQL
Direct Access Facility	None

Languages and Interface Management Systems	
User Languages	QRP/PLP, MAGNA 8, MAGNA View, IIDS, FormsSQL, Reporter
Programming Languages	Cobol, C and Fortranl
User Interface Management Systems	QRP/PLP (Batch Query), Transaction Systems Manager (OLTP Programming Interface), MAGNA 8 (End user and development system), PacBase (Full CASE tool)
Programming Interface Management Systems	MAGNA 8, PacBase

Architectural Characteristics	
Data Constructs	Fields, Records, Record-types, Subschema, Schema
Data Constructors	I-D-S II Schema DDL and DMCL
Search Capability	Partial (DML), Full, Dynamic (SQL)
Data Cross-Referencing (Mapping)	Static (DML),Dynamic (SQL)
Processing Mode	Record at a time (DML), Full (SQL)

Database Programmability	
Command-Based Stored Procedures	No (DML), Yes (SQL)
Event-Driven Stored Procedures (Triggers)	Yes (DML), No (SQL)
Structurally-Defined Business Rule Enforcement	No
Rules Interface Management System	No

Storage Management Profile	
Blocking	Customizable
Buffering	Customizable
Compression	Optional
Clustering	Yes
Sequenced Storage	Yes
Indexing	Yes
Pointers	Yes (Default and ARRAY types)
Scattering/Hashing	Yes

Administrative Profile	
Security	Full Security: Record-type, Area, Subschema, Schema
Concurrency	Locking at Control Interval level (Block)
Backup/Recovery-Logging	Full and Incremental Backup, Full Logging for roll forward and backward by event or time interval

Bull's Integrated Data Store II (I-D-S/II) is a multi-purpose production DBMS with one of the highest OLTP performance rates available on the market. I-D-S/II's predessor (IDS, developed by Charles Bachmann) was used as the primary model for the CODASYL standard and one of the first CODASYL compliant DBMS's on the market. Combined with Bull's TP8 (OLTP Monitor for GCOS 8), it provides the highest TPS ratings in the Enterprise level systems.

I-D-S/II is the anchor of Bull's customer base for production level systems, with many DBA tools, tuning and reorganization facilities.

Bull's relational DBMS (INTEREL - GCOS 8 only) has been highly integrated with I-D-S/II to provide users with high performance CODASYL database systems with full relational manipulation of production databases. Bull was the first vendor to provide such integration from 1983 until the present day. Many customers are taking advantage of this integration from production processing through to full relational DBMS capabilities.

(CA-)IDMS

Architecture	: Relational || Network
Manufacturer	: Computer Associates, Inc.
Platform	: MVS, VM, VSE, PC-DOS

Database Access Method	
Program Data-Manipulation Language (PDML)	CA-IDMS database calls (including FIND, GET, OBTAIN, STORE, MODIFY and ERASE) and SQL
User Data-Manipulation Language (UDML)	SQL
Direct Access Facility	None

Languages and Interface Management Systems	
User Languages	None
Programming Languages	COBOL, FORTRAN, ASSEMBLER, PL1 and CA-ADS (the packaged 4GL)
User Interface Management Systems	CA-OLQ (on-line query), CA-CULPRIT (batch reporting), CA-ICMS (handles data for PCs), CA-GOLDENGATE (PC tools to access mainframe data), CA-INFOGATE (access to mainframe data for spreadsheets and PC databases), CA-QbyX (Windows based query management), CA-RAMIS (end user reporting)
Programming Interface Management Systems	CA-ADS (application development system) CA-DBGENERATOR (code generator)

Architectural Characteristics	
Data Constructs	Fields, records, record-types, schemas, Areas and Databases (nonrelational) || Columns, Rows, Tables, Databases (relataional)
Data Constructors	CA-IDMS schema generation or SQL-DDL
Search Capability	Limited (non-relational) || Full (relational)
Data Cross-Referencing (Mapping)	Static (network)|| Dynamic (relational)
Processing Mode	Record at a time (network) ||Set (relational)

Database Programmability	
Command-Based Stored Procedures	No
Event-Driven Stored Procedures (Triggers)	No
Structurally-Defined Business Rule Enforcement	Yes
Rules Interface Management System	No

Storage Management Profile	
Blocking	Customizable
Buffering	Customizable
Compression	Optional
Clustering	Yes
Sequenced Storage	Yes
Indexing	Yes
Pointers	Yes
Scattering/Hashing	Yes

Administrative Profile	
Security	Full security by record type or table
Concurrency	Locking at record, area and file level
Backup/Recovery-Logging	Full backup and logging available for roll forward and roll backward

The CA-IDMS product is a multipurpose, high-performance database management system, incorporating relational and navigational processing into a comprehensive family of products which together provide a consistent and productive database system development environment.

Until release 12.0 of CA-IDMS, the database was a user-navigated system making use of a network architecture. With the new release, CA-IDMS provides the best of both the navigational and relational worlds.

IDMS has been the "anchor" database product for many large business and governmental organizations for many years, and has a proven history of providing excellent manageability and response time for very, very large and complex applications.

Among the outstanding characteristics of the product are its unique dual-architecture approach, the availability of CA-ADS a powerful application development package which has been in use for many years. The product includes an internal organization which makes the integration of databases across platforms easy.

CA-IDMS is considered by many to be the prototype for an effectively organized network architecture database system, and has certainly become the most popular of the network database systems.

Release 12.0 supports all existing CA-IDMS features with the important addition of full relational processing support via complete support for the SQL language including SQL DML access (select, update, insert and delete) to existing non-SQL defined data.

IMS and DLI

Architecture	: Hierarchical
Manufacturer	: IBM
Platform	: IMS (MVS) DLI (DOS/VSE)

Database Access Method	
Program Data-Manipulation Language (PDML)	Calls to DLI (GET UNIQUE, GET NEXT, GET HOLD NEXT PARENT)
User Data-Manipulation Language (UDML)	None
Direct Access Facility	None

Languages and Interface Management Systems	
User Languages	None
Programming Languages	Most 2nd and 3rd GLs including COBOL, C, FORTRAN and ASSEMBLER
User Interface Management Systems	None
Programming Interface Management Systems	CSP (packaged)

Architectural Characteristics	
Data Constructs	Databases, areas, datasets, segments and fields
Data Constructors	DBDGEN (database generation job)
Search Capability	Limited
Data Cross-Referencing (Mapping)	Static
Processing Mode	Record processing

Database Programmability	
Command-Based Stored Procedures	No
Event-Driven Stored Procedures (Triggers)	No
Structurally-Defined Business Rule Enforcement	No
Rules Interface Management System	No

Storage Management Profile	
Blocking	Yes, customizable
Buffering	Customizable via pools
Compression	No
Clustering	Yes
Sequenced Storage	Yes
Indexing	Yes
Pointers	No
Scattering /Hashing	Yes

Administrative Profile	
Security	Minimal via PCB's
Concurrency	Yes, record and database levels
Backup/Recovery-Logging	Yes, full roll forward and roll back

The IMS and DLI products are basically two versions of the same database. The first and more widely known product is IMS. IMS, which stands for Information Management System was one of the first "truly" production caliber database management systems to become commericially available the second. DLI is a scaled down version of that database, which can run on smaller mainframe computers, and using the less robust DOS/VSE operating system.

IMS, with its hierarchical architecture, was for years the prototype of a successfully implemented large database management systems. In many ways, IMS set the standards for performance, dependability, manageability and ease of use that were in effect before the advent of the relational systems.

The IMS product is available with its own teleprocessing system, called IMS/DC (for IMS/Data Communications). IMS/DC is a packaged product offering from IBM, and does not work the the DLI databae product. It provides the system developer with a highly integrated on line teleprocessing environment that is used to support systems with thousands of end-users. IMS response time optimization is assisted through the use of MSDB (Main Storage Databases) which store the entire database in the computers memory buffers and "Fast Path" systems.

The DLI product provides programmers on the smaller platforms with the same basic hierarchical functionality provided by IMS, but with a less robust call population, and without the benefit of the IMS/DC teleprocessing environment.

INFORMIX

Architecture	: Relational
Manufacturer	: Informix Software Inc.
Platform	: Most UNIX, OS2, PC/DOS and MAC

Database Access Method	
Program Data-Manipulation Language (PDML)	SQL
User Data-Manipulation Language (UDML)	SQL
Direct Access Facility	None

Languages and Interface Management Systems	
User Languages	None
Programming Languages	Informix 4GL (packaged), C, FORTRAN, ADA and COBOL (3GL)
User Interface Management Systems	ISQL (bundled) an interactive query tool and WINGZ (packaged) a GUI front end and DBAccess
Programming Interface Management Systems	Informix RDS (rapid development system) and Interactive Debugger

Architectural Characteristics	
Data Constructs	Columns, rows, tables, tablespaces, databases
Data Constructors	SQL-DDL
Search Capability	Full dynamic search and static
Data Cross-Referencing (Mapping)	Logical, dynamic and Static (with referential integrity)
Processing Mode	Set at a time

Database Programmability	
Command-Based Stored Procedures	Yes
Event-Driven Stored Procedures (Triggers)	Yes
Structurally-Defined Business Rule Enforcement	Yes
Rules Interface Management System	No

Storage Management Profile	
Blocking	Set by platform constraints
Buffering	Customizable
Compression	On indexes
Clustering	Yes
Sequenced Storage	Yes
Indexing	Yes
Pointers	No
Scattering/Hashing	No

Administrative Profile	
Security	Full transaction and table security
Concurrency	Locking at row, page, table and database level
Backup/Recovery-Logging	Incremental and Full Backup/Recovery

Introduced in 1980, INFORMIX has been dedicated to the exploitation of the power and interconnective capabilities of the UNIX environment. INFORMIX provides a complete "end-to-end" database management solution, from the database to the desktop.

The collection of program development and user access tools provided by INFORMIX provides an especially well-integrated set of application development capabilities. The INFORMIX 4GL language provides a simple, but powerful foundation for the building of data based systems, while the Rapid Development System (which automates the 4GL development process) makes it even easier to use.

The WINGZ product provides as especially powerful, GUI-based environment which allows the developer to integrate spreadsheet, database and graphical information into a cohesive user presentation.

Among the more outstanding characteristics of the database itself are its robust database administration capabilities, with developer set characteristics for most of the same kinds of attributes that a mainframe database will require, and the high-performance database engine, based upon INFORMIXs own, ISAM file structure.

The product also provides for the building of cost-effective client-server database solutions, and is one of the UNIX, big four (the four major UNIX based databases).

INFORMIX can store data as numerical, character based or in special fields called BLOBS (Binary Large OBjectS). BLOBS are used to store graphical representations (pictures, diagrams, maps, etc.).

There are several very large, distributed, INFORMIX applications being used to run major corporate intiatives in the retail, hotel and other industries and INFORMIX will continue to be a major force in the UNIX database marketplace.

INGRES

Architecture	: Relational
Manufacturer	: ASK Inc.
Platform	: MVS, VM, Most UNIX platforms,
	: VAX/VMS, PC/DOS

Database Access Method	
Program Data-Manipulation Language (PDML)	SQL and QUEL (the INGRES Proprietery Access Language including the RETRIEVE, REPLACE, DELETE and APPEND commands)
User Data-Manipulation Language (UDML)	SQL and QUEL
Direct Access Facility	None

Languages and Interface Management Systems	
User Languages	None
Programming Languages	BASIC, PASCAL, PL/I,C, FORTRAN, ADA and COBOL (3GL)
User Interface Management Systems	INGRES (MENU, QUERY, REPORTS and GRAPHICS) including ISQL (interactive SQL) and IQUEL (interactive QUEL) interfaces
Programming Interface Management Systems	INGRES/Applications and INGRES/Forms (visual forms editor)

Architectural Characteristics	
Data Constructs	Columns, rows, tables, tablespaces, databases
Data Constructors	SQL-DDL or QUEL-DDL
Search Capability	Full dynamic search
Data Cross-Referencing (Mapping)	Logical and dynamic
Processing Mode	Set at a time

Database Programmability	
Command-Based Stored Procedures	Yes
Event-Driven Stored Procedures (Triggers)	Yes
Structurally-Defined Business Rule Enforcement	Yes
Rules Interface Management System	No

Storage Management Profile	
Blocking	2k
Buffering	Customizable
Compression	Yes
Clustering	Yes
Sequenced Storage	Yes
Indexing	Yes
Pointers	No
Scattering/Hashing	Yes

Administrative Profile	
Security	Full relational security
Concurrency	Locking at page, table and database level
Backup/Recovery-Logging	Full Backup/Recovery including comprehensive journals

The INGRES database, marketed by ASK Computer Systems, Inc., is one of two database products considered to be the ancestor of most relational database products today (the other being System R, the IBM predecessor to DB2 and SQL/DS). The INGRES database was originally developed at the University of California at Berkeley during the period between 1973 and 1975, and stands for Interactive Graphics and Retrieval System.

Among the outstanding characteristics of the database are the many different platforms that it can run on, and the incredibly diverse set of user and programmer productivity tools that come bundled and/or packaged with the product.

Contributing to the success of the INGRES database has been it dual access language capabilities. The INGRES database provides its own proprietery relational access language called QUEL and allows for the use of ANSI standard SQL as well. With both languages the end-user is able to build queries that allow for the expeditious analysis of complex data relationships.

The INGRES system is often portrayed as being made up of two general components, a back-end, which consists of the database engine, and a front-end, which consists of the many Application Development Subsystems including: QUERY: a database retrieval/update/entry system for users, REPORTS: a report definition and writing system, GRAPHICS: which can be used to create business charts, FORMS: for form definition and editing and APPLICATIONS: an application generator.

InterBase

Architecture	: Relational
Manufacturer	: Borland International
Platform	: Apollo, Aegis, UNIX, DEC, HP,
	: SUN, OS2, SCO UNIX or
	: SCO Xenix

Database Access Method	
Program Data-Manipulation Language (PDML)	SQL or GDML (data access subset of commands including PRINT, ERASE and STORE)
User Data-Manipulation Language (UDML)	SQL or GDML (data access subset)
Direct Access Facility	None

Languages and Interface Management Systems	
User Languages	None
Programming Languages	GDML (proprietery 4GL) and ADA, BASIC, C, COBOL, FORTRAN, PASCAL,, PL/I(3GL)
User Interface Management Systems	QLI (query language interface)
Programming Interface Management Systems	FRED (FoRms EDitor), a forms creation and maintenance system

Architectural Characteristics	
Data Constructs	Fields, rows, relations and databases
Data Constructors	SQL-DDL or the GDML-DDL
Search Capability	Full search
Data Cross Referencing (Mapping)	Dynamic and logical
Processing Mode	Set at a time processing

Database Programmability	
Command-Based Stored Procedures	Yes (GDML)
Event-Driven Stored Procedures (Triggers)	Yes including triggers and event alerters
Structurally-Defined Business Rule Enforcement	Yes, referential integrity and domain integrity
Rules Interface Management System	InterBase event manager

Storage Management Profile	
Blocking	Variable sizes (1024, 2048, 4096, 8192)
Buffering	OSdependent
Compression	No
Clustering	No
Sequenced Storage	Yes
Indexing	Yes
Pointers	No
Hashing	No

Administrative Profile	
Security	Robust security capabilties including the development of customized security profiles.
Concurrency	Consistency model (locks records and relations), concurrency model (read-only access via multigenerational records) and distributed capabilities (two-phase commit)
Backup/Recovery-Logging	Backup, recovery and long term journaling

The InterBase product provides a fully functional relational database, with an assortment of additional features. The product was recently acquired by Borlange International and has been fitted into the "family" of Borland database products (which includes the DBASE databases, the Rapidfile flat file product and Paradox).

InterBase is also one of the more popular of the UNIX-based database products.

Among the features that make InterBase distinctive are:

1. A highly sophisticated triggering and event handling architecture which provide for the automatic execution of predefined procedures when certain activities are detected.

2. QLI—the Query Language Interface, which allows end-users and programmers to work directly with stored InterBase data.

3. The powerful and versatile GDML language, InterBases proprietery version of a DML, while still allowing for standard SQL access.

4. Interface capabilties with most 3GL languages.

5. The ability to store text, graphic and sound objects all within the same database structure, and to manipulate them with the GDML language.

Interbase can provide a highly flexible and user friendly environment for the development of many different kinds of commercial applications.

INTEREL

Architecture   : Relational
Manufacturer   : Bull Information Systems Inc.
Platform   : GCOS 8

Database Access Method	
Program Data-Manipulation Language (PDML)	SQL DML
User Data-Manipulation Language (UDML)	SQL DDL
Direct Access Facility	None

Languages and Interface Management Systems	
User Languages	MAGNA 8, MAGNA View, FOCUS
Programming Languages	COBOL, C
User Interface Management Systems	INFOEDGE (SQL Facilities), GLINK, Windows, PC/SQL-Link, FOCUS, others
Programming Interface Management Systems	MAGNA 8, PacBase, FormsSQL

Architectural Characteristics	Name or Names
Data Constructs	Columns, rows, tables, schema
Data Constructors	DDL (SQL)
Search Capability	Full, dynamic
Data Cross-Referencing (Mapping)	Dynamic (either Relational tables or I-D-S/II Areas)
Processing Mode	Set

Database Programmability	
Command-Based Stored Procedures	Yes
Event-Driven Stored Procedures (Triggers)	No
Structurally-Defined Business Rule Enforcement	No
Rules Interface Management System	No

Storage Management Profile	
Blocking	Customizable
Buffering	Customizable
Compression	Optional
Clustering	Yes
Sequenced Storage	Yes
Indexing	Yes
Pointers	Partial (only through I-D-S/II interface)
Scattering/Hashing	Yes (scattering by partitioning)

Administrative Profile	
Security	Full Security (Column/Row and Table)
Concurrency	Locking at Control Interval level (Block)
Backup/Recovery-Logging	Full and Incremental Backup, Full Logging for roll forward and backward by event or time interval

Bull's INTEREL system is a "super set" of the classical relational system. Not only does it provide full relational (ANSI Standard) capabilities, but also can be interfaced to any of Bull's other GCOS 8 files system, like I-D-S/II, UFAS (sequential and indexed), etc. The name INTEREL stands for INTEgrated RELational. INTEREL's INFOEDGE family of host based products allow users to develop comprehensive applications. INTEREL's RDBMS can be accessed in all modes: Batch, Interactive and OLTP.

Some of the features include:

1. ANSI Standard SQL (DDL, DML and DCL)

2. Extensive user facilities like:

   a. BatchSQL

   b. FormsSQL

   c. DBA Utilities

3. Integration and interface to Teradata's DBC 1012 (Bull's Relational DBC)

KNOWLEDGEMAN

Architecture	: Proprietary
Manufacturer	: mdbs Inc.
Platform	: UNIX, OS/2, DOS, VMS

Database Access Method	
Program Data-Manipulation Language (PDML)	KMAN
User Data-Manipulation Language (UDML)	None
Direct Access Facility	None

Languages and Interface Management Systems	
User Languages	NATURAL
Programming Languages	'C', KGL
User Interface Management Systems	Spreadsheet, graphics, report writer
Programming Interface Management Systems	Knowledgeman, commander, paint, forms

Architectural Characteristics	
Data Constructs	Fields, records, tables, databases
Data Constructors	Knowledgeman language
Search Capability	Full search
Data Cross-Referencing (Mapping)	Dynamic
Processing Mode	Record and set

Database Programmability	
Command-Based Stored Procedures	Yes
Event-Driven Stored Procedures (Triggers)	No
Structurally-Defined Business Rule Enforcement	No
Rules Interface Management System	No

Storage Management Profile	
Blocking	Maximum 4096
Buffering	Default 4096
Compression	Yes
Clustering	No
Sequenced Storage	No
Indexing	Binary
Pointers	No
Hashing	No

Administrative Profile	
Security	Encryption, priviledge table
Concurrency	Table and record locking
Backup/Recovery-Logging	Import-export

KnowledgeMan has a diverse user base. From consulting to aerospace, from petrochemical and manufacturing to government and finance, individuals rely on KnowledgeMan to help them manage a wide range of activities including investments, production, planning, marketing, human services, legal affairs and more. KnowledgeMan is the product of choice for these users because it offers the following outstanding knowledge processing capabilities:

. Complete structured programming

. Object-based programming

. Data management

. Standard SQL inquiry

. Spreadsheet analysis with split-screen capability

. Statistics generation

. Elaborate report generation and business graphics

. Text processing

. Screen and forms management

. Remote communication

MODEL 204

Architecture	: Inverted List ‖ Relational
Manufacturer	: Computer Corporation of America
Platform	: MVS, VM, VSE

Database Access Method	
Program Data-Manipulation Language (PDML)	Model 204 user language (HLI calls) (Find, sort, count, add, change and delete) and SQL
User Data-Manipulation Language (UDML)	SQL
Direct Access Facility	None

Languages and Interface Management Systems	
User Languages	User language (4GL)
Programming Languages	COBOL, PLI, FORTRAN, ASSEMBLER, Ada
User Interface Management Systems	Access (query/update facility)
Programming Interface Management Systems	Workshop (screen painter, screen/action generator)

Architectural Characteristics	
Data Constructs	Databases, datasets, files (tables), records (rows), fields (columns)
Data Constructors	Interactive database management commands
Search Capability	Full
Data Cross-Referencing (Mapping)	Dynamic
Processing Mode	Set or record at a time

Database Programmability	
Command-Based Stored Procedures	No
Event-Driven Stored Procedures (Triggers)	No
Structurally-Defined Business Rule Enforcement	No
Rules Interface Management System	No

Storage Management Profile	
Blocking	Customizable
Buffering	Managable buffer pools
Compression	No
Clustering	No
Sequenced Storage	Yes
Indexing	Yes
Pointers	No
Scattering/Hashing	Yes

Administrative Profile	
Security	Interfaces with external security products (i.e., RACF, ACF2, top secret) and provides internal command, application and database access control
Concurrency	Record level locking
Backup/Recovery-Logging	Automatic and manual backup/recovery and logging are available including dump/restore services

The Model 204 database has long been an IBM mainframe standard offering for inverted list database services, and has recently upgraded its profile to include relational support including the use of the SQL language. Computer Corporation of America provides products and services that help organizations to reengineer their businesses to respond to a changing environment.

The Model 204 database is part of CCA's "The Advantage Series" product suite, which features several distinct, powerful components that combine to prove a fast applications development environment. Product offerings that work in tandem with Model 204 include:

User Language—A high performance fourth generation language

Horizon—CCA's distributed and cooperative LU 6.2 development facility

Imagine—A form driven query and report writer which allows access to Model 204 as well and many other IBM supported databases

TextView—A complete full-text retrieval system with Target/204, a comprehensive text application generator

PC/204 and Access/204—Products which allow the integrated accessing of Model 204 data from other platforms

My ^Advanced Database

```
Architecture    : Flat file
Manufacturer    : My Software Corp.
Platform        : Mac
```

Database Access Method	
Program Data-Manipulation Language (PDML)	None
User Data-Manipulation Language (UDML)	None
Direct Access Facility	My Database (part of system)

Languages and Interface Management Systems	
User Languages	None
Programming Languages	None
User Interface Management Systems	My Database (part of system)
Programming Interface Management Systems	None

Architectural Characteristics	
Data Constructs	Fields, records, databases (files)
Data Constructors	Interactive data definition[1]
Search Capability	Full dynamic searches
Data Cross-Referencing (Mapping)	None
Processing Mode	Single record processing

Database Programmability	
Command-Based Stored Procedures	No
Event-Driven Stored Procedures (Triggers)	No
Structurally-Defined Business Rule Enforcement	No
Rules Interface Management System	No

1. The interactive data definition screen is the first record of a database. The first record remains at the top of the database and can be reformatted on the fly, without any loss of data.

Storage Management Profile	
Blocking	OS dependent
Buffering	OS dependent
Compression	No
Clustering	No
Sequenced Storage	Yes
Indexing	No
Pointers	No
Hashing	No

Administrative Profile	
Security	Partial
Concurrency	No
Backup/Recovery-Logging	OS dependent

My ⁻Advanced Database, by My Software Co., Inc., is a low-cost, flexible-list management system. The program has a single-screen interface which provides the user with all the information needed to know the current status of the system, with pull-down menus, and pop-up windows for search, report, and mailmerge functions.

The search window offers two types of sort formats, simple sort, which would allow the data to be sorted on one field, and complex sort which allows the user to specify a calculation for data sequencing.

The report window provides the user with a quick interface for specifying which fields to include in a report, where totals columns should be, and how data should be sorted. Also provided with the report ability is a list of several default formats, from mini address books, to financial summary reports, each allowing the user to specify the sort fields, and appearance of the report.

The Mailmerge feature combines a simple word processor, where the body of a letter can be entered, with the data. A user simply needs to specify where data is to be merged, and the letters are compiled and printed.

The distinguishing feature of My ⁻Advanced Database is the one screen tells all layout. From left to right, the screen shows:

A. An alphabetic listing, for quick access to a key field by clicking on the appropriate letter
B. A listing of database key values in a scrolling window, a user can simply click-on the key value, and the appropriate record will become the current record
C. The Data fields, the center window provides a scrolling view of each record, in a index card format
D. The search, sort, and report window, on the far right, provide the user with quick access to the different capabilities of the system

NOMAD

Architecture	: Relational || Hierarchical
Manufacturer	: MUST SOFTWARE INTERNATIONAL
Platform	: IBM (VM), IBM PC (DOS, OS/2) and
	: compatibles, DEC/VAX(VMS)

Direct Database Access Method	
Program Data-Manipulation Language (PDML)	NOMAD language (data access subset)
User Data-Manipulation Language (UDML)	NOMAD language (data access subset)
Direct Access Facility	None

Languages and Interface Management Systems	
User Languages	NOMAD 4GL
Programming Languages	NOMAD 4GL,
User Interface Management Systems	GLUI, TUI, Access, QLIST, NOMAD windows, Assistant
Programming Interface Management Systems	Flashpoint, collection, Schemgen, Picasso, NOMAD Toolkit

Architectural Characteristics	
Data Constructs	Items (fields, columns), segments, files, databases, defines (virtual items), groups
Data Constructors	SCHEMA
Search Capability	Full
Data Cross-Referencing (Mapping)	Dynamic
Processing Mode	Record||Set processing

Database Programmability	
Command-Based Stored Procedures	No
Event-Driven Stored Procedures (Triggers)	No
Structurally-Defined Business Rule Enforcement	Yes, including limits, members, masks, referential integrity and update restrictions
Rules Interface Management System	No

Storage Management Profile	
Blocking	Customizable
Buffering	Customizable
Compression	No
Clustering	Yes
Sequenced Storage	Yes
Indexing	Yes
Pointers	Yes
Hashing	No

Administrative Profile	
Security	Full and extensive: passwords, profiles defined in schema, encipher
Concurrency	Full
Backup/Recovery-Logging	Full

NOMAD is a powerful database management system that allows you to organize a large quanity of data and use it in a wide variety of ways. NOMAD is an information mangement tool with built-in analytic features that directly increase your ability to access, control and use your information to accomplish your business objectives.

NOMAD is also a comprhensive fourth generation language which can be accessed from a variety of operating systems. It is the existence of this 4th-generation language and the coupling of language and database into one "seamless" offering that makes NOMAD distinctive in the marketplace.

NOMAD combines information processing capabilities usually available only with multiple software packages. The full range of database mangement and reporting activities are performed in one operating environment. This means that NOMAD is ideal for those who use the information for decision-making, as well as for those involved in application development.

The NOMAD product is the cornerstone of the MUST Software International line up of information processing software and the product supports cooperative and client/server processing with MVS, VM, PC-DOS, OS/2, LAN and VMS systems. Multiple database products interfaces make it possible for the developer to access many different database products from within one NOMAD application.

NONSTOP-SQL

Architecture	: Relational
Manufacturer	: Tandem Computers, Inc
Platform	: Guardian 90

Database Access Method	
Program Data-Manipulation Language (PDML)	SQL
User Data-Manipulation Language (UDML)	SQL
Direct Access Facility	None

Languages and Interface Management Systems	
User Languages	None
Programming Languages	C', COBOL, PASCAL
User Interface Management Systems	Report Write, Conversational Interface
Programming Interface Management Systems	None

Architectural Characteristics	
Data Constructs	Fields, tables, partitions, views, databases
Data Constructors	Database definition language
Search Capability	Full search
Data Cross-Referencing (Mapping)	Dynamic
Processing Mode	Set

Database Programmability	
Command-Based Stored Procedures	No
Event-Driven Stored Procedures (Triggers)	No
Structurally-Defined Business Rule Enforcement	Constraint integrity
Rules Interface Management System	No

Storage Management Profile	
Blocking	OS dependent
Buffering	OS dependent
Compression	No
Clustering	No
Sequenced Storage	No
Indexing	Yes
Pointers	No
Hashing	No

Administrative Profile	
Security	OS dependent with SQL compliance
Concurrency	Yes, multiple users on multiple platforms
Backup/Recovery-Logging	Yes, full roll back and roll forward

NonStop SQL is a relational database management system that uses the industry-standard SQL language to define and manipulate data. Non Stop SQL is integrated with other Tandem software so that you can use SQL with COBOL85, Pascal or C programs in online transaction processing applications in a geographically distributed network of systems.

The NonStop SQL environment consists of:

. NonStop SQL conversational interface (SQLCI)— the line oriented terminal interface to a NonStop SQL database. It provides for interactive use of the SQL language, a report writer and NonStop SQL utilities.

. Embedded SQL—the programmatic interface to a NonStOP SQL database. It provides for coding SQL statements in host language programs. The interface supports the COBOL85, Pascal and C programming languages.

. NonStop SQL database utilities—tools for database maintenance.

. Transaction Monitoring Facility (TMF)—a Tandem product that supports concurrent access to a distributed database and ensures it consistency.

. GUARDIAN 90 operating system—the operating system that supports the NonStop SQL database structure and system process. In addition, GUARDIAN 90 authorization for data access provides data security.

Objectivity DB

Architecture	: Object Oriented
Manufacturer	: Objectivity Inc.
Platform	: Unix, Sun3, HP9000, DEC RISC
	: VAX/ULTRIX , VAX/VMS, IBM 6000,
	: Silicon Graphics, SONY News

Database Access Method	
Program Data-Manipulation Language (PDML)	Yes (new() and delete() from C++ or object manipulation library macros including ooNew() and ooDelete() and methods eg. LookupObj)
User Data-Manipulation Language (UDML)	Conditional query thru the data browser
Direct Access Facility	None

Languages and Interface Management Systems	
User Languages	None
Programming Languages	C, C++
User Interface Management Systems	Data browser (bundled)
Programming Interface Management Systems	3rd party (HP-softbench, centerline)

Architectural Characteristics	
Data Constructs	Objects/Classes [federated (global database), database (physical file), Container (Segment of a file), Object (base construct)] Files, Classes, Instances
Data Constructors	Data definition language and class definition use to C++ syntax to provide a superset of C++ facilities
Search Capability	Partial (many key per class) , full via iterators and other object oriented capabilities
Data Cross-Referencing (Mapping)	Association (iterator or named association), conditioinal scan
Processing Mode	Object/page at a time

Database Programmability	
Command-Based Stored Procedures	Implicit in the architecture
Event-Driven Stored Procedures (Triggers)	Implicit in the architecture
Structurally-Defined Business Rule Enforcement	Object-based constraints (via Ovalidate command) and referential integrity
Rules Interface Management System	No

Storage Management Profile	
Blocking	Customizable
Buffering	Customizable
Compression	Can be done by application as a method on the class
Clustering	Yes
Sequenced Storage	Yes
Indexing	Yes (keys)
Pointers	Yes (associations)
Hashing	No

Administrative Profile	
Security	Operating system dependent with DOD C2 planned as an option
Concurrency	Short and long transactions, read and write locks and versioning
Backup/Recovery-Logging	Full and Incremental backup and recovery of backup copies only. Journaling (logging) is only for the life of a transaction.

The Objectivity DB database, provides a fully operational, high performance object-oriented database management system for developing engineering and commercial applications such as ECAD (electronic computer-aided design), CASE, CAP (computer-aided publishing) and CIM (computer integrated manufacturing).

These applications typically require flexible data modeling, involve complex relationships, and demand high performance and large capacity. Objectivity/DB provides full database functionality with a completely distributed architecture that supports networks of heterogeneous platforms. It is designed to manage extremely large amounts of data in a manner transparent to both the developer and the user.

Objectivity/DB meets the feature and performance requirements typical of many complex applications. It combines object oriented technology, the full DBMS functionality required for real-world applications, such as concurrency, security, recovery, versioning, etc., to provide optimal data modeling, performnace, and run-time support.

Among the more pronounced features of the system are included the multi-user support including concurrency control, short and long transactions, two phase commit and atomic updates and database tools including a graphical data and type browser, database debugger, dump/load utility and database administrator utilities.

The Objectivity/DB database is one of the more sophisticated and fully functional object oriented database products on available today and has a large number of successful production implementations.

Omnis 7

Architecture	: SBase
Manufacturer	: Blyth Software Co.
Platform	: MS/Windows, MAC

Database Access Method	
Program Data-Manipulation Language (PDML)	Omnis 7 4GL (data access subset)[1]; SQL[2]
User Data-Manipulation Language (UDML)	Omnis 7 4GL (data access subset) ; SQL
Direct Access Facility	None

Languages and Interface Management Systems	
User Languages	None
Programming Languages	Omnis 7 4GL
User Interface Management Systems	AD-HOC report generator (part of system)
Programming Interface Management Systems	Omnis 7(part of system)

Architectural Characteristics	
Data Constructs	Fields, records, files, windows[3]
Data Constructors	Interactive data definition, file structure copy commands, window paint screens.
Search Capability	Full dynamic searches available
Data Cross-Referencing (Mapping)	Static[4]
Processing Mode	Single record processing

Database Programmability	
Command-Based Stored Procedures	Pushbutton triggered procedures
Event-Driven Stored Procedures (Triggers)	Fully supported
Structurally-Defined Business Rule Enforcement	Field templates and pick lists
Rules Interface Management System	No

1. The Omnis 7 4GL only offers a limited set of data manipulation commands, the remainder of data manipulation features are controlled by the actual data input windows assigned to a particular database. *language examples ; {set main file, enter data, delete, find, import}.*

2. The Omnis 7 program allows programmers to access remote database server tables with SQL, No SQL data management ability is present in the native Omnis 7 environment.

3. An Omnis 7 database window can store any valid procedure in a field or database, this feature gives a data window the ability to perform any procedure Omnis 7 could perform from any program module.

4. Omnis 7 also offers the ability to create relational joins from one table to another via index key joins. Although this is a dynamic mapping (relational) feature, the system is designed, and best used with it's native network architecture.

Storage Management Profile	
Blocking	Controlled within program (menu selection)
Buffering	Controlled within program (menu selection)
Compression	No
Clustering	No
Sequenced Storage	No
Indexing	Yes
Pointers	Yes
Hashing	No

Administrative Profile	
Security	Full
Concurrency	Full roll back or roll forward supported
Backup/Recovery-Logging	OS dependent backup, full logging

Omnis 7 is a MAC, MS/Windows Network Application, applications designed in Omnis can be directly translated to the other platform with no code modification.

The Omnis 7 4GL is a high-level language, offering very powerful commands to perform most database tasks. The example below shows the rich syntax of the Omnis 7 4GL.

```
1. Update Customer list
Set main file to CUST
    Prepare for input  *to prepare the data buffer
    Enter Data         *to open the window
    Update files if flag is true  *to update data files
    quit procedure     *to end the procedure
```

Data integrity and other procedures can be attached to the database window specified by the filename. This feature of the Omnis 7 language makes database programming very efficient, and easy.

The Omnis 7 database manager has the ability to store graphic, text, and BLOB (multimedia) data types. Text and graphic data can be copied from the operating system clipboard into the appropriate field.

The network support for Omnis 7 includes programmatic control of file, and record locking, and programmers can specify the SQL link to most database servers (Oracle, Sybase, Rdb, MS/SQL server, and several other SQL servers.) Additionally, SQL Express is a user interface that allows access to the above servers, SQL Express allows users to click (with the mouse) on the appropriate fields and query statements, and the program completes and executes the query. The ad-hoc report writer is a user interface for quick report generation in the Omnis 7 environment. Users can create reports, on the fly, by making menu selections and clicking "OK."

ONTOS

Architecture	: Object-Oriented
Manufacturer	: ONTOS, Inc
Platform	: SUN, HP, RS6000, DEC,
	: 386/486, OS2, UNIX, SCO

Database Access Method	
Program Data-Manipulation Language (PDML)	Yes, (ONTOS proprietery including Object SQL)
User Data-Manipulation Language (UDML)	ONTOS, Object SQL
Direct Access Facility	None

Languages and Interface Management Systems	
User Languages	None
Programming Languages	C++, Smalltalk
User Interface Management Systems	ONTOS studio
Programming Interface Management Systems	ONTOS DBdesigner

Architectural Characteristics	
Data Constructs	Attributes, instances, objects, pages, areas, segments and logical databases
Data Constructors	C++ class descriptions, programmatic facility thru interactive facility, thru ONTOS DBdesigner or object SQL
Search Capability	Full dynamic search
Data Cross-Referencing (Mapping)	Aggregate classes, sets, arrays, lists, dictionary, direct references, static and dynamic
Processing Mode	Record, object, set, page or closure (complete path)

Database Programmability	
Command-Based Stored Procedures	Via functions (implied)
Event-Driven Stored Procedures (Triggers)	Via functions (implied)
Structurally-Defined Business Rule Enforcement	Implied
Rules Interface Management System	No

Storage Management Profile	
Blocking	By object, page or aggregate (customizable)
Buffering	User setable
Compression	Minimal (strings only)
Clustering	Yes
Sequenced Storage	Yes
Indexing	Yes, dictionary (B-trees)
Pointers	Yes, (list and array descriptions)
Hashing	Dictionary and set descriptions

Administrative Profile	
Security	OS defined
Concurrency	Pessimistic (at acquisition time), Optimistic (at commit time) and Time Based
Backup/Recovery-Logging	Backup, recovery and full journaling

The ONTOS database, like all classical object-oriented database management systems, is a distributed object management system that allows programmers and end-users to access data across a wide variety of platforms. The ONTOS product features an extensible object model, a distributed client-server archictecture a full-featured multi-user database environment, an active data dictionary, multiple storage management options and flexible concurrency control.

Among the features that make ONTOS easy to use and administer are:

1. The DBDesigner product which provides an interactive, visually-oriented tool for looking at and putting together the structure, relationships and content of an ONTOS database.

2. The Classify and Cplus utilities which make it easy to prepare database schemas and to preprocess C++ programs.

3. ONTOS Object SQL—A rich subset of the SQL query language, complete with object extensions which make it possible to work in a relational and object oriented mode with the same access language.

4. The DBA tool—Which provides for the registration and support of ONTOS databases and can be used to define the mapping between logical databases and their physical locations.

5. ONTOS Studio—An interactive front-end development tool for ONTOS databases which constructs user interfaces directly from database schema.

The ONTOS database can be utilized to support many types of applications including engineering, scientific and commercial types of data processing.

(HP) OpenODB

Architecture	: Extended Relational (Object-Oriented)
Manufacturer	: Hewlett-Packard
Platform	: HP 3000 , HP 9000, HP 900, HP 800,
	: HP 700 and RISC workstations

Database Access Method	
Program Data-Manipulation Language (PDML)	Object-oriented SQL
User Data-Manipulation Language (UDML)	Object-oriented SQL
Direct Access Facility	None

Languages and Interface Management Systems	
User Languages	None
Programming Languages	C, C++, COBOL, FORTRAN, PASCAL, ADA, and SMALLTALK
User Interface Management Systems	IOSQL (interactive object-oriented SQL)
Programming Interface Management Systems	Unlimited user-defined types, graphical Browser

Architectural Characteristics	
Data Constructs	Bags, lists, sets, tuples
Data Constructors	OSQL(object-oriented SQL)
Search Capability	On objects, relationships, functions and metadata
Data Cross-Referencing (Mapping)	System defined object identifiers
Processing Mode	Set processing

Database Programmability	
Command-Based Stored Procedures	Via functions created in OSQL or C linkable functions
Event-Driven Stored Procedures (Triggers)	No
Structurally-Defined Business Rule Enforcement	OSQL based or external functions
Rules Interface Management System	Via user defined function

Storage Management Profile	
Blocking	OS defined
Buffering	Yes
Compression	Custom defined
Clustering	Horizontal and vertical
Sequenced Storage	Yes
Indexing	B-tree
Pointers	Yes
Hashing	Yes

Administrative Profile	
Security	Object-level security
Concurrency	Locking of instances and classes
Backup/Recovery-Logging	Yes including online transaction recovery

OpenODB from Hewlett-Packard is an advanced extended relational (objected-oriented) database management system (ODBMS) from Hewlett-Packard for your complex commercial application needs. With OpenODB, you can take advantage of new object-oriented features combined with a robust database mangement system. This combination of capabilities is unique in the industry

OpenODB's object-oriented features will help to reduce your development and maintentance costs by more intuitively representing your business problems. Also, OpenODB stores code as well as data. This means that your application will be simpler and code as well as data can be shared between multiple users and application.

OpenODB's database management features ensure the integrity, security and availability of your stored code and data. At the same time, OpenODB protects your existing data, application and training investments by allowing you to access existing data and application usisng object-oriented structure query language (OSQL).

ORACLE

Architecture	: Relational
Manufacturer	: Oracle Corporation
Platform	: Over 50 including: MVS, VM, VSE, : PC/DOS, MAC, CRAY, UNIX, HP, : UNISYS, WANG .....

Database Access Method	
Program Data-Manipulation Language (PDML)	SQL
User Data-Manipulation Language (UDML)	SQL
Direct Access Facility	None

Languages and Interface Management Systems	
User Languages	None
Programming Languages	C, COBOL, FORTRAN, PL/I, PASCAL, ADA(3GL) and PL/SQL(4GL, packaged)
User Interface Management Systems	SQL*REPORT (a report writer) , QMX (a query manager)
Programming Interface Management Systems	SQL*PLUS (interactive query manager) , SQL*MENU (a menu generator) , SQL*FORMS (a form-based application program generator)

Architectural Characteristics	
Data Constructs	Columns, rows, tables, databases
Data Constructors	SQL-DDL
Search Capability	Full
Data Cross-Referencing (Mapping)	Dynamic
Processing Mode	Set processing

Database Programmability	
Command-Based Stored Procedures	No
Event-Driven Stored Procedures (Triggers)	No
Structurally-Defined Business Rule Enforcement	No
Rules Interface Management System	No

Storage Management Profile	
Blocking	OS dependent but customizable in most cases (2k-8k)
Buffering	Customizable
Compression	No
Clustering	No
Sequenced Storage	Yes
Indexing	B-tree
Pointers	No
Hashing	No

Administrative Profile	
Security	Full SQL-DCL compliance
Concurrency	Row level locking
Backup/Recovery-Logging	Full backup and recovery including the optional use of journaling.

The ORACLE database is another, and the biggest of the UNIX "big four" DBMS products. ORACLE's current installed base on UNIX platforms is somewhere between 40% and 50% or all databases in production today. Because of its outstanding position in the marketplace, the ORACLE database has a large following and continues to improve and enhance its capabilties.

Among the more distincitive characteristics of the database are:

1. The incredibly large number of platforms on which it runs. By far, ORACLE runs on more platforms then any other DBMS considered, from the smallest PC to the largest CRAY.

2. The ORACLE SQL*FORMS product has been used to develop many of the commercially prevelant applications that can be seen today in stores, factories and large commercial environments as well as government and research institutions. With SQL*FORMS, the programmer can quickly and effectively develop complex applications that work intimately with the ORACLE database "engine."

3. The Oracle Corporation is also one of the leading proponents of CASE technology, with several inter-connectible CASE products and approaches.

4. The ORACLE database conforms to many of the standards for open systems developement and enjoys relationships with many 3rd party vendors who provide the user with "front-end" products and programmer enhancement capabilties.

* Information in this review refers to Oracle before release 7.0

OS/2 DATABASE MANAGER

Architecture	: Relational
Manufacturer	: IBM Corporation
Platform	: OS/2

Database Access Method	
Program Data-Manipulation Language (PDML)	SQL
User Data-Manipulation Language (UDML)	SQL
Direct Access Facility	None

Languages and Interface Management Systems	
User Languages	None
Programming Languages	'C', COBOL, FORTRAN, PASCAL, REXX
User Interface Management Systems	QUERY MANAGER
Programming Interface Management Systems	None

Architectural Characteristics	
Data Constructs	Fields, tables, databases, indexes
Data Constructors	Database definition language
Search Capability	Full search
Data Cross-Referencing (Mapping)	Dynamic
Processing Mode	Set

Database Programmability	
Command-Based Stored Procedures	No
Event-Driven Stored Procedures (Triggers)	No
Structurally-Defined Business Rule Enforcement	Referential integrity
Rules Interface Management System	No

Storage Management Profile	
Blocking	OS dependent
Buffering	OS dependent
Compression	No
Clustering	No
Sequenced Storage	No
Indexing	Exists
Pointers	No
Hashing	No

Administrative Profile	
Security	Yes
Concurrency	Yes
Backup/Recovery-Logging	Yes

Database Manager is designed to satisfy the needs of users and programmers alike. For the user, it provides a full-function relational database manager both in a standalone environment or as part of a network on which OS/2 and DOS workstations reside. For the programmer. Database Manager provides utilities and precompilers that support the development of relational database application programs.

As a strategic component of the IBM DRDB (Distributed Relational Database) strategy, OS2 provides the organization that wishes to work with only one vendor for all hardware and software needs the ability to work with an IBM provided relational database on the personal computer.

Although the OS2 data manager is not FULLY compatible with the other IBM relational offerings, it is built in basically the same manner, with many of the same underlying architectural assumptions.

In addition to the additional flexibility provided to the OS2 user with the highly integrated nature of the OS2 operating system and database, the OS2 data manager also boasts an incredibly user friendly query manager interface, which allows the user to build and execute SQL queries from a mouse/icon driven GUI environment.

Although the underlying data storage and management techniques of the OS2-data manager are basic in their design, the database can provide acceptable performance for many applications.

The soon to be realized vision of a fully integrated, cross platform, distributed IBM database environment makes the OS2 database the product of choice for many large organizations.

PACE

Architecture	: Relational
Manufacturer	: Wang Laboratories, Inc
Platform	: Wang VS except VS/80 and VS/45

Database Access Method	
Program Data-Manipulation Language (PDML)	SQL
User Data-Manipulation Language (UDML)	SQL
Direct Access Facility	None

Languages and Interface Management Systems	
User Languages	None
Programming Languages	COBOL, RPG
User Interface Management Systems	PACE Query and Report
Programming Interface Management Systems	PACE application builder and data definition facility

Architectural Characteristics	
Data Constructs	Fields, tables, databases, indexes
Data Constructors	PACE data dictionary: menu driven
Search Capability	Full search
Data Cross-Referencing (Mapping)	Dynamic and Static - both logical
Processing Mode	Set

Database Programmability	
Command-Based Stored Procedures	Yes
Event-Driven Stored Procedures (Triggers)	Yes
Structurally-Defined Business Rule Enforcement	Referential integrity, constraint integrity
Rules Interface Management System	Yes

Storage Management Profile	
Blocking	2K Block
Buffering	Customizable
Compression	Default
Clustering	Yes
Sequenced Storage	Yes
Indexing	B-tree structure (1 primary, 16 alternates)
Pointers	No
Hashing	No

Administrative Profile	
Security	Yes
Concurrency	Yes
Backup/Recovery-Logging	Yes

The VS Professional Application Creation Environment (PACE) is a fully integrated application development and information management environment for the Wang VS. PACE provides easy and timely access to information for both the nonprogramming professional and the programmer/analyst.

As a complete information management environment, PACE includes all of the facilities required to:

. Define and Manage data bases

. Perform ad hoc queries and updates

. Generate reports, documents, charts, and spreadsheets

. Create complete applications nonprocedurally

. Write programs that provide relational access to data and screens

. Access all PACE facilities through system-generated menus

. Integrate with Wang office automation products

. Acess mainframe data bases

PARADOX

Architecture	: SBase
Manufacturer	: Borland International
Platform	: PC/DOS

Database Access Method	
Program Data-Manipulation Language (PDML)	SQL
User Data-Manipulation Language (UDML)	SQL
Direct Access Facility	None

Languages and Interface Management Systems	
User Languages	PAL
Programming Languages	C, PASCAL
User Interface Management Systems	QBE, forms
Programming Interface Management Systems	None

Architectural Characteristics	
Data Constructs	Tables, fields, primary indexes
Data Constructors	Paradox table creation screen
Search Capability	Full
Data Cross-Referencing (Mapping)	Yes via linking forms
Processing Mode	Set processing

Database Programmability	
Command-Based Stored Procedures	No
Event-Driven Stored Procedures (Triggers)	Triggers on forms
Structurally-Defined Business Rule Enforcement	ValCheck on forms
Rules Interface Management System	No

Storage Management Profile	
Blocking	OS dependent
Buffering	VMM (virtual memory management)
Compression	No
Clustering	No
Sequenced Storage	No
Indexing	Yes
Pointers	(Links)
Hashing	No

Administrative Profile	
Security	Yes encryption, password (user, database, table,field), access(table,field)
Concurrency	Implicit locking of records
Backup/Recovery-Logging	Partial and limited

PARADOX is probably one of the most popular screen-based database systems on the market today. By combining the power of its screen-based processing, with an equally effective programming language called PAL, PARADOX has endeared itself to a large population of PC database afficiandos.

From the user-friendly perspective, PARADOX is built around the concept of table based forms, which hold the information that users are processing. By presenting blank tables to the user, the product provides an extremely easy-to-use Query By Example facility.

From the programmers perspective, the PARADOX Engine, with its C, Pascal and MS-Windows interfaces, make it possible for the programmer to develop extremely complex applications programs with all of the robustness of a large mainframe system, while making it possible for end users to access and manipulate the stored data using the friendlier PARADOX front end facilities.

PARADOX seems to be the most popular with end users already comfortable with a spreadsheet, macro-driven type environment. This is probably due to the fact that the PAL language more resembles a macro then a fully procedural programming language.

Both PAL and PARADOX Engine access to the database is managed via the PARADOX defined QBE type screens, making it extremely easy for the beginning programmer to master.

PC-File

Architecture	: Flat file
Manufacturer	: ButtonWare
Platform	: PC/DOS

Direct Database Access Method	
Program Data-Manipulation Language (PDML)	None
User Data-Manipulation Language (UDML)	None
Direct Access Facility	PC-file (part of system)

Languages and Interface Management Systems	
User Languages	PC-file reporting language (part of system)
Programming Languages	None
User Interface Management Systems	PC-file, (part of system)
Programming Interface Management Systems	PC-File macro facility, limited to keystroke only

Architectural Characteristics	
Data Constructs	Fields, records, databases (files)
Data Constructors	PC-File, form paint or interactive data definition[1]
Search Capability	Full
Data Cross-Referencing (Mapping)	Static, limited, cross file lookups are available
Processing Mode	Record processing

Database Programmability	
Command-Based Stored Procedures	No
Event-Driven Stored Procedures (Triggers)	Limited, autolookup across files available
Structurally-Defined Business Rule Enforcement	Limited, field templates, and pick lists
Rules Interface Management System	No

1. PC-file uses XBase .DBF-type files for data storage. This makes the data files compatible with any of the XBase programs discussed in this book.

2. Although PC-file is a flat-file database, the program does allow cross file lookups to simplify data entry.

3. PC-File allows simple versions of XBase template syntax to be included in field definitions (all capital letters, all numbers, several date and time formats).

Storage Management Profile	
Blocking	OS dependent
Buffering	OS dependent
Compression	No
Clustering	No
Sequenced Storage	No
Indexing	B-Tree, XBase .NDX indexes
Pointers	No
Hashing	No

Administrative Profile	
Security	None
Concurrency	File and record locking on networks
Backup/Recovery-Logging	Roll back file recovery with repair program (bundled)

PC-file by Buttonware is a powerful flat file database. The system works with standard .DBF files and provides network support with record and file locking. Working in a proprietary GUI, the program offers users the ability to define data with a screen painter, where fields are laid out on the screen as they appear in a form, or with an interactive data definition screen.

The program offers the ability to make on-the-fly database definition changes, a word processor for creating mailmerge documents, and a cross-file posting ability so that users can update separate files without performing the update manually.

Along with the ability to create several different report layouts, and automatic mailing labels, the product's graphical user interface makes the ability to include graphs of the data tables in reports.

PC-File also provides bar code compatibility, including Zip + 4, and UPC. The bar code facility supports most dot matrix and laser printers. The telephone dialer feature, unique in PC flat file databases, allows users to dial numbers in phone fields, and by clicking on the dialer in the menu, automatically dial the number on the screen.

An easy to use, no frills word processor is also included as part of the system, which PC-File users can write letters in, and specify merge fields for mail-merge.

The import and export capabilities of PC-File include Lotus 123, Microsoft's Excel and Word, WordPerfect, and several other popular applications.

PROGRESS

Architecture	: Relational
Manufacturer	: Progress Sofware Corp.
Platform	: DOS, OS2, UNIX, VMS, CTOS, Windows

Database Access Method	
Program Data-Manipulation Language (PDML)	SQL, PROGRESS 4GL (Data Access Subset)
User Data-Manipulation Language (UDML)	SQL
Direct Access Facility	None

Languages and Interface Management Systems	
User Languages	None
Programming Languages	PROGRESS 4GL
User Interface Management Systems	RESULTS
Programming Interface Management Systems	FASTTRACK

Architectural Characteristics	
Data Constructs	Fields, records, files, databases, indexes
Data Constructors	FASTTRACK: menu driven, data dictionary
Search Capability	Full search
Data Cross-Referencing (Mapping)	Dynamic
Processing Mode	Set and record at a time

Database Programmability	
Command-Based Stored Procedures	Yes
Event-Driven Stored Procedures (Triggers)	No
Structurally-Defined Business Rule Enforcement	Referential integrity
Rules Interface Management System	No

Storage Management Profile	
Blocking	OS dependent
Buffering	OS dependent
Compression	No
Clustering	No
Sequenced Storage	No
Indexing	Exists
Pointers	No
Hashing	No

Administrative Profile	
Security	Yes, Grant and Revoke
Concurrency	Yes, for client/server version
Backup/Recovery-Logging	Yes - full, incremental and partial backup; full Roll foward and Roll back

The PROGRESS RDBMS is a powerful client/server database engine that supports distributed processing and distributed access across a broad range of operating systems, hardware platforms, network protocols and user interfaces. It features automatic crash recovery, flexible record locking controls, on-line backup, two phase commit, referential integrity, a centralized data dictionary and a multi-threaded, multi-server architecture making the PROGRESS RDBMS ideal for high-volume transaction processing.

The PROGRESS RDBMS is a integral component of the PROGRESS Application Development Environment which includes the PROGRESS 4GL, ANSI-standard SQL, the FAST TRACK menu and report generator, the RESULTS end-user query and reporting system and gateways to other data managers including Oracle, RMS, Rdb, OS/400 and C-ISAM.

Q&A

Architecture	: Flat file
Manufacturer	: Symantec Inc.
Platform	: PC/DOS

Database Access Method	
Program Data-Manipulation Language (PDML)	None
User Data-Manipulation Language (UDML)	None[1]
Direct Access Facility	Q&A, (part of system)

Languages and Interface Management Systems	
User Languages	Q&A natural language interface (part of system)[2]
Programming Languages	None[3]
User Interface Management Systems	Q&A, (part of system)
Programming Interface Management Systems	Q&A, (part of system)

Architectural Characteristics	
Data Constructs	Fields, records, files
Data Constructors	Form paint, field definition
Search Capability	Full dynamic search
Data Cross-Referencing (Mapping)	Static, limited, cross file lookups only
Processing Mode	record processing only

Database Programmability	
Command-Based Stored Procedures	Q&A programming interface
Event-Driven Stored Procedures (Triggers)	Q&A programming interface
Structurally-Defined Business Rule Enforcement	Q&A programming interface
Rules Interface Management System	No

1. Although Q&A offers no direct database access with a programming language, Symantec does offer an SQL connect program that allows users to access client/server databases by Oracle, Sybase, and several others. The SQL module is available upon request to registered owners at no extra charge.

2. The Q&A natural language interface is a system that allows users to control a database using a free-form, natural English interpreter. With the IA, (Intelligent Assistant) a user can enter a command like "list all the customers in Cleveland by their last names," and Q&A will display a list of all the customers in Cleveland in alphabetical order of their last name.

3. The Q&A system does have a programming environment, but all commands are entered in the individual fields of the database form. This does not coincide with our description of a programming language. Even though the commands are procedural and have a strict syntax, programming in Q&A is dependent on the database being programmed.

Storage Management Profile	
Blocking	OS dependent
Buffering	OS dependent
Compression	No
Clustering	No
Sequenced Storage	No
Indexing	Yes, referred to as speedy fields
Pointers	No
Hashing	No

Administrative Profile	
Security	Limited
Concurrency	Automatic record and file locking
Backup/Recovery-Logging	QA backup, (bundled)

Q&A, by Symantec, represents the most popular and flexible of the flat file database systems. Running in a mouse-supported TUI, Q&A offers user/programmers the ability to manage sophisticated flat-file databases.

Bundled with the Q&A database is Q&A Write, a full-featured word processor, dedicated to the task of mailmerge with the database. Q&A Write is more than just a text editor, it is a powerful word processor that could stand alone on its own merits in the PC word processing market.

Programming in Q&A is handled through APT (Application Programming Tools). The APTs provide programmers with the following options.
1. Field value definition—a system for defining field defaults, lookup values, and calculations. Field calculations can be defined to include any field, a static value, or a lookup value from another database
2. Field integrity—a method to define the way data is stored, i.e., (111) 111-1111 for phone numbers
3. Field access—a method for defining when and how fields are accessed and edited
4. External file posting—a method for posting changes to lookup databases in case of changes

The APTs are fully integrated, so programmers are free to define only the programming they feel is appropriate. Included with the APTs is a menu/macroing facility, a programmer can create a custom (main) menu, which in turn executes macros that open the database. Once the database is open, the internal programming can maintain all facets of the environment, therefore controlling any actions the user intends to take.

The IA (Intelligent Assistant) is a natural language tool that allows users to perform any task (query, update record, add record, delete record, print report) from a natural language interface. The user simply types (in his or her own words) the task to perform, and Q&A will do it.

RapidFile

Architecture	: Flat file
Manufacturer	: Borland International
Platform	: PC/DOS

Database Access Method	
Program Data-Manipulation Language (PDML)	None
User Data-Manipulation Language (UDML)	None
Direct Access Facility	RapidFile (part of system)

Languages and Interface Management Systems	
User Languages	None
Programming Languages	None
User Interface Management Systems	RapidFile (part of system)
Programming Interface Management Systems	None

Architectural Characteristics	
Data Constructs	Fields, records, files
Data Constructors	Interactive data definition process
Search Capability	Full dynamic searches
Data Cross-Referencing (Mapping)	None
Processing Mode	Record processing

Database Programmability	
Command-Based Stored Procedures	No
Event-Driven Stored Procedures (Triggers)	No
Structurally-Defined Business Rule Enforcement	No
Rules Interface Management System	No

Storage Management Profile	
Blocking	OS dependent
Buffering	OS dependent
Compression	No
Clustering	No
Sequenced Storage	Yes
Indexing	No
Pointers	No
Hashing	No

Administrative Profile	
Security	No
Concurrency	No
Backup/Recovery-Logging	OS dependent

RapidFile, by Borland International, is a list management, word processor package. The system provides users with a menu-driven interface for quick access to all of the programs features.

Combining speed, versatility, and ease-of-use with powerful database, reporting, and word processing capabilities.

Powerful searching and sorting let users create reports that contain only the information they choose. The report writer lets users put titles and headings where they want them on the screen, and that's how they print. Internal functions include column SUM, AVG., Percentages, MAX or MIN.

For a mailing system, the easy-to-use interface, along with a full featured word processor, with spell check and a thesaurus, make RapidFile the perfect tool.

R:BASE

Architecture	: Relational
Manufacturer	: Microrim, Inc
Platform	: PC/DOS, OS/2

Database Access Method	
Program Data-Manipulation Language (PDML)	SQL
User Data-Manipulation Language (UDML)	SQL
Direct Access Facility	None

Languages and Interface Management Systems	
User Languages	R:BASE programming language
Programming Languages	R:BASE programming language
User Interface Management Systems	Menu driven interface and text based
Programming Interface Management Systems	Yes - menu driven application generator

Architectural Characteristics	
Data Constructs	Fields, tables, databases, indexes
Data Constructors	Database definition language
Search Capability	Full search
Data Cross-Referencing (Mapping)	Dynamic
Processing Mode	Set

Database Programmability	
Command-Based Stored Procedures	Forms, reports, labels stored in database
Event-Driven Stored Procedures (Triggers)	No
Structurally-Defined Business Rule Enforcement	Referential integrity, field level constraints
Rules Interface Management System	Yes

Storage Management Profile	
Blocking	OS dependent
Buffering	OS dependent
Compression	No
Clustering	Exists
Sequenced Storage	No
Indexing	Exists
Pointers	No
Hashing	Exists

Administrative Profile	
Security	Yes, grant and revoke with user list
Concurrency	Yes
Backup/Recovery-Logging	Yes

R:BASE is a fully relational database management system that anyone can use.

It has an intuitive interface that gives you a visual map of where you are, where you have been and where you are going. The Application EXPRESS function allows end users and professional programmers to create entire applications using menus. However, for advanced developers, R:BASE has a rich 4GL language and fully supports the ANSI Level II SQL standard.

R:BASE will run on a standalone PC or on a network. It directly reads and writes dBASE III and III+ files even simultaneously on a network while maintaining full concurrency and integrity controls.

For a large number of users, R:BASE has provided the ideal blend of relational database power combined with user friendly programming profile capabilities.

Rdb/VMS

Architecture	: Relational
Manufacturer	: DEC
Platform	: DEC/VAX VMS

Database Access Method	
Program Data-Manipulation Language (PDML)	SQL, RDO
User Data-Manipulation Language (UDML)	SQL, RDO
Direct Access Facility	None

Languages and Interface Management Systems	
User Languages	None
Programming Languages	C, BASIC, COBOL, FORTRAN, ADA, PL/I, PASCAL
User Interface Management Systems	Datatreive, DECdecision, TEAMDATA, DECquery and many third-party vendor interfaces
Programming Interface Management Systems	RALLY, DECforms and many third party interfaces

Architectural Characteristics	
Data Constructs	Databases, tables, columns, rows
Data Constructors	CDD/repository, SQL-DDL
Search Capability	Dynamic
Data Cross-Referencing (Mapping)	Full
Processing Mode	Set processing

Database Programmability	
Command-Based Stored Procedures	No
Event-Driven Stored Procedures (Triggers)	Triggers and field validation
Structurally-Defined Business Rule Enforcement	Referential integrity
Rules Interface Management System	CDD/Respository (packaged)

Storage Management Profile	
Blocking	Yes, Customizable
Buffering	By database and per user
Compression	Data and indexes
Clustering	Physical row clustering and indexes
Sequenced Storage	Horizontal partitioning
Indexing	B-tree
Pointers	No
Hashing	Yes

Administrative Profile	
Security	Full database, table, field, security groups
Concurrency	Full locking
Backup/Recovery-Logging	Full and partial via journals

Rdb/VMS is a high-performance, high-capacity relational database for VMS systems. Rdb supports production applications, end user information management, and transaction processing to provide integration of the enterprise at the information level. With over 17,000 licenses sold worldwide, customers have consistently found Rdb/VMS has the power and the flexibility to manage data and to grow into the furture as their requirements change.

Rdb/VMS can store unstructured data including laboratory, document, digitized voice, and graphic data as a single field in a relation. This feature makes Rdb ideal for business, office, engineering, medical and scientific applications.

RDMS 1100

Architecture	: Relational
Manufacturer	: Unisys Corporation
Platform	: Unisys 1100 and 2200, OS/1100

Database Access Method	
Program Data-Manipulation Language (PDML)	SQL
User Data-Manipulation Language (UDML)	SQL
Direct Access Facility	None

Languages and Interface Management Systems	
User Languages	LINC
Programming Languages	COBOL, FORTRAN
User Interface Management Systems	MAPPER/RDMS
Programming Interface Management Systems	None

Architectural Characteristics	
Data Constructs	Fields, tables, databases, indexes
Data Constructors	Database definition language
Search Capability	Full search
Data Cross-Referencing (Mapping)	Dynamic
Processing Mode	Set

Database Programmability	
Command-Based Stored Procedures	No
Event-Driven Stored Procedures (Triggers)	No
Structurally-Defined Business Rule Enforcement	Referential integrity
Rules Interface Management System	No

Storage Management Profile	
Blocking	Customizable (Table Level)
Buffering	Customizable (Table Level)
Compression	Yes
Clustering	Yes
Sequenced Storage	Yes
Indexing	Binary
Pointers	No
Hashing	No

Administrative Profile	
Security	Yes
Concurrency	Yes
Backup/Recovery-Logging	Yes

UDS RDMS 1100 is the relational system that is table based and can execute SQL commands. RDMS 1100 supports SQL interfaces to standard programming languages such as COBOL and FORTRAN and can also be interfaced with the Unisys MAPPER application development language. The MAPPER Relational Interface (MRI) supports a friendly, menu-driven SQL command build and access to local and remote RDMS databases, along with access to Oracle (UNIX) databases, DB2 databases and CA-databases. With MAPPER the user can create sophisticated reports in a fraction of the time required of normal programming techniques.

Included in the RDMS environment is IPF SQL, the Interactive Processing Facility for SQL. This allows the programmer or user to execute SQL commands directly against existing RDMS tables.

The database is enhanced through the use of the RDMUTL processor which handles the loading and unloading of RDMS tables.

The presence of the RDMS product on UNISYS platforms assures the users of these systems of a manageable migration path from the "traditional" DMS1100 network systems into the new world of relational databases. In addition, the inter-database flexibility of MAPPER means that users and developers can take advantage of other products, like the ORACLE - SQL*FORMS and SQL*PLUS products, as well as the already robust collection of UNISYS development tools like LINC II, ALLY and QLP (the Query Language Processor).

SIM

Architecture	: Proprietery (Semantic)
Manufacturer	: UNISYS Corporation
Platform	: UNISYS large mainframes

Database Access Method	
Program Data-Manipulation Language (PDML)	OML (object manipulation lanaguage)
User Data-Manipulation Language (UDML)	OML
Direct Access Facility	None

Languages and Interface Management Systems	
User Languages	None
Programming Languages	2nd and 3rd Generation languages including COBOL, ALGOL, PASCAL
User Interface Management Systems	INFOEXEC query (packaged)
Programming Interface Management Systems	INFOEXEC programming (packaged)

Architectural Characteristics	
Data Constructs	Classes (object entities), attributes (fields), schemas
Data Constructors	ODL (object definition language)
Search Capability	Full
Data Cross-Referencing (Mapping)	Static and dynamic
Processing Mode	Set and record processing

Database Programmability	
Command-Based Stored Procedures	No
Event-Driven Stored Procedures (Triggers)	Yes, the verify facility
Structurally-Defined Business Rule Enforcement	Yes, semantic relationships, ranges, types (DVA and EVA). (For more information, refer to the chapter about proprietery architectures)
Rules Interface Management System	Yes, UNISYS advanced data dictionary system (ADDS), (NREP/A)

Storage Management Profile	
Blocking	Customizable
Buffering	Customizable
Compression	Optional
Clustering	Yes
Sequenced Storage	Yes
Indexing	Yes
Pointers	Yes
Hashing	Yes

Administrative Profile	
Security	Full attribute and schema security
Concurrency	Object and schema locking
Backup/Recovery-Logging	Full backup and recovery and logging

The SIM (Semantic Information Manager) database, represents a radical departure from the "typical" mainframe computer DBMS.

The SIM product has been developed using the basic concepts established within the definition of databases as outlined under Semantic Data Modeling, and allows for the capture of sophisticated, multidimensional relationships between stored objects.

SIM's distinctive approach to database management, and its equally innovative technique for providing programmatic access to that system, make it a DBMS worth study and use for many types of applications.

This database not only functions as a stand-alone Semantic database, but allows application developers to access DMSII data from within the same programs, making it possible for systems to be developed that make use of existing DMSII data structures, while capitalizing on the more powerful data manipulation capabilties of SIM. DMS II DATA is also available via SQLDB.

Consistent and judicious use of the SIM data relationship mapping functions make it possible for developers to greatly reduce the amount of intelligence that individual programs must enforce, since so much of the logic revolving around issues of data construct interdependency and business integrity definitions can be contained within the database structure itself.

Although still a relatively "young" product, the SIM database is providing valuable input and direction to the tumultuous database industry as a whole.

SIR

Architecture	: Relational
Manufacturer	: SIR(PTY), LTD
Platform	: AEGIS, CGOS, OS/32,
	: NOS, UNIX, COS, CTSSAOS,
	: VMS, TOPS-10, MPX, HP-UX,
	: MVS/TSO, PC-DOS, UNIX,
	: BS2000 EXEC, VM

Database Access Method	
Program Data-Manipulation Language (PDML)	SQL using SIR/ HOST(packaged)
User Data-Manipulation Language (UDML)	SQL+
Direct Access Facility	None

Languages and Interface Management Systems	
User Languages	PQL
Programming Languages	FORTRAN, COBOL, C, ADA, PLI using SIR/HOST
User Interface Management Systems	Graph-PC, forms, easy,
Programming Interface Management Systems	PQL, forms

Architectural Characteristics	
Data Constructs	Database, record type, data fields, foreign keys, primary keys
Data Constructors	SIR/schema
Search Capability	Full
Data Cross-Referencing (Mapping)	Dynamic
Processing Mode	Set processing or record processing

Database Programmability	
Command-Based Stored Procedures	Yes
Event-Driven Stored Procedures (Triggers)	Yes
Structurally-Defined Business Rule Enforcement	Ranges of values, valid values, missing values
Rules Interface Management System	LOOKUP command under the forms subsystem

Storage Management Profile	
Blocking	Dependent on operating system
Buffering	Cache is customizable
Compression	No
Clustering	Yes, optional
Sequenced Storage	Yes, optional
Indexing	Yes
Pointers	No
Hashing	No

Administrative Profile	
Security	Up to 31 levels of read/write secruity
Concurrency	Controlled by a program called MASTER
Backup/Recovery-Logging	Yes, using journalling

SIR is a practical fourth-generation application development environment and relational database management system, practical because they have topped the core relational DBMS with a full-feature set of 4GL capabilities designed for both end users and application developers. This makes the most of the power and flexibility offered by relational theory by having tools to efficiently design, prototype and implement applications.

The SIR product was created in 1976 and is part of an complete product line which includes a 4th-generation language and robust statistical analysis capabilties. The SIR database is most commonly found in medical facilities and government offices.

Because of its history of supporting several different application development platforms, the SIR database can run as well on a mainframe as on a PC and an LAN capabilites product called SIR/LAN makes it possible to use SIR in these types of environments as well.

Among the more user-friendly capabilities of the system is the SIR/EASY user interface management system, which provides a function key driven, query building facility which provides the end-user with a quickie menu system which allows direct interfaces to leading statistical analysis packages such as SAS, SPSS-S, SYSTAT and BMDP as well as many built-in procedures for reports, tabulation and statistical analysis.

Despite its many user-friendly interfaces, SIR is basically a command driven, application development environment which takes advantage of the basic relational internal organization including its own proprietary data dictionary, which serves as the central clearing area for all database activities.

SQL/400

Architecture	: Relational
Manufacturer	: IBM Corporation
Platform	: OS/400 on AS/400

Database Access Method	
Program Data-Manipulation Language (PDML)	Native OS/400 data acess
User Data-Manipulation Language (UDML)	SQL
Direct Access Facility	None

Languages and Interface Management Systems	
User Languages	None
Programming Languages	C/400, COBOL/400, RPG/400
User Interface Management Systems	OS/400 query manager
Programming Interface Management Systems	None

Architectural Characteristics	
Data Constructs	Fields, tables, databases, indexes
Data Constructors	Interactive data definition utility, SQL DDL
Search Capability	Full search
Data Cross-Referencing (Mapping)	Dynamic
Processing Mode	Set

Database Programmability	
Command-Based Stored Procedures	No
Event-Driven Stored Procedures (Triggers)	No
Structurally-Defined Business Rule Enforcement	Referential integrity
Rules Interface Management System	No

Storage Management Profile	
Blocking	OS dependent
Buffering	OS dependent
Compression	No
Clustering	No
Sequenced Storage	No
Indexing	Exists
Pointers	No
Hashing	No

Administrative Profile	
Security	Yes
Concurrency	Yes
Backup/Recovery-Logging	Yes

SQL/400 is a relational database management system marketed by IBM for their AS/400 machine. Due to IBM's pursuit of interoperability across all of their hardware platforms, SQL/400 adheres to the guidelines of System Application Architecture (SAA) and therefore behaves to the user like its mainframe peer DB2.

The SQL/400 database is built to provide full relational functionality, including the full use of SQL-DML (Select, Insert, Update, Delete) embedded within application programs, the creation of native OS400 file structures with SQL-DDL (Create table, index etc.) and security control using SQL-DCL (Grant, Revoke).

The user of an SQL/400 database gets full advantage of the native AS400 file organization when using the relational capabilities which means that application programs can be written to work in both a relational, and in the more traditional "navigational" (key search) mode for more transaction rate intensive kinds of operations.

AS400 native backup, recovery, locking, logging and buffering schemes are utilized by the database, which guarantees low overhead and well integrated administrative services.

SQL/DS

Architecture	: Relational
Manufacturer	: IBM Corporation
Platform	: VM, DOS/VSE

Database Access Method	
Program Data-Manipulation Language (PDML)	SQL
User Data-Manipulation Language (UDML)	SQL
Direct Access Facility	None

Languages and Interface Management Systems	
User Languages	None
Programming Languages	C, COBOL, FORTRAN, PL/I , ASSEMBLER and REXX
User Interface Management Systems	QMF, query management facility and A/S application system (both packaged)
Programming Interface Management Systems	CSP, cross system product (packaged)

Architectural Characteristics	
Data Constructs	Columns, Rows, Tables, DBspaces, Databases
Data Constructors	SQL-DDL
Search Capability	Full
Data Cross Referencing (Mapping)	Dynamic
Processing Mode	Set processing

Database Programmability	
Command-Based Stored Procedures	No
Event-Driven Stored Procedures (Triggers)	No
Structurally-Defined Business Rule Enforcement	Yes, referential integrity
Rules Interface Management System	No

Storage Management Profile	
Blocking	4k
Buffering	Customizable
Compression	No
Clustering	No
Sequenced Storage	Yes
Indexing	B-Tree
Pointers	No
Hashing	No

Administrative Profile	
Security	Full SQL-DCL compliance
Concurrency	Row, page and database level locking
Backup/Recovery-Logging	Full backup and recovery including the optional use of logging

The SQL/DS (SQL Data System) database, is the "little brother" to IBM's DB2 relational database system. Both products' origins can be traced back to the original relational System R prototype develop at the IBM laboratories in the 1970's.

SQL/DS is a mature, dependable DBMS which can be found supporting much of the database activity at IBM based non-MVS sites.

The SQL/DS database organizes data into logical/physical groupings called DBSPACES. A DBSPACE will hold a relational table, and all supporting indexes. By allocating these DBSPACES to private or public ownership the database administrator is able to allocate disk space to individuals, or for globally accessed constructs.

SQL/DS is an important part of IBM's Distributed Relational Database Strategy, and is scheduled for inclusion in the group of IBM database products which will work together in a heterogenous, fully distributed database environment.

SQL/DS is used to support applications of many different kinds including some large financial and commercial applications and it is often used in tandem with the DB2 database, to provide a VM-based user environment where end-users can access copies of their data with products like QMF (Query Management Facility) without encumbering the performance of the more mission-critical DB2 systems.

Along with the 3rd-and 4th-generation language interfaces, is a powerful REXX SQL product which allows programmers to gain access to the SQL/DS database using the high level REXX command language. This makes it possible to write complete application programs with database access, without the necessity of normal program compile and link-edit steps.

SQL Windows (SQL Base)

Architecture	: Relational
Manufacturer	: Gupta Technologies
Platform	: MS/Windows, OS/2
	: UNIX

Database Access Method	
Program Data-Manipulation Language (PDML)	SQL
User Data-Manipulation Language (UDML)	SQL
Direct Access Facility	None

Languages and Interface Management Systems	
User Languages	None
Programming Languages	SAL[1] 4GL
User Interface Management Systems	Report Windows[2] (Bundled)
Programming Interface Management Systems	SQL Windows application development tools[3] (Part of System), Express Windows[4] (Bundled) SQL Talk (Bundled)

Architectural Characteristics	
Data Constructs	Fields, records, tables, datasets
Data Constructors	SQL
Search Capability	Full dynamic searches
Data Cross-Referencing (Mapping)	Dynamic, SQL
Processing Mode	Set processing

Database Programmability	
Command-Based Stored Procedures	No
Event-Driven Stored Procedures (Triggers)	No
Structurally-Defined Business Rule Enforcement	No
Rules Interface Management System	No

1. SAL; the SQL Windows application language, is a 4GL that provides programmers an easy to learn language utilizing the Windows interface.

2. Report Windows is a user tool for creating quick ad hoc reports from SQLWindows databases.

3. The SQL Windows application development tools include SAL, an interactive programming environment, and an interactive debugger, so programmers can run programms, and debug on the fly, without exiting the system.

4. Express Windows is an SQL Windows application developer. Programmers can design Data input screens, menu's, and reports, and the express system will write the source code for the application.

Storage Management Profile	
Blocking	OS dependent
Buffering	OS dependent
Compression	No
Clustering	No
Sequenced Storage	No
Indexing	Dynamic
Pointers	No
Hashing	No

Administrative Profile	
Security	OS Dependent
Concurrency	Full record and file locking
Backup/Recovery-Logging	OS dependent full roll back capabilities

SQL Windows is a complete graphical database application development system for MS/Windows, and OS/2 PM. With SQL Windows, you can build PC applications that combine the elegance and simplicity of a graphical user interface, with powerful multi-user access to data stored in SQL databases throughout an organization.

Designed to realize the potential of client server technology, SQL Windows enables you to build high performance client-server applications that access SQL databases without programming in C, or the Windows SDK (Software Development Kit).

Provided with the SQL Windows system, is Gupta's SQL Base relational database server. Because SQL Windows uses ANSI standard SQL, SQL Windows applications can access multiple types of SQL databases simultaneously. This includes Mini, Mainframe, and LAN servers.

Among other features, SQL Windows provides programmers with an easy to learn 4GL, an interactive application development environment, including all the advantages of a GUI, and direct SQL access to several different database servers.

Within the GUI, SQLWindows has the ability to manage and display text, and Picture type fields, the graphic capabilities are only limited by the hardware, so a true multimedia database application is not far away.

Superbase 4

Architecture	: SBase (Relational, Network)
Manufacturer	: Software Publishing Corp.
Platform	: MS/Windows

Direct Database Access Method	
Program Data-Manipulation Language (PDML)	None
User Data-Manipulation Language (UDML)	None
Direct Access Facility	Superbase (part of system)

Languages and Interface Management Systems	
User Languages	None
Programming Languages	Superbase DML 4GL[1], SBSQL[2]
User Interface Management Systems	Superbase query and database access systems (part of system)
Programming Interface Management Systems	Superbase, form designer, (bundled)

Architectural Characteristics	
Data Constructs	Fields, records, files
Data Constructors	Interactive data definition screen
Search Capability	Full dynamic searches available
Data Cross-Referencing (Mapping)	Static, defined in forms, or during data definition
Processing Mode	Record and set processing both available

Database Programmability	
Command-Based Stored Procedures	No
Event-Driven Stored Procedures (Triggers)	Field lookups[3] and calculated fields
Structurally-Defined Business Rule Enforcement	Field templates and Field validation
Rules Interface Management System	No

1. The superbase DML uses a BASIC like structure for the program management. The DML commands provide programmers with the tools to open and close database files and forms, provide custom windows menus, and execute predefined reports or SBSQL reports embedded within the program.

2. SBSQL is an SQL-like language subset provided within the DML. This SQL hybrid allows programmers and users to create ad-hoc queries, without using the programming language or the database forms. Also provided is an SQL link to the most popular client/server database management systems. This SQL link allows the Server database to be queried, and data management can be performed on the client machine without depending on the servers resources.

3. The Data definition in superbase allows cross file lookups to be defined for data integrity.

Storage Management Profile	
Blocking	OS dependent
Buffering	OS dependent
Compression	No
Clustering	No
Sequenced Storage	No
Indexing	Dynamic
Pointers	No
Hashing	No

Administrative Profile	
Security	Full
Concurrency	Record and file locking
Backup/Recovery-Logging	OS dependent

Superbase 4 is an MS/Windows database management system. The program offers the ability to create sophisticated graphical database forms, for quick access to different facets of a data file.

Provided with Superbase 4 is an example of this capability. With the program running, the form called zmap.sbf provides the user with a map of England. At various locations, pushbuttons appear below certain city names. When one of these buttons is pressed, the form automatically calls up a zoomed view of that particular city. The user can then click on any part of the city, and get all the information about that particular quadrant. This interface allows quick access to data without a user touching the keyboard.

The DML (Database Management Language) provided with Superbase 4, is a procedural, interpreted database system manager. The language does not offer any direct data manipulation, but the structure of the language, along with the use of forms, allows programmers to create sophisticated applications with custom windows menus, and triggers for common command right on the forms.

Data mapping is handled in two ways with Superbase 4. During the data definition process, any fields that are defined as lookup validation fields, automatically create a logical (index key) link to the lookup data file. In data input forms, created with the forms painter (bundled), programmers can define links between data files using logical (index key) links.

The data input form, is the main part of any Superbase application. It is possible for a programmer to create only forms, with no additional programming, and land up with a fully functioning application. The forms in Superbase 4 allow pushbutton triggers, and fields in forms can have stored procedures. This makes Superbase 4 applications very flexible and easy to use.

SUPRA

Architecture	: Relational
Manufacturer	: Cincom Systems Inc.
Platform	: MVS, VSE, VM, VAX/VMS,
	: UNIX, HP, BULL, OS/2

Database Access Method	
Program Data-Manipulation Language (PDML)	SQL
User Data-Manipulation Language (UDML)	SQL
Direct Access Facility	None

Languages and Interface Management Systems	
User Languages	SQL Windows and Mantis
Programming Languages	COBOL, C, FORTRAN, PASCAL, BASIC, ASSEMBLER and PL/1
User Interface Management Systems	Easy, spectra (packaged) quest and SAS interface (3rd Party)
Programming Interface Management Systems	MANTIS and AD/ADVANTAGE (packaged)

Architectural Characteristics	
Data Constructs	Columns, rows, tables, pages, devspaces, databases
Data Constructors	SQL-DDL
Search Capability	Full
Data Cross Referencing (Mapping)	Logical and dynamic
Processing Mode	Set and record at a time (including backwards cursor processing)

Database Programmability	
Command-Based Stored Procedures	No
Event-Driven Stored Procedures (Triggers)	No
Structurally-Defined Business Rule Enforcement	Yes, create domain, create link and referential integrity
Rules Interface Management System	No

Storage Management Profile	
Blocking	4k
Buffering	Customizable
Compression	Default
Clustering	No
Sequenced Storage	Yes
Indexing	Yes
Pointers	No
Scattering/Hashing	Yes

Administrative Profile	
Security	Full transaction, table security via SQL-DDL
Concurrency	Row, page, and table level locking
Backup/Recovery-Logging	Full backup/recovery including incremental backups and full roll forward and roll back

SUPRA is an advanced relational database management system designed for ease-of-use, flexibility and high-performance. SUPRA offers desktop to data center support with client/server and multi-server distributed capabilities. It is portable across multiple hardware and software platforms including IBM, Digital, UNIX and PC environments with a single system image, providing your organization the flexibility to choose the most cost effective hardware to run your business today and in the future.

Based upon industry standards such as ANSI / ISO SQL, the ANSI / SPARC Three schema Architecture and IBM's SAA. SUPRA is an open, multi-server solution that supports such state-of-the-art features as entity and referential integrity enforcement; updatable join view capability; domain support; scrollable cursors; disk mirroring; dual logging; self-reorganization; accounting, auditing and statistical facilities; and Global Directory extensibility.

The unique Three Schema Architecture is a layered architecture that defines an organiztion's data into three distinct levels. The upper level (External Schema) defines how users see the data, independent of how the data is logically organized or physically stored. The middle layer (Conceptual Schema) defines the corporate data model. And the lower level (Internal Schema) defines the physical data structures. This architecture provides insulation from change between layers to free applications from their dependence on physical and logical structures within the database.

SUPRA can also operate in conjunction with Cincom's AD/Advantage, a life-cycle application development and maintenance system. AD/Advantage provides features such as design object generation, reusable component management, documentation management, project/process management, resource management, change management and upper-CASE tool integration.

SYBASE

Architecture	: Relational
Manufacturer	: Sybase Inc.
Platform	: (Clients) - Mac, PC-DOS,
	: OS2, UNIX
	: (Servers) - OS2, UNIX, VMS,
	: Stratus

Database Access Method	
Program Data-Manipulation Language (PDML)	SQL
User Data-Manipulation Language (UDML)	SQL
Direct Access Facility	None

Languages and Interface Management Systems	
User Languages	APT
Programming Languages	Transact-SQL (4GL-packaged), ADA,C, COBOL, FORTRAN, PASCAL (3GL)
User Interface Management Systems	APT workbench, data workbench
Programming Interface Management Systems	Data workbench: APT workbench

Architectural Characteristics	
Data Constructs	Columns, rows, tables, databases
Data Constructors	Data workbench or SQL-DDL
Search Capability	Full dynamic search
Data Cross-Referencing (Mapping)	Logical and dynamic
Processing Mode	Set at a time

Database Programmability	
Command-Based Stored Procedures	Yes
Event-Driven Stored Procedures (Triggers)	Yes
Structurally-Defined Business Rule Enforcement	Yes
Rules Interface Management System	No

Storage Management Profile	
Blocking	2k blocksize
Buffering	Customizable
Compression	No
Clustering	Yes
Sequenced Storage	Yes
Indexing	Yes
Pointers	No
Scattering/Hashing	No

Administrative Profile	
Security	Full transaction and table security
Concurrency	Locking at page and table level
Backup/Recovery-Logging	Full backup/recovery

SYBASE provides a proven, high-performance, distributed relational database management and development system for on-line applications. It consists of two major product families: SQL Toolset and SQL Server. SQL Toolset is a complete set of tools for developing and using on-line applications and SQL Server handles all data management functions, including the enforcement of data integrity rules.

SQL Server delivers a unique level of power and functionality to handle the demanding requirements of on-line applications in large, multi-user environments by providing:

Scalable high performance (high transaction rates and throughput)

Server-enforced system integrity

High application availability (supporting 24-hour run times, and full recovery capabilities)

Open distributed DBMS (SQL Server supports the distribution of applications and databases over networks of heterogeneous workstations and processors)

SYBASE is know as one of the UNIX "big four," the four most commonly used database products within the UNIX environment. The product has established a reputation for itself as probably "the most sophisticated" of the relational database products, especially in the client server arena, and was responsible for a lot of the groundbreaking work that has been done in the areas of stored procedures, triggers and cross platform systems integration.

The product offers the user a fully-functional, integrated relational database environment with a robust set of 3rd-party products to support almost every aspect of system development and maintenance.

(ACP/)TPF

Architecture   : Proprietery
Manufacturer   : IBM Corp.
Platform   : IBM Mainframes and compatibles

Direct Database Access Method	
Program Data-Manipulation Language (PDML)	Yes, FIND and FILE commands only
User Data-Manipulation Language (UDML)	None
Direct Access Facility	None

Languages and Interface Management Systems	
User Languages	None
Programming Languages	ASSEMBLER and C
User Interface Management Systems	None
Programming Interface Management Systems	None

Architectural Characteristics	
Data Constructs	Files - fixed (disk) and pool (memory)
Data Constructors	TPF utilities
Search Capability	Limited (key only)
Data Cross Referencing (Mapping)	None
Processing Mode	Record at a time

Database Programmability	
Command-Based Stored Procedures	No
Event-Driven Stored Procedures (Triggers)	No
Structurally-Defined Business Rule Enforcement	No
Rules Interface Management System	No

Storage Management Profile	
Blocking	No
Buffering	Yes, main memory and FHSP (Fixed Head storage files)
Compression	No
Clustering	No
Sequenced Storage	No
Indexing	Static
Pointers	No
Hashing(Scattering)	Yes

Administrative Profile	
Security	None
Concurrency	Yes
Backup/Recovery-Logging	Capture, recover and exception capture facilities

ACP/TPF is the IBM corporations Airline Control Program/Transaction Processing Facility. This product was originally created for the exclusive support of airlines reservations systems, but has since been modified and turned into a standard facility for the management of many kinds of large, high-data volume, high transaction rate systems. TPF can only marginally considered to be a database product, since its major functionality revolves around its on line transaction processing capabilities. It does however boast its own proprietery database structure in support of this these operations.

Because its primary function is the support of extremely high transaction rates, the TPF database capabilities are extremely rigid and narrow in scope. The database supports only 2 record sizes, small (381 bytes) which is ussually associated with indexing and large (1055 bytes) which hold the processing support data records. In addition to this restraint, the system features only a very simple, record at a time locking mechanism, and supports virtually no batch or reporting activities of any kind. Data to be processed in this manner is offloaded to a "strip file," which can then be read by other systems which have these batch reporting capabilties.

Because of this extremely limited database capability, the TPF database is able to process use input from terminals at a rate incredibly higher then any other IBM mainframe based product can possibly match. Although the TPF database has a narrow range of applications that it can appropriately support, its dependability and performance are unmatched in terms of the currently available database software (where customized hardware is not involved).

(HP) TurboIMAGE/XL

Architecture	: Network
Manufacturer	: Hewlett Packard
Platform	: HP 3000 (MPE/iX)

Database Access Method	
Program Data-Manipulation Language (PDML)	Database intrinsics including FIND, GET, UPDATE, PUT, DELETE, and others
User Data-Manipulation Language (UDML)	ANSI SQL1 Level 2 with SQL2 extensions (via ALLBASE database gateway)
Direct Access Facility	None

Languages and Interface Management Systems	
User Languages	Powerhouse (Cognos), FOCUS (Information Builders), Powerbuilder (Powersoft), Uniface (Uniface), SQL Windows (Gupta), ALLBASE/4GL (Hewlett-Packard)
Programming Languages	BASIC, C, COBOL ,FORTRAN, Pascal, RPG
User Interface Management Systems	Query and BRW (Hewlett-Packard), NewWage/Information Access (Hewlett-Packard), Quiz, UDMS, Inform (third party)
Programming Interface Management Systems	PowerCase (Cognos), Protos

Architectural Characteristics	
Data Constructs	Master datasets, detail datasets, root file datasets
Data Constructors	DBSCHEMA and DBCHANGE (Hewlett-Packard), Adager, DBGeneral, Flexibase (third parties)
Search Capability	Full search on any construct
Data Cross-Referencing (Mapping)	Static logical or physical mapping
Processing Mode	Record-oriented processing

Database Programmability	
Command-Based Stored Procedures	No
Event-Driven Stored Procedures (Triggers)	No
Structurally-Defined Business Rule Enforcement	No
Rules Interface Management System	No

Storage Management Profile	
Blocking	Customizable
Buffering	Customizable via buffer head pool
Compression	No
Clustering	Yes
Sequenced Storage	Yes (serial)
Indexing	Yes (B-tree and inverted list indices)
Pointers	Yes (chained)
Hashing	Yes (calculated) a two-level hashing algorithm

Administrative Profile	
Security	Yes; grantable via user classes, passwords and read/write class lists
Concurrency	Yes; at the database, dataset and record levels
Backup/Recovery-Logging	Full backup and recovery using logging

HP TurboIMAGE/XL is the Hewlett-Packard company's high performance network database management system for mission-critical OLTP applications. As the database used by thousands of customer-written and packaged applications, HP TurboIMAGE/XL has proven its reliability and performance on thousands of systems worldwide. It offers fast, flexible development of applications and provides a comprehensive set of intrinsics, tools and utilities for creating, using and maintaining databases.

The application development environment for HP TurboIMAGE/XL provides greater programmer productivity and increases the speed at which applications can be deployed. HP TurboIMAGE /XL provides easy-to-use tools for:

database and data item security

rapid data retrieval and formatting

program development and maintenance

database reorganization

database schema display and modification

With its high reliability and remote data access capabilities, HP TurboIMAGE/XL supports large, high volume OLTP transaction processing systems with maximum performance and minimum overhead. Scalable performance is provided on all of HP's HP3000 uniprocessor and multiprocessor systems.

HP TurboIMAGE/XL is part of the HP family of integrated information management products, which includes the HP ALLBASE.SQL product line and HP OpenODB, the new object-oriented database management system.

UNIFY 2000

Architecture	: Relational
Manufacturer	: Unify Corporation
Platform	: Most UNIX platforms

Database Access Method	
Program Data-Manipulation Language (PDML)	SQL
User Data-Manipulation Language (UDML)	SQL
Direct Access Facility	None

Languages and Interface Management Systems	
User Languages	ACCELL/SQL
Programming Languages	C, Cobol, ADA
User Interface Management Systems	RPT, ACCELL/IQ
Programming Interface Management Systems	None

Architectural Characteristics	
Data Constructs	Row, column, table, database, index, schema
Data Constructors	Interactive SQL/A or C'
Search Capability	Full Search
Data Cross-Referencing (Mapping)	Dynamic, Static, Physical, Logical
Processing Mode	Set

Database Programmability	
Command-Based Stored Procedures	Data integrity with data integrity subsystem
Event-Driven Stored Procedures (Triggers)	No
Structurally-Defined Business Rule Enforcement	Data integrity subsystem
Rules Interface Management System	No

Storage Management Profile	
Blocking	OS dependent
Buffering	OS dependent
Compression	No
Clustering	No
Sequenced Storage	Exists
Indexing	Exists
Pointers	Exists
Hashing	Exists

Administrative Profile	
Security	Full- ANSI SQL (Grant and Revoke)
Concurrency	Full- row, table and database level locks (Shared (SLOCK), exclusive (XLOCK) and "dirty" (UNLOCK))
Backup/Recovery-Logging	Yes- Full Roll forward and Roll back

UNIFY 2000 is a relational database management system designed to run in the UNIX environment. They UNIFY 2000 kernel is a Transaction Processing System. The UNIFY 2000 Transaction Processing System and its interfaces make up a "next generation," 100% uptime RDBMS for software developers designing on-line, transaction-oriented database applications.

One of the more powerful components of the UNIFY 2000 offering is its companion programming environment product ACCELL. ACCELL is a highly integrated 4GL interface management system that allows programmers to build powerful, flexible applications to run under most UNIX platforms.

UNIFY 2000 includes the following features:

- ANSI SQL standard conformance
- security management
- full transaction rollback and commit
- serializable transaction execution
- multiple-level transaction concurrency control
- recovery from media and system failure
- very large files and volumes
- multiple-level locking
- multiple lock types
- portable and expandable architecture
- multiple interfaces
- multiple access methods
- file, cache, and lock servers
- online backup facilities

VERSANT

Architecture	: Object Oriented
Manufacturer	: Versant Object Technology Corporation
Platform	: SUN, RS6000, DEC/ULTRIX, HP9000,
	: SEQUENT, INTERGRAPH,
	: SILICON GRAPHICS, NEXT, OS2,
	: NCR, BULL

Database Access Method	
Program Data-Manipulation Language (PDML)	Class libraries, C++(commit, connect, locate, version etc.)
User Data-Manipulation Language (UDML)	Object-SQL
Direct Access Facility	None

Languages and Interface Management Systems	
User Languages	Interactive C++
Programming Languages	C, C++, Smalltalk
User Interface Management Systems	VERSANT report writer and interactive object-SQL
Programming Interface Management Systems	VERSANT interactive C++ toolset, VERSANT view

Architectural Characteristics	
Data Constructs	Objects/Classes, containers, databases
Data Constructors	C++ or Smalltalk, runtime with C++(no precompile required)
Search Capability	Key search is available
Data Cross-Referencing (Mapping)	Inheritence, generalization, aggregation, association and dynamic, logical and physical
Processing Mode	Record and set at a time

Database Programmability	
Command-Based Stored Procedures	Implied by the architecture
Event-Driven Stored Procedures (Triggers)	Event notification triggers
Structurally-Defined Business Rule Enforcement	Implied by the architecture
Rules Interface Management System	No

Storage Management Profile	
Blocking	Customizable
Buffering	Customizable
Compression	No
Clustering	Yes, (physical containers)
Sequenced Storage	Yes
Indexing	B-tree
Pointers	Yes
Hashing	Yes

Administrative Profile	
Security	Limited
Concurrency	Exclusive, shared and user defined (customizable) locking levels. Versioning and short, long , nested and multiple transactions.
Backup/Recovery-Logging	Backup by database, and logging for roll forward and roll back processing. Archiving facility. Full recovery of backups and logs.

Versant Object Technology Corporation, which was founded in 1988, is dedicated to the development of an integrated information system development environment which capitalizes on the power and flexibility of object oriented technology. In doing so, they have created a world where application developer's time can be highly productive, while at the same time providing for the support of large, high performance database environments. The VERSANT database is one of the most popular of the "classical" object oriented database environments and features many of the capabilties that make it ideal for the support of large engineering, CASE CAD/CAM, telecommunications or imaging applications.

VERSANT ODBMS has a fully object-oriented client-server architecture with rich functionality for distributed and workgroup applications. It's integrated interfaces for the C++, Smalltalk and C programmers are complemented by the VERSANT Interactive C++ Toolset, which includes an easily learned, interactive subset of C++, many pseudofunctions for developing GUIs, and Interactive Object SQL. VERSANT also provides Gateway products for access to a variety of relational DBMSs from object programs.

WindowBase

Architecture	: Relational
Manufacturer	: Software Products International
Platform	: IBM PC, AT, PS/2 or compatible

Database Access Method	
Program Data Manipulation Language (PDML)	None
User Data Manipulation Language (UDML)	SQL via SQL Access menu
Direct Access Facility	Yes; icons and menus

Languages and Interface Management Systems	
User Languages	None
Programming Languages	None
User Interface Management Systems	Form Access, SQL Access, Table Access, Menu Access and Report Access menus
Programming Interface Management Systems	Form Design, Report Design and Menu Design menus

Architectural Characteristics	
Data Constructs	Rows, columns, tables, databases
Data Constructors	Create database dialog box, DDL thru SQL Access or menu driven thru Table Design, import
Search Capability	Full
Data Cross-Referencing (Mapping)	Dynamic/Logical
Processing Mode	Set processing, record processing

Database Programmability	
Command-Based Stored Procedures	Some
Event-Driven Stored Procedures (Triggers)	Some default procedures
Structurally-Defined Business Rule Enforcement	Referential Constraints
Rules Interface Management System	Some: must match

Storage Management Profile	
Blocking	Operating system dependent
Buffering	Operating system dependent
Compression	No
Clustering	No
Sequenced Storage	Yes
Indexing	Yes
Pointers	No
Hashing	No

Administrative Profile	
Security	Yes; Table privileges, report form encryption, user passwords, levels including system administrator, database owner, database object owners and groups
Concurency	No
Backup/Recovery-Logging	Commit and roll back at transaction units backups and recovery manually done

Software Products International's WindowBase is a PC-based Relational Database Management System (RDBMS) with an exceptional combination of power, flexibility and ease-of-use. WindowBase provide these general features and benefits:

Graphical User Interface. WindowBase operates in the Microsoft Windows environment. This provides intuitive ease-of-use, letting users concentrate on data, activities and forms rather than on the operation of the program. Programs operating under Windows also enjoy a high level of integration with other applications due to its common user interface, multitasking capability and dynamic data exchange (DDE).

Easily Designed and Flexible Forms. Non-programmers can retrieve, manipulate and report on data using mouse-driven screen forms and reports. Event-driven Structured Query Language (SQL) commands can be easily incorporated into forms using push buttons, scroll bars and other features of the Windows interface, insulating users from SQL. Forms can be designed to correspond to your current paper forms, allowing the user a gradual transition from paper to screen forms.

Multiple Queries in Screen Forms. A screen form may contain several different, yet related, SQL queries. This allows updating a table that results from a join, which is not normally possible with SQL.

Configurable Menu Commands. Custom menu applications that conform to each user's needs can be created.

Multiple Levels of Data Presentation. WindowBase provides multiple levels of data presentation depending on user's level of expertise. This includes easy-to-use forms and dialog boxes that provide an indirect SQL interface, as well as direct SQL entry for those fluent in SQL.

XDB

Architecture	: Relational
Manufacturer	: XDB Systems, Inc
Platform	: DOS, OS2, UNIX, Windows

Database Access Method	
Program Data-Manipulation Language (PDML)	SQL
User Data-Manipulation Language (UDML)	SQL
Direct Access Facility (User interface system)	None

Languages and Interface Management Systems	
User Languages	XDB Pro (4GL data language)
Programming Languages	COBOL (micro focus and relia, C, visual BASIC)
User Interface Management Systems	XDB: menu driven
Programming Interface Management Systems	XDB: menu driven

Architectural Characteristics	
Data Constructs	Fields, Tables, Databases, Indexes
Data Constructors	XDB: menu driven and SQL DDL
Search Capability	Full Search
Data Cross-Referencing (Mapping)	Dynamic
Processing Mode	Set or optimal record at a time

Database Programmability	
Command-Based Stored Procedures	Store procedures in server
Event-Driven Stored Procedures (Triggers)	No
Structurally-Defined Business Rule Enforcement	Referential integrity
Rules Interface Management System	No

Storage Management Profile	
Blocking	OS dependent
Buffering	Customizable in Server
Compression	No
Clustering	Clustering is Sequenced Storage
Sequenced Storage	Sequenced Storage is clustering
Indexing	B-tree
Pointers	No
Hashing	Scattering of index and log files

Administrative Profile	
Security	Yes, grant and revoke
Concurrency	Yes, for client/server version
Backup/Recovery-Logging	Yes

XDB is a state-of-the-art, SQL-based relational database management system, with sophisticated application development tools for creating reports, forms and menus. XDB provides a friendly, comprehensive environment for developing and maintaining customized database applications. It provides a high level of compatibility with DB2 and ANSI standard SQL.

It is the systems compatability with DB2 that is responsible for a large amount of its popularity in the database world today. The XDB database can rightfully claim to be the closest thing to being a DB2 clone on the personal computer. XDB not only provides compatible data types, DDL and DML compatability, but even provides a similar API (application programmer interface). The database manufacturers have even seen to it that the error messages displayed by the database match those of DB2 itself.

When combined with the powerful C language API or one of several PC-Cobol interfaces (Micro-Focus Cobol or Realia Cobol), the system developer can actually simulate mainframe application development on the PC.

XDB not only functions as a substitute PC version of DB2, but can also stand on its own merits as a fully functional PC relational database. Its menu driven access and utility functionality and its user friendly query manager make it the database choice for many first time database users.

Bibliography / Suggested Readings

BOOKS

Apple. **Inside Macintosh.** Volume 1. Addison-Wesley Publishing Company, Inc., 1985.

Atkinson, William J., and Paul A. DeSanctis. **Introduction to VSAM.** Hayden Book Company, Inc. 1980.

Bacon, M.D., and G.M. Bull. **Data Transmission.** M.D. Bacon and G.M. Bull, 1973.

Baritz, Tony, and David Dunne. **AS/400.** McGraw-Hill, Inc., 1991.

Chen, P. "The Entity-Relationship Model --- Toward a Unified View of Data." **Readings in Database Systems.** Morgan Kaufmann Publishers, Inc., 1988.

Codd, E.F. "Extending the Database Relational Model to Capture More Meaning." **Readings in Database Systems.** Morgan Kaufmann Publishers, Inc., 1988.

Codd, E.F. "A Relational Model of Data for Large Shared Data Banks." **Readings in Database Systems.** Morgan Kaufmann Publishers, Inc., 1988.

Conference Proceedings of Database World. 1991. Digital Consulting, Inc.

Date, C.J. **A Guide to DB2.** Addison-Wesley Publishing Company, Inc., 1984.

Date, C.J. **A Guide to INGRES.** Addison-Wesley Publishing Company, Inc., 1987.

Date, C.J. **An Introduction to Database Systems** - Volume 2. Addison-Wesley Publishing Company, Inc., 1983.

Date, C.J. **An Introduction to Database Systems** - Third Edition. Addison-Wesley Publishing Company, Inc., 1981, 1977, 1975.

Dockter, Michael. **Data Repair: DB2 Catalog and Directory Inconsistencies.** International Business Machines, Corp., 1989.

Fernandez, Judi, and Ruth Ashley. **The Power of OS/2.** Windcrest Books, 1989.

Fisher, Alan S. **CASE Using Software Development Tools.** John Wiley & Sons, Inc., 1988.

Fitch, Carl, Charles Hinchey, and Hanes Larson. **DB2 Applications Development Handbook.** McGraw-Hill, Inc., 1989.

Fleming, Candace C. and Barbara von Halle. **Handbook of Relational Database Design.** Addison-Wesley Publishing Company, Inc., 1989.

Geller, Joseph R. **DB2 Performance and Development Guide.** Van Nostrand Reinhold Company, Inc., 1991.

Ghosh, Sakti P. **Database Organization for Data Management.** Academic Press, Inc., 1986.

Hammer, M. and D. McLeod. "Database Description with SDM: A Semantic Database Model." **Readings in Database Systems.** Morgan Kaufmann Publishers, Inc., 1988.

528

Hursch, Jack L., Ph.D., and Carolyn H. Hursch, Ph.D. **Working with ORACLE, Version 6.0.** Windcrest Books, 1989.

Inmon, W.H. **Building High Performance Online Systems.** QED Information Sciences, Inc., 1989.

Inmon, W.H. **Data Architecture.** QED Information Sciences, Inc., 1989.

Inmon, W.H. **Maximizing Performance of Online Production Systems.** QED Information Sciences, Inc., 1989.

Jatich, Alida. **CICS Command Level Programming.** John Wiley & Sons, Inc., 1985.

Kapp, Dan, and Joe Leben. **IMS Programming Techniques - A Guide to Using DL/I.** Van Nostrand Reinhold Company, Inc., 1986.

Kenah, Lawrence J., Ruth E. Goldenberg, and Simon F. Bate. **VAX/VMS Internals and Data Structures, Version 4.4.** Digital Equipment Corporation, 1988.

Kerr, James M. **The IRM Imperative.** John Wiley & Sons, Inc., 1991.

Kroenke, David. M. **Business Computer Systems - An Introduction.** Mitchell Publishing, Inc. 1981.

Larson, Bruce L. **The Database Expert's Guide to Database 2.** Multiscience Press, Inc. 1988.

Letwin, Gordon. **Inside OS/2.** Microsoft Press, 1988.

Levy, Henry M., and Richard H. Eckhouse, Jr. **Computer Programming and Architecture: The VAX-11.** Digital Equipment Corporation, 1980.

McClure, Carma. **CASE is Software Automation.** Carma McClure, 1989.

Napier, H. Albert, and Philip J. Judd. **Mastering and Using LOTUS 1-2-3.** Boyd & Fraser Publishing, 1990.

Ozsu, M. Tamer, and Patrick Valduriez. **Principles of Distributed Database Systems.** Prentice-Hall, Inc., 1991.

Page-Jones, Meilir. **The Practical Guide to Structured Systems Design.** Prentice-Hall, Inc., 1988.

Rettig, Tom, and Debby Moody. **Tom Rettig's Clipper Encyclopedia.** Tom Rettig Associates, 1989.

Rumbaugh, James, Michael Blaha, William Premerlani, Frederick Eddy, and William Lorensen. **Object-Oriented Modeling and Design.** Prentice-Hall, Inc., 1991.

Simpson, Alan. **Mastering PARADOX 3.5.** Sybex, Inc., 1990.

Stonebraker, M. "Retrospection on a Database Systems." **Readings in Database Systems.** Morgan Kaufmann Publishers, Inc., 1988.

Stonebraker, M., E. Wong, P. Kreps, and G. Held. "The Design and Implementation of INGRES." **Readings in Database Systems.** Morgan Kaufmann Publishers, Inc., 1988.

Wertz, Charles J. **The Data Dictionary - Concepts and Uses.** QED Information Sciences, Inc. 1989.

JOURNALS

Ahad, Rafiul, K.V. Bapa Rao, and Dennis McLeod. "On Estimating the Cardinality of the Projection of a Database Relation." acm Transactions on Database Systems. 14, 1, (Mar. 1989): 28-40.

Alonso, Rafael, Daniel Barbara, and Hector Garcia-Molina. "Data Caching Issues in an Information Retrieval System." acm Transactions on Database Systems. 15, 3, (Sep. 1990): 359-84.

Bancilhon, Francois, and Won Kim. "Object-Oriented Database Systems: In Transition." Sigmod Record. 19, 4, (Dec. 1990): 49-53.

Borras, P., J.C. Mamou, D. Plateau, B. Poyet, and D. Tallot. "Building User Interfaces for Database Applications: The O2." Sigmod Record. 21, 1 (Mar. 1992): 32-8.

Bass, Len, Ross Ganeuf, Reed Little, Niels Mayer, Bob Pellegrino, Robert Seacord, Sylvia Sheppard, and Martha R. Szczur. "The UIMS Tool Developers Workshop." Sigchi. 24, 1, (January 1992): 32-37.

Can, Fazli, and Esen A. Ozkarahan. "Concepts and Effectiveness of the Cover-Coefficient-Based Clustering Methodology for Text Databases." acm Transactions on Database Systems. 15, 4, (Dec. 1990): 483-517.

Carey, Michael, and Laura Haas. "Extensible Database Management Systems." Sigmod Record. 19, 4, (Dec. 1990): 54-60.

Cesarini, F., and G. Soda. "A Dynamic Hash Method with Signature." acm Transactions on Database Systems. 16, 2, (June 1991): 309-337.

Chang, T.-H., and E. Sciore. "A Universal Relation Data Model with Semantic Abstractions." Transactions on Knowledge and Data Engineering. 4,1, (Feb. 1992): 23-33.

Chignell, Mark H., and John A. Waterworth. "WIMPs and NERDs: An Extended View of the User Interface." Sigchi. 23, 2, (April 1991): 15-21.

Ebner, Rainer, Gunter Haring, Granz Penz, and Gerhard Weichselberger. "A Comparative Evaluation of Graphical User-Interfaces." Sigchi. 22, 1, (July 1990): 12-15.

Geller, J., U. Perl, and E. Neuhold. "Structure and Semantics in OODB Class Specifications." Sigmod Records. 20, 4, (Dec. 1991): 40-3.

Gogolla, Martin and Uwe Hohenstein. "Towards a Semantic View of an Extended Entity-Relationship Model." acm Transactions on Database Systems. 16, 3, (Sep. 1991): 369-416.

Haim, Kilov. "A Review of Object-Oriented Papers." Sigmod Record. 18, 4, (Dec. 1989): 50-5.

Herlihy, Maurice. "Apologizing Versus Asking Permission: Optimistic Concurrency Control for Abstract Data Types." acm Transactions on Database Systems. 15, 1, (Mar. 1990): 96-124.

Hiraga, Rumi, and Yeong-Chang Lien. "Managing Objects in a User Interface System with ROBA." Sigchi. 22, 1, (July 1990): 49-51.

Myers, Brad A., and Mary Beth Rosson. "User Interface Programming Survey." Sigchi. 23, 2, (April 1991): 27-30.

Ramakrishna, M.V., and Per-Ake Larson. "File Organization Using Composite Perfect Hashing." **acm Transactions on Database Systems**. 14, 2, (June 1989): 231-263.

Roussopoulos, N., and A. Delis. "Modern Client-Server DBMS Architectures." **Sigmod Record**. 20, 3, (Sep. 1991): 52-61.

Shaw, Christopher J. "Application And Database Design -- Putting It Off." **Sigmod Record**. 17, 2, (June 1988): 14-22.

MAGAZINES

Bloor, Robin. "Mission Critical View." DBMS. February 1992: 12,13.

Butler, Martin, and Robin Bloor. "Mission Critical View." DBMS. May 1991: 18-20.

Butler, Martin, and Robin Bloor. "Mission Critical View." DBMS. November 1991: 17-21.

Butterworth, Paul, Allen Otic, and Jacob Stein. "The GemStone Object Database Management System." **Communications of the ACM**. October 1991: 64-77.

Celko, Joe. "Front Ends for SQL." **Data Base Programming & Design**. May 1992: 23-25.

Davis, Jack M. "Data Base Decisions and Re-engineering: Part I." **Data Base Management**. June 1991:8-10.

Deux et al, O. "The O2 System." **Communications of the ACM**. October 1991: 34-48.

Kernighan, Lynn R. "Downsizing with Case." DBMS. January 1992: 73-80.

LaBorde, Dominique. "Data Models Revisited: E=MC2." **Data Base Management**. February 1991: 35-7.

Lamb, Charles, Gordon Landis, Jack Orenstein, and Dan Weinreb. "The Object-Store Database System." **Communications of the ACM**. October 1991: 50-63.

Lohman, Guy M., Bruce Lindsay, Hamid Pirahesh, and K. Bernhard Schiefer. "Extensions to Starburst: Objects, Types, Functions, and Rules." **Communication of the ACM**. October 1991: 94-109.

Mattison, Rob. "Selecting the Right DBMS." **Data Base Management**. February 1991: 29-30.

Mattison, Rob. "Selecting the Right DBMS: Part II-Developing a Consensus." **Data Base Management**. March 1991: 34-35.

Mattison, Rob. "Selecting the Right DBMS: Part IV." **Data Base Management**. May 1991: 22-23.

Mattison, Rob. "Selecting the Right DBMS Part III: To Navigate or Not to Navigate." **Data Base Management**. April 1991: 22-26.

Mattison, Rob. "Selecting the Right DBMS - Part V." **Data Base Management**. June 1991: 32-33.

McClanahan, David R. "Physical Database Design." DBMS. April 1992: 62-70.

McClanahan, David R. "The Relational Rules." DBMS. November 1991: 54-58.

McClanahan, David R. " Relational Database Design." DBMS. October 1991: 63-68.

McClanahan, David R. "Logical Database Design." **DBMS**. March 1992: 60-7.

Nelson, Jack. "Model Process." **Data Base Management**. March 1991: 6-10.

Ozsu, Tamer M., and Patrick Valduriez. "Distributed Database: Where Are We Now?" **Database Programming & Design**. March 1992: 46-52.

Partee, Sanders. "The Road to Repository." **Data Base Management**. April 1991: 27-28.

Roti, Steve. "Ingres on Windows." **DBMS**. February 1992: 52-58.

Salemi, Joe. "Database Power Without the Programming." **PC Magazine**. December 1991: 111-168.

Sayles, Jonathan. "Tuning by Design." **Database Programming & Design**. January 1992: 24-33.

Schnapp, Marc. "Windows DBMSs, GUI Applications." **DBMS**. January 1992: 46-65.

Schussel, George. "Distributing: How to take advantage of the SQL environment." **Data Base Management**. April 1991: 20-1.

Silberschatz, Avi, Michael Stonebraker, and Jeff Ullman. "Database Systems: Achievements and Opportunities." **Communications of the ACM**. October 1991: 110-20.

Stonebraker, Michael, and Greg Kemnitz. "The POSTGRES Next-Generation Database Management System." **Communications of the ACM**. October 1991: 78-92.

Tate, Graham, June Verner, and Ross Jeffery. "CASE: A Testbed for Modeling, Measurement and Management." **Communications of the ACM**. April 1992: 65-72.

Tavlin, Barry. "Application Front-Ends and Interfaces: More Than Skin Deep." **Data Base Management**. April 1991: 32-33.

Witterman, Art. "Case System Design and Development Tools Evolve into Viable Data Processing Solutions." **Data Base Management**. March 1991: 14-15.

Index

ABOUT THE AUTHOR

Robert M. Mattison is an internationally recognized
consultant specializing in database management and
CASE. He is experienced in the strategic use and
application of database technologies as solutions to
business and systems requirements and has applied this
knowledge in mainframe, mini, scientific workstation, and
personal computer environments. Mr. Mattison lectures,
teaches, and writes for several publications; he also serves
as editorial director for *The Data Management Review*; and
serves as a member of the National Business
Unit/Database Practice Group for Polaris Consulting L.P.
(a member of Deloitte, Ross, Touche Technologies).